Rethinking Corporate Security in the Post-9/11 Era

Issues and Strategies for Today's Global Business Community

Rethinking Corporate Security in the Post-9/11 Era

Issues and Strategies for Today's Global Business Community

Dennis R. Dalton

An Imprint of Elsevier Science

Amsterdam • Boston • Heidelberg • London • New York • Oxford • Paris
San Diego • San Francisco • Singapore • Sydney • Tokyo

Butterworth-Heinemann is an imprint of Elsevier Science.

 Recognizing the importance of preserving what has been written, Elsevier-Science prints its books on acid-free paper whenever possible.

Library of Congress Cataloging-in-Publication Data

Dalton, Dennis R.
   Rethinking corporate security in the post-9/11 era: issues and strategies for today's global business community / Dennis R. Dalton.
      p.   cm.
   Includes bibliographical references and index.
   ISBN 0-7506-7614-0 (alk. paper)
   1. Corporations–Security measures.   2. Industries–Security measures.   I. Title.

HV8290.D338 2003
658.4′7—dc21   2003043694

British Library Cataloguing-in-Publication Data

A catalogue record for this book is available from the British Library.

The publisher offers special discounts on bulk orders of this book.
For information, please contact:

Manager of Special Sales
Elsevier Science
200 Wheeler Road
Burlington, MA 01803
Tel: 781-313-4700
Fax: 781-313-4880

For information on all Butterworth-Heinemann publications available, contact our World Wide Web home page at: http://www.bh.com

10 9 8 7 6 5 4 3 2 1

Printed in the United States of America

This is dedicated to Walter and Kay Stone, my father-in-law and mother-in-law. Thank you for your years of support, advice, and encouragement. Over the years your insights have helped me more than you will ever know.

I also want to give special recognition to Jim McKeirnan, my best friend for more than 25 years. Thanks for all of your support and encouragement as well, and for introducing me to one of the greatest mysteries of life—golf! It has not only helped me better understand the art of management, but also befuddled the heck out of my weekends!

CONTENTS

About the Author

This is Dr. Dalton's third security management book, following *Security Management: Business Strategies for Success* (Butterworth–Heinemann, 1995) and *The Art of Successful Security Management* (Butterworth–Heinemann, 1997). An internationally recognized expert in the field of corporate security management, his experience spans 35 years in both the private and public sectors. He is a faculty member of the University of Phoenix, the largest business schools in America, and has been president of his consulting firm, Dalton Affiliates, Ltd., in Auburn, California, since 1987. A former security executive for three large multinational firms, his clients are typically among the Fortune 200. Dr. Dalton holds degrees from Michigan State University and the University of Southern California. His professional accomplishments include *Security Magazine*'s Executive Management Achievement Award and several corporate and public service awards. He is a frequent keynote speaker and seminar host. He has appeared on the Fox News Network, MSNBC, and the BBC, and has been featured in *The Wall Street Journal, The New York Times,* the *Los Angeles Times,* and *The San Francisco Examiner,* as well as nearly every major professional security journal.

Prior to his private sector career, Dr. Dalton served as a police officer in Michigan, director of a community college criminal justice program in New York, and a police administrator in the San Francisco Bay area. In that capacity, he served on the board of governance for two of the area's largest police academies.

FOREWORD

Over the ten years that I have known Dr. Dennis Dalton, I have come to value his prolific writing and admire his passion to learn, communicate, teach, and lead. All the while, he also manages to maintain his robust sense of humor, lust for life, and a unique common sense approach to the worlds of business and security.

These attributes are clearly manifested throughout this dynamic new work. *Rethinking Corporate Security,* Dalton's third book in eight years, is written against the backdrop of September 11, and helps usher in the "new era" of the security profession that began on that infamous day in our country's history. I believe this book represents a milestone in the security industry. It is destined to become a classic in our field—a practical "must read" discussion of security management principles for all security professionals and, perhaps more importantly, their organization's executive management.

As you read your way through this insightful and stimulating book, you will no doubt recognize that in many ways Dalton's writing is firmly in the modern tradition established by Peter Drucker, one of our age's leading management consultants, philosophers, and authors. It is said of Drucker that he relishes the role of creative contrarian. His provocative writing is designed not to shock or anger, but to awaken and provoke the reader to look candidly at the facts and make break-through judgments based on well-considered principles and values. Like Drucker, Dalton does not tell us what we want to hear, but what we need to know and think about in this increasingly difficult and complex era in which security professionals work. While Dalton is perhaps one of the most polite and polished men I have ever met, his readers will discover he has little patience for those with closed minds, old world views, and fear of change.

In this regard, Dalton continues to be a pioneering and visionary force in the security profession. Neither this book nor his previous works are manuals or simple (let alone simplistic) "how-to" guides to daily security operations. As helpful as many of those volumes are—such as *Protection of Assets, Encyclopedia of Security Management,* and so many others—Dalton challenges security practitioners to apply universal contemporary management principles to the field of corporate security. This is really very important. First, it reflects Dalton's early recognition that security management is NOT an odd-but-necessary back-lot function, but is instead a vital business function that is essential to any organization's continued viability. Second, it reflects Dalton's deeply felt respect for the security profession and for the difficult job security executives confront on a daily basis. Implicit in this respect for and understanding of the security profession is Dalton's sage insight that for security to be optimally effective, security executives must be able to relate to and communicate effectively with all levels of management. Thus, I believe that applying the best in contemporary management thinking to the security profession is one of Dalton's most important and lasting contributions.

Another related, and perhaps not sufficiently acknowledged, aspect of Dalton's three decades of contribution to the security field is his subtle but persistent and optimistic argument that some CEOs and other important business people are willing—perhaps even eager—to understand and apply the value that security brings to their organizations. From *Security Management: Business Strategies for Success* (1995) to *The Art of Successful Security Management* (1998) to *Rethinking Corporate Security in the Post 9/11 Era* (2003), Dalton has raised his own high bar of expectations for the value that security executives can provide to their companies. If early on Dalton was looking security managers straight in the eye and challenging them to change and grow, today he is talking to corporate security executives who should proudly claim their place in corporate leadership.

Rethinking Corporate Security is not about gross generalizations, ambiguous and inconsistent thinking, or superficial "idea du jour" management principles. Rather, it cuts through the latest management jargon and gives security executives pragmatic insight into management approaches that do and do not work either in security or anywhere else. Equally as important is the gentle and credible guidance Dalton provides about how security executives can most effectively communicate with managers in other business departments as well as with CEOs and other top executives.

Readers will find that *Rethinking Corporate Security* is infused with a perspective that holds new relevance in today's world of change and the related challenges of uncertainty. This book anticipates and lays the groundwork for taking on the post–September 11 changes coming to our profession. The foundation it lays will years from now be viewed as insightful and will become mainstream security management thinking.

If there is one central proposition underlying Dalton's purpose for this book, it is the fundamental and urgent necessity of becoming the best-of-the-best in security management. This is neither a truism nor is it easy to accomplish.

America's most successful corporations spend hundreds of million of dollars annually on comprehensive quality improvement programs and processes. As General Electric and other companies have found, quality pays, but it is hard work. So Dalton argues on virtually every page that successful security executives must be at the top of their game. Security is not for the faint of heart or the semi-retired!

Dalton's imperatives to security practitioners include: "Know what works and what does not. Do you know enough about your employees and senior managers? What conventional wisdom has proven to be utterly useless? Learn to overcome your up-line and down-line obstacles to teamwork. Improve your outsource partnerships through a more clearly defined agreement. Be aware of potential legal threats and challenges that could destroy your program and disrupt your company." This unornamented approach is refreshing and the insights it yields are invaluable.

"Leaders," Dalton writes, "are able to set new direction, new tones, and set the course for a new way of moving the organization forward. The balance must be equally divided amongst the manager's security skills and his required business acumen." He further says, "Security's value needs to be defined and measured in terms of the department's core deliverables." The key is to understand whether you are a manager who executes reactively or an executive and strategic leader who creates and executes against a plan. Dalton believes that this level of self-awareness and perspective is vital to professional success and a successful corporate security program.

Another important dimension of awareness and perspective is benchmarking. Dalton rightly argues that benchmarking is not only insightful, it is healthy and essential. *Rethinking Corporate Security* profiles several security industry giants who have proven leadership skills and who Dalton feels capture the true essence of successful, best-in-class security leadership. Through examples and what he calls "storytelling," Dalton provides vivid case studies that will help readers assess the processes now in place at their establishments and then determine how to improve them in a step-by-step and straightforward way.

It seems clear from Dalton's selection of security's "superstars" that those who have achieved the most success are those who have "sold" security's value to their executive management. *Rethinking Corporate Security* includes important discussions about how security department management must parallel and fully embrace the management programs and practices followed throughout their corporations. These include strategic planning, budgeting, goal setting, hiring, motivation, partner relationship management, leadership, communications, team building, conflict management, defining job descriptions, quality improvement and performance evaluation metrics, and measuring your department against senior management's expectations and challenges.

I consider Dennis Dalton to be one of a few leading security industry thinkers on the practice and study of security management. He time and time again demonstrates the wisdom and skill to insightfully adapt to our industry very technical management principles such as the following:

- The 180-degree rule
- Organizational bracketing
- The looping model
- The ten E's
- The boss's interpretation of risk assessment
- S.W.O.T
- Performance measurement
- Zero-based criteria formatting
- Model service provider agreements
- The impact of 9–11
- Zero-asset-based companies
- RBV
- Metrically based decisions
- The "C" suite
- The era of total loss prevention
- Three pillars
- Defend yourself against ELVIS
- The fishbone
- Panic de jour
- Analysis paralysis
- Morris's seven C's
- Suppliers' ten cardinal sins
- Maxwell's traps, the fear of risk
- Dalton's 20 axioms

As the author Noel Tichy says, "The cycle of leadership defines a road map for business leaders that is both practical and memorable."

Finally, it will be clear to all readers that the terrorist attack of September 11 makes *Rethinking Corporate Security* even more relevant and timely to the security executive. We face a multitude of managerial challenges not conceived prior to September 11. This will be particularly true for security executives who have global responsibility or for those whose companies are high profile and potential targets for terrorist attack. Also, Dalton's strong views about the current and likely future state of "homeland security" as well as the current and likely future directions of U.S. private security service providers will assuredly become important elements in our industry's ongoing dialogue with its stakeholders.

The vision articulated in *Rethinking Corporate Security* has its dark and somber elements as well as its notes of excitement and dynamism. Dalton challenges practitioners to "step out of the little green shack and join the mainstream corporate management team." With the harsh light that the events of September 11 cast on all aspects of homeland and corporate security, the security profession must step up or risk being marginalized. But as Dalton argues, the profession has been and is stepping up and moving forward proudly. *Rethinking Corporate Security* should be required reading for the best and brightest young professionals who are contemplating security management as their career choice.

The security industry is now in a state of flux and major change. As the economy and world affairs continue to threaten our homeland security, the corporate spotlight will now illuminate all corporate security departments, particularly shining on the operating plan and budget. The ability to manage, execute, retain key personnel, and lead in difficult times—including the justification of budget appropriations—will certainly test the talent, resolve, and adaptability of tomorrow's security executives.

Rethinking Corporate Security is an excellent tool for security professionals who have made the deeply personal commitment to become security leaders in this post–September 11 era—leaders who not only provide best-in-class security for their companies, but also hire, train, and inspire future security leaders. *Rethinking Corporate Security* will become a widely read source of insight and inspiration in navigating through the challenges ahead.

David J. Gibbs, CPP
Senior Vice President, On Line Associates
Oakland, California

PREFACE

May you live in interesting times.

Chinese Proverb

The Chinese proverb above is centuries old. Yet for those in the security profession, it has never been more true than it is now. I was approached by my publisher about a year ago and asked if I would be interested in updating my original book, *Security Management: Business Strategies for Success*. For several weeks we discussed whether it was better to simply write a second edition or to introduce an entirely new third book. We surveyed the industry and many past readers to determine the best course of action. After we thought we had the answer, the events of September 11 decidedly changed both our collective thoughts and direction. As I write this, I'm still not sure that a clear path lies ahead. I think our dilemma mirrors the uncertainty that faces the security profession in general.

For the first time in our country's history, we have a presidential cabinet post for a Secretary of Homeland Security. Personally, I find this very troubling. A recent survey suggests that 80% of those polled say they are willing to forgo some freedoms for more security. I find this even more troubling. In the wake of 9/11, private security was summarily booted out of the business of airport screening to be replaced by twice the number of federal employees, earning more than two times the salary and delivering no noticeable measure of true passenger security—some would argue less security and more hassles. No reasonable cost-benefit analysis can justify this "quick fix" approach. In the end, I find the government's approach mind-boggling, but not surprising.

As part of the emotional reaction to the United States' first large-scale terrorist attack, the U.S. Congress passed legislation expanding police powers and allowing federal law enforcement agencies greater latitude in monitoring our conversations and e-mails. I question whether this was the intent of our founding fathers. Through 2002 and into 2003, we have listened almost daily to announcements of imminent threat by some new vague threat or plot to commit another terrorist attack. Yet most of these are followed by some spokesperson backpedaling to soften the original warning of dire consequence. I find myself growing more cynical and, just like the majority of other Americans, jaded to such cries of "Wolf! Wolf!"

By now some of you may have concluded that I am one of those "liberal wackos" whom conservative talk-show hosts like to lambaste. Actually, I'm politically independent, fiscally conservative, and socially moderate. I'm also an American and a security and police management practitioner and specialist of 34 years. I possess a doctorate degree in organizational theory and behavior from one of the country's leading universities, and I am very worried about the direction our country is heading in the name of fighting global terrorism. I voted for George W. Bush and liked his choices for key appointments, but today I am very concerned—not about what lies immediately ahead, since I think he and his staff are honorable people with good intentions. But I do believe that the Bush administration, with congressional support, has unwittingly created the beginnings of an infrastructure that can only lead to a strong police state. History has taught us over and over that key elements of the law enforcement community will abuse this power.

Here's an interesting irony. Despite the widespread belief that Americans are more security conscious and many fear flying or going to crowded public gatherings, corporate America has chosen to talk the talk, but has yet to walk the walk. American business executives have failed to really demonstrate a commitment to protecting their people and assets, both tangible and intangible. You may find this shocking and unbelievable, but it is true.

Immediately following the 9–11 attack, senior managers scrambled to hire more guards and some went so far as to install some new cameras or replace some worn-out devices. Security directors around the country reported that commitments were made to increase both their operating and capital budgets for 2002. In short, for a period of time corporate security managers were a happy lot. Because of the World Trade Center tragedy, it appeared as though the years of pleading their case for a stronger program had finally fallen on receptive ears. Within the first 60 days of the new year, the story had completely reversed. Gone were the commitments for new equipment, expanded staff coverage, and support of security's mission.

Corporate executives and property owners and their agents were faced with a dilemma. The year 2002 dawned on the country in an economic downturn. We were beginning to feel firsthand the bust of the dot.com boom. Supply significantly outstretched demand across all business sectors because of the Y2K panic of 2000. Despite government assurances that the economic indicators showed it was a modest downturn with strong positive numbers suggesting a quick rebound, American corporations continued to send warnings of lower earnings and the need for further cuts. This has extended into 2003, with no certain future ahead. In sum, the hopes of security managers were dashed, as the reality of a down economic cycle always translates into doing without, despite the War on Terror. "Besides," many executives have privately rationalized, "the war is turning out to be quite successful and the threat of another attack has been significantly reduced. Moreover, what are the chances our company will be a direct target?" Such an ostrich approach is pathetic, but is pursued by many otherwise savvy business executives.

For security providers, what started out as a banner business year quickly turned sour. In the last quarter of 2001 contract employees were hired as fast as they could be found, and still the demand exceeded the supply. This hiring frenzy came at the very time private security was being scoffed at over the quality of their work at our country's airports. The media, politicians, and even stand-up comedians had a field day blasting private security's ineptness, while company executives were pressuring their security managers to hire "as many as it takes." Providers geared up to meet the volume only to see such long-term prospects collapse into short-term contracts. As I write this I am reminded of a recent telephone call from one of the country's leading sales representatives for a top security company. He wasn't on the telephone 30 seconds before he exclaimed that business was dead. Within a couple hours I received a similar call from another top-five supplier.

Another phenomenon has been quietly unfolding just below the media's radar screen. It is a trend that began a few years before the events of 9–11, but continues unabated: the face of security's top players is changing. Today if one measures the total revenues of the country's top 40 security companies, the first two have a combined income greater than all of the remaining 38 firms. Sitting atop the list is Swedish-based Securitas North America. They own Pinkerton, Burns, and a host of other companies that less than five years ago ranked among the top 20. Their U.S.-based business accounts for $2.7 billion in revenue. In second place is Wackenhut Corporation with $1.06 billion in annual revenues. They were recently acquired by Group 4 Falck, based in Copenhagen and the Hague. Also among the top ten are Initial Security and AHL Services, both now British owned. When combined, these four firms represent annual revenues of $4.128 billion. The remaining top 40 represent revenues of $3.366 billion. Four foreign-owned companies now account for more than 55% of the top revenue of today's contract security business. This translates to more than 30% of the entire market.

What does this mean for America? If nothing else, I find it ironic that we now have federal legislation mandating that all airport security screeners must be U.S. citizens, yet the company they work for is most likely to be foreign owned. Consolidation, regardless of ownership, would suggest that suppliers will have greater control over their margins. This translates to higher billing rates. In short, we should expect to pay more for security services. One would hope that this means more-qualified and better-trained officers. Unfortunately, since the consolidation drive began in the late 1990s there has been no discernable difference in either the quality of employees or the level of their training. If anything, a number of industry critics believe that some security companies have faltered under the weight of too many mergers over a relatively short period of time. The end result? Although it may be too early to conclude anything definitively, the indicators would suggest higher costs and diminished quality of service.

Uniformed security services are not alone in the arena of foreign ownership. Like many other industries operating here in the United States, most security devices are manufactured in non-U.S.-based plants. Whether it is a camera, an access control reader, or an intrusion alarm, the device's point of origin is well beyond the shores of America. For that matter, it is very fair to say that not a single Fortune 1000 company can boast of having a true U.S.-made security system.

Does this suggest that American businesses are at risk because their security officers and devices are not United States based? No, but it does suggest that when the issue of protecting people and assets is considered, we need to recognize that this is a profession that has been abdicated to others. Foreign ownership means that organizational values and practices differ from domestic values and practices. This seems simple enough, and it is. But the underlying question is whether or not senior corporate executives understand the subtle nuances inherent in their security programs and the potential effects when two differing cultural approaches either merge or clash—I'll have a great more to say about this in the pages ahead. I will also have more to add about the unfolding consolidation phenomenon. After all, as the authors of *Winning the Merger End-Game* (Graeme K. Deans, Fritz Kroeger, and Stefan Zeisel; McGraw-Hill, 2002) suggest, we are seeing the unfolding of the second phase in a four-phase process. Their research suggests that we are in what they refer to as the *Scale Stage*. Yet to come is the *Focus Stage*, in which the market may well be dominated (60%+) by three companies. Finally there is the *Balance and Alliance Stage*, in which the top three players control 70 to 80% of the industry.

When all is considered, today's challenges for the security manager can be somewhat daunting. I have come to the conclusion that the events of 9–11 did not bode well for today's private security executive, due largely to two reasons. First, we are experiencing a great deal of governmental intrusion, especially from their so-called experts in asset protection. Second, the gains made by security programs in truly offering added business value to their organizations have been retrenched. Coupling this with trying to manage business partners across oceans with varying cultural business values (despite the ready access afforded by the Internet) certainly means that the Chinese proverb is right in suggesting that security managers live in interesting times. Only the long term will tell us whether or not the aftermath of 9/11 improved the security industry or, as I suspect, dealt it a serious setback.

So what do we do? What follows is more than an in-depth analysis of the challenges facing American corporate managers inside and outside of security. This book serves as a road map, charting a new course of action for those concerned about protecting people and assets. The book is divided into three parts. The first examines the basic steps of defining an appropriate strategy and the necessary resources. Specifically, we will look at a method for assessing current and future threats—one that is reality based and not as shallow and meaningless as Homeland Security's feeble attempt to generate something politically expedient. The types of risk assessment we will discuss allow the corporate manager to define what type of security program is best suited for the organization; today there are four such programs. In turn, the nature of the program drives the characteristics and skill sets of key management players and their external partners. To this end, we will undertake a detailed analysis of supplier capabilities and their limitations.

The second part of the book examines the need for a strategic approach to today's protection of people and assets. As you will read, strategic planning and implementation is the crucial arrow in the manager's quiver of success. Here we will also review how a metrics-based approach can aid in systematically determining staff allocations and deployment to achieve greater value and contribution to the organization's performance. We will also review the latest additions to my model services agreement, another management tool that first began to take shape in the late 1980s and is now in its fifth generation. Finally, Part Three will examine the latest management approaches and examine their application in today's global and e-commerce centered world of protection. We will see how noted writers and practitioners have translated the challenges of today's turbulent times into opportunities for success.

In sum, in the first two parts of this book we'll look at a deceptively simple process—deceptive because it is easy to identify and articulate, but executing it is quite another matter. The steps are

1. Assess your risk and determine the type of security program that is appropriate.
2. Select a security management team that is best suited for the asset protection charter.
3. Formulate and implement a strategic plan designed to address real and potential threats.

To be successful requires professional experience, business acumen and management savvy. As noted, the third part of this book is dedicated to an analysis of various management tips and strategies that are available to guide the organization's stakeholders down a path of success.

Those who are familiar with my writings, seminars, and lectures know that I have long pushed for a more business-oriented approach to the profession of security. I see this latest contribution as the completion of a three-set volume that has, I hope, helped those currently in the field achieve a higher level of success. I hope that those seeking a career in corporate security will come to understand the challenges that await them and find a few strategies that will aid in meeting them head-on. Finally, for the corporate manager, I hope that you will carry away both an understanding of how you can become a partner in addressing the challenges of today and a sense of ownership that true protection of assets and people begins with your commitment.

ACKNOWLEDGMENTS

Anyone who has ever "put pen to paper" knows that it is not a solitary endeavor. This book is no exception. I want to express my sincerest appreciation to Mark Listewnik, my editor at Butterworth-Heinemann, and Kevin Sullivan and Sarah Manchester from production. Their combined efforts have translated my concepts and experiences into the written word! Thank you. I also want to thank David Gibbs, who not only was kind enough to put his time and name to my Foreword, but also provided me with both encouragement and several key ideas. A special acknowledgment needs to be extended to Ken Wheatley at SONY Electronics. Those familiar with my second book, *The Art of Security Management,* might recall in its acknowledgments that I asked my beloved wife to retire her red editing pen. Little did I realize when I asked Ken that he, too, owned one of those pens! Seriously, though, thank you, Ken, for your careful editing and keen insights. You have made this book an easier read (something you, the reader, will certainly appreciate).

I want to acknowledge my students at the University of Phoenix, especially the RO603 group: Terry Artica, Jennifer Hardin, Pam Herman, Martin Levario, Theresa Londquist, Victoria Maryatt, Ginger Ornelas, Mary Beth Quallick, Randy Raymaker, and Sona Shaw. Thank you. Your keen insights and willingness to share with me your experiences and wisdom helped me considerably. Many of the quotes you, the reader, will find in the chapters come directly from these students' work and class contributions.

In Memoriam
*I also want to acknowledge those security professionals
who committed their lives to serving their fellow
corporate citizens in the events of 9/11.*

Introduction

Many people quit looking for work when they find a job.

Kyle VanderBeek

In 1995 I wrote my first security management book. My purpose was to send a strong message to security managers, which was that their success was rooted in an ability to demonstrate strong organizational and business management skills. Although important, the need to demonstrate professional acumen is a secondary organizational issue for a security manager with a supporting staff. Being experienced in asset protection is necessary, therefore it is assumed by senior and executive management. In other words, it is a basic expectation and does not assure real success. Today my message rings even more true.

It is ironic that part of this book focuses on the need to challenge many of our industry's fundamental assumptions. The impetus is rooted in the way in which our court system is viewing the issue of premises liability, not in the events of 9/11, even though this tragedy serves to underscore the need to question fundamental assumptions. I actually started putting the ideas for this book together just prior to September 11, 2001. That morning's destruction of the World Trade Center changed a great number of other assumptions associated with property and people protection, making the comments, observations, and call for a shift in our thinking even more timely.

In 1998 I followed up my first book with another. This time the message was not only to reinforce the original idea, but also to provide a blueprint for addressing several of the major organizational challenges then facing security managers. The time has come to not only reinforce some of these earlier concepts, but also to push the envelope further. Specifically, whereas the last five years have seen little by way of the "latest and greatest" in management strategies, many of the traditional organizational challenges still have a strangle-hold on today's security departments. Here are some examples: incorporating security on the front end of business decisions related to new markets and products, security's role vis-à-vis human resources, audit, legal, and corporate real estate departments' roles in protecting assets and people, and security's own core deliverables. These are issues that still plague many security managers and their executive management teams, typically as the result of their benign neglect.

Ironically, those who have successfully met these challenges often find that they are not fully equipped to deal with the newer, and often more critical challenges to their professional success. The purpose of this book, then, is twofold. First, it is an examination of the key organizational and management challenges that confront today's security team. From here we examine defined strategies that break through these challenges and allow success to emerge. Second, the book differentiates itself from other management texts by serving as a road map for those who find it necessary to break away from what has become the conventional approach to asset protection and seek new venues for value added contributions.

You may be curious as to why I say "find it necessary to break away." One might suppose that a departure from traditional responsibilities to new ones would be a welcome and voluntarily sought after venture. Would that it were always so. Unfortunately, the landscape of today's security department is being forcibly changed, and the change often is driven by others. In one of my columns for *Security Magazine* I addressed this issue under the cloak of the long-standing adage "when life deals you lemons, make lemonade." In other words, it is becoming almost common to hear of security directors lamenting that their core deliverables are being usurped by other infrastructure business units, most notably facilities management and audit, leaving them essentially without a mission. Left unchallenged, there is only one inevitable outcome: the demise of their programs, their staff, and themselves.

In June of 2001, *Security Management Magazine* published an article of mine entitled "What Should Security's Function Be?" I received more telephone calls and e-mails about this article than about all of my monthly columns over the past three years. (Perhaps this should tell me something about my column!) I think the article hit a raw nerve for many security managers. Not only are they struggling over what security ought to be doing for an organization, but also how it ought to be delivered. Turning to external suppliers for the answer, as many emerging and long-standing Fortune 1000 companies have discovered, is not the answer. In this book we will address this failure, examining both the underlying reasons for this failure and why it will be some time before it can ever be considered an adequate solution.

The core message of the *Security Management Magazine* article was the introduction of a new management paradigm for corporate security. The stage was set with a review of the evolution of security's role in corporate America.

It tracked this evolutionary process beginning with the night watchman era to what I refer to today as the *Total Asset Protection Era*. I outlined three fundamental pillars that serve to define tomorrow's organization: a unit dedicated to business risk assessment, a unit dedicated to employee protection issues, and a unit dedicated to mainstream operational support. Herein lies a core strategy that will allow corporate security to revive from the setback of 9/11 and an opportunity to demonstrate their true added value.

To meet the challenges of today we need to examine security's ability to redefine its scope as it positions itself in today's global economy, both physically and through e-commerce. What is security's value added contribution in a world of tangible and intangible assets? What are the challenges associated with protecting people, both employees and assigned strategic partners? What role does security have in the fight against the loss of competitive intelligence and intellectual property? How does one transition rapidly, but effectively, from a management style of dictating to one of collaboration? What are the issues associated with protecting the rights of individuals when an organization stretches its operation into multiple countries and such rights are defined across the spectrum? Each one of these questions is provocative in its own way, but today's security team must be able to address each within the framework of an integrated approach.

In this latest work I build on the lessons learned from the two previous books. We will see these lessons highlighted because they help establish the context for building a new structure. We will deliberately turn away from the ideas presented by most other security management writers. It is not that their contributions are not important, but they are limited and, quite frankly, fairly basic for an experienced security manager. Rather, we will turn our attention to quite different business environments. Their lessons are both refreshing and incredibly valuable because they allow us to view security management challenges in new ways.

Our examination of the quest for organizational success will draw on the insights provided by such theorists and practitioners as Warren Bennis, Jack Welch, Charles Schwab, Tom Peters, and Peter Senge. We need to revisit carefully and examine in detail Tom Morris' *Seven C's of Success* (I laid the foundation for this in the epilogue of my last book). We will draw on Gary Dessler and read what he has to say in his text, *Management: Leading People and Organizations in the 21st Century,* and examine what Schermerhorn, Hunt, and Osborn say in their book, *Organizational Behavior.* We will also visit what Peter Kline and Bernard Saunders have to say in *Ten Steps to a Learning Organization,* and draw from other books lessons that can be directly applied to the field of security management.

Anyone familiar with my previous writings knows that I am a big fan of Oren Harari. He served as a member's of Tom Peters's consulting staff and is a professor of management at the University of San Francisco. In this book I apply his concept of leading change from the middle. This is particularly relevant because most security managers are organizationally positioned in the middle management strata of their companies. He offers 11 rules that can serve as a guide for leading profound change in an organization. Candidly, not all 11 will work for many security managers. Nonetheless, the essence of his message serves as a springboard into another discussion, one that I can only describe as the fun part of the book, even though the intent is to drive home important management strategies. In this section I present a series of my Best Management Tips. Each is dedicated to operational concerns ranging from the Ten Cardinal Sins of Security Managers to Ten Best Ways to Sell Security's Deliverables.

Finally, I have elected to end the book by asking the reader to consider a long-standing challenge: the need for true research in a profession that is largely based on assumptions. We make management and financial decisions based on a great number of unproven assumptions. Ours is a profession that is both uncodified and largely unproven. We assume that security officers provide some deterrent value. We assume that our state-of-the-art technologies are effective in preventing loss of assets and life. We assume that there is a causal link between a property owner's negligence and harm that may come to an individual. We assume that awareness translates to responsibility and accountability.

The need to conduct objective and targeted research is imperative. Our academic institutions have largely failed us in this regard. The same can be said for our professional associations and corporate sponsorships. Our government shares equally in this failure. One only needs to look to the recent court decisions on the issue of premises liability or to the tragic events associated with the increase in workplace violence and terrorist attacks to prove this point. (I find it scary that I actually wrote this paragraph in mid-August 2001, less than three weeks before the WTC attack of 9/11. Yet I am not all that surprised because terrorism is not new, not even here in the United States. The WTC incident is only the latest in the escalating need for true asset protection. It is a sad and horrific call to security executives to step up to the challenges that define our corporate contribution for the decades to come.)

Before moving on, there are two small administrative notes that need to be addressed. First, throughout this work I will be referring to both of my previous books. When this happens, I will simply use an abbreviated form for the appropriate text. I will refer to *Security Management: Business Strategies for Success* as *Business Strategies*. For *The Art of Successful Security Management*, I will use *The Art*. Also, many of my comments and observations have a link to the actions of September 11, 2001—the attack on the World Trade Center. Throughout this book, when making such a reference I will simply use the abbreviated forms of either *9/11* or *WTC*.

Second, though my friends and colleagues find that I am a man of more than a few words, I have elected to draw on the words of many whose sage advice is offered in far fewer words. I hope you find them helpful and that they add to your insights and are not a distraction. Many have opined on one aspect of business management or their chosen profession in such a way as to leave me saying, "I had not thought of it quite like that." For these people I am indebted to their keen insights.

Recognizing that my essential message cuts across everyone's interests, for this latest book I have charted a course that I hope appeals to everyone. Some of the material will be familiar to those of you who have read my previous work. However, I think you will find that the application is significantly different. I have used many of the ideas and concepts contained within the first two books to help support the points I raise in this book. For those of you who are first time readers, when the idea that I am discussing harkens back to a link with either of my first two books, I have framed the original idea in a way that allows you to bridge the gap. If you would like a fuller discussion on any one topic you can always call or drop me an e-mail at daltonaffiliates@cs.com. I always welcome comments and will gladly answer any questions you may have.

I hope you find the book both thought-provoking and enjoyable!

PART I

THE CHANGING ENVIRONMENT OF SECURITY MANAGEMENT

In the Preface, I began by noting that the events of 9/11 have not benefited private security. There is no doubt that some aspects of the profession have gained and stand to gain more economically. But for the profession overall, it was—and I fear will remain so for some time to come—a true setback. Why? Because corporate security was transitioning from one evolutionary era into a another, one that was held to be very exciting and would have catapulted security from being just another infrastructure element to becoming a true internal business-driving partner. The WTC disaster pulled the profession back to an era with a far more limited organizational scope.

Simply stated, asset protection managers were beginning to make serious inroads into the mainstream of their organizations' business interests. Companies across all sectors and of all sizes were beginning to redefine the mission and contribution of security. The profession was passing from the days of "guns, guards, and dogs" into an era of true proactive protection of all assets, tangible and intangible. Certainly this cannot be said for all organizations, not even for the majority. But the trend was clearly evident—so much so that an entire section of this text is dedicated to this new corporate role.

The security profession has emerged from the days of the classic night watchman to the role of a full business partner, often sitting at the table when critical strategic decisions are being made by senior managers. Yet even before the dust settled at the WTC on September 11, security managers were being summoned to their respective executive rows and grilled as to what measures they had in place to ensure that their company would not fall victim to a similar physical attack. The emphasis on physical attacks underscores a direct reversal in security's new charter. Rather than embracing the events of 9/11 as an added threat to an organization's overall list of business risks, for many security directors the physical threat became the only threat. When you read The Evolution of Corporate Security section this will become even clearer. You will see that those who were on the leading edge of a new dawn were pulled back to responsibilities that had long ago been shifted to others. Or they were directed to forgo their involvement with other (and, I dare say, far more serious) threats to focus on the protection of physical assets—in short, to assume a reactive posture.

Despite decades of discussions about how private security needs to be less reactive in nature and more proactive, little has been done. The WTC disaster only served to reinforce the reactive nature of asset and people protection. Some of you might contend that this is perfectly all right because security is all about reacting to events. Such a position misses the critical point that security, as a corporate function, requires forethought and deliberateness of execution just the same as any other business unit. A true and comprehensive security program entails the ability to address the entire continuum of real and potential threats that logically fall within the purview of a protection program. I make this distinction to avoid confusion over the meaning of risk assessment. There are some risks that are clearly outside the scope of what is commonly referred to as corporate security. For example, in the world of financial services, it ought not be within security's charter to analyze and make decisions regarding consumer loans; yet these become *assets*. Similarly, it is not the mission of security to supplant traditional new-hire screening processes under the governance of human resources (HR) departments, or render legal opinions regarding contractual relationships—a role reserved for the legal department. Yet each of these examples serves as an illustration of how others protect company assets and interests.

On the other hand, security is not about simply reacting, or responding to some sort of adrenalin rush brought on by an emergency, a threat, a loss, or even an investigative pursuit. It is not all about serving as an escort for a concerned employee or ensuring that doors are closed and locked after everyone else has departed for the evening. It is not all about issuing a ticket for a parking infraction or checking someone's company access control badge. It is not all about standing by as HR terminates an angry employee or protecting an executive's home. It is not even all about all of the above combined.

My corporate and consulting experiences have allowed me to interact with many of America's top 200 companies as well as dozens of emerging global organizations. I have interacted with many nonprofit organizations, government agencies, and small companies. Since 1993 I have been retained by more than 250 attorneys representing both plaintiffs and defendants. Consistently, I have listened to two sides of the same concern. From executives I hear that they are concerned that their security program is not as effective as it ought to be. They are often unhappy about, or are at least questioning, their security department's approach or basic contribution to the corporation. On the security team's side I hear about how they are the last to know when something occurs that affects their area, or are so busy fighting the daily fires that they have no time to proactively plan.

Both sides are actually saying much of the same without knowing it. The executives are, in essence, expressing concern for the lack of a strategic plan. Similarly, cries of frustration for being out of the loop underscore the lack of a strategic approach on the part of the security department. In short, the overwhelming majority (I dare estimate over 90%) lack a simple plan of attack regarding the protection of people and assets. Clearly, there is an element of reactivity associated with protecting people and assets. We will revisit a model that I developed years ago and introduced in *Business Strategies* that reinforces this position. I refer to it as the *looping model* because it demonstrates the integration of our proactive and reactive responsibilities through developing practices and procedures, administrating the program, to the resulting response and management of specific incidents. But there is an aspect of effective organizational preplanning that transcends even my looping model. Such a dynamic serves as the foundation for all else to follow. It allows an organization to articulate how it intends to pursue the protection of its people and assets.

The most recent Bush administration would say that they are being proactive with the creation of the Homeland Security Office. They would point to legislation calling for the federalization of airport screeners. They would stress the fact that after the WTC attack, more than $22 billion was set aside to combat terrorism on the home front. They would adamantly insist that all of this was a demonstration of their commitment to being proactive. I'm sorry, but this is wrong on all counts. Whereas the argument could be advanced that these are related to preventive measures, they are certainly not reflective of a strategic plan. Strategic planning requires initiatives that are designed to identify risk, assess its impact, contrast that to the cost of prevention, and then develop an appropriate strategy, complete with a mechanism for ongoing assessments designed to measure the consequences of that strategy. "Wait!!" They might scream. "We have an assessment tool. Have you not heard about our rainbow rating system that ranks threats from green (low) to red (high)?" We'll examine how this so-called tool for the private sector is not now, nor was ever intended to be, a risk assessment for businesses.

Does this mean that security will remain largely reactive? Unfortunately for everyone in the business of asset protection, the answer is yes—at least for a while. Others will remain reactive for a much longer period of time simply because they are that far back on the evolutionary continuum. For them, the events of 9/11 simply reinforced their current role and will do so until other organizational and business drivers push them into the next era. Still others— the majority—will be seen by their organizational counterparts as largely managing a part of the infrastructure that is reaction-oriented over the near to intermediate term. I hope to avoid the trap of timing by simply sidestepping what is meant by the term *intermediate*. I do this because the actual duration will vary from one company to other. The challenge for the corporate security manager is to break away sooner rather than later.

Finally, for those on the farthest end of the continuum—those that entered the *Era of Total Asset Protection*—you, too, have felt the sting of what I refer to as "reactive reactionaries." Those are the senior executives who responded to 9/11 by reordering your priorities and shifting your focus away from the myriad other business threats that pose a much more serious exposure. These threats include addressing physical risks, but they embrace far more. As we shall see, they involve risks on all fronts as your organization continues to compete simultaneously in a global and e-commerce driven market.

Before launching into Chapter 1 and beyond, I think it is important to underscore that I am not saying the role of corporate security is to forgo involvement in matters of physical asset protection. Quite the opposite is true. Protecting assets needs to be an integrated approach. For example, those within the world of information technology (IT) understand that protecting electronic data involves not only software platforms, but also physical barriers. Our courts long ago held that there is a direct relationship between protecting intangible assets such as intellectual property and physical security measures. The issue of security is extremely complex given today's distributed networks. It requires multiple sets of expertise. Corporate security can make valuable contributions to the overall protection of IT in its role as both investigative expert when an unwanted intrusion occurs and as designer of physical protection standards.

Chapter 1

CHARTING THE PATH

All truth passes through three phases. First it is ridiculed. Second, it is violently opposed. Third, it is accepted as being self-evident.

Arthur Schopenhauer

Primary Themes

- Creating the Baseline: Formulating a Risk Assessment
- JLL's Approach vs. Homeland Security's Approach
- Selecting the Most Appropriate Security Response
- The Evolution of Security: Where Do You Fit?

OPENING OBSERVATIONS

Success is not something that just happens. It requires a plan and its execution. It also requires the ability to check in at calculated times to assure that everything is still working. If something is not working, it needs to be attended to—but only if it is really broken. Many managers are meddlers. They simply cannot leave something alone, even when it is doing what it was designed to do. Other managers have the uncanny ability to break that which is not broken simply by virtue of their meddling (I'm sure they would rather that I refer to it as their involvement). Then there are those managers who cannot differentiate between what is working and what is broken. These are the managers who seek quick fixes because they simply cannot live with the stress or uncertainty of something being out of whack, even when being out of whack for a period of time is a necessary part of the resolution strategy.

I think the events of 9/11 underscored how every management approach is represented in the time of crises. There were those who remained calm

5

and focused. There were those who overreacted. There were those who retrenched—a great deal of these, I'm sad to note. And, there were those who saw opportunity in the tragic events of the day. Some opportunities were very self-serving and embarrassing for law enforcement, the security profession, and nonsecurity executives. On the other hand, there were opportunities for reasonable, ethical stakeholders to ask some very important questions and seek out answers to mitigate the likelihood of future incidents.

Long before the dawn of September 11, our federal and state courts challenged those in the security profession to lay the foundation for a reasonable approach to protecting people and assets. Little was done—at least little was done that could be called measured and well thought out. Inherent business drivers such as competition, e-commerce, fluctuating world markets, and political agendas, should have tipped others that the face of asset protection was changing and that a more calculated approach was needed. But times were good and little attention was given to those who called for a strategic-based approach. I'm reminded of what Julius Caesar once said about such times: *In tempore pacis, para bellum*—In time of peace, prepare for war. In the final analysis, what is needed now, as always, is a systematic approach that is grounded in common sense and proven business metrics. We begin our journey with the first two steps: creating a baseline and selecting the best approach. We will then turn our attention to who should lead the effort and who should accompany.

STEP ONE: CREATING THE BASELINE AND ASSESSING RISK

Protecting assets in a dynamic environment can be very expensive. System designs, equipment purchases, modifications to structures, and changes in personnel and operating practices all require substantial investment. The cost for protection significantly increases when intangible assets are calculated into the overall cost formula. How do we begin to determine what is appropriate and what is not? For my clients and others recognized for their pursuit of a best practices approach, the answer begins with determining the level of risk, or threat, inherent in the physical complex or campus. Even the courts have recognized for many years that to prove a company's intent to protect their intellectual property and other intangible assets, the starting point centers on physical controls that limit access.

Over the years, many security experts have offered risk assessment tools. The tools that stress simplicity offer the best results because they can be understood by everyone, which in turn promotes advocacy. More important, regardless of what risk analysis model is used, it must be accompanied by clearly articulated guidelines for what needs to be done for each level of threat. Writing for the June 2002 edition of *Security Management* magazine, David Gibbs, Senior Vice President for On-Line Associates, notes:

Risk assessments should provide a "total picture" assessment of the varied and interdependent assets integrated into a company's operations. Thus, while physically walking specific sites is still essential, a viable risk assessment must also address the company's intellectual property; its electronic networks, databases, and Web sites; the workplaces and movements of key personnel; and distribution logistics.

David goes on to point out that specialized risk assessment software has come into its own. Today several commercial products are available to simplify even the most data-loaded assessments. The latest generations of software can track each element of a comprehensive assessment in relation to the nature and value of the asset, the level of threat, incident history, identified vulnerabilities, and available safeguards. In other words, the drive is to make the information simple to gather and, perhaps more important, simple to interpret. Only then can an appropriate response plan be developed. As David concludes, software based assessment "allows the security manager to ensure consistency . . . when analyzing the deployment and movement of all assets—people, electronic data, and products. The result is a comprehensive, consistent, and dynamic view of the company's total risk. This view becomes the basis for a security and risk management plan and program that factors in such considerations as the cost of security, the cost of risk, and acceptable levels of risk."

Risk assessments need to be realistic. One practitioner noted: "To be meaningful, it has to be meaty, something you can get your teeth into and chew on." I could not have said it better. Here it is easy to fall into the first of many traps to follow. This first trap is in creating something that is more form than substance. The most recent case that best illustrates this for me is the rainbow threat matrix developed shortly after 9/11 by the Homeland Security Office. In their effort to demonstrate that they were being responsive, not to mention in control, they announced their new risk rating system in early 2002. Pundits were quick to dub it the "rainbow threat assessment" because it utilizes five colors to denote certain levels of threat. Ranging from green, representing low risk, to red for high risk, the Homeland Security Office said their intent was to allow the public to quickly and easily assess the state of alert facing the country.

Unfortunately, on closer review, the government's attempt to simplify threat levels becomes more gray than any other color, and a dark shade of gray at that! First, contrary to the media's reporting and the words of Homeland Security czar, Tom Ridge, the color scheme is actually not directed at the general public. Nor does the rating system indicate what criteria are used in determining the level/color of risk. Rather, it is actually for the federal government's use only and is strongly recommended for local law enforcement officials to assist them in developing their response plans. Ridge announced that the intent was to create a common vocabulary between government and industry. He went on to say that the warning system was "designed to measure and evaluate terrorist threats and communicate them to the public in a timely manner." This comment was made the day he announced the color-coded system, thus creating confusion from the start. Knowing that the system was intended only for target users, he confused the matter by saying that it was intended to better assist the general public.

The color-coded system became murkier when Ridge added, "For the first time, threat conditions will be coupled with protective measures." This implies that specific action guidelines would be available to allow individuals the opportunity to better protect themselves. In reality, no clearly articulated guidelines had been developed. Rather, each color simply provided a list of three or four bulleted suggestions. To better understand the form over substance trap, let's take a brief look at the government's well-intentioned risk model, focusing on the first three risk levels. In doing so, hopefully, we can avoid it altogether. With each color, the government assigns a corresponding risk level and provides "guidelines for action." My comments follow each major bulleted guideline. I've chosen to highlight the first three levels only because even the most cursory reading of the last two (orange and red) illustrates that the threat level guidelines are intended for law enforcement use only.

Green: Low Risk of Terrorist Attacks

- **Refine and exercise planned protective measures.** This assumes that some type of preplanned protective measures have been developed. Most companies have never had the need and therefore have no such guidelines in place.

- **Ensure emergency personnel receive training.** This begs the obvious questions of type, duration, and so on.

- **Assess facilities for vulnerabilities and take measures to reduce them.** Since most private companies and public sector organizations do not have this expertise, they will most likely need to turn to the experts. Yet there is no standardization among the so-called experts to assure organizations that they are receiving the best advice and direction.

Blue: Guarded Condition, General Risk of Terrorist Attacks

- **Check communications with designated emergency response or command locations.** This assumes that the local community has identified such command locations and that they have a working model in place. At the time this scheme was developed local law enforcement officials were looking to the federal government for assistance. We see the establishment of a classic bureaucratic catch-22.

- **Review and update emergency response procedures.** Here again, it assumes there is one in place to review and update.

- **Provide the public with necessary information.** This is one of the weakest statements in the entire scheme because it is so general.

Yellow: Elevated Condition, Significant Risk of Terrorist Attacks

- **Increase surveillance of critical locations.** What are the guidelines to distinguish critical from very important locations, and not at all critical locations? This calls for a risk rating scale within a risk rating scale.
- **Coordinate emergency plans with nearby jurisdictions.** This is the first clear indicator that this color scheme is not intended for use by the private sector.
- **Assess further refinement of protective measures within the context of current threat information.** I suggest this is too vague to be meaningful.
- **Implement, as appropriate, contingency and emergency response plans.** Again, this assumes that which in reality does not exist.

Shortly after the rainbow risk assessment was announced, *Newsweek* magazine covered the story (March 18, 2002). They noted that an accompanying brochure published by Ridge's office was "a good, if simple, example of how Ridge's office wants to get the private sector involved." How can they report that? My conclusion is that this is nothing more than an example of bad reporting or falling victim to Washington's spin-doctoring. If, on the other hand, it truly is an attempt by Homeland Security to involve the private sector, they have done less than an admirable job. To further exacerbate the situation, *Newsweek* added the following:

> *"Remember when the SEC encouraged companies to disclose their Y2K protections and vulnerabilities in their prospectuses?" Ridge says. "We intend to do that with terrorism. . . . If companies have to talk about what they're doing they'll do more. . . . There's also the insurance companies. If we help them on best practices and encourage them, they'll push their customers." "If he does that, he'll make a lot of progress," says Jules Kroll, who runs Kroll Associates, a leading corporate-security firm that is already working with insurance companies on rating the security of their clients' buildings and facilities. "It sounds like this guy is prepared to push the right levers," he (Kroll) adds. So far, that's a good summary of what Ridge is doing on a lot of fronts."*

What makes this particularly troubling is twofold. First, Ridge openly states that he expects that companies are going to willingly disclose vulnerabilities and preparations to combat terrorism. Would he offer the same for the government? This is absurd and shows his lack of understanding of the private sector. He underscores this absurdity by drawing the insurance industry in under the cloak of best practices. His own risk assessment is seriously flawed and is anything but an example of best practices. Almost as a kick-in-the-face to the reader, the article then quotes one security consultant who, by the article's own description, renders a self-serving comment in support of using the insurance industry as a tool for disclosure and compliance.

Despite my criticism of the government's coded plan, the whole idea of a threat assessment based on their approach is somewhat academic at best. Ridge noted that it would be several years until the nation's alert status is downgraded to green. For that matter, he, along with Attorney General John Ashcroft, noted that the United States was currently in a yellow status and would most likely remain at that level or higher for several years to come. Given the scope of this country's commitment to ridding the world of terrorism, I suspect they may be right. The argument that this raises is why, then, is there a need to have anything other than a yellow, orange, and red status? I am at a loss to provide an answer. I do know one thing, however. Shortly after their rating system was announced, it fell under a great deal of criticism from the business community and the media, and was the butt of many a comic's joke. I have seen nothing meaningful in the news or government discussions since then. This is another indicator of form over substance—something sounds responsive at first, but falls under its own weight of vagueness and ineptness.

I need to hasten that I am not fundamentally opposed to a five-color-schemed approach. Using a continuum of green to red color-coding is fundamentally sound. The problem arises in its application and, in this case, the lack of clearly communicating its intended audience. I also need to note that this matrix is intended to provide guidance once the actual threat level has been determined by the government. In other words, what we are missing is the actual methodology that is used to determine the announced color code. In this model we, the end-users, are being told the level of threat and what "steps" should be taken, although it is fair to say that the steps are far from clearly defined.

A Working Example

Let's shift gears and examine a different risk matrix model. This one actually allows the end-user to determine the level of risk and offers a plan for action. After 9/11 one of the world's largest property management companies, Jones Lang LaSalle (JLL), developed a threat assessment for their own use. They asked me to review it. The charter was to work with their Technical Services Division to develop a risk matrix that could be used by local personnel to determine their degree of vulnerability. They knew the model needed to be simple to understand, yet based on relevant criteria given the nature of the high stakes involved. Since developing this matrix, I have applied the basic methodology to other business sectors with remarkable success. The model is a decision-making roadmap designed to assist in determining the level of risk the property represents.

The methodology involves three grades of risk: low, medium, and high. It examines five criteria. These criteria serve to measure a property's risk factors resulting from its own prominence or proximity to other highly recognized structures or places. The end result is a Threat Score. The highest possible score is 21. The risk levels, response requirements and score are as follows:

Risk Level	Requirement	Score
Low	Adherence to standard procedures	≤7
Medium	Adherence to standard procedures, plus instituting moderate enhancements	8–14
High	Adherence to standard procedures, plus instituting significant enhancements	≥15

The following sections are guidelines we developed for using this methodology.

Risk Factor #1: Market Importance

This is a measure of the importance the geographic area (a city, region, distinct) carries within the national perception.

- **5 points:** These are areas within the United States that are readily recognized around the world due to population, tourism, business, or government and/or military significance. Examples include Boston, New York City, Philadelphia, Miami, Washington, DC, Chicago, Seattle, Los Angeles, San Diego, and San Francisco.

- **3 points:** These are major urban areas or areas of high technical, military, or commercial importance. These include Atlanta, Northern Virginia, Detroit, Dallas, California's Silicon Valley, and Livermore, California (Lawrence Livermore Labs).

- **2 points:** These cities are population centers of some importance. They may include state capitols, cities with major universities, or commercial hubs. Included are cities such as St. Louis, Denver, Columbus, Ohio, Ann Arbor, Michigan (University of Michigan), Palo Alto, California (Stanford University), Sacramento, and Portland, Oregon.

Risk Factor #2: Site Prominence

This measures a location or property's ability to attract high public, media, or government attention.

- **5 points:** These are high-visibility properties with significant national importance. They include government buildings such as the FBI Building, the U.S. Capitol and Supreme Court Buildings, the White House, national monuments and parks, major military installations, large stadiums, major hotels and convention centers, stock exchanges, nuclear power plants, and hydroelectric dams. Also on this list are properties with importance transcending their commercial purpose. These include the United Nations Building, the Empire State Building, the Sears Tower, Disneyland or Disney World, the Transamerica Building, and several major bridges and rapid transit lines.

- **3 points:** These are places that attract a high regional awareness or traffic. They include major retail centers (Mall of America, etc.), highly visible tourist attractions, large public parking facilities, major state and local government buildings, and trophy office properties. Office properties on this list include New York City's Rockefeller Center, the John Hancock Center and the Prudential Center in Boston, The Museum of Natural Science in Chicago, Fox Plaza in Los Angeles, and San Francisco's 555 California (the West Coast home of Bank of America).

- **1 point:** These are larger office buildings and places of regional interest.

Risk Factor #3: Proximity to Focal Points

This is risk associated with proximity to a site that garners large amounts of public attention.

- **2 points:** Proximity to a site with a 5-point site prominence score.
- **1 point:** Proximity to a site with a 3-point site prominence score.

Inclusion or Proximity to Transportation Hubs

This is risk associated with proximity to centers of high vehicle, cargo, and population traffic.

- **3 points:** Sites that include major ports of entry, large airports, or national rail hubs, such as Grand Central Station, Union Station (Washington, D.C.) and Union Station (Chicago).
- **2 points:** Sites that include regional transportation hubs (regional airports, commuter rail hubs, large metropolitan transit stations), or proximity to a 3-point transportation hub.
- **1 point:** Sites that include local transportation hubs, or proximity to a 2-point transportation hub.

Risk Factor #4: Tenant Exposure

Risk associated with presence or traffic of particular tenants.

- **3 points:** World or national headquarters of high-profile groups or organizations. Examples include the World Trade Organization, Red Cross, B'nai Brith, foreign consulates, political parties, special interest offices, or Fortune 500 corporations such as Citibank, Boeing, Microsoft, Exxon-Mobil. This also includes sites that house a significant governmental presence (FBI, ATF, recruiting centers) or sites that are used for a highly sensitive (major data storage centers) or hazardous purpose (volatile chemical storage warehouses).
- **2 points:** Headquarters of regional high-profile groups or concentrations of national groups. This also includes proximity to a site with 3-point tenant exposure.
- **1 point:** Concentration of regional groups or proximity to a site with 2-point tenant exposure.

Risk Factor #5: Importance to Infrastructure

This rates the importance of a site's role in the functioning of national, regional or local infrastructure.

- **3 points:** Sites with crucial roles in infrastructure functionality. Included are national communication hubs, power plants, and water treatment centers. These places possess the ability to exert a strong influence on public health and welfare.
- **2 points:** Sites that are important in terms of infrastructure, but not crucial, or proximity to a site with 3-point importance to infrastructure.
- **1 point:** Proximity to a site with 2-point importance to infrastructure.

The point assignment that was used to create each category of risk (low, medium, high) simply reflected the total number of points that could be applied per risk factor. In other words, if a property compiled the lowest number of points in each risk factor, its total score would be 6. If the property scored the medium number of points in all categories, its score would not exceed 14. Therefore, a score greater than 14 would automatically place a property in the highest category.

Some might argue that such a scoring strategy is less than mathematically accurate. Technically, I would agree. However, the purpose was to put a working model in the hands of local decision-makers that reflected a reasoned strategy that was conservative in its approach. The team that developed this matrix felt that it allowed managers to make decisions quickly and with a fair degree of accuracy. They also wanted to place in the decision-makers hands a tool that could be shared with others, especially the property owners and tenants. They intended to provide such a tool that would not be criticized or second-guessed based on business metrics, which—as we noted earlier—are not the same as scientific metrics.

The value of this metrics-based approach is that it gives grounded reasoning to the risk assessment process. It serves as a working guide that allows managers the opportunity to ask what their threat level is prior to expenditures. It also drives the issue of coverage. Security managers and corporate executives can come quickly to an agreement that the capital dollars and staff deployment requirements are appropriate for the level of threat. Once the level has been set, the respective parties can begin the work of defining their action plan. We will address this shortly. For now it is important to underscore that this is an example of the risk matrix being applied by a large property management company. As noted, this same approach can be modified for other business sector applications. Likewise, it can be adopted for other operations within the organization.

When applying the matrix to other types of organizations, the threat criteria can be changed. For example, instead of market dominance being used, one might want to consider economic impact; based on either a country as a whole or a specific company. Tenant exposure can be replaced with customer confidence. In other words, the criteria are not rigid, but can be adjusted to the threat interests of the organization. The critical link is the development of criteria with a direct bearing on the company's performance. Once these criteria have been identified, risk rating levels can be developed, whether they are simply categories of low to high or a color code.

Once the matrix has been applied and the risk rating established, what then? For JLL it meant creating a strategy that addresses the present, the intermediate term, and the longer term. In the days following 9/11 each manager was provided a list of 40 considerations. These were essentially broken into three parts, which were staffing concerns; devices and equipment; and operating practices for employees, suppliers, and tenants. Each section identified a number of variables ranging from staff deployment and equipment coverage to notifications. Property managers were provided a simple check-list that could be quickly referenced to assure that the basics were being met.

For the intermediate term, property management teams were provided a more detailed audit instrument that allowed them to compare what was required for a facility or complex that was rated low, medium, or high against what was in place. This prepared list of do's and don'ts/haves and have-nots allowed each property to determine its own disparity between what was required and what was in place. The audit instrument also called for an explanation as to what was required (time, money, etc.) to close the gap, and a determination as to whether such requirements were actually applicable for that particular complex. Similarly, the audit instrument reflected the longer-term requirements and what local management determined to be necessary or not.

As previously mentioned, this is one approach. It is not the only one, nor is it necessarily the most applicable for every security management team, because it focuses on only the issue of proximity. Nevertheless, it illustrates how one company approaches the issue of determining what the baseline is for each property under its direct control. It also demonstrates that there is a reasonable approach—one based on business metrics and not reflective of some arbitrary assumptions.

Canadian-based PPM 2000 has developed a number of software-based programs that broaden the categories for determining threat levels. Their program, RiskAssess, can actually create a threat profile for an organization based on historical crime rates, disasters, system failures, and so on. These elements can be factored into the equation along with security staffing, deployment, operating practices, and a number of related facilities management concerns. When all of the data are entered, a different threat level emerges—one based on past events and current measures.

Regardless of whether the RiskAssess tool is used or the JLL model, both focus on the physical attributes of an organization. Others have developed their own products, which center on the collation of organizational demographics and translate the data into quantifying assets, threats, vulnerabilities, and countermeasures. Unlike RiskAssess or the JLL model, these companies take the issue of risk assessment into the core elements of what drives an organization's business. For example, Akela, Inc. offers a competitive product to Risk Assess. Their program is called Security Analysis Support System (SASSy) and it creates automated survey reports reflecting an analysis of known or anticipated threats.

These examples provide us with demonstrated proofs that the private sector is working toward an approach that not only simplifies the risk assessment process, but also generates deliverables that can aid the decision-maker. Working with a company's information technology department and third-party sources, security can take the lead in collaborating with company executives in determining where threats lurk. Those firms that have yet to develop a full-time security department can draw upon the tools and experiences of others in establishing their baseline asset threat. Can similar approaches be developed measuring threats associated with competitive intelligence, intellectual property, and other key intangible assets? The answer is yes. We will explore this in more detail in our discussion of corporate security as a provider of total asset protection. The process remains constant while the threat criteria change.

STEP TWO: DETERMINING WHICH APPROACH IS MOST APPROPRIATE

As we have seen, the events of 9/11 changed the world for many of us. As a nation we have become so accustomed to this date and all it stands for that we have incorporated it into our vernacular. Today a person need only say "September 11th" or "9/11" and we all know what the speaker is referring to. These two phrases are relatively new to our world of business vernacular and carry meanings that capture our immediate attention. But are they new? Although the actual expressions are new, the underlying threats that both convey are certainly no strangers. As early as the mid 1970s I began writing about policing and security in America. Whereas my articles and books since then have focused on the management side of both, the core principle has always been on the need to adequately address threats to our employees and customers as well as our tangible and intangible assets.

It is amazing how much "press" has been given to the issue of workplace violence over the past decade and a half. This includes violence in our schools and on our highways. When I first began my career in law enforcement there was the inherent danger associated with responding to a bar fight, a domestic dispute, or stopping a dangerous felon on the street. There were other threats as well. I entered policing when the Vietnam protests were peaking and the Black Panthers, the Symbionese Liberation Army (SLA), and the Hells Angels openly talked about "keeping score," a reference to directly confronting the police with the intent to kill or seriously maim them. In response, law enforcement developed a sophisticated officer safety program that is still with us today and has proven to be a double-edged sword. Even though these self-defense strategies have saved many officer lives, these same tactics go to the very root of most of today's complaints regarding excessive force.

As I moved into the world of corporate security I faced other forms of violence. My first for-profit organization was Crocker National Bank in San Francisco. Not only were we the most robbed bank in the most robbed state, but also we had just settled a civil suit involving the shooting death of a customer resulting from an SLA holdup in Carmichael, California. You may recall this as one of the robberies involving Patty Hearst. It is strange to be writing about this, more than 20 years later, knowing that the criminal case is only now making its way through the criminal justice system.

Bank robberies were not our only concern. This was a time when executive protection was on everyone's mind. Reports of kidnapping or extortions were common. Much of this was the result of radical groups, but concern was also related to corporate managers being victimized as a result of their overseas assignments. Companies quietly went about stockpiling marked money for ready access in the event of a kidnapping. Others augmented their security plans with insurance policies, and still others began installing alarms in the residences of their executive staff.

In short, the concept of threats to people and assets is not new. The only difference now is that for a period of time immediately following the events of 9/11 there was a heightened concern for everyone's well-being. For many, this concern remains. For the majority, however, the success of the United States' war on terrorism has put this issue to the back of their minds. Although I believe most Americans today are somewhat more aware of the need to be cautious, they have returned to their daily lives, just as our president pleaded for us to do in the days immediately following the tragedy. I believe this remains so even as talk of inevitable formal confrontation with Iraq, North Korea, and others increases.

About the only ongoing reminders of heightened security are the frequent reports associated with airport security breaches or some new threat issued by the FBI. For example, in the days leading up to the 4th of July festivities in 2002, the media issued daily FBI warnings of some impending disaster that "could likely" occur. Similar warnings were issued just before the Winter Olympics of 2002 in Salt Lake City. Even though these centered on specific high-profile days, such vague and unsubstantiated warnings appeared weekly throughout the first six months of 2002, and the same can be said in 2003. The regulations and procedures that have been put in place at our airports or at special events remind me of something a former boss of mine, Jay Dixon, once said. I don't know if he was quoting someone else or not, but I do remember what he said: "Ah, there is nothing like a crisis to allow small minds to rise to the occasion and think small!" Today, we stand in long lines while screeners check to see if we are carrying plastic knives or nail clippers. Congressional representatives over 70 years old, elderly women in wheelchairs, and even our former Vice President, Al Gore, have been asked to shed their shoes and be subjected to searches while those who wish to do us harm must surely be holding their stomachs and laughing. It is a wonder that a person's eyeglasses are not confiscated, since the glass can be broken out and used to cut someone. Or, worse yet, a person could be pinched into submission by some fanatic who has developed the fine skill of squeezing a sensitive body part with the frames.

Despite this satirical view, the underlying concern is that security professionals tend to be their own worst enemy. When times call for reasonable approaches, ours is an industry sadly quick to overreact. In the mid-1980s corporate executives became frustrated as security experts intimidated them with scare tactics and built over-reaching executive protection programs. International travel advisories became a mainstay for a corporate security program. Unfortunately, such advisories were typically generated by alarmists who portrayed Latin America, the Philippines, Africa, and parts of Asia as places where danger lurked behind every boulder or tree. Executives were required to be driven by specially trained security people, or often by those not specifically trained but who certainly gave the impression that they were so skilled.

This executive frustration later led to a view more cynical than my own regarding today's so-called airport security and other FBI-initiated warnings. The July 3–4, 2002, edition of USA Today carried a cover story entitled "Rules to Rein in Airport Closings." In the article the author, Blake Morrison, reported that as a result of so many orders issued by airport security directors to close terminals or recall airlines after a suspected security breech, the Transportation Security Administration was forced to rescind the directors' powers to issue such directives. Within the first five months of being given such discretionary power, security directors evacuated 124 airports based on a reported security breech and recalled 631 flights to their originating terminal to re-search their passengers.

Many senior managers eventually adopted a fatalistic view of their circumstances. This was (and remains today) most commonly captured by the exclamation, "If it is my time to go, then there is little I or anyone else can do." Such an attitude speaks against not only prudent executive protection, but also leaves the remaining security program without needed senior management support. What has been lacking over the years is a solid, business-based program. Despite my calling for such an approach nearly 20 years ago, most security managers have done little to convince their senior management that asset protection, whether this includes human life or property, is an essential element to the success of the company's bottom line. As we shall see in the pages ahead, security managers are not to be totally blamed for this failure. Senior management and many others share in the culpability of lax security in corporate America today.

Regrettably, we see the same exercise in professional futility being played out by the FBI and Office of Homeland Security. They need to take a lesson from their private security counterparts. As I noted in the previous paragraphs, when corporate security managers inundated their executives with dire warnings of kidnapping threats and danger to the overseas traveler, it did not take long for these executives to become jaded and indifferent to such emotionally loaded warnings. The same thing is happening to the American public. Daily bombardments from the FBI, CIA, and others leave people snickering when the predicted attacks fail to appear and causes the public to lose confidence in these warnings. One would think that the fable of the boy who cried wolf one too many times would resonate with government officials who spend a great deal of effort needlessly scaring people.

Against this backdrop it is difficult for both the nonsecurity executive and the security manager to make a determination as to what type of program is appropriate for their organization. Over time, security has evolved from hiring someone to serve as the town crier or night watchman to hiring a sophisticated core of asset protection professionals. For some companies it may still be appropriate to define their programs largely in terms of employing uniformed guards to be posted at designated points. There may also be the need to install a few security devices such as intrusion alarms or closed-circuit television. For other organizations a much more elaborate approach will be required. To determine the most appropriate approach after having completed the first step (e.g., threat analysis), it is best to begin by having an understanding of how security has evolved. As you will read in my discussion of the evolution of security, the profession has passed through four phases of development. The challenge is for security directors and senior managers to carefully assess which phase is best matched to their particular need.

This is not an easy process because it is intertwined with many personal biases. Obviously, if a case can be made for a more sophisticated approach, the cost of protection goes up. Salaries are higher, equipment needs are more elaborate, and so forth. Likewise, more sophistication increases the potential for more intrusion into the employees' workplace. Whether it is an issue of e-mail monitoring or controlling access to data fields or physical locations, as management increases its need to protect people and assets, there will be an inevitable effect on operations. Such an impact can have a direct affect on morale and productivity—positively or adversely.

Against this backdrop, let us take a short journey through the evolution of corporate security. In doing so, we will discover that today's corporate security program has traversed through four distinct eras. Some programs are still locked into the first era while others are much further along the continuum. But do not draw any hasty conclusions; for some organizations, still being in an earlier era is quite appropriate. This is because each organization has a different set of needs and level of threat. For many, having an early era program may be the most appropriate asset protection response. For others, a more sophisticated approach may be required. By closely examining the characteristics of each era and matching them to an established threat level using a methodology similar to one previously reviewed, the management team should be able to determine where they are versus where they ought to be.

THE EVOLUTION OF CORPORATE SECURITY

Be not afraid of growing slowly; be afraid of only standing still.
Chinese proverb

We can learn a great deal from this Chinese proverb. To meet the challenges of today, security managers need to understand that they cannot stand on their past accomplishments. They need to grow—sometimes slowly—but continuously. To best understand what needs to be done, we have to begin by looking at where corporate security has been. Sadly, many corporations' security programs have not advanced very far, but have been held back, providing a service that can best be described as little more than being night watchmen. Others, such as HP, Capital One, Fidelity Investments, 3M, Exxon-Mobil, and SONY Electronics, have evolved corporate security to the point at which the program actually demonstrates true added value and contributes to the company's mainstream business opportunities. This, in turn, flows effectively to bottom-line profitability.

In June of 2001 I published an article for one of the profession's leading journals, *Security Management* magazine. This article, entitled "What Should Security's Function Be?", set out to describe the evolution of American corporate security. It was set within the framework of where security should report in an American company. I deliberately selected this context because I am frequently asked this simple question. Yet the answer is far from simple. Reporting relationships are a direct reflection of organizational need, emphasis, and support. These three components define both the program's limits and the degree of expertise needed to execute the program. Regrettably, many security managers are either over-qualified, possessing more skills than the job requires, or lack the necessary business acumen to effectively manage what has been given them as their charter.

There was a time when security manager positions were considered the second career of choice for retiring police or military personnel. Some made their way into the corporate halls by way of a career in the intelligence services, but most were either former Justice Department or Treasury Department (Secret Service) agents, or state or large municipal police force managers. In these careers they were very successful. Corporate executives mistakenly believed that if the individual could run a police department, the same individual could manage the company's guard force and a group of investigators. Many times these same executives deliberately sought out former law enforcement personnel to serve more as trophies for their corporate mantel or believed that having a former police manager would provide an inside link to one or more government agencies. I recall how my last boss's boss, an executive vice president for a large financial services organization, once proudly introduced me to a couple of visiting dignitaries. He said: "Let me introduce you to our corporate cop with a Ph.D." Nearly everyone in security with a law enforcement or military background has a similar story to share.

To help us better understand today's security management arena, what follows is an extract from the original article that was submitted to *Security Management* magazine.

We've all heard the old saying, "if I had a dime for every time I was asked that, I'd be a rich person." Well, without a doubt, that holds true for the number of times that I have been asked where Security should organizationally report. It is surprising the number of people who strongly advocate that it should report to the company's president or CEO. In fact, even for medium sized companies, this is rarely appropriate—and I mean rarely. Some contend that Security should report to Human Resources while others offer Administrative Services, Corporate Real Estate, Legal, Audit, and so on. What then is the answer?

Actually, it is quite simple. You need to begin by asking, "What organizational model applies to my particular situation?" Knowing this defines the reporting relationship by function and organizational level. Before we begin discussing models, Security's place on the corporate ladder, and your company's pecking order, I want to stress the importance of how one manages as opposed to from where one manages. I remember a comment made by one of my previous bosses over 20 years ago. I was complaining about my own internal reporting relationship and corporate title. He responded: "Den, it is not so much the box that you fit in that makes the difference as it is the way in which you manage the area in and around the box." Sage advice.

My boss saw that success is far more dependent on managerial ability than managerial positioning. For over 15 years now, I have traveled throughout the United States working with security managers from the largest to some of the smallest corporations. One of the truisms I have witnessed firsthand is how so few understand the nuance of what my boss told me.

Since the early 1960s there has been a dramatic evolution in the role of security. This, in turn, has driven the structure of security within a company. Prior to the 1960s the security industry languished in the role of the night watchman. In this capacity the officer's primary duty was to serve as the eyes, ears, and most importantly, the nose of the organization. That's right, the nose. This is because the job of security was primarily to serve as a fire watch. Even today with national fire codes and sophisticated advances in detection and suppression technology, fire remains the major threat to loss of physical assets.

By the turn of the later half of the 20th century, Security's role expanded beyond fire watches and took on more of the classical security duties. Nevertheless, the scope of responsibility still rested largely within the context of facilities management. I refer to this as the *Green Shack Era*. I think you know what I mean. Simply, a person would approach the main gate and ask for Security. The officer would respond, "Oh, go around back to the little green shack." Never fear, the person knew exactly where to go. For many organizations, Security is still in their green shacks, or in a closet-sized room in the basement. I recently found one in the sub-basement behind the main boilers. It is not surprising, therefore, that the reporting relationship for such organizations is defined within the Maintenance Division.

For most, however, they moved out of these backrooms. They moved to an office location and expanded their role, assuming added physical security duties; hence the *Physical Security Era*. Security continued to perform patrols, but was asked to do other tasks, including responding to medical emergencies, traffic control, escorting employees, and perhaps the most visible of all, staffing the front lobby desk, serving as a receptionist. In this expanded role, the reporting relationship was more the result of which corporate department "made the most sense" according to the company's senior tier. Often, it was not so much which executive wanted it as which executive got stuck with it. Consequently, Security found itself reporting to HR, Legal, Audit, Administrative Services, or most likely, what is today referred to as Corporate Real Estate. I was recently asked to review the security operation for a large consumer products company. Security reports to Corporate Engineering, which translates to the head office unit responsible for all plant engineers.

Again, it is important to note that there is nothing fundamentally inappropriate in Security reporting to any one of these corporate units versus another. The reality is that most security departments today reflect all, or a significant part, of the duties ascribed in this era. The operational model is characteristically one of a large business unit supported by either a resident uniformed staff or a third-party provider. Investigations are performed, but generally are limited to employee violations or thefts below a defined limit.

For a short period of time during the *Physical Security Era*, it became professionally "the in-thing" to rename Security to Loss Prevention. This label is still largely used in the retail sector. The attempt was to better position Security as a value-added contributor. Security professionals wanted something that distanced their operation from the *green shack* image. I personally believe it worked. Other employees, particularly managers, began to see Security more clearly in their expanded role. It positioned them to truly begin participating in proactive initiatives. The whole concept of having Security responsible for developing employee awareness programs took hold. Today, whenever I address a large group of security professionals, I ask how many have well-developed awareness programs. The response is more than 95%. Asking how many have translated awareness programs into employee awareness programs, however, yields a significantly lower percentage.

Despite the daily frustration to be recognized for their contribution to protecting assets and people, a new horizon began to emerge for Security. I refer to this as the *Corporate Security Era*. Retaining its largely operational orientation, many Corporate Security managers began to find themselves being asked to carry on new, and often unrelated, duties. The primary focus, however, remained on protection of physical assets. This era, which is largely the one we are still in, can be best characterized as the *Coming of Age* for Security. As such, many new and innovative approaches have been tried.

Some have experimented with defining themselves as a profit and loss center (largely a major bust since rarely does a corporate manager have the experience to understand how a business is run as opposed to running a department). Others assumed responsibility for a host of corporate services such as mail delivery, shipping and receiving, food services, safety, and so forth. Still, for others, they have expanded their investigative responsibility, assuming the lead on more sensitive security-related incidents. Executive protection and security related systems engineering are deliverables that really took hold in this era as Security defined itself as a true corporate-wide entity. Even so, the reporting relationship remained essentially unchanged from the earlier days of Physical Security and Loss Prevention.

It was during this phase of evolution that companies began to redefine themselves out of competitive necessity. Outsourcing and streamlining became dominant themes. Corporate business units found themselves being required to operate in a *slimmer and trimmer* fashion. For Corporate Security this meant redefining not only their structure, but also their fundamental delivery system. This led to the model that characterizes many security departments today. Specifically, they shifted dramatically away from an operations-oriented program to a small cadre of professionals offering in-house consulting and specialized services.

Typically, for these internal consultancies, they no longer have direct responsibility for uniformed security services. This function has shifted to Real Estate or Facilities Management as an extension of these units' total property care. As their company expanded around the world, for many corporate security directors this meant an expanded identity. Consequently, we are seeing the emergence of another name change, e.g., *Global Security*.

As internal consultants, security professionals are called upon to serve in an advisory capacity. The skill set that tests their ability to be successful is salesmanship. They are not in a role to dictate to end-users *what is* and *what is not* regarding security and safety. Rather, their role is to advise end-users, the internal customer, regarding benefits to be gained or risks to be avoided by following proven security strategies. They defer to the expertise of external partners and understand that their added value is defined in terms of what is commonly referred to as a *best business practice*.

The most distinguishing characteristic to emerge for corporate security directors is their ability to be defined foremost as business managers. They need not prove their professional expertise since this is assumed by those around them. As a business manager there is the expectation that protecting assets need not be intrusive to the company's operations. Moreover, there is a balance of resources, mixing staff with state-of-the-art technology and operating practices. Employee awareness has been augmented with ownership programs that translate directly into bottom-line contributions.

The model is built on collaboration with internal partners and not competition with them. From a delivery of service perspective, this new model still retains some of the traditional security responsibilities. For example, investigations remain, but the emphasis has shifted to more sophisticated and sensitive matters. Security engineering is often retained; however, the emphasis is on developing standards and providing quality review checks as opposed to actual project management. Executive protection remains a responsibility, but like systems engineering, it is focused more on developing standards and policies, expatriate briefings, and event planning.

Within the past five to ten years a new era seems to be emerging. Consequently, today we are in a period of transition. I refer to this as the *Total Asset Protection Era*. A word of caution, however, is required up-front. Just as in the *Corporate Security Era*, we saw that some departments changed their name to Loss Prevention, others have chosen to rename themselves Asset Protection. This can be confusing since the emerging era is significantly different and no other label appears to be more appropriate at this time.

Adding to this confusion is the lack of a clearly defined security program that reflects an exclusive asset protection orientation as described below. This is not uncommon, however, as an industry transitions from one era to the next. What we see today is a significant shift, especially among the Fortune 500 security programs, as security managers begin to assimilate the need for protecting intangible assets into their overall scope of responsibility.

The *Total Asset Protection Era* is characterized by a focus on addressing all of the corporation's assets—tangible and intangible. This is a radical departure from previous charters. Remember, up to now the emphasis was solely on physical assets. It has only been of late that Security has been either asked or on its own initiative taken an active role in addressing the protection needs of intangible assets. This includes collaborating with other business units on matters associated with intellectual property, competitive intelligence, and other aspects of proprietary and/or confidential information.

This new charter doesn't end here. Many Security departments are also being asked to be actively involved in the mainstream of their company's strategic planning and business development. The role of investigation has expanded to incorporate geopolitical forecasting. This involves calling upon their resources to assist in the decision-making process associated with the company's emergence into new and sometimes unstable world markets. Security is also being asked to participate in the due diligence process regarding potential mergers and acquisitions. As companies expand their product offerings to remain competitive, they need external partners and alliances. Often this means developing relationships with privately held companies or those resident in a foreign country. Here Security is asked to draw upon its global network to determine the integrity of the principals.

As a quick example of this due diligence role, a leading consumer goods company wanted to expand their U.S. operations into Latin America. The company's logistics department identified seven trucking companies to provide their transportation needs. Security was asked to "check them out." Based on their efforts, Security discovered that five of the seven were well known to the country's criminal justice system for a variety of previous violations, most of which were felonious in nature.

In the *Total Asset Protection Era*, security professionals need to truly understand their company's business. They are no longer limited to protecting people and real property. To be truly value-added they need to have a working understanding of the business they purport to serve. This means extending their knowledge base into the very heart of what their respective company produces or services. They rely on today's tools including a comprehensive and interactive web-site.

Perhaps the most distinguishing characteristic is Security's collaborative approach. Team management is emphasized more, with Security taking a strong advisory role as opposed to outright management responsibility for several protection areas. For example, there is a close working relationship between the corporate security manager and the data security manager, with each reporting to different executives. Intellectual property protection is defined more universally as each key business unit assumes front-line responsibility, yet looking to Security for appropriate guidance. Competitive intelligence remains within the domain of others, often Marketing or Legal, but they rely on partnering with Security to create both awareness and ownership programs among the general employee population.

Regardless of where you find your department on the era continuum, moving through it and beyond is dependent on the internal organizational model that is adopted. As noted previously, historically the emphasis has been on physical asset protection. It is not surprising, therefore, to find that the department's budget and base delivery system reflects a focus on uniformed security services. Having a defined investigations unit, while secondary, is also a key feature. Beyond these two core competencies, other support functions will vary from security department to security department.

More progressive departments, under the title of Global Security, have created an operating model that reflects a balance between three primary deliverables. Hewlett Packard and Capital One Financial Services are two examples that come readily to mind. Others, such as Fidelity Investments and 3M have similar models. For each, there is a commitment to *Business Risk Analysis*, which supplants the traditional investigative function. Secondly, there is a commitment to providing the necessary resources to address security-related *Human Resource* concerns. The final functional leg focuses on *Global Operational Support*.

This article set the tone for a new way of looking at a corporate security program. In Part II we will not only explore in more depth each of these eras, but also the three cornerstones of the new Total Asset Protection Era. To be successful in today's business world, one which is still on the leading edge of the information revolution, new ways of going about the business of protecting people and assets are in order.

To accomplish this end requires different skill sets and orientations. It requires integrating much of what we have learned in the past with the requisite capabilities necessary to meet today's challenges. These challenges can be in the form of terrorism on the one end and simple incompetence on the other end; both can result in economic loss, loss of market share, and decreased consumer confidence. Threats are real for people and for tangible and intangible assets. These threats need to be recognized and dealt with up front. Failure to do so can only lead in one direction. One need only look at corporate America's recent past to see what can happen to even the largest of companies when fraud, greed, and unethical behavior make their way into the corporate culture or boardroom; Enron, Arthur Anderson, Tyco, Worldcom, Quest, Global Crossing, and Martha Stewart come to mind.

CONCLUDING COMMENTS

In this first chapter we set out to build two of the fundamental building blocks necessary to achieve a successful asset and people protection program. First, we found that the program that is selected is directly related to the type of threats that exist. These threats can be real and present or they can be anticipated. We must, however, always remember that a business will have risks—that is part of the cost associated with doing business. The critical variable is the degree of the threat and the barrier it poses on the organization. Second, the degree of risk will define the most appropriate security strategy. A quick review of security's evolution can help in defining the type of program that is required.

It is obvious that I am particularly critical of the federal government's attempt at making the United States a safer place for its citizens. The same can be said for many state-sponsored initiatives. We need not rehash what has already been said. It is important, however, to emphasize the underlying cause of these programs' eventual failure. Despite their corporate backgrounds, both President Bush and Vice President Cheney reflect the traditional CEO mentality that defines asset protection as a function of corporate policing. This misguided perspective can only result in wasted expenditures and ineffective measures. Law enforcement is about the business of law and order, not about protecting corporate assets. Many a security director has learned this lesson the hard way, sometimes at the cost of his or her job. It is a shame that the lessons of the private sector have not been picked up by government officials. To have done otherwise could have spared them the loss of credibility. Successful asset protection is all about picking a strategy that works and working it step by step. This may seem so fundamental as not to warrant even mentioning it, yet based on the widespread failures reported in today's media, perhaps it is a lesson that merits revisiting.

We must not, in trying to think about how we can make a big difference, ignore the small daily difference we do make.

Marion Wright Edleman

THOUGHT-PROVOKING QUESTIONS

1. The author is critical of the government's efforts associated with risk assessments and the frequent warnings of potential terrorist attacks. Is his assessment accurate or is there another side that needs to be presented?

2. Drawing from your experience and the ideas presented in this chapter, what ought the role of private security be in the country's ongoing effort to root out terrorism, especially in areas outside of the United States?

3. Jones Lang LaSalle developed a risk assessment program that is fundamentally property oriented. The author states that the methodology can be adopted to other threat concerns. Thinking about your situation, what elements can you envision that would best define an effective threat assessment for your area of responsibility?

4. Based on the discussion of security's evolution, where are you? Is it appropriate for your organization, based on a threat analysis? If not, how would you go about closing the disparity gap?

5. Should the role of security administration (e.g., asset protection) stay primarily focused on protecting physical assets and company employees, or should it expand into other business and operational considerations?

Chapter 2

WHO SHOULD TAKE THE HELM?

You cannot master all the elements of management. You take what it gives and learn from it.

Primary Themes

- Determining the Management Skill Set for an Effective Security Manager
- Establishing High Performance Indicators
- Avoiding the Expert Witness Trap
- Avoiding the So-Called Expert

OPENING OBSERVATIONS

When I first sent out the outline for this book, one of my reviewers commented that she would like to know what it takes to be selected as a security manager. In today's turbulent world of organizational management this is more than a fair request. We need to match skill sets with expectations, yet often this is not done. Consequently, we find failure where there ought not be failure. We find frustration on the part of both security managers and other corporate executives when it could be avoided.

As I write this I am reminded of what the treasurer for one of our country's leading software giants once requested. The company wanted some assistance in selecting a new security director. When I met with him to discuss the position, he informed me that his boss, the chief financial officer, and the company's founder—today a very high-profile, and sometimes quite controversial, individual—were interested in getting "the right man for the job." A few days later he called and advised that between the three of them, they had determined that they wanted a second-tier security manager. "One," the treasurer said, "who is young and hungry. Someone who is willing to work for less money, but who has the capacity to grow." I cautioned that such a person might not be capable of meeting the requirements facing the company at that time, especially considering its global challenges. This idea was rejected in favor of the lesser experience. Before I could begin much work, I received another call. This time the treasurer informed me they had turned to an insider with less than a year's experience who had been an investigative supervisor. Less than two years passed before I received yet another call. This time they had concluded that their grand experiment had failed and that a more experienced security manager was needed.

This story is not uncommon. I recall an executive vice president for a major bank once confiding in me that had he the opportunity to hire a new security director, he would not go to the public sector again. His experience led him to believe that successful public servants do not assure success in the private sector. His point has some merit but it is not an absolute. Many managers and directors make the transition from the public to the private sector very successfully. The bottom line is that it is not the sector experience as much as it is the skill set of the holder that determines success. Years ago, as a security executive for a large firm, I hired several public servants who proved to be extremely valuable in meeting our department's mission with a learning curve no different from the personnel drawn from other corporations. Similar experiences can be found among many of today's corporate security leaders. What then are these skill sets?

Step Three: Selecting the Right Leader for Your Security Program

We have seen that the first step to achieving a value-added security program is the creation of a risk assessment. As noted, this is an important management tool because it serves as a road map for action. But the map alone cannot get us from where we are to where we need to be. To close the disparity gap, we need a security team that possesses the requisite skill set—both as asset protection professionals and savvy business partners. When I think about this latter requirement I am always reminded of my golf story.

I was 50 years old when my best friend, Jim, introduced me to the game of golf. Like so many before me, until I had played my first real game I never understood how someone could get excited about this game. I say real game because it was actually my second encounter with the sticks. My first experience occurred the summer I was 12 or 13 years old. Two of my neighborhood chums decided to give their old mashie-niblics (now referred to as 7-irons) a try. They invited me along. We were all about the same age, though Mike and Don had been playing golf for a couple of years. There was a public course not far down the road—an easy bike ride away.

As I think back on that day, I have no idea how good or bad they were. I do know, however, how bad I was. Not just in the execution of the game, but in what can only be described as proper resource management. You see, they each had a set of clubs. Without a niblic to my name, it was incumbent upon us to borrow a few clubs from wherever. That wherever was Mike's dad. We secured four clubs from him, about a half a dozen balls, some tees, and his golf bag.

Slinging the bags over our shoulders, we set out. As I recall, the round of nine holes went okay until we hit the clubhouse and saddled up for the ride home. It was only then that we collectively realized that of the four clubs I started with, I only had one left in my bag. The six balls were long gone and I don't think there was a tee in my pocket. How do you explain losing three clubs in nine holes? You don't. You just pray that the father will have some idea of how dumb it was and maybe, just maybe, not make you pay a lot for this stupid mismanagement of his valued resources. As I further recall, all went well when we returned and explained our predicament. Mike's dad was always a gentle kind of guy. That night he had a massive heart attack and died. Even though his doctors said he had heart disease, I always suspected I had a hand in taking him to his eternal game. Now that I know how much golfers' clubs mean to them, my suspicions are stronger.

So, with this history, you can imagine what went through my mind when Jim offered his spare set of clubs and suggested we go a round. I was petrified and immediately blurted out my "Mike's dad" story in hopes that he would understand and suggest that we skip the round and immediately move to the nineteenth hole, where I would gladly buy the first round of drinks and perhaps even the second. But he passed on this wonderful idea and insisted that we knock the ball around a bit. And knock the ball around is exactly what I did. After a game of 18 holes and a score of 167 on a par 72, we finished. Jim was convinced I would never play again—maybe he prayed I would never play again. Nevertheless, I remember putting our clubs in his trunk—every club I started with, by the way—and suggested we play another round the following day.

That was about five years ago. Today, my handicap is respectable for a duffer. The handicap is actually secondary for me. I am proud to say that after many rounds, several different courses, and a host of playing conditions, I have only lost one club—wouldn't you know it, one of my favorites!! (Dare I think Mike's dad had a hand in it?)

So what has all of this to do with a being a security manager in today's business world? I think there are a number of parallels. I certainly never planned on becoming a golf enthusiast, especially after such an inauspicious beginning. Rather, I stumbled into it. Over the years, I have found that most of today's security managers have likewise stumbled into their careers. Even though they all have their own stories, the common denominator is one of becoming a manager through some indirect route. For some managers, their initial experience was positive; for others it was not. We need to explore this in some depth because it goes to one of the fundamental building blocks of who is successful and who is not. We'll do just that in the pages ahead.

In part, the success of a manager in today's dynamic business world is also linked to that person's readiness in assuming the mantel of leadership. My first experience with golf put me off for nearly 40 years, but when the time was right, I was able to embrace it and continue to thoroughly enjoy it, both as a participant and as a spectator. The same can be said for a person seeking the role of security manager. Timing, as the adage goes, is everything. This same timing extends not only to readiness, but also to future success in presenting programs to senior management and obtaining the go-ahead.

The pursuit of golf has many applications that translate directly to successful management principles. As golfing great Bruce Crampton notes: "Golf is a compromise between what your ego wants you to do, what experience tells you to do, and what your nerves will let you do." Every successful security manager will understand the application here to their own professional lives. Management requires calculated deliberateness, or as Arnold Palmer would suggest, "It is deceptively simple, yet endlessly complicated." Experienced managers know how true this is when applied to their own organizational pursuits. The quote at the beginning of this chapter, "You cannot master all the elements of management. You take what it gives and learn from it," is actually an adaptation from one of golf's great players, Charlie Sifford. I simply substituted the word *management* for *golf*. I think what he has to say is true either way.

It is not absolutely necessary to draw on the life of golf to find parallels to successful management. In *The Art* I related that outside Bend, Oregon, on the Deschutes River, another close friend introduced me to the sport of fly fishing. His objective was to slow me down a bit to enjoy some of the personal pleasures life has to offer. He reasoned that casting a fishing line over and over in 45°F water at 6:00 A.M. should more than slow me down.

He succeeded—somewhat. You may also recall that I said I am always thinking about organizational dynamics. I always have, and I suspect I always will. Standing there casting over and over, I began to think about what he had told me about the mechanics and art of working the river in the pursuit of fish. He told me about the water's depth, color, and speed. These, he said, helped determine the right spot to find fish. As he pointed out, this was the *art* of fly fishing. But one also had to master the *mechanics*. To do this, he also told me about how to work the spot. This involved getting into the river and walking one step forward and one step sideways with each cast. And, after each cast, one needs to mend the line—maneuver the line to exactly the spot you want and the depth you desire. Adhering to these mechanical steps assures that you cover the entire spot, and not just selected areas.

I began to see how all of this advice about the proper fishing technique could be translated into organizational behavior. I saw how the speed of the water related to timing, a critical factor in selling your idea to the powers that be. I saw how the depth of the water translated directly to organizational positioning—the ability to influence decision-making. I began to understand how the color of the water was directly parallel with organizational temperament, determining if your senior managers are ready to receive and accept your ideas.

The mechanics of working the river could also be translated into ready management strategies. By stepping forward and sideways with each cast to cover the entire spot in the river, I could see another important parallel. To be successful, the manager needs to work the entire organization, up, down, and sideways. The manager's own line must be mended to assure that security's message is received in exactly the way it is intended to be received, and at the organizational levels where it can be effective.

The parallels are not limited to golf and fly fishing, either. Again, you may recall how I finished my second book by comparing the stages of becoming a distance runner to the stages of becoming an envisioned leader. I still run several days a week and find that when I am on the treadmill I can lightly hold on to the rails, close my eyes, and work myself into a light trance, allowing the rhythm of my body to keep me from falling off. This, in turn, allows me to work through things that are on my mind or reach insight into a problem. Most of the insights contained in these pages are in one way or another traceable to my running.

In many ways, I think the same can be said for those who find themselves in a leadership role. Some work hard at it, huffing and puffing along the way, but never able to get beyond the first stage. Becoming a distance runner requires hard work and perseverance. The same can be said for leadership. Over the years I have come to believe that there are not natural-born leaders. There are those who have the innate talents that can guide them to excellent leadership, but these talents can go dormant or whither entirely away if they are not exercised. Leadership, in the final stage, is much like my ability for trancelike running; it has qualities that can serve as a guide for an individual, but these qualities need to be nurtured and developed. This requires time, experience, and a strong desire. When the skills are developed, the leader does not have to think about them—they manifest themselves naturally, almost as though the leader is in his or her own world and is able to see things clearly while others struggle to see even shadows.

So, whether in golf, fishing, or running, the parallels to successful management abound. We can draw similar observations from many other sporting venues. As humorist and golfing enthusiast P.G. Wodehouse might have suggested, "It is not mere technical skill that makes a successful golfer (manager), it is also the desire found deep within the soul."

Security managers—those whose full-time employment is as a security person, as opposed to a non–security manager with some protection duties—are referred to by a number of different titles. Three are most commonly used. They are: security manager, security director, and corporate security manager. A few have assumed the title of global security manager. Other titles include loss prevention manager and asset protection manager.

Shortly before 9/11, some of the professional journals began reporting on what appeared to be a new trend. Since 9/11 the "talk" has intensified, suggesting that not only a new title was beginning to emerge, but also a new role. This "talk" made its way into the mainstream media with an article appearing in the *New York Times* on May 27, 2002, by Steve Lohr. The article was entitled "In New Era, Corporate Security Looks Beyond Guns and Badges." At first read, it offers what should be very good news for the security industry. The focus is on what the author terms as an emerging trend among corporations in creating a chief security officer (CSO) position. Lohr draws a comparison between the CSO and today's chief information officer (CIO).

> *The C.S.O. title is meant to suggest that security matters are becoming a more important and integral part of corporate life. Roughly 15 years ago, another three-letter corporate title started to surface, C.I.O., or chief information officer. It was initially greeted with skepticism, even derision. But C.I.O. was more than just a name; it was a recognition that information technology was not just electronic plumbing or a narrow specialty, but something that could affect the mainstream business, strategy and competitiveness. The C.I.O. is now an established and respected executive job at most major corporations. It is too early to tell whether the C.S.O. will eventually reach comparable stature. But even before Sept. 11, the corporate security field had been steadily evolving in response to the major business and technological developments of the last two decades.*

I agree with Lohr that over the past two decades the role of many security departments has shifted from that of corporate cop to more of a contributor to the organization's mainstream business. Unfortunately, as we have already seen, the majority are still largely in the era of providing only uniformed security services. Consequently, any serious consideration of a senior executive position comparable to a chief executive officer (CEO), chief operating officer (COO), chief administrative officer (CAO), or even CIO would most likely be met by such executives with a great deal of "skepticism, even derision," to use Lohr's description.

The title CIO quickly evolved because the very nature of information technology became an inseparable component of mainstream business operations. Virtually no aspect of corporate life can operate effectively today for a sustained period of time without some form of IT support. The same cannot be said for asset and people protection, despite the reality that it, too, permeates each organizational level and is a contributing factor to morale and productivity. Herein lies an interesting paradox. Security is intrusive, in the positive sense of the word, yet it fails to rise to the level of other very senior positions. Why? Because it still serves as an infrastructure function much the same as human resources, audit, legal, and corporate real estate departments. These functions are likewise significant contributors to an organization's health and prosperity; yet they are not under the direct administration of a "chief officer," as the term is understood in today's business environment.

Will there come a time when a majority of corporations have CSOs? Maybe. But the time, I dare say, is a long way off. Some organizational theorists would argue that until a unit rises to the highest level, it can never reach its full potential. Such a belief is based on the concept that power and position are tightly interwoven. However, the exercise of power is not totally dependent on one's formal position. Remember what my former boss had to say about managing from within the box versus managing around it? It was sage advice then, and I think the same can be said of today. Regardless of the title, it is the person that makes the job a success.

To determine what ought to be the basic criteria for a security manager, I asked several of my colleagues and current security executives. As I inquired around, I soon discovered that one of the most basic failings we have today is the lack of a clearly articulated guideline to determine what makes a successful security manager. I found job descriptions galore for captains of the watch, supervisors, investigators, and so forth. Some, disguised as qualifications for a security manager, were little more than a listing of technical skills. But success is more than the mastery of the mechanics; "It is not mere technical skill that makes a successful manager, it is also the desire found deep within the soul."

Do you remember the great football story about the coach who, realizing his team was in a serious slump, decided to go back to the basics. He gathered his players around and, holding the ball high over his head, said: "Gentlemen, this is a football." Pretty basic stuff, but it was necessary to get their attention and reinforce the idea that everything else flows from the ability to set the building blocks. Recently I took a series of lessons from a local golf professional. After watching me swing a few times, he commented that I needed to get in touch with the basics. My swing path was off because I was not setting up properly to the ball and my grip was not aligned properly. For me to be successful I had to return to the basics. The same can be said of many managers today.

As a profession, we should not beat ourselves up too badly. My research went beyond private security, and I found little by way of truly defining the basic qualities necessary to manage a group of people, let alone an entire business unit. Unfortunately, most managers become managers for all the wrong reasons. This is particularly true for private security. When an individual performs very well at the line level or in a specialist capacity, senior management wants to recognize that person's contribution. What is the highest way of demonstrating management's appreciation? By promoting them, of course! Raising them to a level above their fellow employees will show senior management's commitment. Management can use their newly promoted manager as a model for others. They reason that the person has clearly demonstrated a technical competency, and so can be counted on to make further contributions.

Alternatively, senior executives may be faced with a business unit in need of leadership (often confused for management). Not having a person who can readily provide the requisite skill set, they turn to the outside world and recruit from other organizations. Here the accepted belief is that if a person is successful in one environment, he or she surely will be successful in a new environment. Peter Kline and Bernard Saunders, in their book, *Ten Steps to a Learning Organization,* refer to this as one of the basic learning barriers. Labeling this disability the "logical barrier," they explain that it is not uncommon for an organization to hold fast to the belief that what worked for Situation X must work for Situation Y, especially if X and Y appear to be quite similar. The problem is that the nuances that differentiate the two often cause a breakdown in directly applying the lessons learned in Situation X to Situation Y. Here's an example of how a person's success in one arena was mistakenly applied to another and the unfortunate consequences that followed.

Situational Case One: The Promoted-to-be-Fired Security Manager

I will never forget the case of Bill Smith. As a regional security manager, I was responsible for my company's northern operations, including the security at one of the key data centers. At that center there was a dedicated security force. For reasons that I cannot remember now, the resident security manager resigned. For my boss, filling this position was critical—his charge was simple. Fill the position, and fill it *fast*. I set out to execute this directive.

Two days later, my boss called me to his office. There I met my southern counterpart, who had obviously been likewise summoned by the boss (but as I soon discovered, an hour earlier). The boss had thought that a member of my counterpart's staff would be a good candidate for my open position. After dissuading the boss from this idea, they had collectively concluded that the ideal candidate was a recently promoted security supervisor at the northern data center. Their thinking was quite simple: he had been an excellent security officer and was performing well as a newly appointed supervisor. Besides, as they went on in their effort to convince me, he knew the facility and knew the people, especially my boss's boss, who was the resident senior executive.

I pleaded with them to reconsider. The man was simply too inexperienced. This jump was too much too quick, I argued. But the boss had made up his mind, and my task was simply to offer the supervisor the position. Everyone knew he would take it, so it was just a matter of congratulating him on his meteoric rise! Before leaving, I went on record as not only objecting, but also predicting that we would be firing him within six months. They scoffed.

As you no doubt surmised, he took the job, complete with the pay raise and the private office. We set out a developmental plan, but it was obvious within a matter of weeks that he was simply not ready. I updated my boss. He refused to believe it and said that all that was required was a little more time. A few weeks went by and the direction remained straight downhill. At one point I asked the new manager what he thought a manager was. I put it this way: "If you had to describe what makes you the manager over everyone else on your staff, what would you say the difference is?" I'll never forget his reply. "That's easy. I have the private office, the biggest desk and chair, and a view."

Needless to say, it was only a matter of time before the manager "shot himself in the foot," embarrassing both the department and my boss. I cannot recall the exact circumstance, but I remember it had something to do with a missed alarm at the residence of our company president. My boss informed me that the manager had to go—he would not even consider a demotion or reassignment. The day I broke the news to the manager was exactly six months from the day he was promoted. My boss and I never discussed the episode again. The good news is that the manager did learn from his mistakes and today is a very successful security executive for a Fortune 200 company.

It's not how fast you get there, it's how long you stay.

Patty Berg

How did the situation occur? It would be easy to simply dismiss it as a case of paranoia on the part of the boss, and there was some of that. But the breakdown goes much deeper. Here an otherwise excellent up-and-coming security professional was cast into a situation in which he was sure to fail. Yes, he could have declined the promotion, but would you have? The root, I suggest, was a failure to distinguish technical competency from managerial ability. In this case Bill was simply not experienced. This was evident by his response to my question. More important, my boss had fallen into the trap of believing that if Bill was successful under one set of circumstances, he would be successful in another of "high similarity." I set this phrase off because there is no real similarity at all. The fact that Bill knew the facility and the people, coupled with his past accomplishments were, at best, indicators, that he might be successful at an appropriate time in the future.

What makes a good security manager for today? I believe the answer begins in considering the experience of the individual. This means more than years on the job. It is far more than tenure. It also implies the right type of experience. As we noted at the outset, success in law enforcement or the military is no indicator that the individual will make a successful business manager.

Today's business manager also needs to be a leader, and not just the type of leader who can give orders and direct a team from point A to point B. Today a manager needs to demonstrate different leadership styles that reflect the situation. Before 9/11 Rudi Giuliani, the mayor of New York City, was seen as a leader. He had a reputation as being a fighter, someone who fought hard for what he believed was right. Many in his administration agreed with his foes that he was forceful and sometimes obstinate. Then 9/11 caught everyone by surprise and the world watched the city's mayor emerge as a gentle, but visibly determined leader. He was soft-spoken but determined. He knew what was required of him as the leader and he rose to the occasion. His passions were focused and changed from being combative to being stalwart.

Security managers face organizational crises frequently. Like Giuliani, they too need to rise to the occasion and demonstrate gentle, but firm, leadership. A security manager must understand the need for collaboration and set aside dictating. Even in times of crisis, an effective leader can rally more support by demeanor than by barking orders. This can be a difficult personal challenge for someone solely schooled in a military or quasi-military model. Edgar Shein, author of *Organizational Culture and Leadership*, notes that "when an organization faces a crisis, the manner in which leaders and others deal with it creates new norms, values, and working procedures and reveals important underlying assumptions." What Shein is telling us is that leaders are able to set new directions, new tones, new ways of moving the organization forward. Leadership of this kind is one of the essential building blocks for the successful security manager.

> *People are like tea bags. You find out how strong they are when you put them in hot water.*
>
> *Anonymous*

Much has been written about the visionary skill of an effective leader. I conclude *The Art* with a discussion of what I refer to as the *envisioned leader*. This is the individual who has the ability to see what lies ahead—over the horizon—without ever having been there. This leadership quality is fundamental to creating a reasoned strategy that can guide staff members and other organizational stakeholders forward when uncertainties create doubt. We live in dynamic times—some would characterize them as turbulent. Either way, today's business climate has been anything but stable for the past two decades, and there is no indication that it will calm down soon. Such times require leaders who have vision. But a strong caution needs to be made.

Schein warns us that "Much has been said about the need for vision in leaders, but too little has been said about their need to listen, to absorb, to search the environment for trends, to build the organization's capacity to learn. Especially at the strategic level, the ability to see and acknowledge the full complexity of problems becomes critical." He goes on to note that critical roles of leadership in strategy formulation and implementation are:

- To perceive accurately and in depth what is happening in the environment
- To create enough discomforting information to motivate the organization to change without creating too much anxiety
- To provide psychological safety by either providing a vision of how to change and in what direction or by creating a process of visioning that allows the organization to find a path
- To acknowledge uncertainty

- To embrace errors in the learning process as inevitable and desirable
- To manage all phases of the change process, including especially the management of anxiety as some cultural assumptions are given up and new learning begins

Leadership is not managerial in the sense that there are managers—those who can execute—and there are leaders—those who can guide through their execution. What do leaders need to demonstrate? Most authors would include:

- Perception and insight
- Motivation
- Emotional strength
- Ability to change others
- Ability to achieve collaboration
- Ability to learn

I would add that today's security leader needs to have (1) a keen insight into how the world of organizations and business is changing, (2) the necessary motivation to keep moving forward when the environment is uncertain and clouded with confusion, (3) maturity and emotional stability (especially when anxieties arise resulting from uncertain times and calls to action into uncharted arenas), (4) the ability to question long-standing assumptions, (5) the capacity to elicit participation and involvement, and (6) a willingness to accept new environments, new responsibilities, and new people.

Kline and Saunders offer their list of 26 characteristics that define what makes a good leader. Some of them include:

- Cross-disciplined awareness
- Ability to respond to confrontational questions comfortably
- Ability to re-frame ideas
- Business acumen
- Strong marketing ability
- Ability to think on your feet
- Ability to take criticism
- Sense of paradox
- Regard for the quantification process
- Ability to think like a child
- Proactive orientation
- Sense of humor

- Sense of universal patterns and relationships
- Ability to admit mistakes
- Flexible thinking
- Lack of need for immediate closure
- Willingness and ability to listen sensitively
- Willingness to conduct research

This is a great list and significantly different from most management texts that try to define what qualities to look for in selecting a leader. Several of the items are very provocative and require quiet reflection. For example, how many leaders have a sense of paradox? As the authors note, there are many paradoxes in our lives. The more we know about something, the more we understand how much more there is to learn about it. To reduce the number of mistakes, you actually have to increase the tolerance for them. People who are too by-the-book and controlling will have difficulty dealing with these subtleties.

Likewise, effective leaders have not lost their ability to think like a child. Even the most complex problems find their resolution in simple answers and strategies. Moreover, like the child, facing a difficult situation can often have a successful outcome based on the ability to think creatively (today we call this *thinking out of the box*). Today's security director needs to have patience and live with open-endedness. Quick solutions are not always the best. After the initial assault on Afghanistan, in America's War on Terror, many criticized the president's team for not capturing the ringleaders. It took great courage to stand before the sea of microphones and suggest that success comes in time and that sometimes the best strategy comes farther down the road.

When I have been asked to provide my own criteria for effectively managing a security program, I always begin by offering the following:

- *Frank, effective, savvy managers with strong business acumen and proven success driving creative solutions designed to mitigate loss and reduce risks.* Those of you who know me should not be surprised that I start right off with a call for being a frank and savvy manager with strong business acumen. Most managers of professional support groups miss this critical building block altogether. Remember, success is first measured by one's contribution as a proven business manager. Executives assume that by the time one ascends to the lead management position of their support unit they have the necessary technical expertise. Having the ability to drive creative solutions aimed at mitigating loss and reducing risks is part of that technical expertise.

- *Demonstrated success in developing programs reflecting recognized best business practices based on the application of metrics designed to reflect added value.* As we go forward in this book I will have a great deal more to say about the importance of using a metrics-based approach. Today's executive needs proof that the investment in security has a beneficial return. This can be achieved only by using some form of reliable metrics. The call for a best business practices approach simply makes prudent sense. This should in no way suggest that novel and unique solutions are undesirable. Best business practices allow for the unconventional, when the circumstances warrant. Pushing the envelope is often necessary to achieve a desired outcome in today's turbulent management times. The caveat, however, is that any approach needs to be business based and well calculated.

- *Adept communicators able to lead the creative process and significantly contribute to the collaborative process among business unit managers, demonstrating credibility through professional expertise and an understanding of advanced management issues.* Gone are the days of "going it alone." Such days have actually been gone for quite some time. Unfortunately, many security managers did not receive the message. There are those who continue to reflect a management style characteristic of a completely top-down accountability. In other words, the manager assumes strong centralized control of the operation and believes that because security is the holder of the expertise, it is either their way or no way. The overwhelming majority of today's corporate cultures are moving toward, or have already arrived at, a style that invites participation and collaboration. This does not mean that decision-making is done in an atmosphere of democratic voting. Rather, it reflects consensus building and soliciting input from a variety of sources to achieve as complete an assessment as possible before the final decision is made.

- *Demonstrated track record of success with an ability to reflect and learn from past failure.* We are all human and we all make mistakes. This fundamental observation about life and the human condition sums it up nicely. Senior managers look for individuals with a successful track record. At the same time, they recognize that everyone who has ever achieved success has done so via a path cluttered with mistakes and losses. The ability to acknowledge shortfalls is what propels the successful person forward, because he or she understands what will work and what will not.

- *Energized by challenge, driven by successful results, and capable of inspiring a team with the same degree of enthusiasm, loyalty, and respect for individual differences.* This is the hallmark of leadership. Demonstrating the ability to inspire others requires not only enthusiasm—this demonstrates your commitment—but also loyalty and respect. Team building drives the unit to success. One need only look to the world of organized sports to see how a team that receives loyalty and respect from their coaches wins. Leadership is different from management. One creates and builds while the other executes and delivers.

■ *Intelligent, assertive, and comfortable in a changing environment; capable of adapting to new business paradigms and leading a team to effective solutions.* As noted, today we live in turbulent times. We will continue to do so for a long time to come. I am not just referring to the terrorist threats stemming from 9/11. Today's turbulence transcends any one factor. It is a reflection of global competition, economic cycles, the information revolution, the integration of e-commerce business paradigms, and a score of other dynamic forces currently in force. The successful security manager has to have an ability to be flexible and work in an uncertain environment. Equally important, today's business world has no place for timidity. The very essence of being savvy requires intelligent assertiveness vis-à-vis opportunistic aggressiveness.

■ *A comprehensive knowledge of operational and capital budgeting processes and an ability to stay within approved levels, seeking cost efficiencies without diminishing the integrity of a quality-driven security program.* Business, when all is said and done, is all about money. For-profit companies exist to make a profit. It is as simple as that. They also need to demonstrate a compassion for people and have a strong sense of community responsibility and morality—these are basics. The true test of a successful manager is the ability to identify necessary resources and leverage them in an ethical manner. To do so requires basic knowledge and a demonstrated ability to allocate resources acceptably. This translates to being able to develop and live within the parameters of both an operating budget and a capital budget. Most recent transfers from the public sector have not had a prior opportunity to hone this skill. Consequently, it is not unusual to see them struggle and often actually stumble, sometimes calling into question their unit's tactics.

■ *An ability to effectively evaluate asset protection challenges and offer integrated solutions reflecting state-of-the-art technologies, appropriate staffing models, and written policies and procedures.* These are the three fundamental legs of a well-balanced security program. State-of-the-art technology helps to control annual recurring costs associated with labor. Staffing models are the tools for effective deployment. Written policies and procedures create the framework for assuring that everyone transcends awareness and moves into actual ownership, or responsibility, for managing threat mitigation.

I'll have more to say about each of these in the chapters ahead and how they can serve as the arrows in any successful security director's management quiver.

To the man who only has a hammer in his toolkit, every problem looks like a nail.

Abraham Maslow

These eight basic skill sets serve as the basis for a high-performance security leader. They require both management savvy and professional expertise. They serve as the basis for defining an experienced security business-oriented manager from one still in waiting. I hope I have met the challenge my reviewer laid down in defining what it takes to be a successful leader of today's security management team.

THE EXPERT WITNESS TRAP

By now it is probably apparent that a successful security manager can use all of the help that can be mustered. Sometimes events call for engaging the services of an external expert. This most commonly occurs when litigation is involved. Despite the manager's best efforts, sometimes things can go awfully wrong and there are legal consequences. The organization suddenly finds itself the subject of a civil lawsuit and an expert is needed to explain whether or not the security department acted within the limits of what is referred to as the "custom and practice" of the industry. The legal department calls and says that they need an expert witness, someone with recognized expertise in the field of asset protection. The security director wants to cooperate, so he or she reaches out to colleagues and professional associations. Suddenly, the director is in the less-than-desirable position I call the *expert witness trap*.

Today there are a number of so-called experts at the ready. Many of them are recently retired law enforcement officers. As we noted earlier, reasoning that they have had a successful career in policing, these people offer their services to the legal community on the mistaken belief that there is a direct transference of their experience to private security. Unfortunately, the security consulting profession is unregulated. Well intentioned, but mistaken, lawyers can fall into the same trap-like thinking when it comes to considering the use of law enforcement personnel instead of a proven security professional. We have also noted that many executives fail to understand the difference. Therefore, it should not be a surprise when an individual whose only credential is law enforcement is hired as a security expert in matters of premises liability, guard operations, or asset protection over another individual far more qualified.

If only the expert witness trap were limited to just this challenge. There are other contributors to this phenomenon, including the employment of what might best be described as the "I can testify on any security matter" expert. This is generally the start-up consultant who is desperate for any engagement just to stay in business. I would estimate that at least half of the 300 experts retained in opposition to me should never have been so in the first place—not because of me, but because they simply were not qualified to serve as experts in the area in which they had been retained.

Security professionals who find themselves between corporate careers or who have recently retired will often turn to expert witness work to fill the void. When initially approached, they convince the hiring attorney that they have the expertise to render opinions in matters in which, if the truth were told, they have no background on which to base such a claim. This type of so-called expert may in fact have a degree of expertise—it is just not in the area under consideration. Frequently, I have found retained experts attempting to testify in retail cases when their entire professional background has been in school safety or banking. Similarly, I have found these same "experts" rendering opinions on matters of guard management when their career has focused on corporate fraud investigations or fire and life safety matters. The really good expert is the one who knows his or her limits and has the ability to say no and direct the attorney to someone else.

Perhaps the most troublesome contributing factor to the expert witness trap is the true expert who has become either complacent or arrogant. As I sit here writing this, no less than a dozen of these individuals come readily to mind. Tragically, each enjoys a degree of national notoriety and is therefore often called on. Based on their reputations, they commonly charge their clients extremely high fees and have no compunction about milking their retainer for literally tens of thousands of dollars more than what they can contribute to the case.

More important, they often do a disservice to their client. Let me give you a few examples. In what is now considered a landmark case in California, one security expert was branded by the appellate court as a "so-called expert" based on his testimony. This highly unusual step by a high court reflects their frustration over testimony rendered by individuals that is not fact based. As they noted: "where an expert bases his conclusion upon factors which are speculative, remote, or conjectural, expert's opinion cannot rise to the dignity of substantial review." They continue: "While an expert may, in his area of expertise, reach conclusions beyond that of the ordinary layman, he may only do so on the basis of established facts. *He may not himself create the facts upon which the conclusion is based.*" (Emphasis added by the court.) The otherwise experienced security professional and expert witness in question fell into his own trap of becoming assumptive. He projected what he believed to be the facts of the case as opposed to letting the facts speak for themselves. He is not alone.

In a case on the opposite side of the country another established expert rendered opinions in his deposition that caught everyone off-guard, including the attorney who had retained him. In this case, two innocent shoppers were killed following a botched robbery of an armored car. At the outset of the attack, the assailants opened fire on one of the guards, striking him and a customer. The customer's sister was next to him when he was hit. She, along with the guard and the driver of the armored car, testified that her brother was hit by the initial volley of gunfire from one of the assailants. The police reports affirmed this conclusion. Miraculously, the guard survived being shot in the head and was able to return gunfire.

The expert in this case came to the conclusion that the brother was hit as a result of the subsequent exchange of gunfire between the assailants and the guard. He never explained how he arrived at this conclusion. This was but only the tip of the iceberg. Following is an excerpt of his testimony.

Q. Would it be as important to you as an expert asked to provide opinions in this case to have the testimony of anybody who actually was an eyewitness to this incident?
A. No.

Q. It would not be important?
A. No.

Q. Was your mind made up regarding your opinions even before you were provided with any of the 1 to 19 items by [retaining counsel's] office?
A. My mind was made up before [retaining counsel] engaged my services or retained me.

Q. Was your mind made up as to the opinions you've expressed at the time you first learned of this particular incident during that interview with the news reporter on the phone? [Here, I should note that this expert earlier testified that shortly after this incident he was contacted by a local reporter and asked what he thought about the shooting.]
A. The interview with the news reporter was apparently after the incident occurred.

Q. Yes.
A. And I have no independent recollection, number one, when the article was published. I never read it. I have no independent recollection as to the date that [retaining counsel] called me and I have never—I have seen, I have glanced at the article today. I have not read the article. Still to this day I have not read the article, but I am told that there were no differences between my opinions here than what's in that article.

Q. And regardless of when that article appeared, regardless of the date, whatever that date is, and you've been told that your opinions in that article are the same as you're expressing now in your report. Am I correct so far?
A. I think so.

Q. At the time you expressed those opinions that appeared in the article had you done any investigations into the incident which occurred [date]?
A. No.

Q. Getting back to testimony of eye witnesses—and [retaining counsel] made a note to himself—[Decedent] was entering the mall along with his sister. [Sister's name] was deposed and gave certain testimony and I'm not going to represent to you what it was. Would her testimony as to what she observed and what happened at the time this incident occurred be of any value to you in reaching any of your opinions that you're expressing in this case?

A. Not unless the decedent was carrying a gun and was facing his assailants with a gun.

Q. I'll make a note of that.

I bet he did!! You may think this testimony is unbelievable. What is even more disturbing is the fact that this expert has positioned himself within the security expert witness community as an instructor for new experts. He not only prides himself as having created one of the definitive lists of do's and don'ts, but also believes he is one of the country's best.

It should be evident from this testimony that he has apparently fallen deep into the trap of professional arrogance. It is almost inconceivable that an expert would ever testify to having come to any opinions without having first heard and read all of the evidence. I'm not sure who is more of a cancer on the expert witness profession, the arrogant ex-police officer with no experience or the arrogant experienced expert.

Complacency can be just as ruinous. In another case, a nationally recognized expert was asked to file a declaration in support of a plaintiff's contention that a security firm was negligent in the hiring, training, and supervision of one of their officers. The officer admitted that he had deliberately set a fire inside a client location to cover up another crime he had committed. Unfortunately for him, his plans went askew and the resulting fire burned the entire building down.

The security expert, testifying in support of the plaintiff, was cited by the court as not having done his homework. He failed to support his position with any facts. In his declaration he simply stated that he had years of experience and was familiar with the industry's standard of care in the hiring and retention of security personnel. The court characterized his declaration as "devoid of any foundation, and thus lacked any evidentiary value. The expert never laid a proper foundation for his opinions, showing for instance that he investigated, surveyed or called any professional contract security company to formulate an understanding of the standard of care."

Additionally, as published in *Verdicts and Settlements*—one of the legal community's professional news journals—the expert "failed to discuss the factors he considered and the reasoning he used in reaching his opinions. To make matters worse, (the expert) commented that (the security company) failed to administer a written test to evaluate the officer's trustworthiness was wrong.

Had (the expert) properly reviewed the officer's employment file, he would have discovered that the officer took and passed numerous pre-employment written tests concerning honesty/trustworthiness."

This lack of following through on even the most basic expert witness work cost the plaintiff. The court ruled on summary judgment for the security company and dismissed the lawsuit. This loss may not have been exclusively the fault of the expert, but his failure to properly do his job certainly brought the plaintiff's contentions into question and was definitely contributory to the loss.

Another example is important because it demonstrates something more insidious than incompetence and arrogance. Many experts fail to distinguish their role as an objective witness from that of an advocate for their retained client. For expert witnesses to have credibility, there is a need to demonstrate that they are primarily interested in expressing opinions that are based on fact. Irrespective of whether or not their testimony helps or hurts either side, the opinions should represent objective analysis and conclusion based on fact. The courts, as noted above, are very clear on this point.

More important, retained experts are actually agents of the court. Even though they are retained by one side or the other, experts have an obligation to render opinion based on established criteria. In short, they are not there to serve as an advocate for their client. This was illustrated recently in a case involving a woman who filed suit against a very high-end retailer, alleging that she was wrongfully detained for shoplifting and falsely imprisoned after being held more than eleven hours.

The expert for the defendant store, another nationally renowned security consultant, was convinced that the plaintiff had shoplifted certain items. Under examination by the plaintiff's attorney, this very experienced expert became very upset and yelled angrily: "I know what happened that day. I know exactly what happened." In a very calm voice, the plaintiff's attorney responded by asking the expert if he had his appointment calendar with him. The expert, somewhat puzzled by such a response, answered that he did not. Plaintiff's counsel retorted: "Is it fair, nonetheless, to say that if you had it and were to have opened to the date of this incident, it would indicate that you were not at the store on this day?" "Yes," the expert sheepishly responded, knowing that he had allowed himself to be pulled into his own assumptions, having emotionally declared that *he knew* something that was only speculation. After having charged his client more than $35,000 for this engagement, he and the client were chagrined when the jury came back with the unanimous verdict upholding plaintiff's claim of false imprisonment.

How does the expert witness trap affect the security manager and the profession in general? Often the manager is called on to recommend an expert to the legal department. Referring an expert who is not effective brings into direct question the credibility of the security manager. Corporate counsel or an outside law firm representing the company's interest has a great deal at stake.

Norman Bates, president of Liability Consultants, Inc., routinely surveys the legal field and analyzes settlement and verdict values in cases involving security matters. His company reports that the average out-of-court settlement for a premises liability case approaches $1 million. A jury verdict averages in excess of $3 million. In other words, the stakes are high for both sides. Having the right expert is more than a matter of being right or wrong. In civil cases, it can mean significant dollars for both parties.

What can a security manager do to maintain credibility? Logically, one would think that the prudent manager would turn to either trusted colleagues or a professional association. These are good avenues, but possess their own inherent traps. Though well intentioned, these sources fail to address the critical test of whether or not the recommended expert is really appropriate for the manager's need. In other words, just as our examples demonstrate, relying on the word or reputation of an expert provides no assurance of success at all. Professional associations can only offer what has been fed to them, generally by someone advocating a particular expert over another, or based on their involvement with the association. Again, these can sometimes yield a positive result, but never can they assure success.

Where then does the manager go? The answer is simple: where the expert has been tested and proven to be a success. Before recommending someone, the security director needs to check out the expert(s) being considered.

Seek out sources that identify experts. Despite their limitations, a starting point might be a professional association such as the International Association of Professional Security Consultants. Their Web site is packed with experts on everything ranging from airports to zoos. Other sources include directories, several of which are underwritten by the local chapters of the American Bar Association or the state's trial lawyers' association. Others have their own Web sites. A simple search using the keywords "security expert, litigation" will yield a number of sources.

Certainly a check with your colleagues is well worth the effort. They may have used an expert in the past and have very definite opinions, pro or con. Universities are another source; however, caution is warranted. If a member of the university's faculty is an expert, you can rest assured that this individual will receive a high recommendation, whether it is appropriate to the manager's application or not.

So, now you have a list of potential experts. The next step is to contact them. Talk to them about their experience. Don't discuss the particulars of your case—that may put them on the clock. Rather, discuss what their experience is and what cases they have testified in regarding matters similar to the case at hand. Ask for a list of former attorney clients they have worked with, both for plaintiff and defense, on the matter similar to your circumstance. This exercise alone will weed out more than 75% of your potential list. Call the attorneys they suggest. In your discussion ask for the case citations and have your legal department pull them. Read the expert's testimony. Recall what you have just read above. This should scare you. If not, reread it. After all, this is testimony involving some of the industry's most self-proclaimed authorities regarding security expert witnessing.

Finally, call back the experts you think might best serve your company's interests. Listen to them and how they respond to you. It is not only what they say, but how they say it. Remember, arrogance runs rampant in this area. Pass over those who brag about their accomplishments or give you the impression that they are doing you a favor. They are in it for their ego and will not represent your best interests. This four-step process increases the chances that a proven and effective expert witness will be selected. It weeds out the undesirable and builds your credibility.

Concluding Comments

In this second chapter we continued building our model for determining the best security strategy for an organization. In Chapter 1 we concentrated on the first two steps: establishing a model for determining the level of risk an organization faces, and determining the appropriate security approach. In this chapter we took the process one step further by deciding what skill sets are necessary for today's security manager. Clearly, the characteristics that I have outlined call for a business manager with strong professional expertise. If your organization is not ready for such a person, you will quickly become frustrated if your skills are closely aligned to what has been outlined. The inescapable fact remains that sometimes the wrong person ends up in the wrong organization. That holds true whether one is overqualified or underqualified.

If there is a mismatch, it is incumbent on the security manager to pursue one of two courses. First, make an effort to determine whether the organization is willing to close the disparity gap. This means "putting out your feelers." Is senior management receptive or are they still stuck in a limited mindset? Perhaps it is not a matter of anyone being stuck at all. Rather, the organization may simply not need an individual with the level of experience that I have outlined. I recall the time when an information technology administrator was convinced she needed an electronic access control device on her tape library. After a few probing questions, we quickly established that only three people had access. Our recommendation was simply to change the mechanical lock. For her, the answer was cemented in the need for the latest state-of-the-art equipment, at a much higher operating expense. Sometimes the obvious is what is missed the most.

If there is a mismatch, it may mean exercising the other form of career development—moving on. As difficult as this may be, it is often the more desirable alternative over the long run. When an organization is mismatched to the capabilities of those asked to manage business units, it is the individual who suffers the most. Many security managers find themselves ready to assume greater responsibilities and new directions, but senior management's myopic beliefs about the role of their security director and the assumed limitations that often accompany specialized functions may keep the security manager from this career development. Such a position should lead the security manager to the decision that his or her contributions will be better received in another environment.

Life is 1% what you are dealt and 99% how you deal with it.

Anonymous

This chapter also drew attention to another trap that can cause unintended consequences for the unsuspecting security manager. I speak of the so-called expert who can cause more damage or serve more as a liability than a resource. In this chapter I highlighted the failed attempts of several security professionals widely recognized for their expertise who, through their own complacency and arrogance, did not serve their clients well. That is because they failed the most basic rule of all—they took on the role of advocate instead of expert. In one of the cases the expert charged more than $35,000 for his services. In another, the expert lost his credibility among the legal profession by believing that just because he said it was so, it was. It is little wonder then that some judges have wondered aloud that ours seems to be more a profession of court jesters than agents of the court.

The best executive is the one who has the sense to pick good men to do what he wants done, and self-restraint enough to keep from meddling with them while they do it.

Theodore Roosevelt

Thought-Provoking Questions

1. At the outset of this chapter the author relates his golf story. That experience leads him to conclude that timing is a critical variable for determining the success of one's career. He also concludes that golf, like other sport analogies, can help explain key organizational dynamics. What is your experience? Would you agree with the author when he says becoming an asset protection manager is rarely through a direct route?

2. In this chapter the author draws attention to the latest efforts to create a new and powerful organizational role for security; the chief security officer (CSO). Advocates of this new role liken it to that of a CIO, CFO, or CAO. What do you think about this role? Is the time right for it? Will a CSO be viewed with the same degree of credibility as a CIO or CFO?

3. There should be a set of high performance standards that clearly define the skill set necessary to assume a leadership role in asset protection management. The author offers eight specific skills. Can you add to the list?

4. This chapter concludes with a caution. The author warns that even recognized security experts can serve as a liability due to their arrogance. Have you found this to be true for your organization?

5. Should security consultants that serve as expert witnesses in civil litigation be required to undergo some form of certification process?

Chapter 3

UNDERSTANDING OUR
BARRIERS TO SUCCESS

Never take a knife to a gunfight.

Anonymous

Primary Themes

- The Organizational Challenges Facing Security
- Digging for the Root Causes
- The Barriers to Achieving Long-Term Success
- Nine Principle Contributors

OPENING OBSERVATIONS

I estimate that more than 85% of all security departments have direct responsibility for physical asset protection. I wish I could say this with some of degree of proof, but I am not aware of any definitive studies on the subject. I'll have more to say about the absence of such research efforts at the end of this book. For now, however, my experience and that of many others is all that I have to come to such a conclusion. I raise this point because it helps to create a context that needs to be set to go forward. Because the overwhelming majority of security teams have accountability for physical asset protection, we need to examine the dynamic forces that define the organizational contributions of these teams.

Any discussion of physical asset protection almost always focuses on the issue of uniformed security services at some point. Over the years there has been a great deal written regarding the use of a resident staff versus reliance on third-party providers. In *Business Strategies*, I made the point that there is no clear-cut answer. This is because each organization is different and requires its own unique strategy. In some organizations the use of a resident staff is exactly what may be required, and the same can be said for external partners in other organizations. For still others, a combination of both may be the better fit. Regardless of the strategy selected, the decision should be based on sound business criteria. These include:

- Quality of the workforce
- Loyalty of the workforce
- Turnover/attrition
- Economic gain
- Risk transference: hold harmless and indemnification
- Management flexibility
- Experience in specific business sector
- Ability to develop global alliances
- Access to new markets
- Focusing resources on core competencies
- Cyclical influences and nature of the work to be performed
- Training and promotional opportunities
- Employee and customer acceptance
- Litigation requirements
- Acquisitions and consolidations
- Access to confidential information

These sixteen variables apply to either side of the outsourcing versus residential workforce issue. Each must be considered before a final decision is made. And yet, these are not the only variables. After assisting more than 200 clients and assessing over 600 security operations, I have found that there are more than 1,300 decision points that need to be considered. On the surface some appear to be minor. However, even the most mundane factor can have a dramatic effect on the entire process.

For today's security manager the issue of workforce configuration is only one in a series of underlying dynamics that can define success or failure. To effectively contribute to the organization's business aims, the security management team needs respect. Only then can it obtain the critical support it requires to be effective. Unfortunately, such respect is often weak or lacking all together. Sometimes there is outright opposition. Therefore, it is necessary to probe the root causes underneath this lack of respect to discover what needs to be done to reverse the situation. That is the focus of what follows.

The Organizational Challenges Facing Security

In the 1990s corporate America became obsessed with the idea of redefining itself as a "lean, mean, competitive machine." Layoffs were the call of the day as organization after organization shifted from a reliance on proprietary, or resident, workforces and turned instead to third-party providers. Noted management writers fell into step one after another touting the wonders of external strategic partnerships and how such a management move actually positioned the company to yield significantly greater returns for its investors. The large consulting houses such as McKinsey, Anderson Consulting, and others, raced to the executive suites of our largest corporations, selling the occupants on the concept of hiring them at seven figure retainers. In return, these so-called sages of profitability and global competition would reengineer the company, casting out middle managers and restructuring the organization's infrastructure. They promised significant and long-term economies once the company shifted from a reliance on hiring its own workers and yielding to the expertise of the suppliers.

The mantra of management consultants was "stick to your core competencies and leave support functions in the hands of the experts." Maybe this was true for other support functions, but rarely did corporate America find a comforting level of assurance in the expertise of most security providers. Despite valiant efforts on the part of some providers, the sad reality was that contract companies failed to provide true expertise in the management of a company's security program. The same can be said today. Although I have seen significant improvement over the past 30 years of my career, it is no understatement to say that we have a very long, long way to go.

But that is only half of the picture. Often these same consulting firms turned their attention on those resident managed programs and proclaimed that they, too, needed reengineering to bring added value. Hence we saw the introduction of total quality management, continuous quality improvement, ISO 9000 derivatives, and a number of other remedies. When each of these failed, the band of would-be corporate saviors threw their hands up in frustration and left, leaving a bitter taste in the mouths of many. Often their parting shot was directed at the "incompetence of the security staff" or "a business unit that was not in step with the corporate culture." Either way, the fact remained that security directors were looked on as being outside the mainstream of the organization. For many this perception remains today.

Following the days of 9/11, Marc Bradshaw, president of the International Association of Professional Security Consultants, noted that the security profession is at a crossroad. I believe one of the factors that have drawn us to this junction is the need to address the underlying causes that keep security personnel cast as second-class corporate citizens. When the nation scoffed at Argenbright's airport screeners, did they address the problem? No, instead they cast the lot out, replacing them with federal employees as though that simplistic, but highly expensive alternative was the answer. Once again the security profession saw a nation, led by the federal government, strongly pressured by the media and openly criticized by local law enforcement, abandon them in a critical hour of need.

I will cut to the bottom line. Today's corporate world cannot possibly look to third-party contractors with any sense of confidence that, as a group, they can effectively manage the issue of people and asset protection. Nor can we rely solely on resident staffs. Let there be no mistake that within the profession there are a number of quality-driven security companies. Likewise, there are dedicated resident security professionals that deliver high-quality service each day. Unfortunately, these are the exceptions. A far better characterization of today's security staffer is one bound by misconceptions and misunderstandings. Until each causative factor is identified and dealt with, the security professional will remain disadvantaged.

Why does such a state exist and is there any possible light at the end of this seemingly very dark tunnel? To answer the "why" question will take a few pages, which we will begin shortly. The answer to the longer-term question about any future hope is simple: yes. Nevertheless, it is sometime off. From where I sit I do see a flicker of light, and my reconnaissance team tells me that it is not the headlamp of a speeding train. There is actually some hope, but to achieve it will require new attitudes, new strategies, and new commitments. Having established exactly where we are today—as painful as it may be to read—I think we can see the holes and traps and begin building a new foundation toward a brighter and more effective future. We need to do this, if for no other reason than because our own safety and security demands as much. Despite the dollars committed in the post-9/11 era by local, state, and federal agencies, they simply cannot do the job of ensuring that people can go about their business or enjoy a vacation with family and friends without being victimized by a terrorist or common street thug. Moreover, today's emerging and established corporate giants cannot rely on public law enforcement to protect their people and their most valued assets—tangible and intangible.

> *In war, the stronger overcomes the weaker. In business, the stronger imparts strength to the weaker.*
>
> *Frederic Bastiat*

On a personal note, I find it professionally embarrassing that our industry continues to be a business enterprise that remains so downtrodden when other infrastructure support elements are coming into their own era of respectability. I also feel that we, as a country, should take note of how we value private security and recognize that among many other nations—both developed and underdeveloped—we rank pathetically low. Why? I'm not totally sure, but, as you will see, I offer some insights in this chapter. Perhaps our learned sociologists can provide some insight. As a practitioner, consultant, writer, and teacher in this area for over 30 years, I can conjecture that, as a society, we place little value on selected professions—among them are security officers. Whether originally deserved or not, lack of commitment to heighten our expectations of private guards only feeds the self-fulfilling prophecy that they are second-class citizens. Simply stated, Americans are rather snobbish when it comes to sanitation workers, janitors, and guards, to name but a few of the "lower-caste careers."

As I was writing this section, I received Bob McCrie's latest edition of *Security Letter*. Bob had recently returned from an extended business trip to Europe and was reporting on the recent efforts underway to improve the training for security officers. In a previous edition he had written about his positive impressions regarding the role of security among the Euro countries. He was most favorably impressed by how much farther advanced they are than their American counterparts. This caused me to think about an observation I made in the early 1990s. I was asked where U.S. security services ranked among the other nations of the world. Having traveled extensively and worked with many global companies, I stated that I was not sure because I had never actually conducted a formal study. For that matter, I was not aware of any such study.

Nevertheless, I stopped for a moment and considered my own experiences and recalled comments and observations made by other well-respected security managers, both here in the United States and from other countries. I also reflected on the work I had done for the Canadian government when I was asked to review their nationalized security services standards. I began to tick off in my mind the names of countries that were clearly ahead of American security services across a wide continuum of comparative factors. These included respect for the officers, training, compensation, tenure, and so forth— in short, those variables that define a country's commitment to the security profession. As I did so, several European countries came to my mind as being more advanced than the United States. Canada certainly flashed through my mind, as did Russia, several Latin American countries, and a number of countries along the Pacific Rim. I recalled such countries as Israel and others in the Middle East. When my list was completed, I was somewhat surprised to realize that the United States could do no more than place 15th, and that was being generous.

This is admittedly anecdotal, but I would challenge anyone to consider the same question and using objective, measurable criteria, generate a list that identifies the United States among the top 10, let alone the top 5. I do not know that it could have been done then, and it cannot be done now or for anytime in the foreseeable future. This is because Americans look down on private security. They do not value security as a meaningful career pursuit, whereas in other parts of the world, private security is regarded as a respected career choice. Officers are fairly compensated and can make the pursuit of private security an admirable career. Elsewhere (e.g., the U.S.), security personnel are commonly the butt of jokes or portrayed as losers.

In the 2002 Hollywood release of the movie *John Q.*, the hospital guard is portrayed as an obese, cowardly character who refuses to do his job because he is only paid $8.50 an hour. This movie speaks volumes as to how influential scriptwriters view the security profession. The movie drips with nearly every politically correct message possible regarding the plight of a poor factory worker and his battle against a cold and heartless healthcare system. The director goes out of his way to make one point after another about how medical "fat cats" are arrogant and inconsiderate. His portrayal of uncaring bureaucrats and their indifference to blue-collar people is designed to elicit viewer sympathies and stir up feelings of indignation. Yet, running through every scene at the hospital is his stereotypical representation of the totally unprofessional security guard. If it were not so pathetic, it would be amusing to watch the director hoist himself on his own petard.

Despite the lack of "expert" responsiveness, senior executives followed the advice of their high-priced consulting firms and began rampant outsourcing. In some cases the transition worked well, but in most cases there was a discernable decrease in the quality of the security department's deliverable. Plagued by the lack of Standards that could ensure consistent quality across both geographic boundaries and functional responsibilities, external providers in particular demonstrated an acute inability to effectively *manage* even the most basic security programs, let alone the complex. Note that I stress *managing* as opposed to simply providing a service.

I stress the word *Standards*, with a capital S because the security services profession is a noncodified profession. The same can be said for criminal and corporate investigations, preemployment processing, and background verifications. In other words, there are no national standards that can serve as a measuring rod for performance. There are no federal laws that define minimums. At the state level there are significant disparities between what is required and what is not even addressed. Few states require more than two weeks of preassignment training. Today most police agencies require an officer to undergo some form of supervised training for nearly a year before being allowed to patrol solo.

As I noted in my opening observations, perhaps one of the most visible examples of this lack of standards was found within the airline industry and the pounding that third-party security providers took. The criticism rang loud after the 9/11 incident. Politicians, talk shows, news commentators, and even stand-up comedians found easy prey across America's media skies as they zeroed in on Argenbright Security and other providers. For Argenbright Security it meant the end of their service as one of the largest airport screening companies in America.

For now, the right question to be asked is: Why has the security profession as a whole failed to rise to the occasion and demonstrate a consistent approach, providing management acumen? Is it because they are inept? Is it the fault of the organization or client? Is it the lack of national standards? Perhaps at least part of the blame rests with the public at large for failing to see security as a profession meriting respect and confidence. Or is it simply a matter of economics—you get what you pay for?

The answer to these questions is, as you may have guessed, all of the above. When it comes to assigning blame, there is plenty to go around for everyone, even the hallowed halls of academia. The success of a physical asset protection program rests on a capable management team and workforce as one of the three key pillars of today's security program, so let's take a closer look. Following is a list of the culpable, not necessarily in order of contribution.

■ Law enforcement at all government levels and the Fraternal Order of Police

■ University and college criminal justice programs, and the absence of these programs from business schools

■ Professional associations and their internal politics or lack of management focus

■ Insurance companies, as underwriters of contract service with limits of liability

■ The courts, as learned bodies unwilling to define security's role

■ Corporate executives and employees who view security as a necessary evil

■ Third-party security providers, as poor business owners and unwilling participants

■ Resident security managers, as distracted business managers

■ Ourselves, as a society with a cultural bias against private security (e.g., rent-a-cops)

Quite a hit list, isn't it? In short, we are all to blame. Let's look at each briefly and explain why there is such universal sharing of culpability.

Law Enforcement

A common misconception among the ranks of the sworn police community is that they are qualified to speak definitively on matters involving private security. Many believe that after a career in law enforcement they can simply proclaim to the business world that they are experts in matters of security and stand ready to serve as corporate managers or expert witnesses in matters of civil litigation. The problem is that their fundamental orientation is not aligned to protecting corporate assets. Similarly, corporate security managers, regardless of their success, are not necessarily experts in law enforcement. In short, the two professions are truly worlds apart.

First, policing operates from a law and order perspective. Police have been charged with enforcing laws and maintaining order. This is grilled into police personnel from the first day of their academy training. It is reinforced by the courts and extends into the fundamental teachings of criminal justice. This is an appropriate role for them. Conversely, corporate security is about the business of protecting assets. Sometimes these assets are tangible (this includes people) and sometimes they are intangible (intellectual property, for example). As an asset protection specialist, the primary focus is on assuring that such assets are not placed unduly or inadvertently at risk. Sometimes it means assuring that certain laws are obeyed, but it does not involve the enforcement of laws or the maintenance of public order.

Because there are two dichotomous perspectives, we have different approaches, requiring different skill sets. Unfortunately, police personnel are typically not educated to see, let alone understand, the fundamental differences. They have been chartered to protect—that is, to enforce and maintain. They reason that protection in law enforcement equates to protection in the private sector. Authors Al Germann, Frank Day, and Robert Gallatti explained this difference in their classic text, *An Introduction to Law Enforcement and Criminal Justice*, in the early 1960s. Unfortunately, many a police student failed then— and now—to learn this fundamental principle.

How does this translate directly to the problem of inconsistent private security management? Simply, this inherently arrogant attitude on the part of American policing creates a failure to support private security and leads directly to an arena of competition. It never ceases to amaze me, then, when a police officer retires early and seeks employment among the ranks of private security. While carrying the badge, law enforcement personnel are quick to jibe private security personal. Often the butt of their jokes, security people are labeled as "want-to-be's," "police rejects," or "rent-a-cops." But once the police officer retires, all too often the corporate security director hears a knock at the door from the inquiring retired police officer turned instant security expert.

Perhaps the best example of this lack of support comes from the ranks of the Fraternal Order of Police (FOP). As law enforcement's leading lobbyist and labor representative, the FOP has actively lobbied against every major piece of legislation designed to improve the lot of the private security officer. Major bill after major bill introduced at the national level aimed at creating national qualifying and performance standards for the private sector has been strongly opposed by the FOP or blocked by their legislator of choice. Why? Because they are intelligent enough to recognize a threat from far off. They fear that just as mandated national standards for policing changed their status and significantly improved their lot, so too will similar standards alter the face and character of private security.

Many FOP members fear loss of their employment if government entities consider privatization to reduce annual operating expenses. Many cite the inroads made by civilian employees employed as police dispatchers, crime lab technicians, and community service officers. Still others point to Wackenhut's correctional institutions arm, which employs the largest nonsworn group of correctional officers. All in all, police union officials fear that once even the most minimum standards are cast into law, it is only a matter of time before their livelihood is threatened.

In reality, this is bunk. As we have discussed before, security is about the business of protecting assets and not about law and order. There is no doubt that many police-related infrastructure activities can be handled by nonsworn personnel, but there is a limit. Eventually, we expect there to be a group of individuals empowered to investigate and arrest to enforce the laws. Failure to take a bold position and support the idea that a professionally recruited, well-trained, and well-compensated security force is actually a benefit to law enforcement's efforts, is indicative of Neanderthal thinking that can only work against the best interests of everyone in the long run.

I must be quick to add that there is a remarkable irony at work here. Although it is true that attempts have been made to introduce higher standards for private security, such standards are meager at best. For example, the proposed standard for training typically calls for a minimum of 8 to 12 *hours* of classroom instruction for new hires. This compares to more than 20 *weeks* for the average police officer. The irony is that even if such standards were to become law, they are essentially weak and effective.

Prior to the introduction of the Law Enforcement Assistance Administration (LEAA) in the early 1960s, policing was not a respected career alternative for young Americans. The police were looked down on and considered the profession of choice for anyone who could not make it in another career. Police officers were viewed as bullies and the strong arm of not the law, but of crooked politicians and crime figures. They were seen as uneducated, unprofessional, and uncaring. Their reputation had sunk to such a low that reformists found it an easy task to secure the necessary legislation to assure a radical change. The public demanded it because they were tired of being victimized by their "men in blue."

LEAA was not without its faults, but there was no mistaking the fact that its overall impact was highly successful. Police officers were given grants to seek college degrees, with increased salaries as bonuses for completing their degree. Police departments at every level received grant monies to improve their equipment and facilities. Community police programs sprang up, giving birth to police–community relations programs, the precursor to today's highly regarded community policing programs. It is not coincidental that Robert Trojanowitz, considered by many as the father of community policing, began his academic studies at Michigan State University—at that time considered one of the foremost institutions in Police Administration—under Louis Radlett, one of the leading advocates and founders of what was then referred to as police-community relations.

In short, American policing was called to task by the public, its customers. The response was a rapid escalation in the quality of policing across the country. The Police Executive Research Forum was founded at this time and propelled to national prominence under Patrick Murphy, former commissioner of New York City. This was the same Patrick Murphy who was seen as a reformist and credited with cleaning up the widespread corruption within the NYPD, as portrayed in the movie *Serpico*, which is based on the true story of a vice officer who testified against many of his fellow officers for their involvement in corrupt police practices.

Today private security has been called to task, especially since the events of 9/11. There is a basic lack of respect for security officers. Yet, the FOP resists standards to improve private security because they fear that once the camel's nose is under the tent flap, it won't be long before the camel is in all the way. What does this possible competition really mean? The fears range from the introduction of private policing (e.g., loss of jobs) to widespread civilian management of police organizations. Whether such fears are warranted or not is really no excuse for law enforcement to continue an obstructionist role.

It is impossible to win the great prizes of life without running risks.
Theodore Roosevelt

Universities and Colleges

In *Business Strategies* I made the point that our halls of academia are failing us as well. That was nearly a decade ago but, sadly, I still stand on this position. Some anecdotal evidence exists that indicates progress has been made to differentiate criminal justice from corporate asset protection; however, there is no discernable pattern of true progress. Some universities have created security management programs dedicated to the study of applying business management principles to the concepts of asset and people protection. Most still insist on incorporating private security as a subset to criminal justice.

Would these same learned professors move human resources, accounting, auditing, marketing, and manufacturing out of the school of business to criminal justice? It would be ludicrous to suggest such a thing. Yet when it comes to protecting the people and assets of a corporation, the widespread belief is that somehow it makes sense as part of the college of social sciences and the school of criminal justice. Again, I ask why?

Moving the study of corporate security to the business school is no easy task, despite all of the evidence to suggest that it is not only the wise thing to do, but also just makes common sense. Unfortunately, academia, like all other sectors, suffers from its internal politics, power struggles, and indifference. Internal politics arise when the criminal justice department head or college dean refuses to give up the corporate security program because it means a loss of power and influence. Conversely, business school deans remain largely ignorant of the value that a truly well-run comprehensive security program brings to a company's bottom-line profitability. (We've already touched on this contribution and will do so again.)

The end result is that private security students are short-changed, as are business students. Absent an exposure to the risks and threats associated with the loss of assets and physical suffering resulting from workplace violence, business students of today fail to develop a full appreciation of corporate net worth when they become the executives of tomorrow. Often seen as a second-rate stepchild, the security management student is looked down on as someone who cannot cut it in the real world of policing. Security students are required to pack their core curriculum with police-related courses, yet the reverse is not true for the classic criminal justice student. Security students are expected to know the laws of search and seizure, the powers of arrest, juvenile custodial rights, and a plethora of other police-related topics. Why are these commonly required courses instead of electives?

Some may argue that security personnel do respond to incidents that require custody of individuals, sometimes juveniles. Knowing the basic legal requirements assures a satisfactory arrest or detainment, not to mention proper handling of evidence for later criminal prosecutorial consideration. This may be true, but the overwhelming majority of security incidents do not have such requirements. Just as there are specialty areas for law enforcement (i.e., e-commerce frauds, embezzlements, gang management, etc.) that require added training in addition to core requirements, the same can be said for the private sector. In other words, those students desiring to specialize in retail security, school safety, and so forth should surely be given the opportunity to consider appropriate electives to study. Conversely, the fundamentals of strong business management of a corporate security program should not be usurped for coursework that is secondary at best. In short, knowing criminal law and police tactics does little to assure executive management that their assets will be properly protected.

Academicians have failed in their research efforts as well. I will have more to say about this at the conclusion of this book. For now, however, it is important to underscore that basic assumptions about the business of asset protection remain just that—assumptions. Yet entire security programs are designed around such assumptions. Budgets are created and pushed before corporate executives based on these assumptions, all without the empirical evidence to support them. I am reminded of Yogi Berra's observation: "Before you build a better mousetrap, it helps to know if there are any mice out there."

Before moving on, here is a simple test for academicians. Survey a dozen security managers. Ask if having a degree from a well-respected criminal justice program gives one job candidate an advantage over another. As I and my colleagues discovered years ago, the answer is never an unequivocal yes. Rarely, it is a qualified yes. Rather, the common refrain is more likely to be a definitive no. This is because the majority of security managers have learned that, just as in the world of policing, there are some things that can be taught after the individual is employed. What is far more desirable is an understanding of how businesses operate, what assets are, and how they can be protected.

As a final note regarding the role of our universities, allow me to draw one last observation. In early 2002 the University of Phoenix, the country's largest private university serving more than 60,000 working adults, announced that it was launching a degree in criminal justice. UOP is recognized as a business management school founded for the purpose of providing college degrees to those engaged largely in the private sector. Over the years their student body has attracted many in the public sector, but the emphasis has largely been focused on corporate America. I find it fascinating that this school, like the vast majority of its business school counterparts, elected to offer a degree aimed at addressing public administration issues, yet it does not offer one course designed to help business students better understand the importance of protecting their company's valued assets. Moreover, the school does not spend as much as *one hour* in its degree programs dedicated to this critical topic. The business schools of Harvard, Stanford, the University of Virginia, and the University of Michigan suffer the same pathetic inadequacy.

We keep moving forward, opening new doors, and doing new things, because we're curious and curiosity keeps leading us down new paths.

Walt Disney

Professional Associations

Like most other sectors of our society, the security industry is not without its multitude of professional associations. Such associations can be wonderful resources for both the newcomer and the experienced professional. They serve as a resource for training and education, introduction of the latest state-of-the-art technologies, and professional networking. Some serve as strong lobbying interests for the benefit of the overall profession. Others have amassed comprehensive resource libraries and sponsor grants for new research. Associations have become so diverse that they serve multiple interests and needs. Today's security constituencies are grouped by gender, ethnicity, religion, professional specialty, and corporate size. Some are international and others are limited to regions. When I was in Chicago, I was a member of APEX, or Asset Protection Executives. This was a group limited to 20 members, each representing a business sector such as banking, retail, and transportation.

Most associations have their own charters and promote professionalism as one of their main tenets. Some subscribe to a specific code of ethics. All in all, the industry does not want for opportunities to gather and discuss the challenges of the day. Yet many associations are bogged down by internal politics, jealousies, personality conflicts, and bureaucracies, and these organizational distractions get in the way of their being truly effective. Some associations have appointed executive staffs who, in turn, have come to believe they know what is better for the association than the membership they have been appointed to serve.

Chapters and their national parent will often advocate their commitment to bettering the profession, but they can easily fall into the trap of promoting the social agenda over their professional aims. For years the International Association of Professional Security Consultants has been comprised of two camps. There are those who believe they should promote professional standards and address the pressing challenges of the day. Opposed to them are several of the founding fathers who believe that the charter was designed to sponsor camaraderie and fellowship as its foremost purpose. The industry's largest professional association, the American Society of Industrial Security (ASIS), budgets tens of thousands of dollars for the entertainment portion of its annual meetings and other sponsored events, dollars I would like to see spent on meaningful research and promoting a higher level of professionalism and business acumen.

It is appropriate for the specialized associations to focus on ways to improve the core deliverables. The larger and more comprehensive associations, however, need to set aside petty differences, individual agendas, and self-serving interests. They need to rededicate themselves and their resources to promoting standards and finding new ways for their members to garner executive sponsorship. Year after year, legislation has failed to materialize that would require improving the security industry, yet there is no concerted effort on the part of the major professional associations to form a unified front to push for such passage.

If you cannot get rid of the skeleton in your closet, you'd best teach it to dance.
George Bernard Shaw

Insurers of Contract Security Companies

Few underwriters will cover third-party security suppliers. Their position is that the cost of coverage is offset by the exposure. Stated another way, the risks are so great that they cannot make a profit. Why do a few provide the coverage then? Because they know the business and understand what limits can be placed on the insured—thus reducing their exposure—and charge high premiums. Although all of this makes good business sense, it also contributes to the inconsistency of security management. By limiting coverage, insurance companies contribute to limiting a security officer's role to a nominal contribution. This, in turn, limits skill sets and responsibility—both of which downplay the importance of security.

Security officers are not obligated to intervene in a situation when they are likely to put themselves in harm's way. This includes incidents involving the clear and present danger to others. There is no legal, ethical, or moral obligation to intervene except as a private citizen governed, in some jurisdictions, by Good Samaritan laws. For that matter, should a security officer engage in an activity that results in the death or injury of a third party, the officer's company would most likely not be covered. This is because the officer acted outside the limits of coverage. Insurers are reluctant to provide comprehensive coverage for acts involving potential injury or death. Unless special riders are in place, the intent is to hold security officers to the classic roles of observing, reporting, recording, and intervening only in a manner that does not place persons in peril.

The net effect of such coverage forces contract employers to deny claims filed on behalf of their clients, or to admit ownership of the officer's actions and seek economic relief. For small security firms this often means filing bankruptcy to avoid a costly payout. In addition to the economic restrictions, there is a more insidious factor at play. Failure to fully support security operations creates a credibility gap between provider and client. Companies engage the services of their provider because the supplier represents itself as the security expert. This creates a false expectation on the part of the client that, over the long run, works directly against the interests of the relationship.

Moreover, as early as 1995 in *Business Strategies,* I cautioned that it is troubling to note that even if hold harmless and indemnification language is in the client–supplier contract, this is no assurance that the underwriter will step up and provide the necessary coverage in the event of litigation. As companies continue to set aside traditional vendor relationships and pursue strategic partnerships, many underwriters see this as an opportunity to claim that a co-employment relationship exists between their insured (the supplier) and the supplier's client. Consequently, should a supplier's officer be the subject of litigation while servicing the client account, the underwriter may refuse coverage. This forces suppliers to either honor the hold harmless and indemnification intent on their own or seek other economic remedies. As noted, this later course often translates to filing for bankruptcy, once again creating a credibility gap between the supplier side of the equation and the client side.

Finally, the insurance industry has yet to create employment, training, and performance criteria for their insured's employees. One would think that this might be the most logical and demanding source for creating acceptable standards—after all, failure to hire and train qualified personnel increases risks. One need only turn to the daily filings of civil litigation by plaintiffs seeking damages against unqualified security officers and their employers to prove this point. But the underwriter rarely requires adherence to a delineated set of performance criteria. The only notable exception is in the area of requiring the employer to assure that they are in compliance with local laws governing guard certifications. Although nearly two-thirds of the states have some form of guard qualification, these requirements are minimum at best (e.g., free of criminal convictions, able to pass a written exam administered by the supplier, and—when required by the prospective client—be bondable). Whereas the onus for requiring higher standards for security officers should not be placed disproportionately on the insurance industry, the fact remains that they share in contributing to the inconsistency of many security accounts across all business sectors.

Caring is a powerful business advantage.

Scott Johnson

The Courts

As long as I have been in the industry, I have watched with interest the number of court cases involving security operations. Subscriber newsletters are packed each month with anywhere from 15 to 25 cases—all different—reporting the latest court rulings. Since 1993 I have been augmenting my own consulting business with expert litigation support for both the plaintiff and defense. In this capacity I have had the opportunity to testify in several states and at the federal level. Of the more than 250 attorneys retaining my services, most have focused directly on matters of either premises liability involving inadequate security or negligent security operations. This workload has provided me the opportunity to research how the courts have viewed similar cases. Frequently, judicial decision-makers struggle with the role of private security, yet fail to clearly and succinctly define what should be the baseline.

Some would argue that this is not the role of the lower or higher courts. I disagree. Absent a national standard, and recognizing that the security services profession is not codified, some external source is required to provide the necessary metrics for acceptable performance. Given this absence, and considering the issue of personal damages that are at stake, having our judicial system provide a uniform standard for security's role is certainly reasonable. If legislators refuse, the security profession itself refuses, and the insurance industry refuses, then, by default, the courts need to intervene. And, slowly, that is exactly what they are doing. However, until there is ultimately a defined standard, private security will continue to hobble along.

As noted, much of today's litigation involving security ties the issue of premises liability with the concept of inadequate security. Plaintiffs seek to demonstrate that had the property owner been more diligent in establishing security practices based on sound and reasonable standards, their injuries would not have been suffered. Tragically, some state courts such as California's have rendered rulings that disproportionately distance property owners from this liability. Let us briefly look at California, because they are often viewed as a precedent setting state.

Beginning in 1993, the California courts began limiting property owner liabilities. This, in turn, lessens the need for developing a professional standard of performance for private security operations. Although the courts profess to be concerned strictly with the issue of an owner's liability, the net effect of limiting their liability means that property owners will require less from their security teams. "After all," they reason, "why pay more when you do not have to?" When the California high court set aside the concept of *totality of circumstances* in reversing the *Issacs vs. Huntington* decision in favor of the defendants in *Nola M. vs. the University of Southern California* in 1993, they started down the path of what is today known as the concept of *foreseeability*—a very slippery slope indeed! This simply means that for defendant property owners to be held liable, the act causing injury to a third party needs to have been foreseeable. As one of the dissenting justices cynically, but accurately noted, this is tantamount to allowing "one free rape."

For purposes of our discussion here, however, the concept of foreseeability limits, by its very nature, any requirement to have a professional security force that should properly advise its clients as to inherent dangers based on the experiences of other accounts or what is generally known in the industry. Remember, without proof of a foreseeable event the property owner can claim—and they now do—that all they need is a minimum security force with minimum job duties (skill sets). Since 1993 the state courts have handed down ruling after ruling in favor of property owners.

Perhaps the biggest blow the California higher courts have struck to date in this arena is their decision in the *Marianne Saelzler vs. Advanced Group 400 et al.* decision in 2001. Here they stretched the envelope even farther by ruling that even if a property owner was shown to be grossly negligent, absent plaintiff's ability to tie such negligence to the direct issue of causation, the property owner is not liable. Stated another way, unless the assailant admits that the crime was perpetrated based on the assailant's knowledge that the property owner was grossly negligent and so took advantage, the property owner is not liable. This ruling is the latest in what I refer to as the *Alphabet Soup* cases. This is because beginning with Nola M. (when minors are involved in court cases, their name is replaced by the first initial of their last name) there have been a series of pro-property cases. These include Ann M., Pamela B., Pamela H., and Leslie G., each of whom were victims of rape while on private property.

California is at least consistent. The same, unfortunately, cannot be said of many other state courts. The Florida, Georgia, Texas, and Massachusetts courts have rendered inconsistent opinions on matters of security. Attempting to focus on the nuances of each particular case, the justices have often rendered opinions that conflict with all or parts of previous cases. This creates confusion within the corporate sector because there is no clear baseline for creating policies and establishing operating practices.

To summarize, the courts have contributed to creating an inconsistency in security management through their judicial rulings. They have done this by failing to clearly establish standards of performance and by rendering decisions that actually work against the interests of raising the security standards bar. It is sad that even when there is an appropriate venue for determining such standards, we see nothing but failure.

Good people do not need laws to act responsibly, while bad people will find a way around the laws.

                                                                    Plato

Corporate Executives and Their Employees

As I have noted, many corporate executives and their employees see security as bringing little value to an organization. Others see security as a necessary evil. The majority of working Americans remain indifferent, despite the events of the WTC bombing in the early 1990s and the later attack in 2001. The first 45 to 60 days following the 9/11 terrorist attack saw a very clear heightened awareness. Emotions ran high as Americans for the first time felt nervous going to work. After numerous incidents involving workplace violence episodes and school shootings prior to the 9/11 attack, Americans had become jaded. While believing that such incidents were tragic, corporate executives were quick to rationalize that they were something that could never happen to their company. The WTC attack altered this perspective—but only for a very short period of time.

With the United State's quick victories over the terrorist forces in far away places, most American workers settled back into their old habits and perspectives. Corporate executives slipped back into their fatalistic attitudes regarding their potential of falling victim to a kidnapping or injury at the hands of disgruntled employees or radicals. For them, it was all a matter of "when your time comes, there is little anyone can do." Such an attitude could be seen developing for a long time. In the mid-1980s security directors engaged in the business of creating elaborate, and often unrealistic, executive protection plans that served only to create paranoia among senior managers. Citing hot spots of terrorist activity or anti-American sentiment around the world, it was not uncommon for security managers to warn of dire consequences to those traveling abroad. So loud was their cry that it was not long before executives felt stifled and tuned out such warnings, believing them to be much ado about nothing. For many security directors there was a loss of credibility, one that continues to manifest itself today.

To demonstrate how executives and their employees become jaded, we need only go back to what we have already covered—the daily barrage of reports regarding one possible terrorist threat after another from Homeland Security, the FBI, or the CIA. Some are absolutely mind-bending and encourage the lack of credibility. For example, in June of 2002 the head of California's Stateland Security appeared before a group of computer security experts. His remarks were picked up by the media when he warned of an imminent terrorist attack in California sometime in the summer. The next day he backpedaled on his comment, telling the press, "Even when I read this aloud, I knew it did not sound right." He then went on to clarify what he had intended to say, noting that the FBI was concerned that such an event might happen. But note the underlying issue: he had not read his prepared remarks in advance. In short, he was not prepared, opting instead to blindly read what was in front of him. No one from the media challenged this point, opting instead to focus on the fact that he had retracted his comment and that all was once again safe—for the time being.

Senior decision-makers of corporations are not innocent bystanders. When the government announced its intent to provide federal airline screeners, airline executives were quick to support such government intervention because this shifted the responsibility away from them and they could move on, leaving the issue of professionalizing security to someone else. This is another way of saying, "Let them (the government) handle this hot potato. That way, when things go wrong—as it invariably will—we cannot be sued. In short, it's not our problem."

As we have seen, corporate America in general turned its back on security after the immediacy of 9/11. Not wanting to be inconvenienced, and blaming the economic downturn of 2001 on their company's inability to fully support heightened security measures, senior managers failed to render the necessary support. For example, in the days following the WTC attack, three of the country's largest property management firms, whose client lists represented a portfolio of America's best-of-the-best in multitenant, Class A high-rises became very interested in developing risk profiles and seeking recommendations that were consistent with their owners' business plans. They sought the advice of experts to develop an approach that was both cost-effective and responsive to their individual properties. Before going ahead, however, each had to consult with their clients, the owners of the high-rises.

Sure that the owners would want something done, if for no other reason than to calm the nerves of their tenants, each property management company sought what they believed would be quick approval. Not one of the owners, in virtually every major market in the country, wanted to spend the money. They offered their own litany of *why not*s, including recessionary woes that forced low occupancies and therefore reduced operating capital. Also, they feared that by having an independent assessment of what might be appropriate, they would be criticized and possibly held liable if they failed to act.

In other cases, the property management companies reported there was disagreement among the tenants as to the level of desired security. In one case, within a week of 9/11 a major law firm, the largest tenant of a high-rise less than a block from Chicago's Sears Tower, vehemently objected to having its employees and guests register in the lobby during business hours. This, despite the fact that only the day before, the national media played a video over and over showing a young Islamic fundamentalist defying America and waving a picture of the Sears Tower and chanting, "This one's mine."

In December of 2001, less than 90 days after the WTC attack, *Security Magazine* reported that approximately one-third of respondents to their Web site survey indicated that they would see an increase in their security budgets for 2002. Even though many reported that their budgets increased immediately after the attack, few indicated that the dollars were spent on long-term strategies. Rather, the money was to be spent on quick fixes designed to address long-overdue requests or the temporary assignment of added staff. In the middle of February 2002 I canvassed dozens of security directors representing America's

Fortune 500 and heard the majority candidly report that "things had returned to normal" regarding a general lack of support for true long-term strategic support for security initiatives among their senior and executive management ranks.

This admittedly informal survey speaks volumes. What it demonstrates is the lack of support for improving the lot of security. If the absolute destruction of one of America's most notable landmarks is not enough to shake decision-makers into realizing the need to improve security standards and practices, what will? As further illustration, over the years I have hosted a variety of workshops for security managers. I often ask them to identify which room in a house security represents in their organization. The common answers include the basement, the garage, the bathroom, or the attic—in other words, places that are out of sight and therefore out of mind.

> *It ain't no fun fight'n for a man when, no matter what you've done, it ain't good enough.*
>
> *Steve Crane*

Third-Party Security Providers

Thus far we have looked outside the security profession to find our pockets of culpability.

Unfortunately, blame can be found just as easily within the security profession itself. As a group, third-party security suppliers are reluctant to take their share of responsibility for the current state of affairs. Owners are quick to shift the blame. The common cry is, "We cannot control our clients. We only provide what they want." Or, "We are on the receiving end. We want to improve our lot, but the paying clients hold us down by their insistence that ours is a commodity business driven by low-bid pricing."

Recalling my discussion of commodity busting in *The Art*, you should not be surprised that I categorically reject such statements—or, rather, such admissions of failure. When I hear suppliers lament their sorry position, I categorize it as *welfare rationalization*. This means a willingness to accept what is handed down without asking questions and being happy with what is given. Perhaps this is somewhat harsh, but it illustrates the pathetic nature of such rationalizing. Security services are not commodities. When clients, actual or prospective, voice this belief, they should be challenged directly and forcefully. Before its acquisition by Securitas, the fourth-largest company was American Protective Services (APS). Dwight Pederson, APS's CEO, adamantly held to the standard that security was not a commodity and refused to accept accounts driven by such a client attitude.

Is a corporation's HR department a commodity? Are the auditors commodities? Are their lawyers? Is their marketing department a commodity? Perhaps their R&D is a commodity. Would executive row describe itself as a corporate commodity? Why then should there be an assumption that security is a commodity? Left unchallenged, this belief will only perpetuate. When management views security services as a commodity, they foster the notion of cost over quality. Price becomes the determinant, not standards of performance, and certainly not quality of service. In sum, executives who define corporate services as commodities and suppliers who accept this are both getting in the way of effective business thinking and value-added asset protection.

Consolidations

With the recent wave of consolidations within the security industry, I fail to see any significant change in priorities among service providers over the near to intermediate terms. By the late 1990s we had seen a number of strong regional security companies pushing clients to consider best value for lowest price. Companies such as American Protective Services, First Security, Doyle Security, Allied, Spectaguard, and a host of others fell victim to acquisition mania. These companies, despite their continuous tug-of-war with clients insisting on compressing profit margins and resisting efforts of true partnering, were making headway in the battle to upgrade the security profession's role and image. Each, in its own way, is now part of a much larger company, the driving force of which is to maximize shareholder value.

As I noted before, many of those acquiring companies are European based. At first glance, one might be lulled into believing that security companies operating in the United States under European control might be the dawning of a new era marked by an effort to upgrade the stature of private security. Recalling my previous comments regarding how positively security officers are viewed in other parts of the world, might suggest that this is very good news indeed. Note, however, that I say *lulled into believing*. To date, there is no evidence to support this line of thinking. This is because a security firm, regardless of how it may be viewed on its home turf, is powerless in changing basic attitudes, at least over the foreseeable future, in a host country. Security services are not like items such as automobiles and electronics that Americans can see and touch to determine their quality and therefore be persuaded to purchase. Rather, the challenge is rooted in an ability to demonstrate continuity of a delivery system based on day-in and day-out encounters with a professional staff—something that, at least for now, most Americans do not place much credence in, all the while knowing that they share in the culpability of security's inconsistency.

Some industry experts have conjectured that the pace of foreign acquisition may slow in the years ahead. This would conflict with the research efforts conducted by Graeme K. Deans, Fritz Kroeger, and Stefan Zeisel. Regarding industry consolidations they note: "Regardless of industry, consolidation activity follows a distinct pattern. It progresses through four phases of different lengths. In addition, the number of mergers varies in reverse proportion to the extent of the consolidation."

In their book, *Winning the Merger Endgame* (McGraw-Hill, 2002), they identify the four phases (or stages) as:

- The Opening Stage
- The Scale Stage
- The Focus Stage
- The Balance and Alliance Stage

They also note that the time frame for an industry to go through this process varies, but it typically spans 20 years. They add: "Starting at the low level of concentration, an industry increases its merger and acquisition activity until saturation is reached. Toward the end of the cycle, streamlining and ultimately the formulation of alliances move into the foreground." Within the security industry, merger and acquisition activity has been part of the mosaic for years as small companies aligned with one another in local or regional markets. Burns International was one of the first to aggressively position itself as a national player through its acquisition program dating back to the early 1980s. Yet the real push for major acquisitions finds it roots dating back a relatively short time ago, circa the mid-1990s. Today, Burns is part of an even larger merger, owned by Securitas.

The evidence suggests that the security industry is early in the four phases of the Deans et al. model. As they suggest, the opening phase is characterized as a fractured market filled with players of all sizes. Their data suggests that the largest suppliers account for 10% to 30% of the market. Clearly this was the case for the security industry entering the 1990s, with the top ten companies representing an aggregate market of less than 20%.

The second phase, the scale phase, sees an aggressive round of consolidations as the larger companies push to lower operating costs and ward off hostile takeovers. For security, there remains but a handful of publicly traded companies. Nonetheless, largely seeing themselves as being under the influence of the commodity syndrome, they fought to lower expenses and increase margins by essentially eliminating the competition and gaining a broader market share. It is not surprising, then, to find that the top players of today account for 30% to 45% of the market. This is directly in keeping with Deans et al.'s findings.

Based on the latest reported earnings, it would appear that the security industry is at some point in this second phase. It is a trend that began a few years before the events of 9/11, but continues unabated. The faces of security's top players are changing. Today, if one measures the total revenues of the country's top 40 security companies, the first two have a combined income greater than all of the remaining 38 firms. Sitting atop the list is Swedish-based Securitas North America. They own Pinkerton, Burns, and a host of other companies that less than five years ago ranked among the top 20. Their U.S.-based business accounts for $2.7 billion in revenue. In second place is Wackenhut Corporation with $1.06 billion in annual revenues. They were recently acquired by Group 4 Falck, based in Copenhagen and the Hague. Also among the top ten are Initial Security and AHL Services, both British owned. When combined, these four firms represent annual revenues of $4.128 billion. The remaining top 40 represent revenues of $3.366 billion. Percentage-wise, four foreign-owned companies now account for more than 55% of the top revenue of today's contract security business. This translates to about 30% of the entire market.

What does this mean for America? If nothing else, I find it ironic that we now have federal legislation mandating that all airport security screeners must be United States citizens, yet the company they work for is most likely to be foreign owned. Consolidation, regardless of ownership, would suggest that suppliers will have greater control over their margins. This translates to higher billing rates. One would hope that it might mean a more qualified and better-trained officer. Unfortunately, since the consolidation drive began in the late 1990s there has been no discernable difference in either the quality of employees or the level of their training. As noted in the Preface, industry critics suggest that some security companies have faltered under the weight of too many mergers over a relatively short period of time.

Uniformed security services are not alone in the arena of foreign ownership. Like many other industries operating here in the United States, most security devices are manufactured in non-U.S.-based plants. Whether it is a camera, an access control reader, or an intrusion alarm, the device's point of origin is well beyond the shores of America. It is very fair to say that not a single Fortune 1000 company can boast of having a true U.S.-made security system.

Does this suggest that American businesses are at risk because their security officers and devices are not U.S.-based? No, but it does suggest that when the issue of protecting people and assets is considered, we need to recognize that this is a profession that has been abdicated to others. Foreign ownership means that organizational values and practices differ from domestic values and practices. This seems simple enough, and it is. But the underlying question is whether or not senior corporate executives understand the subtle nuances inherent in their security programs and the potential impact that can fall-out when two differing cultural approaches either merge or clash—I'll have a great more to say about this in the pages ahead.

This all suggests that the industry has yet to experience the remaining two phases of *focus* and *balance and alliance*. Being halfway through also suggests that the industry will continue to consolidate for several years to come. By the end of the focus phase we should anticipate a 60% concentration of the top three market leaders. By the time the alliance phase is underway, Deans et al. suggest a concentration of 70% to 80% of the market. They conclude:

> *The industry becomes apportioned and desirable M&A becomes a rarity. Antitrust laws block further consolidation, and megamergers are out of the question. In addition, potential partners have long disappeared from the*

scene. The battle for the biggest and the best pieces of the market is over. Many former competitors have either become part of the family, parent companies or equal partners. The remaining companies become the object of alliances. The last acquisitions in the industry are still in the offing. Alliances are formed at all levels of the value-added chain.

If we follow the Deans et al. model, in time, the alliance relationship represented by the Transnational Group will be commonplace, although the incumbents may well have departed. Similarly, independents, such as fourth-ranked Memphis-based Guardsmark, will have either conquered or been conquered. Whether such consolidations will yield an improvement in the state of inconsistent security management has yet to be determined. If the early consolidations are any indicator, however, such consolidating will do little to improve the lot of the security professional.

Despite the consolidation phenomenon, third-party suppliers today are often their own worst enemy for several reasons. Of the estimated 10,000± security companies licensed in the United States, fewer than 50 have annual revenues exceeding $1 million. This means that more than 99% of the security services industry is dominated by small firms, often run by a family or two partners with a history in either security or policing. Typically, these boutique companies are very poorly managed. As surprising as it may be, if it were not for the presence of a handful of multimillion-dollar corporations (only one company can actually boast of sales in excess of $1 billion—e.g., Securitas), private security service companies would be considered a cottage industry in the United States. And, as is so often the case with a cottage industry, these companies lack the necessary business acumen to be competitive and deliver truly quality-oriented service. Rather, they lack the infrastructure and, often times, the desire to reinvest in their firms.

I have frequently been asked to review the business operations of small security companies as the result of pending litigation involving contentions of improper hiring, training, and supervision. Recalling that security services are fundamentally a noncodified industry (lacking written codes or laws that govern such matters), it is not surprising to discover that the actual custom and practice among providers is woefully inadequate. Among the "big boys," such as the top 25, the custom and practice is significantly different regarding hiring, training, and supervision. But when this group accounts for less than half of the marketplace, it is difficult to suggest that what they do should be considered representative of the industry. In other words, there are actually two baselines for comparison. When there is a situation such as this, there can only be one outcome: a lack of credibility and a resulting inconsistency.

Even larger regional suppliers have candidly confided that their primary aim is to drive up account revenue to draw the attention of larger companies to be considered as acquisition candidates. Hoping for a quick sale (less than five years), this group of business owners have little or no desire to reinvest in their companies and develop an adequate infrastructure. They argue that such an investment only robs from their personal net income. They reason, "why spend the money if a larger company is only going to come around and replace everything I have with something of their own?" This type of shallow thinking leads to a failure to develop adequate hiring criteria, little to no training, poor supervision, and high turnover resulting from minimum wages and little consideration for employee benefits. It is little wonder that security officers come and go faster than a traveling carnival through rural America in the middle of summer.

Several years ago I asked a group of security service owners who were attending one of my seminars to write down on a piece of paper what they believed to be their unique selling proposition to prospective clients. I instructed them to hold their answers tight so as not to inadvertently give away this most cherished piece of competitive information. After each executive team conferred and arrived at their super-secret answer, I wrote a single word on the easel pad behind me. I then asked each of the 37 companies represented (all, by the way, among the top 50) to compare their answer with my word. It was only a few moments before we all heard the laughter break out as everyone realized that their answers were all the same. The word? Training.

I wasn't finished yet. I then turned to 15 of my special guests. These were the security decision-makers for various companies. All were current or former clients of mine. Together they represented more than $200 million in annual contract revenue. I asked them to rank order the following six business considerations, ranking as #1 their highest concern and #6 as their lowest. The six were:

- Recruitment
- Administrative support
- Cost
- Training
- Supervision
- Account management

As all of them began their separate considerations, I asked the security services executives to do the same. When everyone was done, I returned to my easel and flipped the first of two pages over on the easel. At the top of the first it read "Contractor's Rating." The list read:

- Cost
- Training
- Supervision
- Recruitment

- Account management
- Administrative support

Again there was laughter. But this time, it was noticeably nervous. I then turned over the second page. At the top it read "Client's Rating." It read:

- Account management
- Supervision
- Recruitment
- Training
- Administrative support
- Cost

There was silence. I asked the client representatives, by a show of hands, to indicate if their list matched mine. The audience gasped when 15 hands rose. I then asked, again by a show of hands, how many suppliers had a list identical to my list entitled "Contractor's List." Nearly every one of them raised their hands. Some suggested there was collusion between the clients and myself. There was none. If someone were to repeat this experiment I can say with almost complete certainty that the results would be the same. At the time I did this Burns Security was not owned by Securitas. Their executive vice president for marketing thought that somehow I had rigged the results and asked permission to survey some of his company's clients using this same list. I agreed. A few months later I received an interesting letter from him. He reported that his company had surveyed 2,000 of their clients and that over 90% had ranked the six categories the same as the group of 15 in the seminar.

Why am I so sure that the results would be the same today? First, I have conducted similar tests since then. Each time the results were almost identical. Second, experience has shown that there are some very basic forces in operation that, sadly enough, have not changed. These forces were present long before this demonstration and continue unabated today. The problem is that they directly contribute to the issue of inconsistency and each can be controlled by the third-party suppliers. Yet, they fail to do so.

I have written extensively about each of the six variables and why they are ranked in the order I presented in the "Client's List." Since this state of security still exists today, it is well worth revisiting this disparity and briefly exploring why it continues to exist. First, suppliers believe that cost is the primary driver in defining the relationship. This is a myth. Cost is certainly a variable that is strongly considered at the time of the relationship's beginning. But once the relationship is established, clients consider cost to be a "done deal" and begin to focus immediately on how their account is managed. Consequently, for the client, cost is a fixed factor that warrants the least of their attention.

Unfortunately, the supplier is fixated on operating within an acceptable profit margin, one that may well have been negotiated away from the very outset. Immediately, a serious disparity between outlooks arises.

The irony here is that while suppliers lament the fact that clients force their profit margins to near nonprofitability, clients counter that if they can be assured that there are no hidden pockets of profit, they are willing to pay for a 5% to 6% profit mark-up. While this margin would be viewed by many other business sectors as low, it is far higher than the suppliers' claim that to be competitive they must maintain margins closer to 2% or lower. Even if the 2% margin is accurate, it is only common among the larger accounts. Rarely have I seen single-digit margins for accounts that average less than 300 hours per week of security officer coverage.

Clients become more frustrated with their supplier's inability to properly manage their account than with anything else. Many have heard me contend that 90% of all long-term account relationships (e.g., those running for several years) are the direct result of satisfactory local account management. Conversely, 90% of all lost accounts are directly related to poor local account management. Neither resident security managers nor contract security owners have ever challenged me on either statistic, and in fact agree on its accuracy. If this is true, then why is it not obvious to suppliers that their first cardinal sin in client relationships is the failure to provide account management that warrants satisfaction, which in turn leads to long-term client loyalty?

Second, clients want their accounts to be supervised. They recognize early on that the quality of the security deliverable is closely linked to the quality of supervision. The ratio of customer satisfaction to the level of professional supervision is one to one. I have often observed to my clients that security officers' performance is directly related to the degree to which they are supervised. Why? Because supervisors influence morale, control performance, and set the tone of the supplier's client relationship.

Equally important, supervisors are typically the most senior supplier representatives on the account. Even with a fully assigned account manager, a shift supervisor is responsible for maintaining the operation for far more hours per week than the manager. Just consider the fact that a typical 24-hour, 7-day-a-week security account translates to 168 hours per week. An account manager works 40 of those hours. Who is accountable for the remaining 128 hours? The shift supervisor is accountable. Given this level of accountability, why is that so few security companies have a formal program for identifying security supervisors and developing (grooming) them for this position? Sadly, most supervisors are promoted within a matter of months because they are the most senior or the favorite of either another supervisor or the account manager. Developing a solid cadre of professional supervisors is so basic, yet so very, very ignored.

Recruitment is certainly the bane of the supplier. Finding and attracting quality personnel is a formidable challenge. This is especially true when economic times are robust and the unemployment rate is very low, or when a significant event such as the WTC terrorist attack occurs and there is a sudden and strong demand for security officers. Regardless, there is little creativity used in meeting this challenge. Suppliers are typically content to rely on newspaper advertising in the help wanted section. Some expand their efforts beyond print media and register for career fairs or provide incentives to their employees for successful referrals. These strategies are good, but often inadequate in meeting the demand. In early 2000 I offered readers of my *Security Magazine* column, "Dalton's Tips," these 20 ways to attract and maintain quality-driven officers:

Part One: Challenges to Attracting Qualified Personnel During Times of Full Employment

1. Compensation—it is what counts for most people.
2. You are competing with the local business market and not your comparative market.
3. Other professions are drawing from your labor pool—more often than not, more effectively.
4. Your organization may well be your worst enemy.
5. Considering an alternative workforce is not always the sure-fire answer.
6. Shifting the full-time to part-time ratio to more part-timers rarely works.
7. Traditional recruitment strategies and retention incentives will not be sufficient.
8. Clients—integrate security personnel into the organization.
9. Educate them to the big picture.
10. Draw the family in. If the officer's family has a vested interest, they will support the officer and the client's organization.

Part Two: Tips on How to Attract Qualified Personnel During Times of Full Employment

11. Work together to create a positive work environment image.
12. Market the job as being fun.
13. Consider sharing the job with other clients.
14. Work together to transform the security job into a multitasking career.
15. Expand your bonus pool.
16. Consider redefining your candidate pool (e.g., advertise for customer service reps, not security officers).

17. Explore extended recruiting hours—evenings and weekends, including Sundays.

18. Recruit where others fear to go, or have not even considered.

19. Ask yourself: Do prospective employees see working for us as a career, not a way-station to something else?

20. Don't forget the Internet and other electronic alternatives.

Even though our economic times have shifted since these tips were first published, most of the fundamentals that support them are just as relevant today. And, because they are timeless in their design, they will remain effective strategies for years to come. The secret to breaking inconsistency due to inadequate recruitment is to venture outside of the conventional recruitment box and take measured risks. As Milton Berle once commented, "If opportunity doesn't knock, build a door."

The next great disparity is in the perceptions of officer training. Despite the claims of suppliers, their secret competitive advantage is not their training. Unfortunately, few acknowledge this. Most believe that their training is second to none. Clients who have had experience with two or more suppliers are quick to point out that the opposite is true—they generally see no difference. Each supplier's initial training program is a carbon copy of the others. It is common to see a difference in hours, ranging from a low of eight hours to a maximum of 24, with the average being 12 hours. On closer examination, however, the curriculum topics are rarely different. The difference is in the amount of time spent on each topic.

What is far more interesting is the lack of a learning module dedicated to quality customer service. This is interesting because security suppliers are quick to tell their clients that 90% of a security officer's job is customer service. That only leaves 10% to asset protection. Yet, their training programs focus on such "customer relevant" topics as:

- The rules and regulations of the supplier
- Report writing
- The laws of search and seizure
- Public relations
- The care and handling of a fire extinguisher

Whenever they are asked where the module on customer service is, they typically respond that this is a concept that is woven into the very fabric of all the other topics. I beg to differ. Ask for a copy of the lesson plan for any topic and see if you can find this finely woven thread. I have reviewed hundreds and have yet to see it. It must be very fine indeed!

Setting the cynicism aside, the point is that customer service is closely related to client perceptions, which determine whether or not security personnel are seen as professional or not. Absent a dedicated module, security suppliers are only setting themselves up for a serious, if not fatal, fall. Moreover, it is not fair to the line-level employee. As President Lyndon B. Johnson once observed: "We must open the door of opportunity. But we must also equip our people to walk through those doors." When suppliers do not create this opportunity for their people, they carry a great deal of the burden for fostering continued inconsistency in their deliverables.

Finally, we come to the issue of administrative support. Many of the larger companies have spent considerable capital developing information support systems. Unfortunately, most of the smaller companies have failed in this regard. For the small-time players, developing an adequate infrastructure is costly. Lacking a commitment or the capital to do so puts them at a clear disadvantage, especially when they solicit large corporate accounts.

As cold as it may seem, security suppliers need to understand their limits and pursue only that segment of the market that is willing to accept their limitations. As they grow in both resources and commitment they can then consider broadening their client base. Conversely, for some there is the issue of overexpanding. I recall one mid-Michigan security firm that was highly desirous of breaking through the annual revenue ceiling of $3 million. They had achieved this level over a number of years and had stalled. Their new goal was to plow through the $5 million mark and reach annual sales of $10 million in five years.

But how? They believed that by expanding their infrastructure to incorporate Internet-based payroll, patrol tours, and alarm monitoring they could position themselves as a formidable competitor for much larger accounts. They did not stop there. They opened several new branches in hopes of securing added accounts. This required adding staff and entering into long-term leases. It also meant adding to their automotive fleet and administrative staff. The overhead, needless to say, exploded. The result? An operating loss that nearly bankrupted them. Why? Because they misdirected their resources. As opposed to marketing and seeking new venues, they turned their attention to what might best be described as the "bells and whistles" of the profession. They failed to understand their market position and leverage their reputation to draw the attention and interest of new clients. By the time a prospective client showed interest, the supplier was unable to demonstrate a positive cash flow that assured the would-be client that doing business with the supplier was a sound business decision.

Let me make one final note. I started this part of the discussion with the comment that contract suppliers are their own worst enemies. I firmly believe this, and once again offer a warning. Despite the fact that many corporations have solidly entrenched themselves into considerable outsourcing of their support units, I see definite cracks in their fortress walls. Company executives will tolerate only so much poor delivery. Some have already reached that point. If suppliers cannot rise to the occasion, executives will seek alternatives. This includes not only considering a return to proprietary operations, but also seeking new resources.

Companies that are not necessarily in the contract security services business will consider expanding their core deliverables to incorporate security services. Some have already begun. We see this with security consulting companies, temporary personnel agencies, and even the creation of security divisions within property management companies. I was engaged recently to assist a group of very influential investors in Chicago exploring the possibility of asking an entrepreneur they knew to start a security company dedicated to meeting their specific business interests. They were very negative on the local security services market and believed this nonsecurity businessman could be more successful, based on their previous dealings with him. Knowing the individual and having evaluated his previous initiatives, I agreed with the investment group— these owners of several of Chicago's largest properties would be further ahead in placing their confidence in an outsider than in one of the security industry's so-called experts.

RESIDENT SECURITY MANAGERS

Today's security managers, when taken as a whole, still lack the proper management skills to actively promote the value of their security programs. Clearly there are exceptions, but by and large there remains more frustration and missed opportunities than successful hits. Much of what I just commented on regarding contract suppliers being their own worst enemy can be applied to resident programs. What is even more troubling is the fact that I have often witnessed security managers becoming sidetracked and directing their efforts against those that could be of the most help. Among these supporters are third-party suppliers! I refer to this as their dark side because they have sought ways to sabotage their suppliers, often overtly and actively. Why? Because of their inherent dislike for having to be responsible for a contract operation. This dislike is the result of one or more common myths or personal experiences. Let's briefly examine the myths first.

You may recall in *Business Strategies* that we covered the common myths associated with contract providers. The myths that were present then and continue to be today relate to:

- Quality of the workforce
- Loyalty of the workforce
- Turnover of the workforce

Here's what I said then. When reading it, bear in mind one question: Is this still applicable today? I think you may be surprised.

When the question comes up regarding the use of a proprietary versus contracted forces, security experts tend to define their positions along adversarial pro–con lines based largely on a number of myths. The consequence of such debates pits the merits of one against the other, spinning the dialogue into a highly emotional discussion. Often they focus on factors that may have been true once but are not necessarily so today; consequently, they miss considering the merits. The challenge is in the decision-maker's ability to determine whether having a proprietary or a contract force is most advantageous for their organization. Such appropriateness must be based on sound business principles that survive the scrutiny of those beyond the security department. The asset protection manager must clearly see the reasoning associated with using a proprietary force over a contractor.

The decision to employ a third-party or an in-house workforce should be based on economic imperatives, corporate culture, and operational synergy. Unfortunately, among security professionals I find that these three dynamics are often set aside for other sacred cows that cannot be justified with empirical data. This is particularly true for the proponents of proprietary operations who are quick to conclude that contract service is less than adequate because of three factors: quality of the workforce, loyalty of the workforce, and turnover of the workforce.

Quality of the Workforce

I find the issue of quality particularly interesting since it assumes that there must be two or more labor pools to draw from. For proponents of proprietary workforces, the implication is that contractors somehow recruit from a less-qualified group. The fact is there is only one labor pool from which all employers choose. Regrettably, organizations intent on lowering operating costs typically focus on labor costs and require lower-paid, lesser-experienced individuals. Not only is it unfair, but also it borders on absurdity for a manager to ask for such employees and then claim that outsourcing provides a lower level of service due to inadequate staffing.

Loyalty of the Workforce

Like the issue of quality, the concept of loyalty is equally misrepresented. Whether an organization uses contract labor or not, loyalty is built on trust, acceptance, and integration. Each of these can be effectively administered without breaching the issue of co-employment. Astute security managers can provide opportunities for the supplier's employees to develop a strong identity with their client's organization. Through a series of properly managed target incentives and activities, contract employees can develop a strong identity with the client organization and therefore a high level of loyalty. If the corporate culture distances itself from vendor employees, then the blame lies squarely with the organization, not the contractor.

Turnover of the Workforce

Finally, there is the myth that security suppliers have a higher turnover rate. This apparently is not true. Annual studies conducted by a variety of industry sources continue to reflect the same findings first reported in the early 1990s. The 1992 National Private Security Officer Survey found that turnover is less than 60% annually. Prior estimates ranged from 200 to 300%, but these were never statistically proven. Whatever percentage is used, however, turnover need not be an issue if the force is properly managed. Contract language can specify a turnover rate comparable to that experienced by the organization's own back-office support functions. Failure by the supplier to hold to a preset level (generally 35% annually after the first 60 days of operation) triggers a financial penalty. Conversely, if the supplier can hold turnover under the established rate, an appropriate incentive is paid. My model contract has incorporated such an approach since the early 1980s. After hundreds of contracts, less than 5% have ever had to pay a penalty.

As you can see, these myths are deeply entrenched, but empirically do not stand the test of what is reasonable and based on common sense. Yet they continue to be perpetuated, especially by those who strongly support the use of a resident force. This forces us to ask the second question: What personal experience have these pro-proprietary supporters had that has so disillusioned them? There are several.

First, some believe that their organizational influence, and therefore, their position within their own company, is lessened if they are charged with administering a contract workforce. Actually there is a great deal of truth in this. Human Resource departments are blind to the overall contribution a manager can make to the company when the staff they are charged to administer is not one of the company's own. Time after time, organization after organization, I have found that a security director's managerial grade and compensation are tied to whether or not the director manages a resident uniformed force. There is this simplistic, and rather arcane, belief a person who does not manage a proprietary workforce somehow has less responsibility than a person who does manage a proprietary workforce. Here, HR, in its overly simplistic view of functional management, has tried to tie something as arbitrary as proprietary headcount to managerial contribution. This is about as bizarre as believing that support services are commodities because there is more than one supplier and they compete based on marketing factors, only one of which is price.

Security directors do not want to assume a lower position in their organization. If they are so categorized based on something as artificial as workforce configuration, it is easy to see why they turn away from actively supporting third-party suppliers. Still, there are other considerations. For example, whether or not most security managers are willing to openly admit it, they see a pecking order among their own colleagues. Just as they do not want to be seen as someone with less responsibility within their own company, they do not want to be viewed similarly among their peer group.

Unfortunately, over the past several decades security directors have built their own ranking of importance. For some it is based on the size of their operation, both in terms of functions reporting to them and, more importantly, the size of their staff. This is a classic military view that is also alive and well within the police community. Security directors with former careers in either the military or law enforcement have been reared on the concept of "more means more power." They fail to see that when it comes to the concept of "more," corporate executives want more contribution to profitability. This invariably translates to lower operating expenses. Ironically, setting the issue of quality aside for a moment, the smarter security director is the one who understands that "less is more." In this case, less direct expense often translates directly to bottom-line profitability.

Note that I postured this last point with the caveat that we needed to set the issue of quality aside for the moment. We cannot, however, stray too far from this critically important driver. Quality, or the lack thereof, is often the root cause underneath so much of a security manager's distrust (dislike) of third-party providers. It is the lack of quality delivery, as discussed in the previous chapters, that turns managers off. They get tired of being "organizationally burned" by poorly performing providers—particularly those whose marketing staff promises far more than the company can deliver.

Regarding the issue of quality delivery, we have the proverbial catch-22. The contractor performs badly. The security manager pulls back support. The contractor fails to address the performance issue in a timely or acceptable manner. The security manager points the accusing finger and calls for a change in either the supplier or for serious consideration to instituting a proprietary staff. The supplier claims to be doing the best they can given the limited resources and limited support from the manager. In other words, there is a continuous loop that eventually spins out of control. There can only be one outcome, and it is not a desirable one.

Resident managers cannot blame their inability to be more effective solely on their suppliers. As I noted, this is often more of a diversion and fails to address the more serious issues. Security managers have come a long way over the past few decades in becoming more business oriented, but there are many more miles to go before they, as a profession, can stand equal to other business unit heads. We'll address this in much more depth in Part III.

Ourselves, as a Society with Disdain for Private Security

In many respects this is nothing more than an extension of the attitude held by corporate executives and the other employees. As a society, America has a cultural bias against private security. When the news media reports that a person has "gone postal," killing or seriously wounding others, and adds that the assailant was a security guard, we snicker and cynically say, "Well, what did you expect?" We get angry when we hear about security officers failing to do their jobs (e.g., bank guards not drawing their guns and single-handedly shooting all of the robbers, or not stopping a fight between two barroom patrons when one or both have a knife). We are quick to blame and ridicule, especially when dealing with an officer who does not have command of the English language. But we are even quicker to turn our backs and fail to support them.

Americans recognize that security personnel are commonly little more than minimum-wage employees. And yet we criticize them when something is stolen from an office or an individual is the victim of workplace violence. It is a curious phenomenon that executives go home, leaving billions of dollars in assets or the well-being of their employees in the "trusted" hands of a minimum-wage employee who is not very well trained, and think little about it. It is even more curious when these same executives are quick to look for someone to blame when things go terribly wrong.

I routinely interview the key executive staff of my clients when asked to do a management analysis. More often than not, it is clear that senior managers are unaccustomed to being asked questions about their security program and their level of satisfaction. They are generally dissatisfied but have chosen to do nothing about it, deferring instead to me—the expert—to tell them what should be done when just as often the answer is obvious.

Recently the CEO, his chief legal counsel, and the senior vice president of corporate real estate of a global software company met with me to discuss the state of their security. The CEO commented that he believed there was not one element of their most-cherished intellectual property (their source code) that was not in the hands of their competitors. His legal counsel agreed. The three went on to voice a high degree of concern that there was a need to hire a security director, a first for this multibillion-dollar company. When I asked if it was not in some regard too late, they disagreed, fearing more losses. When asked why they had delayed this long, the CEO thought about the question while the other two looked for his lead. Finally he said, "I guess we never took the time to seriously think about it." It was as simple as that. This same scene has been played out with me time after time over the past 15 years. Once again, all of this is anecdotal, but it illustrates the point that there is a genuine indifference when it comes to our support of the security function.

We do not see things as they are. We see things as we are.

Talmud

CONCLUDING COMMENTS

We conclude Part I with a review of what I consider to be the nine principle barriers facing security managers today. Corporate executives need to pay close attention to each of them and ask what they can do to break through these barriers. Bradshaw's comment about the security profession being at a crossroad is certainly proven to be very accurate. It is interesting to note that security is something on the minds of most Americans, but very little is being done to actually improve the lot of security professionals. Progress is slow and advances are achieved often by only one step at a time. I would like to see some real breakthroughs, but none appear to be on the horizon.

The challenges that face today's security manager are complex and the barriers are tightly integrated. One needs a plan of attack that hits on multiple fronts simultaneously. We need a paradigm shift to occur, beginning with how Americans view the profession. As we have seen, the problem is rooted in our criminal justice system, our academic institutions, our professional associations, our industry, and ourselves. Obviously, it will take more than a 9/11 disaster to awaken the need within our minds and hearts to make the necessary changes. The security profession cannot go it alone, but it can be a driving force. How to do this is the aim of the next two parts of this book.

The ocean is made of drops.

Mother Teresa

THOUGHT-PROVOKING QUESTIONS

1. At the outset of this chapter the author lists 16 variables that he describes as business metrics for determining which type of workforce configuration is best suited for an organization. After reviewing each of them, do they apply to your organization? Are there others that need to be added?

2. The point is raised that a set of national standards for private security is long overdue. Based on your experience, would you agree with this position? Even if national standards were created, how would they affect the nine culpable principals the author discusses?

3. It was pointed out that third-party suppliers are often their own worst enemies. Do you agree? If so, what do they need to do to improve their own lot? If not, why not?

4. Should security administration be a part of a college or university's business department, or should it be resident in a criminal justice curriculum? Does it really matter where it resides? Should business students be required to take at least one course fully dedicated to asset protection and workplace violence issues?

5. The author suggests that consolidation in the contract security sector is only about half completed. Do you believe that eventually service quality will improve once the industry is fully consolidated? What influence do you think foreign acquisitions will have over the long run?

PART II

THE MECHANICS OF SUCCESS: USING A STRATEGIC APPROACH

Over the course of the first three chapters we have tracked the four critical steps toward achieving a successful security program. First, we need to properly assess the degree of risk that our organizations face. Next we need to identify what type of overall approach is appropriate. To determine this we reviewed the evolutionary progress of America's asset protection program. This allowed us to determine where security is today and thus provide some insight as to the gap between the degree of risk and an organization's current state of security. Step three was an examination of what skill sets are required in selecting the person charged with leading the security management team. Finally, we examined the critical barriers that represent the organizational challenges facing the security team, particularly one that is largely dependent on third-party suppliers.

The delineation of these four building blocks is necessary if we hope to move forward. They create a foundation that allows us to better define a strategic approach that can move an asset protection program to a new and more respected level within the corporation. Note that I use the term *strategic approach*. All too often security directors and their teams miss this essential component to organizational success. Thomas Jefferson once quipped, "I find that the harder I work, the more luck I have." But his was not aimless hard work. Jefferson, one of the principal architects of our country's founding was also noted for always having a plan, a strategy. He understood that having a plan was essential to success. For me, having a strategic plan is another one of those essential arrows in any well-stocked management quiver.

ASSET PROTECTION DEFINED

Despite decades of discussions about how private security needs to be less reactive in nature and more proactive, little has been done. The WTC disaster only served to reinforce the reactive nature of asset and people protection. Some of you might contend that this is perfectly all right because security is all about reacting to events. Such a position misses the critical point that security, as a corporate function, requires forethought and deliberateness of execution, just the same as any other business unit. Reinforcing the point I made earlier, we must understand that security is not about simply reacting, or responding to some sort of adrenalin rush brought on by an emergency, threat, loss, or even an investigative pursuit. It is not all about serving as an escort for a concerned employee or ensuring that doors are closed and locked after everyone else has departed for the evening. It is not all about issuing a ticket for a parking infraction or checking someone's company access control badge. It is not all about standing by as HR terminates an angry employee or protecting an executive's home. It is not even all about all of the above combined. It can be said that all of the above things are incorporated into a well-organized plan, but it is more than that.

Asset protection, and here I include the protection of people, is the formulation of an over-arching plan that is designed to enhance the workplace by assuring that every reasonable thing is done to promote a secure environment and mitigate the likelihood of loss or injury. Therefore, asset protection certainly entails those tasks I just enumerated. However, it extends itself into the very fabric of the organization's overall business plan. It is a contributor to profitability because it protects those valuable resources capable of generating the very profit the organization seeks. To accomplish this requires a dual character—a proactive capability and a reactive capability. This, therefore, is the definition and application of true asset protection.

REVISITING THE LOOPING MODEL

This goes to the very core of what I introduced in *Business Strategies* as my Looping Model, which remains as strong today as it was when I first introduced it. You may recall that the model identifies the duality of an effective security program proactiveness and reactiveness. It states that the two dimensions co-exist and are made up of four key components: developing your policies and procedures (the control variables), bringing the program to life through the administration of the program, establishing an effective response plan for when the inevitable occurs, and having a well-coordinated program in place to manage the event. The loop is not complete, however, until the recommendations that flow from the event management are translated into modifications of policies and procedures. All of this is illustrated in Figure PII-1.

There is an inherent assumption that underlies this model that I failed to emphasize when I first introduced it. It is so subtle that it is easy to take for

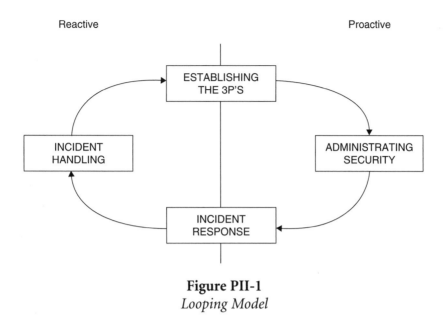

Figure PII-1
Looping Model

granted: these four components do not exist in a vacuum. They are encompassed under an umbrella of strong customer service, but even this is dependent on a more fundamental element. What I am referring to is the need for a well-constructed strategic plan. Before we can begin to consider what control variables are necessary, let alone how we are going to execute them via our administrative program, we need to have a game plan, a vision of what we are setting out to accomplish. And yet, the vision must be applicable to your particular environment. In other words, an effective strategic approach requires a plan of attack that is compatible with the organization's environment. If it is out of whack, it will not work—you cannot force a plan on an organization that is not ready for it. Golf great and course designer Robert Trent Jones, Jr., commented, "No two courses or rounds are ever so alike that you can attack them with exactly the same plan." The same holds true for developing a strategic plan—no two organizations are ever so alike as to warrant the same game plan. Just as a new round of golf on the same course calls for a new plan because the ball is never hit in the same place twice, so too, as events change in an organization, so must the plan. But there must always be a plan. Chi Chi Rodriguez summarizes it best: "Golf is a thinking man's game. You can have all the shots in the bag, but if you don't know what to do with them, you've got troubles." The same can be said for security managers who do not know how to create a strategic plan and use its many components.

TWO SIDES OF THE SAME ISSUE

As I noted earlier, my corporate and consulting experiences have allowed me to interact with many of America's top 200 companies and with dozens of emerging global organizations. I have also interacted with many nonprofit organizations, government agencies, and small companies. As I also noted earlier, I have listened to two sides of the same concern. I hear senior managers question the effectiveness of their security program, and their department's approach to protecting the corporation's people and assets. On the security team's side, I hear about how they are the last to know when something that affects their area occurs, or that they are so busy fighting the daily fires they have no time to proactively plan.

Executives are, in essence, expressing concern for the lack of a strategic plan. Similarly, cries of frustration at being out of the loop underscore the lack of a strategic approach on the part of the security department. My experience leads me to conclude that most security programs lack a simple plan of attack regarding the protection of people and assets. *Proactive* is an overused term. It also smacks of a concept that many would say is "so 1980s." Unfortunately, it is as misunderstood and poorly applied, if at all, today as it was then, yet it stands as one of the key cornerstones of managerial success. The pillar that serves as the brace for proactive security is strategic planning and implementation. John Pearce and Richard Robinson, in the 7th Edition of *Strategic Management* set the stage by identifying the nine critical tasks that are commonly associated with a comprehensive approach to strategic management. Abbreviated, they are:

1. Formulate the mission
2. Assess internal conditions and capabilities
3. Assess external environment's competitive and contextual factors
4. Define options and match resources with the external environment
5. Identify most desirable options
6. Select long-term objectives and strategies aimed at achieving desirable options
7. Develop annual objectives/short-term strategies compatible with the longer term
8. Implement the strategic choices, emphasizing collaboration and resource integration
9. Evaluate the success as input for future decision-making

Some security teams do some of these things, but few do all of them. Many corporate executives will do all of these critical tasks when dealing with certain aspects of their business, but few do any of them, on their own, when specifically considering their security needs. Yet, as noted, both nonsecurity executives and security teams will lament the lack of a coordinated approach. Pearce and Robinson add that these nine variables reflect that strategic management involves planning, directing, organizing, and controlling (PDOC) a company's strategy-related decisions and actions. This is not anything new.

When I first began reading management texts in the mid-1960s the introductory themes stressed PDOC. In the mid-1970s I came across a collection of writings entitled *Papers on the Science of Administration*, edited by Luther Gulick and L. Urwick in 1936. The collection is a compilation of writings offered by some of the brightest management minds at the time and served as a research reference for the President's Committee on Administrative Management. Here the editors noted that the job of the chief executive is to pursue POSDCORB, or planning, organizing, staffing, directing, co-coordinating, reporting, and budgeting.

In other words, the job of organizational leadership is to take a strategic approach toward achieving the goals of the company. Such a strategic plan cuts across the entire continuum of organizational entities, each contributing to the other. None of this is new, yet the perplexing question remains as to why so few have yet to lift this banner and carry it forward. Most organizations are content to wait until confronted with a crisis in people or asset protection before reacting.

Consider the following: shortly after 9/11 I was approached by a property management company that represented the owner of one of the highest-profile buildings in a large metro area. They had particular concerns because one of their tenants was the Israeli consulate. As we discussed earlier, as the government's War on Terror unfolded, significant gains were made early on in eliminating the terrorists' network. Concern for the threat of future attacks began to wane, especially for this property owner.

Author's Note: This point is so intriguing that it warrants a quick review. The reaction of property owners and corporate executives illustrates their failure to develop a strategic approach to security. You may recall that I pointed out that despite pleas from the management agents, owners pulled back, citing recessionary hardships, concerns for extended legal liabilities, and a host of other excuses. The end result was swift in coming—nothing happened. And owners of high-rises were not alone. Corporate security managers, initially buoyed by promises from their own executives that security enhancements would be forthcoming, soon found that they, too, were left "swinging slowly, slowly in the in the wind."

As for the management company charged with taking care of the property housing the Israeli consulate, they, likewise, were left without their owner's commitment—until the spring of 2002, some seven months later. It was then that the warring actions between Israel and the Palestinians heated up and new threats against the building itself began unfolding. To say that their contacting me was panic motivated is an understatement. When they called, the building had been the object of four days of escalating demonstrations. As the crowds were growing larger, so too were the threats and fear of a terrorist attack. It was only when the danger was imminent that the owners decided the time had come for action.

I could go on and on about other examples of inattention and inaction on the part of those charged with making critical decisions. The events of 9/11 should have been the loudest wake-up call for property owners and corporate executives. But it was not, at least not over the long run. There were a great number of knee-jerk reactions, but few took the time to see this as a true warning and begin approaching the protection of human life and assets—tangible and intangible—in a strategic manner.

Few strides have been made to taking a holistic and integrated approach to the function of asset protection. Absent such an approach, it is little wonder that security managers and their teams feel frustrated and disillusioned with their charter. It is also little wonder that the cost of victimization is so high in the United States. No one can accurately give an accounting for just how much is suffered or lost in a year as a result of inadequate security. We know that premises liability claims that are settled total in the hundreds of millions each year. Other watchdog groups and accounting offices estimate that more than $50 billion is lost to theft of all kinds, chief among them the loss of intellectual property through competitive intelligence means.

I remember a study we did at Montgomery Ward, before it went out of business. The study was actually completed in the mid-1980s. We discovered that Ward's could offer a permanent 5% reduction on the cost of all goods sold if theft, particularly employee fraud, could be eliminated. Despite Ward's demise, other retailers report similar findings. How can such staggering losses occur annually? A significant part of the answer lies in the fact that, without a strategic approach, loss prevention people are left primarily responding to reported incidents.

Retail is not alone. There is not a business sector I am aware of that does not have the same challenge. Perhaps the reported losses may vary, but the theme remains constant. Absent a plan that is developed in a collaborative environment, supported by executive management, and executed in a timely and effective manner, asset protection will remain continuously—to borrow a pocket billiards expression—"behind the eight ball."

WHAT PART II IS ABOUT

If the first part of this book can be defined as the building blocks, then the last two parts can be likened to the mechanical and artistic aspects of security management. In Part II we will examine the technical aspects of repositioning the security program. To accomplish this we will draw on those who can best help us in defining what a strategic approach ought to encompass. We begin in Chapter 4 by stressing the need for a measured approach to protecting people and assets. Such an approach requires the integration of defining risk (we covered this in Chapter 1). We will follow this discussion with an examination of three applications for security: a staffing model that was actually developed a number of years ago but has been updated and applied recently to other business sectors with a great deal of success; one consultant's approach to aiding his client in defining the terms and conditions for the application of security systems and devices; and an update to my model services agreement, first introduced in the early 1990s. These high-performance-based approaches involve more than creating a set of metrics-based criteria. Each involves the added need to create critical buy-ins and an ability to deploy the program rapidly, bearing in mind that reviewing for quality is a must. Once this is completed, we will then turn our attention to the latest stage in the evolution of asset protection and see the role it will play in tomorrow's organizations; for many, however, it is something they are living with today.

The premise of Part II is simple: *To be successful, today's security team must seek a strategic approach to the issue of protecting people and assets.* Note that I do not put the onus on the security manager. Certainly the head of security plays a central role, but he or she is not alone. Many share in this responsibility. We will examine the others and see what happens when they fail to meet this basic organizational responsibility.

Chapter 4

THE CORPORATE SECURITY MANAGER AS ORGANIZATIONAL STRATEGIC PLANNER

People with goals succeed because they know where they are going.

Anonymous

Primary Themes

- Strategic Planning As a Process
- Keeping Strategic Planning Simple
- Controllable and Uncontrollable Factors
- Developing a Corporate Security Strategic Plan
- Empowerment through Policy Formulation

OPENING OBSERVATIONS

When managers lament that they are too busy fighting the daily brush fires to strategically plan, I can only wonder if this is not one of the greatest admissions of failure. Another way of looking at this is as operating from the perspective of *panic du jour*. I first heard this phrase from my brother-in-law, Robert House. He was describing how some management teams operate. They have no real plan, so they spend much of their day in a panic, running from crisis to crisis. Success must be planned—it does not come as a result of being reactive. Managers who find themselves rushing from one operational crisis to another are *transactional* in their approach. By this I mean that they have no plan of attack. Rather, theirs is a day spent engaging in one transaction after another. Simply put, they remind me of a puppet at the end of a marionette's wire.

The underlying principle of good strategic planning can be summed up as doing the right things, the right way, to achieve a desired outcome. To achieve the desired outcome requires a plan, executing it and modifying it only when

95

it is obviously broken. As every coach knows, to win the game you need a game plan and resources. The lesson is so obvious you might wonder why it needs to be reduced to writing in a management textbook. I am not quite sure I know the answer to this question. I do know, however, that a great number of security managers have not taken the time to learn it. When I think of those who race through their days reacting to events, I am reminded of what Lee Iacocca once observed: "The speed of the boss is the speed of the team." True enough. But there are always two directions in which the boss may be moving. Forward and slow is not good enough. In reverse and fast is worse. When a strategic plan is absent, the organization is flying backwards.

There are a number of reasons strategic planning is necessary.

1. It mitigates the likelihood that problems will turn into insurmountable obstacles.

2. It forces collaboration, which is short for ownership among the stakeholders.

3. Everyone knows what is at stake and what his or her role is. This leads to higher motivation, thus higher productivity, thus higher profitability.

4. Wasted effort resulting from duplication, or "the left hand not knowing what the right hand is doing," is minimized.

5. Finally, as Pearce and Robinson note: "Resistance to change is reduced. Though the participants in strategy formulation may be no more pleased with their own decisions than they would be with authoritarian decisions, their greater awareness of the parameters that limit the available options makes them more likely to accept those decisions."

Strategic planning is not a panacea. It can have its drawbacks. Managers can become so fixated with the process that they lose sight of the intended objective. This is what happened to the great total quality improvement programs of the 1990s. TQM strategists literally lost sight of the intended mission, focusing instead on internal processes, which produced frustration, resistance, cynicism, and lost dollars that could have otherwise gone to the bottom line.

Strategic planning can also mean missing the mark simply because of bad planning or false assumptions. When this happens, it is easy for the naysayer to jump up, wag an accusing finger, and yell, "I told you so!" Smart managers, on the other hand, are quick to ignore such exclamations, seeing that they are obstructionist, and begin the process of analyzing what went wrong. They understand that the process is not flawed, just the underlying assumptions.

Another risk is the assumption on the part of lower-level employees that their ideas will be implemented. Although their involvement is often important, lack of understanding of the bigger picture can limit what they can offer. If the strategic planner is not adroit in handling subordinate expectations, morale can actually become lower because the line-level employees believe they have been set up.

Finally, strategic planners can fall into the trap of over-complicating what is to be achieved. Perhaps the best example of this can be found in the development of a mission or vision statement. I'll have a great deal more to say about this later in this chapter. Suffice it to say, there is always the temptation to add things when they are not required. Worse yet is the temptation to add that which distracts or misdirects valued resources.

> *There seems to be some perverse human characteristic that likes to make easy things difficult.*
>
> Warren Buffet

Before tackling the issue of strategic planning and its role in defining a security manager's success, I would like to draw your attention one more time to Pearce and Robinson. They report that corporate executives and managers were asked to what degree strategic planning was important in the success of their firms. They note that in a survey of over 200 executives from the Fortune 500, Fortune 500 Service, and INC 500 companies, "corporate America sees strategic management as instrumental to high performance, evolutionary and perhaps revolutionary in its ever-growing sophistication, action oriented, and cost effective. Clearly, the responding executives view strategic management as critical to their individual and organizational success."

I raise this point because it would be easy for security managers to ask if their strategic planning efforts are necessary. Those who have taken the time to develop a strategic approach have found that is hard work. Consequently, it is only fair to ask whether the return on this investment in a strategic approach is going to be realized. Certainly the chief executive officer and other senior managers see the value.

Going Where Others Have Already Gone

In developing the outline of this chapter I turned to some of the more noted writers in security management to see what they have had to say about the value of strategic planning. I was amazed to discover only one author who even approached the topic of corporate security directors as strategic planners. That was Chuck Sennewald, and even his attempt is cursory at best, devoting only a couple of paragraphs to the subject. Moreover, a casual read reveals immediately that he is talking more about goal setting than actual strategic planning.

The failure to address such a critical role for security managers speaks volumes about how far the profession has yet to go before its incumbents can be taken seriously as proven business managers. Not until the manager can break away from the demands of daily activities and find some time—regardless of how little it may be—to concentrate on the development of a strategic approach will the security department stand a chance of being seen by senior managers as fully contributing.

When I hosted seminars for police executives I would always ask them to write down how they envisioned their department in five years. I asked them to set forth how they saw the department being organized, what resources they would be relying on, and what their core deliverables would be. I would then ask each of them to share their vision with the others. Most would simply describe their department as it existed in its present form. On the other hand, a few were bold and you could see that they were not content to maintain the status quo. It was to those few that I would turn my attention and ask: "Why the change? Change for the sake of change or change because you see your customer base changing?" As you can imagine, I received mixed answers.

There is a dynamic present that underscores a very important consideration. Those who sought change for the sake of change may have actually been putting their department at more of a disadvantage than their counterparts who intended to do nothing more than maintain the status quo. Those that saw the need to change because their market was changing can be described as strategic planners. They understood that organizations and environments are fluid. This requires planned change.

What was true then for police executives applies today to security managers. Business is changing. As we have noted, business is dynamic, even turbulent. It is not static. Just as a company may find itself in an environment that requires continuous adjustments, the same can be said of their internal infrastructure units. It is the organization's infrastructure that enables a company to be flexible and responsive to changing market conditions, especially regarding competition.

Situational Case Two: Cisco As Market Leader

An excellent example of how business climates change can be seen by analyzing Cisco Systems Inc. A global leader in network support for the Internet, it stands on the threshold of bursting through the $10 billion mark in annual revenues; this is remarkable for a company that is less than 20 years old. Under the direction of CEO John T. Chambers, the company incorporated strategic planning into its culture at every management level.

Chambers set his eye on being known as the next Jack Welch, former CEO of General Electric. To accomplish this he relied on both human interaction and its integration with technology. As he described it, "the network is the glue for the internal workings of the company. It ties strategic partners to resident staff and makes it appear seamless to their customers." The same approach is applied to the company's own internal customers, and therefore impacts corporate security.

Another key to the company's success is its reliance on customers to share in the development of key strategies. Cisco's management team actively solicits feedback. As a company, it is not assumptive about what is best for its customers. Cisco challenges the age-old notion that they are the experts and therefore know what is best. Chambers readily admitted that his company might have a great product, but if it was not relevant to his customer base, it was money unwisely spent—a bad investment.

It is within such a climate that I think you can see that traditional security management models will fail. The types of organizational structures advocated by many of the security profession's leading management writers and practitioners simply do not fit. At the core of a security director's responsibility must be an effort to strategically position the security department for the challenges that lie ahead and not focus on just what confronts them here and now.

The key is playing the ball to the best position from which to play the next shot.

Arnold Palmer

Strategic Planning: Three Approaches

Gary Hamel, writing for *Harvard Business Review* in their July/August 1996 issue, introduces us to the concept of strategy as revolution. He notes that there are three categories of strategists: the rule makers, the rule takers, and the rule breakers. It is a fascinating concept because some security managers believe they are pursuing strategic planning when, in fact, they are doing little more than pursuing a course of maintaining "business as usual." They are rule makers. They may have been seen at one time as being pacesetters among their peers, but have fallen into a strategy of essentially protecting what they have built. Rule makers set yesterday's standard. They are the ones known for their bold thinking of old, but they haven't delivered anything new for a long time, opting to live on their past accomplishments.

The rule takers, on the other hand, follow what the rule makers produced years ago. They subscribe to a philosophy that says "what was good for them must be good for us." As Hamel describes it, "they essentially pay homage to the rule makers." Rule takers mirror the same methodology and are not willing to risk going beyond the bounds of what has already been developed by others. Often, they are successful in meeting daily operational requirements, but they are less economical and need to wait for the "new" standard to be developed before making any progress.

The rule breakers are neither hindered by that which has gone before them, nor do they have any desire to fit into the conventional mold of what asset protection should be all about. They are often seen as those who pursue best business practices, because they have tried conventional ways and found them wanting. In their own pursuit of finding smarter, better ways to accomplish their intended goals, they seek new perspectives and try new approaches until they find the approach that is best for them. They become, in essence, the new rule makers.

We'll revisit Hamel at the conclusion of this chapter. For now, I wanted to share the concept of rule making, taking, and breaking because it can help in setting the stage for what follows. As asset protection managers, we can continue to accept the way things are or we can make a change—it is as simple as that. Strategic planning, as a management tool, is designed to make the change happen.

Strategic Planning Is a Process

So how do we do this? How do we become strategic planners? First, we need to understand the value of setting priorities and delegation. This is pretty basic stuff, but it is at the root of the complaint that a manager never has the time to be a proactive planner. Until we can clear away the clutter, all of our best intentions about strategic planning will be transformed into an overbearing monster. We will see it as something to be avoided because we simply cannot get to it. Guilt will lead to stress, which in turn feeds frustration and poor performance.

The success-driven manager must rank what needs to be done, when it needs to be done, and by whom it needs to be done. Prioritizing is an opportunity to challenge core deliverables and ask if they are still relevant. More often than not, when a manager gets behind or is overwhelmed with all that needs to be done, the root cause is attempting to deliver on things that are not a part of the security department's primary mission. Today more than 90% of a manager's time is dedicated to attending meetings—someone else's meetings, for the most part. This is not new. The 90% average has haunted managers at all levels for nearly two decades. Yet we continue to attend. Am I advocating that we stop attending? No, but I do question whether all of them are necessary and whether they need to last as long as they do.

My own consulting practice took a dramatic turn when I discovered that I could tell clients that meetings they thought were important could often be dropped, rescheduled to a different time, or conducted in an alternative manner. I spent years flying from coast to coast, often to attend a series of client-driven meetings that were spread out over several days. These same meetings could be reduced in number and scope once they were reduced to teleconferences or videoconferences. The quality of the end deliverable actually improved because people were focused. The cost in terms of time and consulting fees was also reduced. This was good news for them and good news for me because it gave me the time to do other things, including time to strategically plan how I want my company to move forward. Lest someone think that this may simply be rationalizing the loss of income, the truth is that my business has actually flourished, reaching new highs each year (part of my strategy).

Strategic management also means delegation. Looking to other staff members may not be the answer. They are probably in the same fuddled way. This may mean turning to others outside the organization. Sometimes it requires going to the external environment and securing the services of a consultant or a third-party supplier. Other times it may mean going inside and seeking partners resident in other departments. *No manager is an island and no security department is a corporate entity unto itself.* In today's world of collaboration, security does not even have to take the primary lead. Rather, the security management team can serve in an advisory capacity and still achieve the desired result.

Once priorities have been set and selected accountabilities properly delegated, the actual process of strategic planning is ready. Depending on the approach one follows, strategic planning can consist of several steps or can concentrate on a few core elements. The former is far more process oriented and can often get the planner sidetracked simply because of the number of required steps. Here's a typical list:

- Establishing a vision and mission statement
- Analyzing the external environment
- Analyzing the internal environment
- Developing long-term objectives
- Creating generalized strategies (organizational and environmental road maps)
- Honing the direction with short-term objectives
- Defining functional tactics
- Empowering resources to accomplish the defined tasks
- Creating a mechanism for continuous improvement

When I review this list I recall again Peter Drucker's observation: "There is nothing so useless as doing efficiently that which should not be done at all." It is easy to become sidelined and miss the intended end result. Strategic management is about following a process that takes you from where you are to where you want to be. It is deliberate and it is systematic. It requires planning, collaboration, and empiricism (which we will read more about in the next chapter about metric management). It requires two additional elements, however, which are rarely addressed in the writings of recognized strategists. They are patience and discipline. Without either, success is not going to be achieved. It is as simple as that. Patience is required because the manager will encounter challenges along the way. Some of these challenges are controllable, and some are not. Discipline is required lest the manager get distracted along the way. That is one of the reasons that the traditional approach, with its many elements, can become a treacherous path very quickly.

I noted earlier that today's business world is dynamic and continuously fluid. What may be a sound long-term objective today may well be a short-term functional tactic tomorrow. It is therefore important to identify what the overall business objective is, formulate a strategy that is action oriented, implement the strategy, and evaluate it regularly to assure that the business objective will be met. Nike Corporation's motto of "Just do it" became an instant success because it captured the reality of today's business world. Timing is critical, but it cannot become the controller.

Gary Dessler, in his text, *Management, Leading People and Organizations in the 21st Century*, suggests that there need not be nine steps, but only five. He outlines them as shown in Figure 4-1.

Dessler's five-step model contains the essential elements of the traditional school, but Dessler has simplified the process by combining some of the elements of the former into one or two of his steps. Nevertheless, he suggests that five steps are necessary as opposed to the four that I mentioned in my opening observations (e.g., define, formulate, execute, and modify when broken). Despite the traditionalists and authors like Dessler, I believe the four-step model is the most effective because it allows the management team to remain tightly focused and allows the group leader to set a tone of urgency. Regardless of the model you chose—the nine-step traditional approach, Dessler's five-step model, or my four steps, the essential point is that there needs to be a process that serves as a guide for accomplishing the end objective.

Setting the academic debate aside, many of today's noted practitioners have "cut to the bottom line" and agree that strategic planning is all about the following:

- Defining what you are all about in the most easily understood terms
- Formulating your game plan
- Executing it

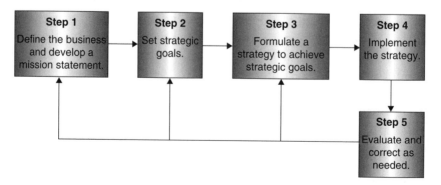

Figure 4-1
Strategic Management Process Model

- Reviewing it at selected times to ensure that you're on track, modifying the game plan only if it's broken

Who supports this school of thought? Jack Welch, former CEO of General Electric, and Herb Kelleher of Southwest Airlines agree in principle, but warn of creating specific work units or divisions dedicated to the function of strategic planning. For them, strategic planning is more about defining who they are, what they want in terms of market position, operational strategy, and financial health. Sam Walton, the founder of Wal-Mart, and Louis Gerstner of IBM were hard-hitting executives who believed that planning is necessary to stay focused, but ought not become cumbersome. In other words, strategic planning is more about identifying who you are, getting down to the business of developing a plan of attack, executing it, and staying on top of it to assure that it is appropriate—if it is not appropriate, change it rather than staying with something that is sure not to yield the desired return.

Even if the list of supporters ended there, many would argue that it is long enough. Luckily for us, there are many more. Where can you read more about these four steps? I don't know that you can pick up any one book versus another and find them articulated exactly as I have them here, but the underlying message is consistently found among the writings of not only these corporate giants, but among many other less-known contributors.

Let's examine each step briefly and see how they apply to corporate security.

Define What You Are All About in the Most Easily Understood Terms

Strategic management writers almost always begin by calling for the development of a vision statement, and then follow this up with a mission statement. To the uninitiated, this can lead to immediate confusion and distraction. Do you need one or the other, or both? Actually, a strategic approach does rely on a defined goal, something that everyone can understand and accept as the direction in which the organization is headed. Vision and mission statements create the basic framework; they define purpose. Yet both are unique.

A *vision*, as Peter Senge refers to it, is a process of setting up creative tension, in which the gap between the future and the present is the source of creative energy. This is too esoteric to be meaningful for the practitioner. Vision is what sets the tone—the road, if you will—that the organization will follow in meeting its end objective. Susan Clayton describes it as the "path for future achievement. And, it is on this path that strategists find their journey."

Let us get even more concrete. A vision is that which allows all stakeholders to know why the organization is pursuing the course it has chosen. Generally, the vision incorporates some degree of social responsibility, such as, "to make the world a better place for everyone as a result of the organization's products or services." It establishes the ethical context in which everyone is expected to operate. The organization's vision is often described in metaphoric terms (i.e., its heart and soul).

Whereas vision statements are easily understood, they provide such a broad perspective that it is difficult to get one's arms around them. That is the purpose of a mission statement. Mission statements define purpose, the business philosophy, the culture. Mission statements are typically steeped in their own emotional language. They are typically designed to make employees feel a passion for what they are doing. This zeal is supposed to drive them forward to accomplish things they thought were out of their reach. But they know they can accomplish these things because the organization promises to support them—again, at least by inference, in what is said within the mission statement.

Here is what Clayton has to add:

A statement of the mission will encapsulate in a cohesive whole the purpose, vision and strategy for achieving that vision. The statement is not a vision of the future, although it carries the vision within it. A mission statement will guide management and staff in their work, in the present. A mission can provide the glue for bringing people together in working towards a common goal. Because the mission is a vessel which carries the vision, purpose, values, and strategy of the business, it is the guiding principle for decisions and actions of management and staff. It can help people understand the reason for doing the things that they do and the way that they do them.

Communicating a mission is not about putting a statement in pretty colors on the wall of the foyer or the office, but rather drawing in your team and staff to take onboard the mission as an all-embracing concept that they can work with. An organization's mission has to be integrated into the system; the heart, mind, body and spirit of the whole organization, starting from the top. It should not just be pinned to the wall in some vain hope that something worthwhile will seep into the woodwork.

My graduate and undergraduate students are working managers or professionals; my clients—with the exception of the lawyers—are all practitioners, the majority of whom are security executives. Despite Clayton's attempt to define what a mission statement is and how it is differentiated from the organization's vision, her explanation still leaves these practical folks scratching their heads. They know what is intended, but they persist in asking, "Sure, but make it relevant, something I can relate to." To do this is quite easy. As a manager intent on formulating a mission statement, Keep It Simple (KIS).

That's it. KIS. To be relevant, the first step is to make the mission statement easily understood and something everyone can relate to. Here's the test I put in front of students and clients: Define what you are about in three words or less. That is correct, three words or less. The best way to do this is to phrase what your department is all about in the form of a motto. Let me give you some examples. Disney's motto is "We create happiness." Nike's motto is "Just do it." Nordstrom's motto is "Use common sense."

In each of these examples the mission is straightforward and easy for everyone to grasp via their motto. The mission underscores the organization's vision. By creating happiness, by just doing it, or by using common sense, each staff person knows that the company is committed to the well-being of the employee base, the customer, and the shareholders. There is no second-guessing or head scratching. It is simple and achievable. It is also challenging and creates a framework for working harmoniously.

Can a security department develop its own vision/mission motto? Try it. Here are some that my clients have developed:

- We Protect Assets, or We Provide Security
- Protect and Serve (a play on many police department mottos)
- We Manage Risk, or We Control Risk
- We Deter Crime (though I think this is impossible to prove)

Some cynics have offered the following mottos:

- Search and Destroy
- We're Watching You
- You are Busted

Either way, they all have it. These managers have encapsulated their direction and their deliverable in three words, and in a motto that everyone understands. The security strategist, with the help of staff, needs to create something similar.

Situational Case Three: Mission: Impertinent

Before moving to the second step, I need to offer one caution. Whether the security management team can create what they are all about in three words or not, there is a trap that needs to be avoided. In November of 1997 the *San Jose Mercury News* ran a wonderful cover story in their Sunday supplement, *West Magazine*. The article was entitled "Mission: Impertinent," and featured a corporate trick that Scott Adams, of *Dilbert* fame, pulled on one Silicon Valley company, Logitech International. He approached their co-founder and vice chairman, Pierluigi Zappacosta, with a unique challenge. Adams believed he could lead a group of corporate executives in the development of a mission statement that was so impossibly complicated that it would have no real content whatsoever. He further challenged that he could do it in an hour. The vice chairman said it sounded interesting and gave the idea his blessing.

After disguising himself, Adams was introduced as a management consultant of high esteem, and offered his qualifications: "I did the Harvard MBA thing and then went to Procter & Gamble, where I worked on the Taste Bright Project." He began by telling a group of nine executives: "I try not to become too familiar with the companies I'm consulting for. I find that otherwise, generic solutions might not fit as well." Having said this, he proceeded without so much as one eyebrow being lifted.

The article provides a humorous accounting of what followed. In the end, and just shy of his 60-minute mark, he had lead this group of highly paid executives—the organization's leadership, from a mission statement that read: "The New Ventures mission is to provide Logitech with profitable growth and related new business areas," to "The New Ventures Mission is to scout profitable growth opportunities in relationships, both internally and externally, in emerging, mission inclusive markets, and explore new paradigms and then filter and communicate and evangelize the findings."

Armed with this new direction, the article's author observes: "Zappacosta nods exuberantly. His executive team looks satisfied." But the article does not end there. Adams has more. He cautions the team not to become overly enthusiastic—that is, not until the rest of the employees have bought in. To accomplish this Adams suggests that the group put their new mission statement to music. He observes: "Because what I've found is that some companies have created, like, a division song around the mission statement."

Were there any takers? You bet. The vice president of the video division nervously admitted that he "wrote a little music" and consented to write something for the mission statement after the others encouraged him. It is only then that Adams revealed who he really was and that the vice chairman had been in on the trick from the start. The news was met with stunned silence and then followed by applause as they accepted the folly of their adventure. One of the tricked executives commented that the new statement actually read better than the first, which he had helped write. Others observed, "Who dares to challenge this guy since he's brought in by the vice chairman who says he's top notch?" But it was the vice chairman who probably best described the experience: "When you look at management consultants, it's a little scary actually. It is indeed prone to witchcraft."

Perhaps Zappacosta is right. I think, however, there is an equally troubling dynamic that arises. Just as the gurus of quality improvement programs (TQM, CQI, Six Sigma, etc.) have lost their way by concentrating on internal processing, mission statement writers can fall into the trap of meaningless, but well-intentioned, guiding lights. The answer? As noted earlier: Keep It Simple.

The accepted view is that the game is complex, difficult, and inherently frustrating. I just don't buy that.

                                                                    Arnold Palmer

Before bringing this part of the discussion to a close, I think it is important to underscore what Warren Bennis and Bert Manus have to say: "To choose a direction, a leader must first have developed a mental image of a possible and desirable future state for the organization. This image, which we call a vision, may be as vague as a dream or as precise as a goal or mission statement. The critical point is that a vision articulates a view of a realistic, credible, attractive future for the organization, a condition that is better in some important ways than what now exists." Defining what the corporate security mission is all about can be an emotional morass for many. Therefore, Bennis and Manus are correct in noting that it must be seen as realistic and representing a serious departure from the current state of affairs to a more inviting organizational place.

Recap and Application

The first step for the strategic planner, then, is to define the vision and state it in the simplest terms so everyone knows the vision and can relate to the end objective. Based on all of the above, let us assume that a corporate security director wants to manage a program that is recognized as a world-class operation that brings true value to the organization. Certainly this is a laudable goal, but it remains too vague. What, after all is meant by "world-class"? Further, what defines "brings true value"? I think each of us can get a feel for what the security manager desires, but its grandiose language leaves us unsettled. A more defined statement of purpose might be, "To be viewed as a leader in the business of protecting people and corporate assets." This is a straightforward mission. By saying "to be viewed," the security department puts itself out front, both in terms of its industry and its organization. It defines the point of comparison and customer base concurrently. The use of "leader" connotes professionalism and ethical responsibility, valued resources. The use of "in the business of" defines exactly what the security department is all about. It is *in* business; it has the purpose of offering something of value to someone else. And, as a business, it expects to receive a return on its efforts. "Protecting people and assets" defines the department's scope of services. Their three-word motto could be as simple as "Leadership in Protection."

Formulating Your Game Plan

Many managers struggle a long time before they come to grips with the reality that they need a strategic approach to their management style. Others recognize the need to be strategic but take a long time figuring out just exactly where they want to take their departments, or what core deliverables make the most sense for their organizations. Either way, once they have defined what they are all about, they waste little time in getting started. This can lead to a serious trap.

Formulating a strategic direction requires knowing what obstacles are in the way of success. These obstacles can originate either internally or externally. Often they are a combination of both. Until they have been identified and the limits of their obstruction defined, little progress can be made. Internal obstacles can take on many forms, some of which are directly outside the control of the manager. These might include a recent announcement by senior management that the company will soon be closing an entire division, or that the decision has been made to outsource several infrastructure units. These are but two internal variables that can significantly influence a security manager's strategic goal with little opportunity for the manager to voice concern or offer input. The end result may well mean a change in the strategic goal altogether.

Internal obstacles that the manager and security team can impact may include:

- Capital and/or operating budget
- Employee awareness and ownership
- The degree of advocacy from key decision-makers
- Direct reporting relationships
- The existing core deliverables

In the world of business, money *is* the bottom line. Dollars represent the driving engine that propels the security department forward. It is therefore essential that the management team understand the tactics necessary to assure their fair share. Historically, security managers have used the emotional appeal approach. They would paint scenarios of nearly insurmountable losses, injury to employees and customers, and any other catastrophic event that would get attention and approval for their budgets. But this is not an advisable approach, as we discussed in Part I when commenting on the need for the FBI and other government agencies to take their lead from security directors who have already gone this route and failed.

The smarter approach is to look for the motivating hook that drives the decision-maker to the manager's request, thus making both partners. As noted in *The Art*, the "hook" can only take on one of three forms. First, the decision-maker will be motivated only if there is a demonstrated ability to solve a problem facing the decision-maker. Second, there must be an opportunity to receive a gain. For the decision-maker this may mean a promotion, an opportunity to look good, to demonstrate good will, and so forth. Finally, is there an ability to relieve the decision-maker of some pain that is present? When people are in pain, cost becomes a secondary concern. They simply want the pain to go away and are willing to make a quick and positive decision.

The goal of the security manager is to ensure that financial requests make their way through the approval process as expeditiously as possible. At times, this requires more knowledge about psychology than financial acumen. Knowing what motivates people defines a tactical strategy in itself. Without this knowledge and knowing how to use it, even the best vision will flounder.

We have already addressed the need to gain employee awareness and convert it to ownership. This is closely linked to the third challenge, developing advocacy. There is a similarity in the strategic approach for each of the first three elements (monetary approval, awareness/ownership, and advocacy), which is understanding the trigger points that drive each (problem solving, gain, and pain) and adroitly applying them to each element.

Reporting relationships and core deliverables are perhaps the easiest factors that a security team can manage. Typically, the relationships a security director has with superiors and subordinates are well defined. Given today's organizational fluidity, however, it is not unheard of for a security manager to have three or more bosses over a relatively short period of time. Even when this happens, it is only a matter of time before the security director and the boss know what is expected of each other. Likewise, subordinates demonstrate their capabilities sooner than later. The end result is that these given "knowns" dictate reciprocal relationships.

Yet, to assume that eventually everyone will come to know one another, see capabilities and limitations, and learn how to deal with them accordingly is somewhat naive. To assure strategic success, the security manager needs to first understand the organization's culture. Only then can there be an opportunity to gain control and direct the desired outcome. In 1998, R. Goffee and G. Jones wrote *The Character of a Corporation*. In their research they identified four distinct organizational cultures based on two dimensions. The first is *sociability* and the other is *solidarity*. The first relates to the degree of socializing that drives organizational behavior. The culture is described as friendly, naturally collaborative, and focused more on process than outcomes. The second is based on the organization's participants as task oriented. Here people focus on common interests and goals and less so on personalities, biases, and social interaction.

Within the context of sociability and solidarity they define four different cultures: networked, mercenary, fragmented, and communal. These are reflected in the typology in Figure 4-2.

Networked cultures view members as family and friends. They are high in sociability and low on solidarity. This type of culture can often be found in smaller organizations and start-ups, but long-standing family-owned companies can fall into this group as well. For example, McKee Foods of Collegedale, Tennessee is such a corporation. This billion-dollar family-run business produces baked goods for consumers across the country and has expanded overseas. Employees are often viewed as extended members of the family, and organizational relationships are given very high consideration in the decision-making process. Stephen Robbins, author of *Organizational Behavior*, describes Unilever and Heineken as two other companies that serve as examples of a networked culture.

Mercenary cultures are low on sociability and high on solidarity. These are organizations that are tightly focused and extremely goal oriented. Corporate politics is not significant because employees understand their position within the organization. These organizations are quick to position themselves in the marketplace and remain focused on what they do best. *Forbes* magazine's

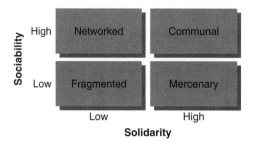

Figure 4-2
Four-Culture Typology

January 21, 2002 issue describes such a company in the cover article, entitled "The Man Who Sees Around Corners." They describe Siebel Systems as a highly focused, no-nonsense company that has emerged as the fastest growing software company in the industry's history, out-performing Oracle, PeopleSoft, and Microsoft. Siebel is so focused that every employee—including security officers—completes at least five Web-hosted tutorials on its products every quarter. These tutorials include exams on which workers must score 90% to pass. The test results become part of their quarterly performance reviews.

A fragmented culture is low on sociability and solidarity. Typically, such organizations recognize individual behavior and job tasks. The professional does not strongly identify with the organization, and is judged on transactional performance. In other words, they "earn their keep one job at a time." Universities, law firms, consulting houses, and other professional firms usually fall into this category. For me, a good example is the Apollo Group. This publicly traded company owns and operates the University of Phoenix (UOP), along with a large publishing firm. The university is a for-profit educational institution offering degrees in selected professions and business management. With more than 90,000 registered adult students, it is the largest university in the United States.

With thousands of adjunct professors, UOP has one of the largest faculty groups in academia. Each adjunct professor is an independent contractor and is awarded a separate contract for each course of instruction. If the instructor does well, additional contracts are offered. If the instructor falls below the University's standard, no additional contracts are awarded and the instructor loses affiliation with UOP. The University is also a leader in on-line instruction and individual studies (one-on-one between student and instructor). Although these new forms of instruction are well received by the students, these forms of instructor–student relationships distance the instructor's identity from the University as a whole.

A communal culture is high on sociability and solidarity. Here both friendship and performance are highly regarded values. Leadership has a clear vision of the company's future and is often described as charismatic. One of their hall-marks is the development of disciples as opposed to followers. The Hewlett-Packard company under the direction of its founders was an example of this type of company-driven culture. Similarly, Herman-Miller enjoyed such a reputation for years until it lost its way with the current senior management team. Wal-Mart and Disney are other examples of past communal cultures, but like Herman-Miller, with the passing of Sam Walton and Walt Disney, these companies have likewise shifted in cultural orientation. Today, companies such as Starbucks and Krispy Kreme can be described as communal cultures. Along with Southwest Airlines and Veritas Software, these highly successful companies rely heavily on strong interpersonal relationships and individual performance.

Each of the four cultures can be understood in terms of the overall organization, but they can also be applied to work units within the framework of the company as a whole. In other words, departments such as corporate security can reflect similar cultural ratings. Determining which culture best describes the security team is critical if the manager hopes to control relationships from above and below. Culture defines the limits for employees and supervisors for such factors as risk tolerance, acceptance of change, and team relationships.

The security team needs to identify whether their culture is a reflection of sociability or solidarity, or is a combination of both. Knowing the culture is what drives the type of strategy and the style of management that will be required to achieve the stated goal. I recall one security manager who failed to understand this requirement. The end result was that he not only missed his strategic objective, but also lost his job in the process.

Situational Case Four: The Wrong Cultural Perspective

Frank was fairly new to the world of corporate security, having made quite a name for himself in the law enforcement community, where he was a successful vice officer. Before being named corporate security manager for a rapidly emerging global company, he was an investigator for another large company. Despite his lack of corporate management experience, Frank soon realized that the success of his department lay in its ability to control costs and define a strategic initiative that complemented his company's overall business objectives.

He had been hired by this emerging company as a start-up manager and charged with the responsibility of creating the company's first security program. To assist him, he set about hiring several key managers, most of whom had a background similar to his. He trusted his staff from the beginning and saw himself as more than boss to everyone. To many, he was their mentor. From his perspective, he had seen the emergence of what we have just defined as a networked culture. Some of his direct reports were long-standing professional colleagues from their mutual days within the law enforcement community.

However, he knew a time would come for his department to shift to more of a communal culture.

From this perspective he adopted a management style that was open and highly relationship based. He believed everyone got along with one another and that, as a family-oriented team, they could accomplish just about anything they set their sights on. He had watched his unit grow each year and as new staff members were added he felt the department could only continue to bring real value to the parent company. It wasn't long before the scope of his department began to expand, especially geographically. As the total organization developed a presence in one country after another, Frank's team correspondingly grew. Soon his management and professional staff totaled nearly 30 employees. Initially he was not concerned about the growing size of his staff, rationalizing that the company had a presence in nearly 60 countries and security needs abounded. The economy was pushing forward and so was his company and, most important of all, his plans.

Frank was astute enough to recognize that growth for the sake of growth was not sound. He knew that his growth should be measured against a strategic plan that reflected protecting the assets of his company. He turned to an external consultant to help him in the development of his plan. Why? Because he knew that despite the skills of his staff, they were not accustomed to thinking in business terms. As he put it to his consultant, "The team is good, but there are too many cops. They don't see the bigger picture. We need a change and we're going to get it whether they like it or not." Thus sounded the first clang of his undoing.

The two set out to develop measures of performance, and his consultant said he would "create metrics designed to demonstrate value." Skill sets were assessed and decisions were made to replace some of the staff with others more qualified. It did not take long before Frank felt that he was making all of the right management decisions. He had purchased several leading management texts and read them from cover to cover. Here he discovered a world of management concepts filled with such daring concepts as hyperarchies, political boundaries, and how to build team-based organizations. As he became more informed, he discovered that he could *talk the talk* and set out to show that he could *walk the walk*. His consultant was proud of the progress Frank had made in so short a period of time and sought out Frank's boss to tell him about what was going on in corporate security. The boss felt confident that Frank had done the right thing in bringing in an outside expert.

Frank had originally created a department around a given culture. Yet he failed to take those steps necessary to assure that any change in that culture was done in a calculated manner. He and his consultant sought change to stave off criticism from any would-be naysayer arising from the senior management ranks regarding his department's rapid growth. Yet, in doing so, they failed to take into account that one culture cannot supplant another without the proper strategy. It wasn't long before another culture began to emerge. Unfortunately, it was not the cultural shift that had been anticipated.

Frank was oblivious at first, but eventually found that mistrust began to replace the strong trust that he had once counted on for his department's success. Team members began to divide according to unit responsibilities. Cast aside was the willingness to exchange resources and ideas as members of the management team began to draw lines of accountability. As the staff saw their ranks shift from long-standing friends and colleagues to "the new breed," and performance measures tracked their daily activities, they questioned Frank's motives and labeled the consultant as the enemy. Others felt that their jobs were at stake based on arbitrary measures. It was not long before some felt disenfranchised and began seeking employment elsewhere. Others took a wait-and-see posture, and still others began to make their unhappiness known to senior executives, each with the idea of undermining Frank's credibility.

What Frank and his consultant had done was to create a *fragmented culture*. Instead of achieving the communal culture Frank had wanted, he mismanaged the process and instead engineered a culture that was divisive and, worse yet, nonproductive. His old team and new team members were spending time and effort fighting among themselves. Something had to be done. In less than a year Frank had fallen from being a rising corporate star to being offered a severance package and shown the back door. The damage to his reputation as an effective business manager had suffered a fatal blow. Senior management was quick to conclude that Frank simply was no longer the right man for the job. The company and his department had outgrown his skill competency, or so executive row concluded.

But it was not a matter of incompetence, per se. Frank provides a classic example of moving too fast and in the wrong direction. He had hired the wrong consultant and, despite reading the "right books," failed to understand that theoretical constructs can only be successful if properly executed. His consultant was a security specialist, not a management consultant. Between the two of them they knew about technical security issues. Together they lacked the sophistication needed to understand the nuances associated with changing organizational cultures and their impact on team behavior.

If you think education is expensive, try ignorance.
                    Derek Bok, former president of Harvard

This situational case has been played out many times by many others. Frank is far from alone. I recall a former police chief who was considered one of the most progressive chiefs in the country (actually his reputation was equally strong among many non-U.S. police executives). He was a true visionary and set out to replace sworn officers with civilian administrators and specialists (jailors, dispatchers, crime lab technicians, trainers, etc.). His idea was to put as many sworn officers as he could on the street to provide police protection. He reasoned that it was inefficient to spend time and money training officers to do nonpolice duties. The end result was a conversion of his department from nearly 100% sworn personnel to a ratio of 40% civilian and 60% sworn personnel—the highest such ratio in the country at that time.

His idea may have been right on target, as was eventually proven by the adoption of his strategy by police agencies across the country. Unfortunately, he, like Frank, was not a good change agent. The chief had set out to replace one culture with another. He failed to demonstrate strong organizational acumen by mismanaging the change process. His sworn ranks became resentful of the loss of their positions. They felt their jobs were not secure, and many complained that they had worked hard for an "inside" job that was now being denied them. Conflicts between the sworn and civilian staff became a daily occurrence and countless hours were spent trying to negotiate settlements between what had become warring parties.

I studied this police chief and his attempt to *civilianize* his department in 1978. He was considered a pioneer in police management by many of his contemporaries and academicians. Yet those who worked for him found his management style far from acceptable. I drew the following conclusion in *An Analysis of Civilian Management in an Urban Police Department* (1979):

As Ida Hoos once observed, "Despite all of the evidence to the contrary, we continue to believe that somewhere there are 'grown-ups' who know what they are doing." This is particularly true in the arena of public administration. Most people seem to assume that their leaders know what they are doing. Unfortunately, this is not always the case. When it comes to civilianization of police management, most police and city executives find themselves in unfamiliar territory and must negotiate their way by trial and error around numerous obstacles.

The present study has attempted to identify some of these obstacles and to provide some guidance for their circumvention. The data collected suggests that there are many potential advantages to the employment of civilians in police management positions, ranging from cost savings to enhanced productivity. But the evidence also suggests that, in the absence of careful planning and special efforts to ensure that civilians will be accorded legitimacy and acceptance, any civilianization program is likely to fail.

Whether it is a police department or a private-sector business organization, I find it sad that the lessons of nearly a quarter of a century ago are still ignored today. When I wrote those words I did not know how prophetic they might be. Shortly afterwards the state of California passed a voter-driven proposition calling for a radical cut in property tax. Known as Proposition 13, it rolled back tax revenues slated for municipalities. Government officials, seeking ways to cut costs, fell to the pressure of their police unions, and soon many civilians were replaced with sworn personnel at a much higher cost. The unions prevailed because they argued that in the long run it was more cost-effective because a police officer could fulfill the dual role of street patrols and internal operations and management. Such an argument is false and self-serving, yet the public is not now—just as it was then—interested in supporting anything that might upset their police officers.

External obstacles, by their nature, are more difficult to control. In Chapter 3 we found a litany of such external variables, ranging from society's overall attitudes to special interest groups that work hard at creating barriers for the security manager's organizational success. Other external elements include:

- How competitive forces shape strategy
- Supplier demands and capabilities
- Social and political forces (especially for global security programs)
- Technology limitations
- Organizational alliances with other companies

Competitive forces influence the company's executives to make decisions that can run directly counter to the expectations and needs of the security manager. Such decisions can cause a shift in focus and a call for more attention in unplanned arenas. For example, loss of intellectual property to a competitor, legitimately or otherwise, can require a shift in security's deliverables. Plans that are made at one time in the fiscal year can be radically altered as a result of external forces on the company in general.

Global economics once upon a time had little impact on how a company's security program was shaped. Today's e-commerce business models can have an immediate impact. Many businesses resident outside the United States receive strong financial support from their government. This can give them both an economic advantage and a resource to gather information about U.S. businesses that might not otherwise be available to their U.S. counterparts. Lest you get the impression that this is purely a one-way street, I hasten to add that much of the same can be said for many U.S.-centered businesses. The end result is that the corporate security team can have its own agenda changed on short notice and without much, if any, input from the team.

Another external source that is not directly controlled by the security manager is the quality and capability of external suppliers. In *Business Strategies* I discussed the difference between traditional vendors, preferred vendors, and strategic partners. I also discussed strategic alliances, but these still remain few and far between. In the previous chapter I discussed the limitations of today's security suppliers. Despite the numerous calls for external suppliers to become business partners with resident security programs, most have failed to step forward. Product suppliers still push sales for the sake of sales as opposed to working out real solutions, even it means missing a sale or two. Service providers continue to miss the mark, still opting to take direction instead of pushing for a share in the risks and rewards of jointly defining management strategies that are solution oriented.

Social and political events, as evident by the War on Terrorism, are external variables that shift the fortunes of corporate security. Sometimes such events can be a positive influence in defining a strong asset protection strategy. At other times, as we have already discussed, social and political events can mean the end of one strategy and the possible redefinition of another. Judicial decisions and legislative measures can radically alter the direction of security. In the mid-1990s the state of California passed healthcare legislation calling for the training of nonsecurity healthcare workers in workplace violence prevention scenarios. Coupled with a rise in infant abductions and gang-related activity in their emergency wards, healthcare administrators and politicians reacted quickly to stem the tide of growing public criticism. Security directors needed to develop a workable strategy that appropriately responded to their call for assistance.

Technology can be another external element that influences security strategy without the direct control of the security director. In today's world of high-tech response to protecting tangible and intangible assets, there is a strong reliance on devices and systems, but often the need runs ahead of the technology. Following are some examples.

- **The events of 9/11:** One of the government's immediate concerns following the WTC attack was proper screening at the nation's airports. To properly screen individual travelers would require extended delays at assigned checkpoints. A technology was needed that could ensure proper screening without causing long delays. Since that time no real solution has been found. Despite several creative attempts to define a suitable solution, as of this writing, technology has lagged behind the need. Yet, in time, a reasonable solution will likely emerge.

- **Increasing labor costs:** As business cycles fluctuate, owners and senior executives continuously look for ways to manage annual recurring costs (e.g., labor). One way is to substitute labor with technology. For years it was understood that the operation of a security control room required at least two security officers. One was for monitoring alarms, cameras, and so forth. The other officer was needed to respond to anything the control officer observed. Such a belief remains largely with us. Yet for many security applications, technology is now beginning to catch up with the need to reduce labor expense; through the use of affordable paging systems, cellular communications and real-time Internet based monitoring, one officer can literally patrol an area and monitor systems (including closed-circuit television) from a handheld device that can mount on the officer's uniform belt.

- **Expand response capability:** Similar to the one-officer patrol capability just described, security managers for years have wanted the ability to allow vehicle patrol officers expanded response capability. Specifically, by installing a remote camera control ability inside a vehicle, the patrol officer could monitor externally mounted cameras in one location from another. In a retail mall parking lot, for example, an officer could park in one area and operate a pan-tilt-zoom camera in another section of the lot from the vehicle. This would eliminate the need for a console operator serving as the officer's eyes. Today's technology is not quite there to assure reliability at a price that is cost-effective, but it is coming—and soon.

Finally, the security manager does not always have direct control over the company's strategic alliances with other companies. Although there is a close and formal relationship between strategic alliances, often these relationships are distinct and unique. The very nature of a strategic alliance recognizes that two or more companies join forces to share resources for a period of time without each taking an equity position in the other. For the security team of one company, this means having to work in an environment where policies, practices, and norms may be radically different from each other.

From the perspective of protecting competitive information and intellectual property, the challenge can be daunting. Strategic alliances are designed so that each collaborator learns from the other. As Pearce and Robinson note: "Such relationships are tricky since in a sense the partners are attempting to 'steal' each other's know-how." They go on to note that in some instances, strategic alliances are synonymous with licensing agreements. This means that, out of necessity, one company is transferring industrial property rights to a motivated licensee. How such transfers are accomplished and what protections are built-in against future abuse or exposure is of high concern for the security manager. Unfortunately, such deals are typically made outside the sphere of corporate security's influence.

At the outset of this discussion I noted that a successful strategy means for-mulating your plan of attack. To do so requires knowing both the internal and external obstacles that face the management team. Once they have been iden-tified, a sub-strategy can be developed to overcome them. In our analysis we looked at several such obstacles; however, our list was not intended to be exhaustive. Each organization is different, operating in its own unique envi-ronment with its own culture. Consequently, obstacles will vary. The challenge is to be assured that each obstacle is identified and that the weight of its influ-ence is taken into proper account.

About the time we make ends meet, someone moves the ends.
Herbert Hoover

SWOT Analysis and the Resource-Based View

Whether the manager is focusing on internal or external obstacles, before a strategic plan can be developed some type of analysis of the obstacles must be completed. Of late, a method known as SWOT analysis has proven to be very effective. This is a strategic planning tool for analyzing an organization's strengths, weaknesses, opportunities, and threats (SWOT). Formulating a strategic approach takes into account those actions that are designed to balance the strengths and weaknesses with the organization's external and internal opportunities. Clayton identifies each as follows:

- Strengths are areas of value within the organization.
- Weaknesses are the liabilities within the organization.
- Opportunities are favorable or advantageous combinations of circumstances that provide the organization with opportunities to explore new directions.
- Threats are possible risks that could threaten the viability and future success of the organization.

SWOT analysis has been used over the years by many managers because of its ease and ability to match opportunities and threats to strengths and weaknesses. There is one caution that needs to be made, however: SWOT analysis has the tendency to reflect very general capabilities. To provide greater specificity, many have augmented their SWOT activities with what is known as the resource-based view (RBV).

RBV's basic premise is that the organization possesses its own "bundle" of resources that differentiates it from other organizations. This is a particularly valuable tool for many of today's security managers who are confronted with the added challenge of demonstrating their value over the services of an external provider. These resources—tangible and intangible—and the organization's capability of making use of them, become the source of its competitive value. The RBV emerged as a way to more effectively measure the worth of an organization's core competencies.

To understand how RBV can be applied, one need only recall that a resource-based view identifies the organization's tangible and intangible qualities (assets) and organizational capabilities. For a security organization, tangible assets would include a knowledgeable resident staff, organizational advocates, technologies that are integrated into the physical environment, and programs that involve nonsecurity personnel. Some security organizations would include the actual physical assets of their department (offices, control rooms, lobby consoles, etc.) because these are known locales for employees, customers, and visitors to seek out security services.

Intangible assets include security practices and procedures, company policies, and the department's reputation, expertise, industry contacts and liaisons, company loyalty, and knowledge of key decision-makers. Organizational capabilities include the security management team's ability to act as a cohesive unit to accomplish objectives. There is more, however. It also incorporates the department's way of integrating assets, creating collaborations, and executing processes in ways to accomplish the desired result. The manager demonstrates organizational capability by knowing "what buttons to push and when to push them."

A security director armed with staff input regarding the department's RBV can better define the elements necessary for an effective SWOT analysis. Let us briefly look at some factors that might be included in a SWOT analysis.

Strengths

- Knowledge of the organization's products and markets
- Knowledge of the organization's culture (how to get things done)
- Knowledge of key decision-makers (formal and informal)
- Established reputation (assuming that it is good)
- Known entity (employees recognize security team members)
- Industry knowledge and technical expertise

Weaknesses

- Overhead or excess capacity (both in terms of headcount and inventory)
- Staff turnover (particularly if an external provider is on the front line)
- Lack of management depth or professional skill sets
- Established reputation (assuming that it is not good)
- Inability to deliver consistent value

Opportunities

- New deliverables/core competencies (i.e., tangible versus intangible asset protection)
- Expanded internal customer base (geographically and functionally)
- Creating new partnerships (externally and internally)
- Redefining delivery system (i.e., controlling to collaborating/consulting)
- Research and development/beta testing

Threats

- Lower cost from external suppliers
- Challenges to long-standing operational assumptions
- Governmental or regulatory interference
- Judicial decisions that create limitations
- Merger or acquisition

Only when this type of analysis is completed can the security management team develop a strategic plan that carries them from the *here and now* to *then and there*. Once the team has identified the internal and external obstacles and matched them with demonstrated strengths and capabilities, a proper framework can be developed. Whether the manager opts to employ SWOT, RBV, a combination of both, or some other analytical tool, the important point is that some form of analysis must be completed before a realistic assessment can be achieved. From here new opportunities and value can be identified.

Execute the Plan

Despite all of the preparation, there comes the time when it is necessary to execute the strategic plan. Organizational strategists refer to this as the *action phase*. This means:

1. The strategy must be translated into action steps for those involved.
2. The strategy must be accepted and woven into the very fabric of the organization's values and beliefs.
3. The management team needs to take direct responsibility for directing the process.

To accomplish the strategic goal, the action phase requires the development of incremental steps that lead to the end objective. These are, in essence, stepping stones that serve as a defined path that allows everyone to stay focused and assures periodic checkpoints. It also requires the formulation of specific tactics. Just as a sports team creates its own game plan, these tactics serve as the management team's game book. The action phase also calls for the empowerment of *stakeholders*, those who have a vested interest in the outcome. Such empowerment allows them to make critical decisions and act on them. Finally, to keep everyone motivated, the action phase often recognizes individual and group efforts through a series of incentives.

Stepping Stones and Tactics

Otherwise known as short-term objectives, these stepping stones transform the great strategy into incremental parts that can be managed. When considering this initial aspect of strategy implementation, I am reminded of the riddle, How do you eat an elephant? Answer: One bite at a time. The same can be said here. Achieving a strategic plan can be a daunting process, especially for the uninitiated. It can become so overwhelming as to create anxiety and frustration before the plan is even given a chance to begin. Absent a game plan, people can quickly become *reluctant warriors*—a concept we discussed in *Business Strategies* when discussing the need to create reasonable performance measures for external suppliers. Without reasonableness, partners and employees will balk at the change and become reluctant to do battle.

These stepping stones serve to achieve the goal in three ways. First, they serve to "operationalize" long-term objectives. If the plan calls for a three-year dedication of resources, short-term objectives allow the management team to create a one-year or 18-month milepost. If the plan calls for corporate security to expand investigative capabilities to include e-commerce frauds, the short-term objectives may reflect the hiring and training of appropriate staff as initial markers to assure that the plan is on track. Second, they point out that discussion of short-term objectives creates a forum to raise issues and potential conflicts. By identifying them up-front, sub-strategies can be developed to mitigate the likelihood of organizational conflict or some otherwise unintended consequence. Finally, stepping stones can serve as a means of generating feedback to keep the project on course.

Short-term objectives also create accountability. They define specific steps, time frames, and identify who is responsible for what. We are all familiar with the *who, what, when, where,* and *how* paradigm. This is the substance of defining action steps. By implementing this basic organizational plan, measurable results can be generated. Defining the who, what, when, where, and how becomes the tactical aspect of strategic planning. It moves the process from generic statements to very specific requirements.

A strategy I employed when I was a corporate manager, and continue to employ with my clients, is a bi-weekly status meeting. Each person is charged with coming to the meeting with a three-part progress report. The first part identifies the action step. The second part identifies what has been done to move toward accomplishing it. The third part is the projected completion date. Each person is also allowed to identify any obstacles they cannot manage. We discuss these obstacles and develop a plan to either work around them or through them. If no progress is made between status sessions, when the time comes for the next one employees (and clients) understand that there will be consequences.

An important dimension to objective setting is the need to establish priorities. Some action items follow a logical sequence. For example, one cannot train an investigator until the investigator has been identified (e.g., hired, promoted, reassigned). Other items require a deliberate decision. If priority setting does not occur, confusion and miscommunication are sure to result. Conflicting assumptions between stakeholders also will arise. Creating stepping stones and prioritizing them creates what I refer to as the *decision-making road map*. In other words, it shows the way. Perhaps it is not the only way, but more often than not it is the most direct way to accomplish the strategic objective.

Recalling the strategic goal example I offered earlier—"To be viewed as a leader in the business of protecting people and corporate assets"—what might be a set of stepping stones? The following are a few suggestions to consider.

- Assess threats to tangible and intangible assets and assign an accurate level of risk.
- Deliver performance-based uniformed security services.
- Design and install a security system reflecting state-of-the-art technologies.
- Provide high-level investigative services, identifying culpability and control deficiencies.

Each of these stepping stones transforms the overall strategic objective into a set of measurable objectives. Lacking is the actual breakdown of what action steps (tactics) each stepping stone is going to need, the person(s) responsible for each supporting action step, and a completion date. Tactics take the short-term objectives, or stepping stones, to the next level of specificity. Table 4-1 shows a matrix that demonstrates how the process unfolds. In this matrix the strategic purpose is identified. In turn, it is supported by the four stepping stones detailed in the second column. The third column identifies the individual tactics that are necessary to support the first stepping stone. There is actually another column that is required, but not illustrated here: each of the four tactics needs to be assigned to a person or team who will be accountable for assuring that the tactic, or action step, is completed. Further, there is a need to identify a due date for the completion. This added level of detail must be developed for each of the remaining stepping stones in the second column.

Table 4-1
Corporate Security Strategic Plan

Strategic Purpose	Business Strategies (Stepping Stones)	Operational Tactics (Action Steps)
To be viewed as a leader in the business of protecting people and corporate assets	Assess threats to tangible and intangible assets and assign an accurate level of risk	Meet with end-users to identify risks
		Develop risk matrix for each tangible and intangible asset
	Deliver performance-based uniformed security services	Apply matrix
	Design and install a security system reflecting state-of-the-art technologies	Develop action plan for each threat
	Provide high-level investigative services, identifying culpability and control deficiencies	

This type of *leveling*, moving from the general to the specific, allows the security management team to monitor its progress and ensure that the end objective is met. There are several strategic tools that can be used to identify and accomplish both the stepping stones and their corresponding tactics. In *Business Strategies* I briefly introduced my readers to the concept of fish bone analysis (pages 119–120). This is a long-standing tool that forces decision-making based on a process of cause and effects. An examination can be made concerning what factors affect other factors and why. There are a number of other tools and techniques that are available to the strategist. Some of them are in the following list, several of which you may be familiar with.

- **Dialectical inquiry:** Evaluation of conflicting points of view
- **Delphi method**: Evaluation of points of view through carefully constructed questioning and feedback of opinions derived from earlier feedback
- **Focus groups:** Hosting a group discussion, generally of experts or qualified individuals (though sometimes involving representative stakeholders) to evaluate points of view on particular topics
- **Simulation:** Typically computer-based technique for simulating future situations
- **Benchmarking:** Comparative analysis with like organizations
- **Multiple scenarios:** Unfolding narratives describing assumed future events or circumstances through a sequence of time frames and snapshots
- **Metagame analysis:** Analyzing viewpoints on a contemplated strategy from the perspective of competitors or competitive responses
- **Strategic gap:** Extrapolation of current performance levels and desired performance objectives

Empowering and Motivating the Stakeholders

Empowerment is policy driven. By this I mean that empowerment comes as a result of developing written policies and disseminating them to everyone. The written word is a powerful tool in and of itself. It puts the organization on record as supporting what the policy says. It is senior management's commitment. It defines purpose and serves as the basis for the procedures and practices that follow.

Many managers do not understand empowerment or its role in today's organizational environment. Because a great number of other writers have dealt with this topic in great depth, I will not go there. Rather, my purpose here is to highlight that a successful strategic plan requires a level of stakeholder involvement. Empowerment is the machinery that makes action plans come to life. It is the mechanism that drives the process forward. Policies serve as the basis for legitimizing what employees and others do or do not do. Well-written policies designed to promote empowerment have clear benefits for the organization, which include:

- Serving as the forum for clarifying intent
- Creating a level playing field for everyone involved
- Defining fair and equitable treatment
- Providing a basis for authorized decision-making and action
- Promoting delegation while reinforcing accountability

Pearce and Robinson identify their own eight ways policies promote empowerment.

1. Policies establish control over independent action by stating how things are to be done *now*.
2. Policies promote uniform handling of similar activities.
3. Policies ensure quicker decisions.
4. Policies institutionalize basic aspects of organizational behavior.
5. Policies reduce uncertainty in day-to-day decision-making.
6. Policies counteract resistance to or rejection of chosen strategies by others.
7. Policies offer predetermined answers to routine problems.
8. Policies provide a mechanism for avoiding hasty and ill-conceived decisions.

In short, policies allow people to act.

Rewarding behavior that complements the overall strategic plan is also essential. Such rewards can take many forms. Some rewards are outside of the direct control of the security manager, and others are not. Senior management stays motivated through compensation plans that are tied directly to performance. Over the recent past this has been criticized by many, not because performance-based compensation is bad, but because the level of compensation can be very high. My intent here is not to discuss the value of compensation as much as it is to recognize that monetary compensation can be a strong motivator for many people. David Gibbs once noted: "There are those that are camped on money, and there are those camped on fame." He was right— some are motivated by the dollar but others find motivation in other forms of recognition.

Few security directors can offer golden parachutes or apply golden handcuffs. Likewise, few can offer stock options or bonus plans beyond prescribed limits set by senior executives or their compensation committees. This does not mean that they are prohibited from petitioning these people to create compensation incentives for lower-level managers that meet the department's strategic planning requirements. Rewards can take many other forms, however. As I described in *Business Strategies*, reward scan be as simple as entertainment certificates or passes. One of the most effective motivators I found when I worked for Continental Illinois National Bank was arranging for my entire staff to watch a Chicago White Sox baseball game periodically from my company's sky box. Even those who were not baseball fans looked forward to the experience because they knew it was a night of "good eating and drinking," and a time to relax while being treated as a VIP. The experience was so enjoyable, few cared about the game's outcome.

Other incentives can include reassignments, promotions, title changes, attending conferences, compensatory time-off, and special recognition ceremonies. CapitalOne Financial Services allows the security manager to budget quarterly team enhancing days. This allows each work unit to select a day's activity away from the office for everyone. Some units opt for a day of golf, and others seek alternative outdoor activities. Some elect to spend the day at a local art show or museum. Regardless of the activity chosen, the security budget absorbs the cost. It doesn't matter so much what type of motivation program is developed—the important point is that one is developed and offered. Employees need to know that their efforts are being recognized and that they enjoy the support and commitment of the manager.

Reviewing to Assure That You're on Track, and Modifying Only if It's Broken

The final leg of a solid strategic plan calls for an ability to modify the plan—but only if it is broken. Many managers are driven to change things for the sake of change. Or, if something runs askew once, they believe the entire plan is off-track and demand changes. Sometimes they may be right, but often they are not. A plan requires patience and has some measure of trial and error. Quick fixes are not remedies—they are simply delay tactics that can truly lead the team astray.

But there are times when the plan does break. There are occasions when parts or entire sections of the plan need to be revised for any number of legitimate reasons. Environment shifts, senior management changing the business course, bad assumptions made at the outset, and internal customer expectations or needs that reverse themselves are but a few of the reasons calling for a modification to the plan.

The management team does need to continuously ask themselves a series of questions. These include:

- Are we still on course?
- Are our advocates still supporting us?

- Are our assumptions still valid?
- Are we doing the right things at the right times?
- Are deadlines being met?
- Are we still within budget?

Answers to these "are we" questions will drive a second set of "do we" questions. These include:

- Do we need to make adjustments?
- Do we need to include anyone else?
- Do we need to validate any of our data or results?
- Do we anticipate any changes that will affect us adversely or beneficially?
- Do we want to stay the course or redefine ourselves?

Neither set of questions is intended to be comprehensive. Rather, I offer them to stimulate thinking. Strategists need to understand that there is a time to question things. There is nothing wrong with questioning. However, taking action is dependent on a number of considerations. We saw a great deal written in the 1990s about continuous quality improvement (CQI) processing. Unfortunately, the concept of CQI was often interpreted to mean that some form of action was expected. Quality gurus would not be content with the concept that sometimes the process was working even though occasional glitches occurred. Here they failed to follow their own advice and did not conduct a root cause analysis to determine whether this was an anomaly or an indicator of something more seriously wrong. Rather, the assumption was that the system was ultimately tied to human interaction and must automatically require some form of continuous adjustment.

Making mistakes simply means that you are learning faster.

Weston Agor

How do we know if the process is broken and needs fixing or if we should exercise patience and wait to see if there are further unwanted fallouts? What if the circumstances are such that we simply cannot risk another indicator of something being wrong? The answer to these questions lies in the development of strategic controls. These controls serve as a process barometer. They allow the strategist to make adjustments when adjustment is required. Schreyogg and Steinmann introduced the concept of strategic control as having four distinct elements. In their article *Strategic Control: A New Perspective*, which appeared in the *Academy of Management Review* (No. 12, 1987), they identified four types of control: premise control, implementation control, strategic surveillance, and special alert control.

Premise control is designed to systematically assure that the assumptions and facts (premises) on which the strategy is based are still valid. To accomplish this, someone on the management team needs to be assigned the task of continuously monitoring influencing factors that drive the overall strategic approach. Sometimes a single individual may not be able to handle this and the process will require others. Still, there are times when events will occur that may not appear to directly impact the plan, but upon further analysis will. The acquisition of a company whose products and services appear to be synergistic could, from an operational perspective or as a result of the acquisition terms, alter the security team's strategic plan.

Likewise, judicial decisions, regulatory changes, legislative enactments, world events (e.g., 9/11), a new product announcement, and mergers among suppliers or competitors are all environmental or industry factors that can alter a plan. Some may have an immediate and direct effect and others may not appear to have an effect at all, but they may have significant affects further down the road. Regardless, premise control is simply a means of requiring someone to be accountable for continuously asking the basic question: What does this do to our plan?

Implementation control assesses whether or not action is required as a result of incremental changes that occur as the plan is unfolding. As we have seen, strategic planning is a process carried out over a series of steps. Along the way stakeholders change, priorities shift, new factors are introduced, and special programs outside the influence of security are introduced that have an effect on the strategic plan. The two basic types of implementation control are monitoring strategic thrusts and milestone reviews.

Monitoring strategic thrusts is fairly obvious when the event is widely published or becomes public knowledge. Others may be less apparent. For example, the international division of a major U.S.-based manufacturing firm made the decision to eliminate direct production over a period of months and quietly shift to a third-party contractor. The security department was caught unaware because the decision was kept fairly low-key to avoid any type of inadvertent leak. This shift had a direct effect on the security department's staffing plan because they were ramping up to provide a new investigative initiative designed to counter threats from the loss of competitive information. This shift in production operations meant a new focus for security, and perhaps even a halt to their staffing plans. Milestone reviews typically are large undertakings. These are periodic reviews that are planned in advance and serve as checkpoints to assure either that all is well or that something is in need of adjustment. On the other hand, milestone reviews can take on a much more informal tone. All that is required for the planning process is a design element that calls for periodic reviews. I liken this to quarterly performance reviews versus annual reviews. Both serve as a check valve, yet one is far more formal than the other. I prefer the quarterly reviews simply because of their frequency. If something is going to go askew, it is better to catch it early on and not be caught off-guard at a point that may be difficult to recover from.

Strategic surveillance can best be characterized as the *soft side* of implementation control. This activity is designed to monitor activity that is general in nature. It can be likened to the collection of competitive information insofar as it is a process of gathering information from a variety of sources without a specific intent. In other words, this is an activity that consists of scanning trade journals, talking to other security professionals, and attending conferences and professional association meetings. It can also involve paying close attention to e-mails, even those to which the security manager is a copy recipient only. This activity allows the management team to uncover information that may be relevant to the overall strategy.

Special alert control is a decision-making session that results from an unexpected event. Typically, this session is pulled together quickly, is very short in duration, and is decisive. Throughout this book we have been using the events of 9/11 as such an event. For global organizations this could also involve coups or a shift in policy regarding American-based companies. Natural disasters can be strategy-altering events, as can manmade crises such as the power blackouts that rolled through California in the summer of 2001. Such events trigger immediate and intense assessments of the strategic plan.

Concluding Comments

In *Business Strategies* I offered a series of management axioms. One of them advised that if you are going to wait to be recognized, you should pack a lunch because you are going to have a very long wait. Admittedly, the comment was intended to be humorous, yet there is a great deal of truth in the observation. Why? Because success is a planned event. Success does not typically fall into someone's lap—rather, it is earned. In this chapter I stressed the point that success requires deliberateness based on the development and execution of a strategic plan. The only way I know to break from the chaos of reactive management is to force a process into one's management approach that allows time for proactive planning.

In this chapter we found that the security industry, by and large, has yet to incorporate strategic planning into its everyday activities of business management. Some security directors have seen the necessity and implemented some very worthwhile initiatives. Most have not, and continue to lag behind their organization and other professional sectors. Strategic planning, as we saw, need not be cumbersome. It can be as simple as defining what you want to deliver, developing a game plan, executing it, and modifying the plan only if it is broken.

We also discovered that success comes by charting a course that is simple to understand, simple to follow, simple to measure, and makes obvious to everyone what has been accomplished. To help us I proposed an exercise that requires the development of a three-word motto that reflects what corporate security is all about. We also analyzed the variables that are under the direct influence of the security team and how they can be leveraged to promote the strategic plan. We found that there are variables that are not so readily controllable. However, these too can be managed. As a cornerstone for any strategic plan, we reviewed how organizational culture comes in at least four varieties and serves as a driving force in determining success.

Next we found that there are several tools that can be put in the manager's strategic planning toolkit. Beginning with SWOT and resource-based view analyses, or some other recognized approach, strategic planning also incorporates the use of special stepping stones and tactics. When used, each allows the management team to create a matrix-based corporate security plan that moves from a generalized statement to a specific plan of attack. Finally, we explored how the entire process can be controlled to ensure that the plan stays on track.

To wrap our discussion up, I would like to draw back on a few key insights that Hamel offers us regarding the process of strategic planning. First, he notes that strategizing is more of a quest. The stages cannot be expected to simply fall into place. They require manipulation. Second, we must recognize that strategic planning results in change, and change can be very threatening, especially to stakeholders who have a vested interest in maintaining the status quo. This usually involves senior managers—the power brokers. Third, change is not the problem that confronts most managers when pursuing strategic planning. Rather, it is the engagement. To be successful, those affected must be brought into the process; this means that strategy making must be democratic. People should have a say in their destiny, a chance to influence the direction. This is not, however, to say that everyone has an equal say. Nonetheless, without some opportunity to be heard and have their input seriously considered, buy-in will be adversely affected. Hamel offers several other key insights that can serve as a reference for us. For now, however, I leave you with an adaptation from his concluding comment, one with which I think he would agree: To invite new voices into the strategy-making process, to encourage new perspectives, to start new conversations that span organizational boundaries, and then help to synthesize unconventional options into a point of view about asset protection— this is the challenge for the security management team.

Diamonds are nothing but chunks of coal that stuck to their job.
Malcolm Forbes

THOUGHT-PROVOKING QUESTIONS

1. In Part II I offer a definition of asset protection: *Asset protection, and here I include the protection of people, is the formulation of an overarching plan that is designed to enhance the workplace by ensuring that*

every reasonable thing is done to promote a secure environment and mitigate the likelihood of loss or injury. Would you agree or disagree with this definition?

2. In this chapter we introduced the need for strategic planning. We noted that most security management teams have yet to fully integrate this process into their programs. Do you agree? If so, why do you think this is the case?

3. Strategic planning is a process. For some authors it involves may substeps. Others believe that it can be fairly simple, involving only four fundamental steps: defining the vision, developing the plan, executing it, and modifying it only when it is broken. Based on your experience, which approach seems to be more appropriate?

4. Take the time now to develop both a strategic vision and a mission statement that appropriately reflect what a global security department should be. Can you develop a three-word motto that captures the spirit of this vision?

5. In this chapter a corporate security strategic plan was introduced reflecting four stepping stones. Based on the vision and mission statements you just completed, can you identify the critical stepping stones necessary to accomplish your goal?

Chapter 5

THE CALL FOR A METRICS-BASED APPROACH TO TOTAL ASSET PROTECTION

You must be the change you see in the world.

Mohandas Gandhi

Primary Themes

- Using a Statistically Based Staffing Model
- Applying a Tailor-made Security Approach
- Updates to the Model Services Agreement

OPENING OBSERVATIONS

"You must be the change you see in the world." What a wonderful way to begin this chapter. These words of Gandhi speak volumes for the world of corporate security. The security industry has been reluctant to embrace a metrics-based approach. There is no doubt that many within the profession have applied metrics, and with amazing success. Yet, for the most part, this approach has not spread to the industry at large. Despite a great number of calls for this by many over the years, the resistance has been strong.

Trying to explain why has eluded me for years. It would be easy to conclude that most security managers resist this approach because they are not familiar with it, fear it—or at least its possible consequences—or are simply comfortable with the traditional approach. It would be easy to fall back to a comment once made by Albert Einstein: "Great spirits have always faced violent protest from mediocre minds." Others might more readily identify with Groucho Marx's observation: "I've had a wonderful time and this wasn't it." I think such conclusions would be misleading, however. I have come to see that there is more to this resistance than these easy answers, although they certainly play a part. It is my conclusion that the resistance is rooted much deeper. Most security managers are put off by the term *metrics* because it is perceived as a management fad that can lead to only one conclusion—if you cannot measure it, it must not have value. There's more. I think they also fail to see the relevance of metrics. After all, security is essential and even though it is not an exact science, it is relevant because without it losses would occur and people would be hurt—or so they reason. Such an argument as this, unfortunately, is circular and fails to really address the issue.

Many security managers resist a metrics-ased approach because they have been burned by such approaches in the past. For this I cannot blame them. Over the past 30 or so years we have seen MBO (Management by Objectives) come and go, along with Theories X & Y, and later Z. To add to this list there have been the Zen Way of Management, the One-Minute Manager, CQI (Continuous Quality Improvement), and the infamous TQM (Total Quality Management). Now we have Six Sigma. Each in its own way has promoted new processes, new measurements, new tests, new views, new proofs of success. If any one of these were as successful as their inventors would have us believe, one would need to ask the obvious question: If the former was so successful why was there the need for any of the others to follow?

In their book *The Six Sigma Way*, authors Peter S. Pande, Robert P. Neuman, and Roland R. Cavanagh are quick to point out the numerous companies that have proven the success of Six Sigma. They showcase GE, Motorola, Allied Signal. They include Black & Decker, Bombardier, Dupont, Dow Chemical, Federal Express, Johnson & Johnson, Kodak, Navistar, Polaroid, Seagate Technologies, Sony, and Toshiba. Whereas most of these companies are household names, one is compelled to ask how much shareholder value they have returned in the past three years. Recently, several of these Six Sigma successes have reported their lowest earnings in decades, and some have filed for court protection against their debtors. Nearly all have struggled to maintain their market share. During high-flying economic times these companies may have recorded double-digit successes, but this has certainly not been the case during down times when such processes as Six Sigma should assure their ability to rise above the rest.

> *Anyone can hold the helm when the sea is calm.*
>
> *Publilius Syrus*

Maybe the day will come when students and practitioners of business management will see the folly in trying to apply technical production concepts to a world of human motivation, customer perceptions, and stakeholder interests. Later in this book we will look at the seemingly unending pursuit of corporate managers to find the holy grail of the *one best way*, when it has always been directly in front of them. For now, just as Oren Harari rejoiced at the death of TQM, I look forward to the death of such management fads as Six Sigma—despite the accolades of Pande, Neuman, and Cavanagh.

It is not surprising, therefore, that many managers, both inside and outside corporate security have come to be gun shy (no pun intended) when it comes to a discussion on metrics. Some still hold tightly to a management style spun around the idea that "it's so because I'm the expert and say it is so." The good news, however, is that many have come to the awareness that some form of metrics-based performance and decision-making is both necessary and relevant in today's dynamic times. They want a sense of measured value because they can demonstrate their added value. These are the enlightened managers who recognize that they can contribute to their organization's business mission. More important, they want to be seen as savvy business managers. For them the challenge is one of pursuing a metrics-based approach that is viable and relevant.

So how can they make this happen? That is the focus of this chapter. In the pages that follow we will look at three ways that are both practical and demonstrate relevance. If followed, at least in concept, they will position the security director as a participating business-oriented manager. The first method deals with a company's work at developing a statistically based staff deployment model. This model has been applied to several other business sectors with amazing success. Second, we will read how one security consultant aided in helping a company define its basic security program using a system of factors that can be manipulated based on need.

Finally, we will revisit my model contract—or at least a couple of key articles that have been revised over the recent past. Between the three methods I hope that you will walk away with a better understanding of how a metrics-based approach can work and that it need not be cumbersome.

Before venturing further into our discussion, I would like to stress one underlying principle that is often overlooked in a discussion of metrics-based performance. Not all business metrics need to be entirely scientifically or mathematically based to be successful. Business management is, by its nature, an inexact science at best. It reflects the best efforts of those pursing what we have come to refer to as *best practices*. Such practices are not always clearly defined. There is no one source that can definitively say Approach A is truly the one best approach over all others.

Rather, a solid business metrics-based approach is one that is based more on fact than on opinion or assumptions. It is an approach that identifies clearly stated criteria and adheres to them. It acknowledges the subjective value inherent in each criterion and is open to change if it can be demonstrated that the criteria are flawed or have been misapplied. Metrics-based performance is common-sense rooted. It is not capricious or arbitrary. Those who miss this point are obstructionists, often without realizing it. A metrics approach simply calls for a rational approach, one that does not reflect biases and is not subject to manipulation by zealots or opportunists.

If you do what you've always done, you'll get what you've always gotten.
Tony Robbins

Failing to Lay the Appropriate Groundwork for Support

Recently, a client asked me to visit one of their Florida locations. On arrival, I met their senior vice president. In addition to his business unit responsibilities, he was also designated as the site's primary decision-maker. In other words, his word was final on all matters related to infrastructure support, including security. As I sat down to discuss physical asset protection with him, he informed me that he was glad I had come. "Finally, someone may be able to explain to me why we have the number of guards we have and why we have all of these cameras and access control devices!" he exclaimed.

This example underscores a fundamental flaw made by many security managers. As the experts, they may know why they assign the number of officers they do and the number of closed-circuit television devices, but they often fail to share their plans and conclusions with the end-users. It is not uncommon for a security manager to fail in seeking out the primary customer and explaining the various elements of the asset protection program, including the staffing, the technology, and the operating procedures. In the case just cited, the senior manager was a supporter of security, but was left questioning essential security expenditures because the why's and wherefore's had not been explained to him.

A much better approach would have been for a security manager to sit with the senior executive first and solicit his concerns and identify his needs. As a part of this discussion a review of the looping model's elements would most likely have better positioned the overall program. The effort doesn't end there, however. Once the theoretical construct has been laid out, the security manager needs to demonstrate that the various elements are allocated based on a measured response. Using a measured approach creates credibility. Often its use verifies decisions that have already been made. It takes the guesswork out of the decision-making process. It moves allocations from being assumptive based to a more fact-based approach. It encourages ownership because the end-user is drawn into the process and better understands the why's and wherefore"s of the security program. Unless the end-user shares this understanding, there is little chance for the security manager to obtain true advocacy for the security program. The end result is that the security management team's decisions are often second-guessed and lack support. It is little wonder that so many security managers become frustrated when their programs are curtailed or scuttled altogether.

Sound security business planning requires three fundamental steps. Omit any one of these and the program is doomed for failure sooner rather than later. The steps are quite simple to identify but require true acumen in their execution. They are: (1) develop a plan that is metric based (therefore, justified), (2) achieve buy-in from the critical decision-makers (end-users), and (3) rapidly deploy the plan and include a process for ongoing quality assurance. Here is how these three steps become integrated.

We can become hopelessly snared into very limited options if we allow our-selves to think only as we have been trained to do so.

D. Dalton, Business Strategies

Metrics-Based Planning

Metrics-based decision-making is certainly not new to the business world. In security-related matters, however, it has become extremely important. This is especially true during tight economic cycles, when closer scrutiny is given to returns on the company's investments. This is essential to understand, because security should not be a central business driver. It is certainly an important consideration, but it ought not be so cost invasive as to offset the allocation of resources necessary to assure profitability. Unfortunately, the historical view of many security managers is that their measures are so important that they will argue strongly for expenditures and allocations that are not fact based but are assumptive, at best. This position lessens the credibility of their initiatives and paints them as obstructionists, or, at the least, out of the loop in terms of the final decision-making process.

In *Business Strategies* I discussed the "Chicken Little concept" of corporate security management. This phenomenon is still very much alive. In it the secu-rity manager calls for constant doom-and-gloom, much like Chicken Little who was always crying that the sky was falling. After a while, executive managers tune these security managers out and resist their otherwise legitimate claims. A test of this is what I referred to as the "snicker test." This occurs when the security manager briefs an executive on a topic or offers professional advice. The executive nods obligingly, but after the security manager has left, snickers to himself or herself and thinks, "You've got to be kidding me." Metrics-based planning eliminates both the Chicken Little syndrome and the snicker test. It demonstrates in the best of business practices that careful and deliberate thought has been put into the analysis and that it is supported.

The will to succeed is important, but what's more important is the will to prepare.

Bobby Knight

Allocating Staff Based on Threat Level

Only after a property has been properly assessed regarding its threat posture can one pursue the three core elements of a sound security program. These ele-ments are: proper staff deployment, integration of state-of-the-art technolo-gies, and operationally friendly procedures and practices. Each of these needs to be metrics based. We begin with staff deployment.

One Healthcare Provider's Approach to Statistically Based Staffing

In the late 1990's I was asked to be part of a team to assist one of the largest healthcare providers in reviewing a statistically generated staffing model. Their security staff needed a model that could help them determine the appropriate level of security staffing. Additionally, they required a model to help them identify the best assignment of personnel based on time of day, day of week, and so on. The healthcare administrators were facing severe economic times and cost reduction was the organization's first priority. Security was not the only infrastructure unit to feel the pressure. All units, even those generating fees, were being squeezed to reduce where they could, without jeopardizing the well-being of the patients.

When I first began the analysis I was highly skeptical that a statistically based staffing model could work, especially when I first heard what criteria they were using. I have long advocated that it is dangerous business to build comparative models based on per capita data, the size of a complex's square footage, or the number of guests. Yet I could relate to the challenge facing the corporate security staff members. I listened carefully as the security director explained that hiring and deployment of security personnel had been historically predicated on subjective decisions rather than objective criteria, due to differences in perceived need, unique circumstances, and the organizational culture. He had grown tired of trying to defend staffing levels that he himself could not always justify. Recognizing that the executive management was accustomed to basing decisions on such drivers as square footage and patient load, the security director wanted to present his plan built on a set of criteria that would be readily accepted.

I agreed that the road to success is paved by establishing a common language between the presenter and the receiver. His approach was fundamentally sound. As you may recall from the discussion in *Business Strategies*, retailers think in terms of sales, manufacturers in terms of units produced, bankers in terms of deposits, and hospital administrators in terms of number of patients and beds. The challenge was to create a set of criteria that were acceptable and valid. Realizing that we were charting new ground, we set out to identify a set of workable criteria.

Author's Note

At this juncture I want to reiterate that what is important for our discussion here is not so much the final criteria as it is the process. Note that the director was attempting to create a context for decision-making that was metrically based. He needed a rational business approach to determine appropriate security levels and deployment.

Regardless of the final criteria, we agreed that the model needed to be zero-base formatted. This would force us to set aside traditional assumptions and rely instead on historical incident and service call frequencies, established statistical indicators (known crime rates, demographics, etc.), the physical attributes of each campus, and end-user needs and expectations. Because this client was a national healthcare provider and had multiple facilities, we knew that a field staffing model would need to reflect local administrative support (i.e., access control and parking permit administration, systems engineering, investigations, etc.)

We also recognized the need to identify our base assumptions and delineate them in a manner that the hospital administrators would not criticize. These assumptions had to reflect realistic limitations. For example:

- The model, which was constructed with limited data availability, is dynamic and will need continuous updating as more data becomes available. To this end, the model serves as a guideline and is not intended to be an absolute.
- The model assumes support, both in terms of administrative commitment and the integration of technology.
- Unique security considerations such as major construction projects, special events, or heightened levels of threats are not reflected.

In total, we identified eight primary assumptions. Once these were articulated we set out to identify the necessary criteria. When we were finished, 16 factors were identified. We knew that square footage did play a part because the size of a complex directly affects response time, physical control of the environment, and both type and frequency of patrols. Therefore, it was reasonable to incorporate square footage as one of the 16 variables but not rely heavily on it, as is typically the case among administrators.

Analyzing the incident history and calls for service, we discovered a direct correlation between the number of officers and the number of patients resident at any one time. We noted that patient load was often a driver in determining visitor traffic volume, employee staffing, patient utilization expectations—especially in such units as intensive care and the emergency ward—and turnover in the parking structures and lots. Hence, the number of patients was a base factor in establishing our criteria.

As our analysis unfolded we also identified the remaining list of factors. In this application they were:

1. Number of visits
2. Area crime rate
3. Internal incident frequency
4. Service requests
5. Command center operations

6. Emergency standby and assistance
7. Parking enforcement
8. Motorized patrol
9. Administrative complexity
10. Legal and regulatory conditions
11. Third-party security supplier liaisons
12. Ancillary facilities
13. Medical staff training
14. Customer-driven requirements

This last factor was particularly noteworthy since we knew that, despite our expertise, the corporate culture needed to be reflected. We knew that some end-user expectations were not necessarily "required security considerations," but reflected demand-side wants and desires. For example, the doctors often insisted that a security officer needed to be present in the physicians' parking lot. In most cases this was not a security requirement. Instead of going to battle with the doctors, it was decided that such customer-driven expectations would be reviewed by the local administrator. If the administrator acquiesced to this demand, security would certainly reflect it as part of the facility-specific requirements. If the administrator elected not to approve of the medical staff's demand, the matter would be left to the two parties to work out.

Each criterion was further defined to correlate volumes and complexity to a staffing ratio. This allowed the team to identify both the number of full-time equivalents (FTE's) needed at each facility and how they should be deployed. For example, using the available crime rate data for the area and past incident history for the targeted medical facility, three levels of crime threats were determined (e.g., low, medium, and high). Studying the amount of time required to handle each incident and dividing that by the average work year (2,080 hours, minus paid leaves), the staffing ranges were determined. The following table compares the total crime/incident history rate to the number of required officers.

Category	# of Incidents Annually	Required FTEs
Low	<350	0.5
Medium	351–650	2.8
High	>650	4.2

Similar calculations were determined for service requests. For example, calls for service might include escorts, patient assistance, missing or recovered property, and lock/unlock requests. After compiling the frequency of such requests and determining the amount of time needed to handle them, it was determined that up to 1,000 requests could be handled by 1.9 FTEs. A frequency approaching 2,000 required nearly 4 FTEs, and levels above this aggregate could require as many as 9 FTEs. For this particular organization, a total of 9 patrol-directed FTEs was never exceeded at any facility.

Similar numerical measurements could be determined for staffing a command dispatch center, on-site investigations, training, and administrative support (access control, parking permit issuance, key control, etc.). When each criterion was developed, every medical facility had a working understanding of the total number of officers required to maintain acceptable levels of routine preventative patrols, response time capabilities, and incident management.

Once the total FTE count was determined, another initiative was undertaken to determine the actual deployment. This required localizing activities and arriving at agreements regarding how certain positions were to be staffed. For example, the hospital administrators decided that most lobbies were to be staffed by receptionists and volunteers. Therefore, security did not have to consider staffing this position. On the other hand, security was responsible for the exterior lots and parking facilities and for providing a staff person for the emergency ward, loading docks, and internal patrols. Some facilities, as noted, had very specific customer-driven requirements that might not otherwise be staffed if the decision had been based strictly on security-related criteria.

Obviously there was some overlap between a few of the staffing model criteria and the required positions. Because of this overlap, adjustments were made to eliminate any potential duplication. When the project was completed, a comparison was made between the new staffing levels and the existing levels. The healthcare provider had 11 major hospitals that were the subject of this study. Before the project the total staff was 530.32 FTEs. After the staffing model was applied the total number dropped to 453.46 FTEs, a reduction of 76.86 FTEs.

This statistical approach proved to be very surprising. As I noted earlier, I was skeptical when first asked to become a part of this project. By the end, I realized that even if the staffing model had arrived at an allocation level similar to the original level, its strength lay not so much in the end result as in the ability to justify the allocations and deployment. Officers were assigned based on reliable measures and not on assumptions. The obvious question, however, was whether or not the results could be sustained and applied in another business sector.

Two years after the new allocations were instituted, the security department reported no loss on several fronts. First, there was no loss in customer satisfaction. Critical internal users such as the medical staff (doctors and nurses) reported no noticeable loss in the delivery of security's service. For that matter, most healthcare centers were not aware that the number of uniformed personnel assigned to their respective facilities had diminished. Second, there was no measurable loss in terms of stolen assets. Theft rates remained constant. The same result was reported for parking violations and incidents involving employee and patient safety. Finally, there was no reported loss in confidence on the part of employees, patients, and visitors.

Having realized these "no loss results," the next challenge was to determine whether or not the same results could be achieved when the method was applied to other business sectors. The important point to note is that this was not an exercise in determining whether or not the statistical model could reduce staffing levels. Rather, it was an attempt to establish the validity of an organization's current allocations. As I ventured out, I was reminded what Cervantes said centuries ago: "Many have gone out for the wool only to return shorn themselves."

To test the model, I turned to two different Fortune 200 companies, one on the East Coast and one on the West Coast. The first was a national financial services company with over 60 office buildings scattered over seven campuses. Their particular challenge was to curb their escalating cost of security coverage. Over the previous three years the security operating budget had exploded from just under $3 million to more than $14 million. Although the fact remained that the company was in an aggressive expansion mode, security's costs appeared to be outpacing other support units. The second application was an established West Coast firm that had undergone a series of mergers and wanted to assure themselves that security's allocation was consistent with their comparative industry. They, too, were feeling the pinch of the impending 2001/2002 recessionary downturn and wanted to either reduce security officer coverage or justify the current staffing levels.

The model was applied in the first case, altering several of the variables to best reflect the new business environment. For example, the number of patients was converted to the number of visitors and employees who entered or were assigned to a particular facility. This allowed the security management team to set allocation parameters based on the number of people entering and leaving over the course of a business day (similar to the number of patients identified by the healthcare facility). This client found that greater emphasis needed to be placed on the nature of the facility's operational business, and therefore added this variable to the model, opting to set aside local crime rate as an influencing factor because all of their facilities were located in very low crime rate areas.

As for the second application, the West Coast client was a major corporation in the high-technology business sector. Like the financial services company, this corporation also had multiple campus locations with several overseas operations. Their primary concern was protecting four data centers that were critical in their effort to establish an effective competitive intelligence protection program. In this application, the importance of a well-constructed, business-based allocation model was essential. They needed to be assured that security officers, when combined with state-of-the-art technology, provided the appropriate level of access control. Likewise, they needed to be assured that security personnel were effectively deployed because they were under an obligation to do so as a result of a recent lawsuit. The company had been sued because of a past workplace violence episode in which several employees were seriously injured and one was killed. The claim centered on the issue of proper deployment of the security force; consequently, the company was very concerned that a similar claim could not be filed.

Using the statistical staffing model, this second company was able to establish a deployment plan that not only met the legal liability concerns, but also actually expanded security's coverage. Prior to the model's application, it was assumed that security officer's were not needed to provide coverage in the parking lots and loading docks. There was also a great deal of resistance to having them conduct internal roving patrols through work areas. Using the model, the company was forced to review past incidents. Volume alone justified an increase in the number of officers and assignment to areas that had heretofore been banned.

These three examples, each representing different business sectors, demonstrate that a metrics-based approach to both staffing allocations and deployment can be used. They demonstrate the power that a planned, systematic approach to one of security's more difficult operational issues can create credibility and advocacy. This approach demonstrates business acumen, on which executives place considerable value. It positions the security management team to explain the why's and wherefore's of the staffing model without becoming defensive. It also reflects a collaborative spirit, because end-users are brought into the process and allowed to not only provide input, but also to become an actual resource for the ultimate resolution.

A Consultant's Application of Security Standards

Our second determinant of a metrics-based approach draws us to the work of Steve Kaufer. A few years ago I was asked by the large credit card company, CapitalOne Financial Services, to provide them with a methodology for determining a set of basic security system specifications. To assist them, I employed the services of Steve's company, InterAction Associates, located in Palm Springs, California. As a systems engineer, Steve had worked with a number of large, multifacility organizations. His methodology complemented my metrics-based approach. Steve also recognized the need to assure that any systems approach reflected the integration of a staffing model and a set of operating procedures and practices that were based on collaboration.

After consulting with local site managers, representatives from the asset protection group, and members of the company's engineering and real estate departments, Steve was able to draft a comprehensive set of guidelines. These standards were intended to serve as a baseline. Should one or more threats become elevated, this baseline would serve as an effective decision-making tool for both security and nonsecurity managers. Steve's aim was to develop these guidelines based on the function of each property, CapitalOne's role (e.g., property owner or tenant), and the campus location.

Following is an extract from the introduction of the Security Standards Manual developed by Steve. The final product varied slightly. Also included is an example of one of the many matrices Steve developed to serve as a quick ready-reference for the decision-maker and end-user. After reviewing Steve's work, a few comments are in order.

Facility Security Guidelines

Introduction

As an organization with a large number of facilities of varying sizes, uses and occupancies, CapitalOne faces a considerable challenge to provide the right balance of security. Effective security must be designed to protect the associates, assets and business operations of the corporation, yet not restrict the ability to conduct business efficiently.

Complicating the security design issues are the facilities themselves. CapitalOne is the owner or sole occupant of some offices, but in other facilities is one tenant in a building shared with other organizations. In the instances where CapitalOne is one of several tenants, the security program, systems and procedures may have been developed and administered by others. In approximately one-third of the facilities occupied by CapitalOne the building is owned by CapitalOne, another one-third are leased from others, and the final one-third are "synthetic" leases. The direction for future facilities is that of CapitalOne being the sole occupant.

Additionally, due to the nature of its business activities, some security policies, procedures and systems are dictated by various regulations, including but not limited to:

1. Federal Deposit Insurance Corporation (FDIC), including Regulation P
2. VISA and MasterCard "Security Standards for Vendors"
3. Internal Audit requirements and guidelines on restricted access
4. Individual Department/User guidelines
5. Corporate Security guidelines

The continuing growth of CapitalOne has created a need for a set of guidelines that will assist architects, facility planners, CapitalOne associates, and others to implement the desired level of security for each type of facility utilized by the corporation. The Corporate Security Department of CapitalOne has developed these guidelines as a tool to be used when considering a site location, designing a facility, incorporating security in a facility, and during the on-going operation of that facility.

While these guidelines incorporate recommendations of the Corporate Security Department, understandably there will be instances where not all the recommendations contained in the Security Guidelines are adopted. Given the wide range of facilities and uses, it is understood that not all facilities can or should utilize all portions of these guidelines. Deviations from the Security Guidelines can be made to adapt to local conditions, hours of operation, local ordinances, lease requirements or restrictions, specific concerns, business changes and other factors or conditions.

Site Managers working with representatives of the Corporate Security Department should confer to determine if changes to the implementation of Security Guidelines for a specific facility should be made. The Security Guidelines detail the process used when a variance from the guidelines is desired.

Design Features

Physical security consists of hardware, systems, procedures and barriers. Barriers are often the first line of defense in a security program, and can be natural, such as a river or cliff, or more commonly, man-made. The concept of Crime Prevention Through Environmental Design (CPTED) holds that security can be increased by the architecture of buildings, often creating barriers to crime or removing elements that contribute to security weaknesses.

In the case of facilities constructed to the needs and specifications of CapitalOne, incorporating security features is a task more easily accomplished. Where the corporation utilizes an existing structure, it may be more difficult to make physical changes that impact security of the facility and its operation in a positive manner.

The Corporate Security Department works cooperatively with all other Departments within CapitalOne to create a work environment that protects associates, business operations and assets. It should be standard procedure to consult with the Corporate Security Department prior to major renovation of existing space or the selection of a new facility, to ensure the attendant security issues are addressed in the best interests of CapitalOne and its associates.

In addition to the development of these Security Guidelines, the Corporate Security Department is a resource during the planning, site selection, design, and construction phases for a new facility. In the Building Design portion of the Security Guidelines issues that should be addressed in the facility design are detailed. These guidelines are to be used beginning at the inception of a project, to ensure that the desired level of security is incorporated at each stage.

Technical Security Systems

Electronic security systems are an integral tool in effective and cost-efficient security. All CapitalOne facilities will have electronic access control and related systems. As facilities are developed, a Project Manager from the Corporate Security Department will assist in the design of the electronic security systems in coordination with the Site Manager and the security system vendor selected by CapitalOne.

To assist in the implementation of electronic security systems in CapitalOne facilities, the Corporate Security Department has developed a set of Security System Specifications that guide the selection of approved security equipment and systems, and control the manner in which these devices are installed. These Security System Specifications help ensure a uniformly high level of quality for the electronic systems used by CapitalOne.

Here the system guidelines are articulated for a variety of security devices. These include:

1. Access Control

2. CCTV & other surveillance tools

3. Intrusion Alarms, etc.

Administrative/Procedural Controls

Here Steve continues by articulating standards for the following security-related topics. These include, but are not limited to:

- Visitor and contractor access
- Use of a photo ID system
- Employee safety features
- Package control
- Mail and deliveries
- Employee awareness and ownership training

Security Operations

In most CapitalOne buildings the security planning, design and implementation functions are the responsibility of the Corporate Security Department and the designated on-site Security Manager. The Corporate Security Department has developed a comprehensive Security Staffing Model to determine the requirements for security personnel for each type and size of CapitalOne facility. (Emphasis added by author.) In addition, the members of CapitalOne Corporate Security staff are a valuable resource of expertise that can, and should be consulted with specific questions or concerns.

Based on a host of factors, the Security Staffing Model allows the proper allocation of resources to provide on-site security personnel. Variations to the Model can only be made with the approval of the Corporate Security Department and the Site Manager based on a justifiable business reason.

The Corporate Security Department will assist in the development of security procedures for each facility. The Department will also assist in offering initial and on-going security related training. Training should include the associate's security-related responsibilities, protection of proprietary information, CPR, and other topics as needed. In-service training should be regularly offered to provide as needs indicate.

CapitalOne has developed guidelines to select qualified contract security service providers. Included in these guidelines are the factors that influence the quality of the service and personnel. The Corporate Security Department will provide guidance to Site Managers in the implementation of a security guard program, in accordance with the approved Security Staffing Model.

Having set forth the basic philosophy of the systems approach, Steve then broke out the various components of the security program, providing a description of each element and how it applied to CapitalOne specifically. To protect CapitalOne's proprietary information regarding the application, the actual description has been deleted here. The following is an extract and reflects some of those components commonly found among organizations; however, I think you can get a very good idea of how Steve approached this client's need.

Building Design

Term	Definition/Description
1. Security Control Center (SCC)	This side of the matrix has
2. Security Control Center/BR	been left blank to protect
3. Security/Reception Desk	the company's proprietary
4. Optical Turnstiles	information.
5. Mantrap	
6. Access for applicants/trainees	
7. Exterior lighting	
8. Call Boxes in parking lot	
9. Bollards at entrances	
10. Landscaping design contributes to security	
11. Fire alarm panel in SCC	
12. Interior stairwell doors controlled	
13. Exterior fencing	
14. Electronic systems per CapitalOne specifications	
15. Contact with local law enforcement	
16. Liaison with building management	
17. Liaison with security provider	
18. Develop Emergency/Crisis Response Plan	
19. Development of ID issuance procedure	
20. Implementation of document destruction procedures	
21. Asset inventory and tagging	
22. Generator testing program	
23. Fire alarms testing program	
24. Visitor screening	
25. Mail handling/package inspection	
26. Designated location for courier deliveries	
27. Key issuance and control program	
28. Emergency drills conducted	
29. Initial Associates training	
30. On-going Associates training	
31. Periodic security evaluation	

Having broken down each component, Steve concluded the manual with a quick reference matrix for the appropriate decision-makers. A sample is illustrated in Table 5-1. As with the other information, I have deleted the action steps for each category to protect CapitalOne's privacy. Each element, however, identifies whether or not it is optional or required.

Table 5-1
Sample Security Guidelines Operational Matrix

Facility Type	Security Assists in Site Selection	CAP Index Report	Contact with Local Law Enforcement	Liaison with Building Management	Liaison with Security Provider	Completion of Security Staffing Model	Security Contractor to Receive Building Plans	Develop Emergency/ Crisis Response Plan	Emergency Contact Information
Risk Center—owned	Yes	Yes	Yes	N/A	Yes	Yes	Yes	Yes	Yes
Risk Center—leased sole tenant	Yes	Yes	Yes	Yes	Yes	Yes	Yes	Yes	Yes
Risk Center—leased multitenant	Yes	Yes	Yes	Yes	Yes	Yes	Yes	Yes	Yes
Professional—owned	Yes	Yes	Yes	N/A	Yes	Yes	Yes	Yes	Yes
Professional—leased sole tenant	Yes	Yes	Yes	Yes	Yes	Yes	Yes	Yes	Yes
Professional—leased multitenant	Yes	Yes	Yes	Yes	Yes	Yes	Yes	Yes	Yes
Data/Operations	Yes	Yes	Yes	N/A	Yes	Yes	Yes	Yes	Yes
Mail	Yes	Yes	Yes	N/A	Yes	Yes	Yes	Yes	Yes
Embossing	Yes	Yes	Yes	N/A	Yes	Yes	Yes	Yes	Yes
Warehouse/Storage	Yes	Yes	Yes	N/A	Yes	Yes	Yes	Yes	Yes

Table 5-1
Continued

Facility Type	Security Communication Equipment	"No Weapons" Signage	Visible ID Display	ID Issuance Procedure	Document Destruction Procedures	Asset Inventory and Tagging	Generator Testing Program	Fire Alarm Testing	Fire Equipment Inspection
Risk Center—owned	Yes	Yes	Yes	Yes	Yes	Yes	Yes	Yes	Yes
Risk Center—LST	Yes	Yes	Yes	Yes	Yes	Yes	Yes	Yes	Yes
Risk Center—LMT	Yes	Desired	Yes	Yes	Yes	Yes	Yes	Desired	Yes
Professional—owned	Yes	Yes	Desired	Yes	Yes	Yes	Desired	Yes	Yes
Professional—LST	Yes	Yes	Desired	Yes	Yes	Yes	Desired	Yes	Yes
Professional—LMT	Yes	Desired	Desired	Yes	Yes	Yes	Desired	Desired	Yes
Data/Operations	Yes	Yes	Yes	Yes	Yes	Yes	Yes	Yes	Yes
Mail	Yes	Yes	Yes	Yes	Yes	Yes	Yes	Yes	Yes
Embossing	Yes	Yes	Yes	Yes	Yes	Yes	Yes	Yes	Yes
Warehouse/Storage	Yes	Yes	Yes	Yes	Yes	Yes	Yes	Yes	Yes

Table 5-1
Continued

Facility Type	Visitor Screening	Mail Handling/ Package Inspection	Designated Location for Courier Deliveries	Key Issuance and Control Program	Emergency Drills Conducted	Initial Associates Training	Ongoing Associates Training	Periodic Security Evaluation
Call Center—owned	Yes	Yes	Yes	Yes	Yes	Yes	Yes	Yes
Call Center—leased sole tenant	Yes	Yes	Yes	Yes	Yes	Yes	Yes	Yes
Call Center—leased multitenant	Yes	Yes	Yes	Yes	Yes	Yes	Yes	Yes
Risk Center—owned	Yes	Yes	Yes	Yes	Yes	Yes	Yes	Yes
Risk Center—leased sole tenant	Yes	Yes	Yes	Yes	Yes	Yes	Yes	Yes
Risk Center—leased multitenant	Yes	Yes	Yes	Yes	Yes	Yes	Yes	Yes
Professional—owned	Yes	Yes	Yes	Yes	Yes	Yes	Yes	Yes
Professional—leased sole tenant	Yes	Yes	Yes	Yes	Yes	Yes	Yes	Yes
Professional—leased multitenant	Yes	Yes	Yes	Yes	Yes	Yes	Yes	Yes
Data/Operations	Yes	Yes	Yes	Yes	Yes	Yes	Yes	Yes
Mail	Yes	Yes	Yes	Yes	Yes	Yes	Yes	Yes
Embossing	Yes	Yes	Yes	Yes	Yes	Yes	Yes	Yes
Warehouse/Storage	Yes	Yes	Yes	Yes	Yes	Yes	Yes	Yes

For now, I would like to draw your attention to several attributes of Steve's model and demonstrate how it pulls together our previous discussions regarding risk analysis, staff modeling, and systems integration. First, note that Steve relies on the need to develop such specifications independent from CapitalOne's desire to have them. Rather, in keeping with a best business practices approach, he cites that several regulatory organizations require as much. Next, he recognizes that the client operates in different environments and that his guidelines will vary according to the ownership, environment, function, and so on. He then acknowledges that circumstances change. When they do, regardless of whether they are temporary or long lasting, there is a need to modify both the elements and actions accordingly.

Steve also draws on a highly regarded and well-recognized external source to support his methodology; he notes that his approach is consistent with the Crime Prevention Through Environmental Design standards. These are promulgated by the National Institute for Crime Prevention Institute, an organization noted for its work in developing fact-based criteria. He also calls specific attention to corporate security's role as both a valued resource and collaborator.

The "meat" of his guidelines is in the development of specific components and the document's comprehensiveness. He augments this with the integration of a performance-based staffing model and the involvement of nonsecurity employees. His end product reflects the full range of security devices ranging from access control (electrical and mechanical) to surveillance and intrusion monitoring and communication. The strength of his approach is in the development of an easy to follow set of matrices that allow the decision-maker to determine what is mandatory and what is optional, based on the degree of risk that is assessed.

This approach pulls together our discussion on a metrics-based approach to security. It begins by defining a methodology that offers local management the ability to determine the level of inherent risk present. From here a metrics-based approach acknowledges that assignment of risk is only the first step. The true measure of effectiveness is the development of a staffing model that is integrated with operating practices and security devices, each complementing the other.

Revisiting the Model Services Agreement

I provided a copy of my model service agreement in the appendix of *Business Strategies*, and I do so here as well. Those of you familiar with the previous version will note that there have been several changes. The most significant can be seen in Article 8, Standards of Performance. As you will note, this has been considerably expanded to allow the decision-maker to choose from a wide variety of performance indicators. These indicators were originally developed for one international client. Since then, several other companies have incorporated many of them into their corporate agreements. There are 46 criteria, more than most agreements need. They have been developed to allow the parties to choose those most applicable for them.

Article 8. Standards of Performance

As a condition of this agreement the following standards will be required of CONTRACTOR. All personnel assigned to this account will:

A.8.1. Possess proof of having met the requirements for Private Security Guards as required by (STATE or DISTRICT)

A.8.2. Possess a high school diploma, GED or equivalent training or job experience.

A.8.3. Demonstrate the ability to read and write in English equivalent to a high school graduate. Have the ability to verbally communicate in English, particularly in emergency situations requiring clear and definitive articulation to assure confidence, control and safety of those involved.

A.8.4. Have the ability to demonstrate psychological stability under a variety of conditions as illustrated by passage of appropriately administered testing consistent with national standards and as allowed by law.

A.8.5. Pass a physical fitness examination, including drug testing, by a licensed physician or laboratory, which demonstrates an ability to meet the requirements of this account.

A.8.6. (IF DESIRED BY CLIENT) Possess CPR and First Aid certification as set forth by the American Red Cross or equivalent association.

A.8.7. Pass a test on Customer Service Relations, to be set forth by mutual agreement between CLIENT and CONTRACTOR and undergo periodic training as agreed to from time to time by CLIENT and CONTRACTOR.

A.8.8. Receive a 24-hour course of advanced officer training annually, the curriculum to be mutually agreed upon between CLIENT and CONTRACTOR, reflecting changes in law, customer relations, corporate policies, etc.

In addition, CONTRACTOR shall:

A.8.9. Be responsible for providing, at a minimum, all legally required employment benefits to the CONTRACTOR Employees. These costs shall be included in the overall bill rate to CLIENT Corporate Security.

A.8.10. Assure employee duties and responsibilities be performed in accordance with, (i) the duties and responsibilities and the rules and regulations contained in the site-specific Security Procedures for each site being serviced, and (ii) any subsequent additions, deletions or revisions to the Procedures which CLIENT'S Corporate Security Department, at its discretion, may make from time to time. CLIENT'S Corporate Security Department shall promptly notify the CONTRACTOR, or its representatives, of any such additions, deletions or revisions.

A.8.11. Ensure that its personnel are dressed in the complete uniform, appropriate for the assignment; that they present a neat appearance, paying particular attention to their personal hygiene, bearing, uniform and equipment; that they are prepared for and are performing the assigned security duties in accordance with established operational procedures and policies; and that they prepare and submit all required recorded and reports.

A.8.12. Require CONTRACTOR employees to comply with all CLIENT policies and procedures related to the personal conduct of individuals working at CLIENT.

A.8.13. Ensure that CONTRACTOR employees do not tamper with personal papers, desk, or cabinets, or use CLIENT telecommunications or computer and related network systems or any other equipment or systems except as authorized by CLIENT'S Corporate Security Department.

A.8.14. Except with the written consent of CLIENT'S Corporate Security Department, not permit any CONTRACTOR employee to possess, on CLIENT premises, a firearm, night stick, club, liquid and/or aerosol mace or any other device, object or instrument reasonably considered for use as a weapon which may be used against another person while on CLIENT premises and while engaged in providing Security Services under this Agreement.

A.8.15. Promptly assign a qualified CONTRACTOR employee to fill the position of any CONTRACTOR employee who fails to report for duty, is absent from his/her assigned post, or requires relief from his/her assigned duties. CONTRACTOR employees shall be both qualified and available to personally staff assignments immediately when a CONTRACTOR employee fails to report for duty (or such assignment otherwise becomes vacant) and shall remain at the assignment until such time as a CONTRACTOR employee is made available.

A.8.16. Use its best efforts and all available resources to promptly furnish temporary CONTRACTOR employees requested in the event of unforeseen emergencies. CONTRACTOR shall be capable of providing a minimum of two additional certified CONTRACTOR employees (per shift) on 24 hours' notice. These personnel may be billed at a premium rate not to exceed 1 1/2 times the contracted billing rate for the work being performed and only for a maximum of 48 continuous hours.

A.8.17. Not permit CONTRACTOR employees to work on CLIENT premises in excess of 12 consecutive hours in a 24-hour period, or more than 48 hours during any five-day work week, unless specifically requested or authorized by CLIENT'S Corporate Security Department and Senior CONTRACTOR Management. Nor shall any security officer report for duty with less than 12 hours off from having worked a previous shift, unless such reporting is necessitated by an emergency. Further, no security person may be assigned to work a post or work site alone without first having been tested and successfully demonstrating a comprehensive knowledge of the job functions and responsibilities.

A.8.18. Assure employees assigned to CLIENT shall not be assigned to any other CONTRACTOR accounts while such employees are regularly assigned full-time to CLIENT.

A.8.19. Promptly inform CLIENT'S Corporate Security Department of any and all incidents which require or appear to require investigation. CONTRACTOR shall not conduct investigations where CLIENT is a party unless approved by CLIENT'S Corporate Security Department. CONTRACTOR shall inform CLIENT'S Corporate Security Department in the event they conduct an investigation of any CONTRACTOR personnel assigned to CLIENT. CONTRACTOR shall cooperate fully in any investigation conducted by CLIENT'S Corporate Security Department.

CONTRACTOR shall install at its expense and use an automated management reporting system comparable to the PPM 2000 product to track incidents and generate reports for CLIENT'S Corporate Security Department. This system will be interfaced with CLIENT'S Corporate Security Department, allowing them direct access as necessary and appropriate.

A.8.20. Supervise and administer CONTRACTOR employees through designated on-site and off-site supervisory personnel, who will be responsible for the performance of the security services. These supervisory personnel shall have operational and administrative experience in security services at a level commensurate with the scope of work of this Agreement and shall be responsible for maintaining high standards of performance, professional appearance, and conduct. Off-site CONTRACTOR supervisory personnel shall inspect on-duty, on-site CONTRACTOR employees a minimum of once per week including CONTRACTOR employees working weekends and holidays.

A.8.21. Assure that CONTRACTOR management personnel will be available 24 hours a day at designated locations and telephone numbers provided by CONTRACTOR to the designated CLIENT'S Corporate Security Operations Center (SOC) and designated CLIENT'S Corporate Security Department Representatives.

A.8.22. Assure that CONTRACTOR managers, where they directly or indirectly manage the site security, shall accomplish daily coordination with the CONTRACTOR employees assigned to the responsibility for security at the protected site, to ensure that the requirements/needs of CLIENT'S Corporate Security Department Management are met.

A.8.23. Maintain an office within 15 miles (or its equivalent in kilometers) of the CLIENT site to be serviced. It is possible that additional facilities may be occupied by CLIENT during the term of this Agreement and may require CONTRACTOR services there as well. CONTRACTOR shall, upon request of CLIENT'S Corporate Security Department, provide a Supervisor on any specified CLIENT site within one (1) hour, a Manager on site within two (2) hours, or an Executive officer on site within four (4) hours. A current copy of CONTRACTOR's organization chart is to be continuously on file with CLIENT'S Corporate Security Department. If CONTRACTOR is part of a multi-location organization, CONTRACTOR shall demonstrate, in writing, how the local office fits in the corporate structure, and identify the reporting lines between management at the local level and corporate.

A.8.24. Provide a detailed plan to CLIENT'S Corporate Security Department which states how Key Performance Indicators will be measured and results reported and the strategies employed to ensure the continued quality and improvement of the CONTRACTOR. Key Performance Indicators are attached as (EXHIBIT X).

A.8.25. Develop and submit a one-year business plan prior to the start of the contract. This plan shall clearly detail the strategies, tactics, milestones, and execution methodologies that will be employed by the CONTRACTOR during the plan period, which will ensure the successful management and support of this critical element of the CLIENT'S Corporate Security Department Program.

A.8.26. Assure that CLIENT'S Corporate Security Department will have the sole and absolute right to prohibit any CONTRACTOR employee from entering CLIENT premises or to eject any CONTRACTOR employee therefrom without stating cause.

A.8.27. Assure that CONTRACTOR employees must read, understand, and endorse a CLIENT'S Non-Disclosure Agreement (NDA). CLIENT'S Corporate Security Department shall maintain completed NDAs.

A.8.28. Prior to commencement of services under this Agreement, furnish CLIENT'S Corporate Security Department with description of the uniforms to be worn by the CONTRACTOR'S employees and satisfactory evidence that such uniforms comply with legal requirements. CONTRACTOR shall, at CONTRACTOR'S expense, provide any other clothing or equipment required in the performance of the services. CONTRACTOR shall require each CONTRACTOR employee to wear the complete and issued uniform at all times while engaged in providing services.

A.8.29. Periodically review operational policies and procedures intended to ensure optimum performance and submit recommended changes to CLIENT'S Corporate Security Department.

A.8.30. Collaborate with CLIENT'S Corporate Security Department in establishing and implementing mutually satisfactory procedures for meeting the needs of the site to which Security Services are provided.

A.8.31. Take receipt of, secure, and account for all property and equipment assigned to the CONTRACTOR by CLIENT. CONTRACTOR shall maintain and care for such property and equipment and replace or compensate CLIENT for property and equipment that is lost, stolen, or damaged by CONTRACTOR Employees. CONTRACTOR shall conduct a semi-annual inventory of CLIENT property assigned to the CONTRACTOR and submit a written report to CLIENT'S Corporate Security Department.

A.8.32. Advise CLIENT prior to any CONTRACTOR employee being assigned to or reassigned, disciplined, promoted or transferred within or away from the account.

A.8.33. Assure CLIENT all staffing will be in compliance with established EEO standards for the geographic area.

A.8.34. Provide annual testing of all assigned personnel on CLIENT'S emergency procedures plans.

A.8.35. Assure CLIENT that all personnel assigned to operate a motor vehicle or other such equipment requiring special licensing shall have such certification and appropriate levels of insurance.

A.8.36. Assure CLIENT that all assigned personnel have passed a comprehensive pre-employment background reference check. CONTRACTOR shall submit to CLIENT, within seven (7) days before the commencement of service or concurrent with assignment, a background investigation report for all personnel assigned to CLIENT under the terms of this agreement. The background investigation report will include, but not be limited to:

- Police Record Check
- Credit Check (if permissible)
- Confirmation of Previous Employment
- Verification of All Application Information.

The criminal history check as prescribed in this document is to be updated annually in the anniversary month of each year of the contract for all CONTRACTOR employees assigned to CLIENT. In the event a misdemeanor or felony conviction is discovered, CLIENT Corporate Security Department shall be informed immediately for consultation. CONTRACTOR shall institute requirements, which will obligate CONTRACTOR employees to "self report" interactions with Law Enforcement that results in arrests resulting in either misdemeanor or felony convictions.

A.8.37. Acknowledge that CLIENT reserves the right to fingerprint and photograph all personnel assigned under terms of this agreement. If CONTRACTOR receives an unsuitable report on any of CONTRACTOR'S employees subsequent to the commencement of service, the employee will not be allowed to continue work, or be assigned to work, under the terms of this agreement.

A.8.38. Provide CLIENT with a Letter of Affidavit on each person assigned to the account certifying that the individual has met all of the hiring and training requirements as set forth in this agreement.

A.8.39. Assure that all services, equipment or material furnished or utilized in the performance of services and quality of service provided by CONTRACTOR will be subject to inspection and testing by CLIENT without notice. Such inspections and testing will be conducted in a manner so as not to unduly interfere with CONTRACTOR'S ability to carry out the terms of this agreement.

Should CLIENT determine, as a result of these inspections and testing, that services and/or equipment or materials used by CONTRACTOR is not satisfactory, CLIENT shall inform CONTRACTOR in writing. CLIENT reserves the right to: (a) require CONTRACTOR to take immediate action to bring such matters into compliance with the terms of this agreement; and (b) impose monetary deductions in accordance with a schedule to be mutually agreed upon between CLIENT and CONTRACTOR prior to the initiation of this agreement.

A.8.40. Acknowledge that, should CONTRACTOR fail to take necessary measures to ensure conformity with the requirements of this agreement, CLIENT reserves the right to (a) procure or furnish services as required by CLIENT and charge CONTRACTOR any cost that is directly related to the performance of such services; or (b) terminate this agreement for default in accordance with the terms set forth in Article 2.2 governing Termination of Agreement.

A.8.41. Further acknowledge that, within 60 days of the initiation of this agreement, CONTRACTOR will develop a set of measurable performance objectives for CONTRACTOR'S employees. These objectives will be developed for each position assigned to this account. Personnel assigned to this account must satisfactorily complete each of the performance objectives to be eligible for an increase in base wages. Performance objectives will be evaluated on an annual basis and be responsible for 75% of any consideration for an increase in wages. The balance of the performance evaluation will be based upon the officer's compliance with general orders, absenteeism, personal bearing and professionalism.

A.8.42. Assure that each security person will receive an interim evaluation every 90 days, to be administered by CONTRACTOR. This evaluation will be a brief overview to allow the officers to know and understand the quality of their performance. A thorough review of performance will be conducted every 180 days.

A.8.43. Assure that CONTRACTOR employees will read, comprehend, and satisfy all training, certification, and vetting requirements set forth in this document and/or the attached Exhibits prior to assignment to any CLIENT site unless specifically permitted an exemption by CLIENT Corporate Security Department in this document or a formal letter.

With the prior approval of CLIENT Corporate Security Department, CONTRACTOR may temporarily assign CONTRACTOR Trainee Employees who have not satisfied the qualifications required of CONTRACTOR employees under this Agreement. Provided, however, that such temporary assignments shall be made only for the purpose of preparing CONTRACTOR Trainee Employees for regular assignments as CLIENT assigned employees. Or, such CONTRACTOR Trainee Employees are accompanied at all times by a certified CONTRACTOR Employee who satisfies all qualifications required under this Agreement. CLIENT shall not be charged for CONTRACTOR Trainee Employee services.

A.8.44. Require CONTRACTOR employees to comply with all CLIENT policies and procedures related to the personal conduct of individuals working at CLIENT.

A.8.45. Assure that no CONTRACTOR employee, including those serving the CONTRACTOR in a managerial capacity, or those controlling the CONTRACTOR through stock ownership or otherwise, will have been convicted of a felony or have been dishonorably discharged from any branch of the Armed Forces. Affidavits are required for each CONTRACTOR employee attesting to meeting this requirement as well as accomplishing background checks.

These 46 performance indicators have been developed to establish a set of client expectations for their third-party suppliers. These expectations set forth the criteria that will drive the operation day to day. Articles 6 and 7 are also closely related because they, too, define performance indicators; they deal with matters governing specific conduct and job responsibilities. Like the previous versions of the Model Contract, the aim here is to put the supplier on notice that standards of performance are expected. Failure to adhere to them places the relationship in jeopardy. Conversely, as covered by another article, adherence or performance beyond those subscribed standards can result in any number of financial and relationship-building incentives.

In short, the service agreement defines the union between client and supplier. Even though it falls short of a marriage license, there is a similarity in expectations. Both parties clearly know what is expected and how performance will be measured. It allows suppliers to assess whether or not this is a relationship they want to pursue. Likewise, it allows the client to state up-front what is needed to meet their expectations and needs. Another way of viewing this is to say that both agree to a set of metrics that is easily understood and fair.

The three examples in this chapter of a metrics-based approach serve a number of purposes. First, they illustrate that not all metrics have to be the same. For that matter, it is not the metric, per se, that is important, because this can change from one circumstance to another. Rather, it is the actual creation of a metric that is far more important, because its creation defines how performance is going to be measured. Second, each example serves to illustrate that metrics represent an attempt to introduce objectivity into the process. Metrics are not *bias bound*. In other words, one party cannot be held accountable by another without just cause. Metrics define relationships and expectations. They establish parameters among stakeholders. Finally, a metrics approach builds credibility. Senior executives and other key decision-makers can develop advocacy for a program when it represents measures they can relate to and support. Metrics set aside claims that the pursuit of one program over another is the result of someone's vested interest. In other words, success is achieved or fails based on measured results.

DEVELOPING CRITICAL BUY-IN

As we noted at the outset, developing a metrics-based set of criteria is the first step. Success comes when the critical buy-in on the part of the ultimate decision-makers is achieved. As we have seen in the looping model, critical buy-in occurs when the end-user is transformed into an advocate. To do so requires that the security manager meet and explain the rationale that supports the program designed for a particular application. This harkens back to our discussion of explaining the why's and wherefores of the security program.

But buy-in is more than this. Often the end-user has a misguided understanding of what is needed, or may not even know what is appropriate. Having deferred to security in the past, the end-user may have trusted security's expertise and not questioned the allocation of resources. But now, times have changed. Today it is common for a nonsecurity senior manager to ask some very tough questions. This is especially so when the same manager is being held accountable for the expenditure. Today it is common for local managers to pay for security within their local operating budgets. As more and more companies define local operations as standalone profit centers, there is a great deal of fiscal decision-making left to the discretion of the local on-site senior manager. For corporate security this means that the success of their program is critically linked to having this decision-maker understand and support the asset protection plan.

Critical buy-in goes much deeper than securing the support of the ultimate decision-maker. An organization is vulnerable if the rank and file do not fully support the aims of the security program as well. Obtaining critical buy-in requires that all employees understand the limits of a security program and are willing to accept ownership (responsibility) for certain asset protection requirements. My experience in dealing with hundreds of organizations of all sizes over the years has led me to one consistent observation: there appears to be a direct correlation between the size of the security organization and the general employee's sense of security ownership. In other words, the smaller the security organization, the more responsibility is demonstrated on the part of the average employee. Conversely, the larger the security organization, the less ownership is assumed by the average employee.

There appears to be a corollary to this phenomenon. The smaller the security organization, the fewer demands there are by the average employee, and more notably, unit managers. Conversely, the larger the security organization, the more common it is to hear, "Why should I be concerned about safety and asset protection? After all, isn't that why we have a security group?" When employees do not assume their share of the responsibility for protecting themselves, others, and company assets, there is a higher degree of risk.

Part of the buy-in also requires a realistic set of expectations and needs on the part of employees and their bosses. In *The Art* we discussed the concept of demand-side versus supplier-side allocations. Here you may recall that I noted: "trying to reduce or redefine internal user demands can be fraught with frustration and danger. Corporate politics, unrealistic demands, and fears of personal safety all fuel the emotionalism associated with cutting security services to a more realistic level. It is, therefore, easier for corporate managers to apply pressure on their suppliers to lower their charges than it is to force their employees to demand fewer services."

Unrealistic expectations drive up the cost of security, or can cause a dysfunctional allocation of limited resources. As the security management team tries to address these misguided or unreasonable expectations, they jeopardize their ability to effectively respond and manage other incidents. This creates a kink in the asset protection looping model and causes it to become vulnerable to criticisms, resulting in a loss of credibility. The next case study provides an example.

Situational Case Five: The "Need" for More Security Escorts

In downtown Oakland, California, there is a large complex referred to as Oakland City Center. The complex consists of several mixed-use high-rises and many smaller retail establishments. When the complex was first built the decision was made among the primary owners to have a consolidated security program supported by one dispatch center. Of the six owners, it was decided that they would pay their share based on total square footage. This allocation formula did not last very long, because some buildings had less square footage but higher tenant occupancies, thus requiring more security services. Chief among the security services was the end-of-the-business-day program of escorting employees to their vehicles or to one of many nearby bus stops. Like many urban centers, parking in remote lots was considerably less expensive; therefore the time to conduct one escort could take a considerable period of time.

The City Center was located in a high crime area. It was simply not safe for employees to walk to their vehicles, especially during hours of darkness. Consequently, there was a continuous battle between the various owners over the cost of this security service. Even though some attempts were made to compromise and have employees walk in groups, there was a constant struggle because most employees did not want to wait. Another attempted solution was to reassign more officers from other shifts to be available for escorts. This resulted in fewer officers to respond to incidents occurring at other times of the day and overtime cost increasing. The situation deteriorated to the point where several of the owners began exploring the possibility of breaking away from the consolidated program and forming their own security force.

Security suffered considerable loss of credibility because they could not offer a solution that worked well for everyone. Their customer demand was unrealistic for the level of available security resources. Although the need was there, the expectations were out of whack. The answer was found in shifting the view away from the escort service being primarily a security service, but rather as a transportation issue. Simply stated, employees needed to get from Point A (their place of work) to Point B (their vehicle or bus stop). When viewed from this perspective, security—or their safety—was seen more as a value-added benefit. Making it a transportation issue, also allowed security to return to the former staffing model on the other shifts and regain the needed balance.

The solution involved pooling the owners' resources and contracting with a third-party shuttle service that ferried people to and from locations, both in the morning and at night. For very early arrivers and those needing to work late, special arrangements could be made with security on an as-required basis.

This simple solution was missed by nearly everyone for the longest time because it was viewed as a security problem. Yet it was always doomed for failure because the escort service was a severe drain on security's resources. This, in turn, lead to frustration for everyone—business owners, security personnel, and the employees. Once critical buy-in was achieved in defining this more as a transportation issue than a security problem, the resolution was quickly identified.

If you don't know where you want to go, it doesn't matter how you get there.
Lewis Carroll

One caution about this: In deciding what is truly needed and what can be either shifted to another operating unit or discarded altogether, security managers need to be sensitive to the underlying politics associated with workplace violence perceptions. This is especially true since 9/11 and the ongoing continuance of enraged employees (or ex-employees) violently acting out their anger at the workplace. You may recall in *The Art* I wrote about one manager's reaction to a suggestion of reducing security coverage.

A large meeting of several corporate managers was assembled to discuss how the company could reduce their security costs without impacting the quality of service. Billed as a brainstorming session, managers representing various segments of the company were invited. Since security was a current "hot topic," the majority showed up to voice their input. As the meeting started, the manager for their largest retail segment began voicing her opinion, which centered on the need for more security.

The manager was quickly joined by a corporate attorney who talked about the dangers of reducing protection in view of recent decisions on premises liability. The lawyer discussed the issue in general terms, spending a great deal of time on the issue of workplace violence. She failed, though, to cite any one of the six recent case decisions that were pro-owner and reduced the conditions associated with an owner's duty and foreseeability regarding third-party injuries.

At the conclusion of the attorney's remarks, she was supported by the company's risk manager, who also monopolized the discussion with anecdotes about increased losses and rising premiums. Finally, the security manager joined the discussion and reinforced the necessity for increasing demand based on "history trends and rising crimes rates," even though that very morning's newspaper ran a feature article about the three-year downward trend in crime, especially in this company's industry.

After these "impromptu" presentations, the facility manager asked to have the floor to offer his observations. He was an external property manager and, coincidently, a lawyer. He began by informing the group of the recent court cases and reminded them about the decreasing crime rate. He went on to ask for specifics from the risk manager, only to be told that she would "have to research her sources." He explained that the meeting's purpose was to discuss possible ways to lower demand in light of the recent trends. When he finished, the retail manager pushed her chair back, stood up, and announced that she was leaving. She stated that she felt she had a "moral obligation" to increase security and would do so—with or without the group's approval. She then left, stating that she had no intentions of lessening security.

Set against the current concerns regarding workplace violence, internal customers want more, not less, security. This is often in direct conflict with executive management's mandate to reduce operating expense as part of their restructuring plan. User demand remains high until they are asked to pay for it out of their budget. This only escalates feelings of bitterness between opposing parties. Since most unit managers do not budget for security as a direct charge or are a cost center and cannot off-set the expense against revenues, they will balk and point accusing fingers at anyone who suggests a reduction in coverage, warning that resulting injuries and deaths will be their burden to carry.

The security manager should definitely attempt to bring balance to such a situation. The underlying point is that internal customer demands are very difficult to break down. That is because much of what is believed to be required is mixed with perceptions, emotions, and often an *entitlement philosophy*—they simply believe it is due them.

Demand-side requirements need to be worked out rationally. As a part of this rational approach to demand-side requirements, internal users need to break away from the traditional perspective of the "haves and have-nots." This is extremely difficult because it is deeply rooted into the very fabric of our society. This same concept drives how operating units function on a daily basis. One of the most important tools for success under this way of life is the concept of competition. As a psychiatrist friend of mine notes: "We are a society built on the warrior metaphor. To us everything—religion, education, business, government, even personal relationships—revolves around one side winning, the other losing."

We need to find ways to define what is essential to operating the business versus what would be nice to have. The answer begins by developing a strong and pragmatic sense of ownership. Here's a simple question business unit managers need to ask themselves when seeking allocations: "If I owned this company, would I spend the money?"

Rapid Deployment with a Strong Quality Assurance Component

It has been a long journey through the concept of building a sound security business plan that is metrics based. We began by exploring the very need for a metrics approach. We then ventured through the need for obtaining critical buy-in. Finally, we arrive at the need for rapid deployment with an ongoing quality assurance review. This last module is as important as the previous two. Once the plan and corresponding measures have been developed and people have bought in, they want to see results—and fast. Later we will explore Oren

Harari's 11 suggestions for effectively managing from the middle. One of his key factors is the ability to demonstrate results quickly and accurately. I think he would agree that a quality assurance (QA) component is required, provided it measures properly and generates results. QA, properly administered, is the manager's checkpoint for improvement. Without it, even the best intentions can fail.

We do not see things as they are. We see things as we are.

Talmud

To borrow from one of former Mobil Oil security manager George Murphy's maxims, rapid deployment means seizing the moment. There is little else that compares to a missed opportunity, especially when everyone is expecting action. As I noted earlier, people are motivated to action when they perceive that there is a problem and they want it fixed, or when they feel pain and are crying for immediate attention. They may believe that there is a potential gain for them and they, too, want to seize the moment. Regardless of their motivation, if it is there, it requires action sooner rather than later.

Rapid deployment must not be action for the sake of action, however. It must be deliberate, planned, and executed properly. This is where true leadership enters and separates those managers who might be technically proficient from those who can rally widespread support and advocacy. In *The Art* I referred to this as pursuing *envisioned leadership*. The envisioned leader has the ability to look over the horizon and see what is there without actually having been there. Armed with the vision, the manager is capable of aligning the necessary resources, defining the measures, and acting decisively.

Situational Case Six: The Procrastinator

Many managers engage in what we might term as *analysis paralysis*, or the inability to arrive at a decision and act on it. I recall one security director who assumed the mantle of her first directorship. She wanted to be seen as a success and went about politicking her senior managers for the need to develop a business plan for the upcoming fiscal year that was performance based. They agreed and bought in on the need. Knowing that she was new to the organization and her position, they were willing to give her what they believed was a reasonable lead time to put her plan in place and execute it.

She hired a business plan consultant, and together they agreed on a strategy involving her management team and several other key individuals. Originally, they thought the plan could be worked out in a matter of weeks. But time dragged and the weeks turned into months. After six months she had in hand what she believed to be the final version of her plan. She set a date to present her plan to senior management. They quickly agreed to the meeting date, many grumbling that it was long overdue. A few days before the meeting she wanted to "tweak it a bit" and postponed the presentation. Days once again dragged into weeks. Finally the presentation date arrived, the meeting took place, and everyone agreed that it was a fine strategy and endorsed its immediate implementation.

Unfortunately for her, she did not have the staff capability to execute the plan. Some staff members needed additional training, and others were simply unqualified. She needed time to jump start her team, so she returned to her boss. He had made commitments to his senior group and was caught by surprise when she advised that implementation would be more than four months off. He could not allow the delay, and pushed her to implement at least some aspect of the plan. He pleaded, "Show them something, anything! We can't put them off any longer. They need to see action." Reluctantly she agreed, and pushed her staff to launch even the least of what the plan called for in terms of deliverables.

Her staff wanted to perform, but lacking the necessary skill sets, they couldn't even manage delivery of the minimum. Loyal to her staff, she held off on acting, and again days turned to weeks. Finally, she received an unexpected visit from her boss. He demanded to know what the hold-up was. She tried to explain, but he was not of a mindset to listen to her explanation. The meeting ended in disaster. She lost her credibility, and the urgency that everyone felt at the outset was gone. By the time she was ready to deploy, she heard the one expression no manager wants to ever hear: "Sorry—too little too late." A few months later I received an e-mail from her asking if I knew of any job openings.

> You can't build your reputation on what you are going to do.
>
> *Henry Ford*

As I write this situational case I can think of dozens and dozens of similar episodes. Many managers expend a great deal of energy planning and politicking, but fail to execute in a timely manner. In some respects this has never been proven better than in the aftermath of 9/11. As I write this, more than 17 months have passed from that day. Beyond the call for immediate interim steps, I know of only a handful of security managers who have completed their long-term strategy and begun implementing it. Sadly, most have missed the opportunity— most have failed to seize the moment. It is no wonder that many of the Fortune 500 companies who once "committed" dollars to upgrade their security programs after 9/11 have withdrawn their support. Although it is easy to blame this retrenchment on the recessionary woes that followed the WTC destruction, I am left wondering if this is not a red herring for some security managers. Rather, the truth lies somewhere between corporate executives' reluctance to commit and the security manager's inability to execute rapidly.

I remember asking Mike Farmer at Exxon-Mobil what he thought was a major contributing factor to his success. He reflected on this a moment and then said, "Den, more than anything, my team delivers. We deliver on the big stuff and we deliver on the small stuff. We build our credibility based on the motto that we are the 'can do' team. People come to us because they know we will get the job done—quickly and accurately, and with discretion." These are powerful words that demonstrate recognition of the importance of being able to deploy rapidly.

Mike's former boss, George Murphy, had another phrase, which you may recall from *The Art*: "man on the way." Mike not only followed this advice, but pushed it hard among his own team. The phrase simply means that as soon as something happened, no matter the time of day or location in the world, there was a security representative en route, and with the promise that the representative would be there within 24 hours. This gave security 24 hours to meet and devise a response, so that when the representative arrived he or she knew that a plan had been worked out and was ready to execute.

The Need for a Truly Effective QA Component

Yet, as we noted in our discussion of the looping model, response is only half the measure of success. There is also the need to properly manage the incident. This is where an effective QA program comes into play. Over the years there has been a great deal written about quality assurance plans. Entire schools of management thought have come and gone, not the least of which was total quality management (TQM) and its second cousin, continuous quality improvement (CQI). Each has had its beneficial components; however, they have also had their downsides.

In the late 1990s, the American Management Association published a book by James R. Lucas entitled *Fatal Illusions: Shredding a Dozen Unrealities That Can Keep Your Organization From Success*. In addressing the issue of quality, Lucas observes that organizations have fallen victim to what he refers to as the *quality illusion*. He notes that managers mistakenly believe that customers always know what they want. A second illusion is that managers assume everyone in their organization knows what quality is. He goes on to note that these two illusions are fed by other illusions. He observes:

We believe that on any given problem, we have to get all possible information before deciding (we can't), or, conversely, that we don't need all possible information before deciding (we must try).

We believe that mistakes are bad and convey the idea to people around us by conducting witch-hunts, crucifying those who make mistakes, fixing the blame rather than the problem, and even shooting the messengers. Except for those with malice or repetitive hard-headedness, mistakes aren't bad; they're opportunities to grow and improve and hone. One measure of organizational quality is how little (or how much) time and energy are spent generating defenses, creating "cover ourselves" paper trails, and reinterpreting reality to point organizational fingers in a different direction.

We can believe that complexity and sophistication are symbolic of world-class operations, while the reality is that these are often the things that drive up costs, extend lead times, compound and disguise problems, and color everything with a gray haze of confusion. Few things can mislead us as effectively as the illusion of quality and success that impressive and costly systems can project.

The whole idea of measurement provides fertile ground for illusions. In one sense, the management dictum "If I don't measure it, I can't manage it" is true. But we can deceive ourselves at the extremes. We can believe that if we can measure something it must be important, giving us a feeling of control, when the reality is that we can measure hundreds of things that are easy to measure and worthless to report. On the other end, we can convince ourselves that if we can't measure something (at least easily), it must not be important, leading to a sense of smugness, when what we're not attempting to measure can be necessary for the organization's survival.

Even if we get past the smugness, we can still end up believing that we can measure more difficult or nonrational factors in the same way as the easily measured or rational ones. The reality is that all of these success criteria must be measured and managed, but in different ways. Rational factors are measured by numbers and charts and graphs. Nonrational factors are measured by dialogue and intuition and instinct. All important things can be measured—and must be.

Even if we pick the right things to measure, we can measure them the wrong end or with the wrong perspective. Many measurements are of inputs (what we are doing) rather than of outputs (the results that our customers want). Organizations caught up in their illusions usually focus on inputs, methods, and processes rather than on outputs, possibilities, and results.

Perhaps one of the biggest illusions in the quality movement is that we can and should measure quality from a negative perspective: number of defects, number of errors, number of customer complaints. But the essence of quality is that it is a positive outcome. Only massive illusion can cause us to believe that we can measure a positive criterion in a negative way and at the same time inspire a passion for positive outcomes in our organizations.

Lucas gives us a blueprint that is vital to our success, a blueprint that is typically missed by even the best of the so-called quality gurus. Entire corporations have been duped over the years into a position of requiring their unit managers, including security, to pursue quality based on all the wrong assumptions. In *The Art* I demonstrated how even the best intentioned can be sucked into the deep well of absurd quality pursuits. You may recall my discussion of one company's quality program that I termed the "alphabet soup of QA." Their program was commonly referred to as TQRDCE, with each letter standing for some supposed component that measured quality (e.g., from *T* for technology to *E* for environment). Each component was represented by a checklist of measures that were, in turn, rated on a scale of 0 to 4, representing "consistently failing to meet expectations" to "consistently exceeding expectations." Was the end result the measurement of quality? Far from it. Rather, it was an exercise (an expensive one at that) in futility. Suppliers could not measure up. Nor, for that matter, could internal units. The company put all of its effort on process and loss sight of the very thing it wanted to achieve. Tragically, this company is but one example of hundreds of organizations that were likewise duped by "quality experts."

This obsession with numeric measures is not only distracting, but also demoralizing. As Lucas notes, quality is more about attitude than it is about being a system or process. He goes on to make the point that quality is a way of life, the result of an intelligent effort. How does this tie into our claim that a successful security program requires an element of quality assurance?

Note that Lucas agrees that all important things can be measured. For emphasis he adds "and must be." To know that we are still on the right track, QA—as an intelligent process—can be a beacon in an otherwise murky organizational environment. To do so requires that we begin by overcoming entropy, relying on statistical measures that only add confusion and misguide our best intentions. We need to recognize that conventional measuring of all component parts does not reveal much in support of pursuing quality. Rather, the truer measure of success comes by focusing on what is really important to our delivery system or actual deliverable.

For security departments, this means the ability to assess the degree of risk and the development of strategies based on sound business practices. It means casting aside measuring how many doors are found open or the number of coffee pots left on after everyone has gone home. Assuring that doors are locked and that coffee pots are not left on is important from an operational perspective, but they are no measure of the quality of security's ultimate deliverable. As Lucas points out: "Ask our people to list the worthless or low-payoff measurements. After we have ferreted out the real time wasters, we can take what is left and ask employees to prioritize them on the basis of their usefulness in achieving results."

True QA involves learning how to measure the unmeasurable, or at least the difficult-to-measure. This most often requires collaboration with resident staff, suppliers, and the end-user. It requires hard thinking and thinking out-of-the-box. The truer measures for a security program may well focus on the number of mistakes that were saved by security's intervention, the number of new ideas or approaches generated for end-users, the number of unnecessary supplier specifications or purchases avoided. These measures are significantly different from the conventional security statistics (cases opened/closed, parking tickets issued, etc.).

When QA becomes an ingrained part of the organization's culture, the need for statistical measures involving customer complaints or the number of overtime hours reduced melts away. People are judged on their contribution and not on whether or not they clocked so many hours in one week. In *Business Strategies* I told you about my experience at Le Meridien Hotel in Boston. I was so impressed by the way I was treated over many stays that I commented to the manager that it must take a considerable investment in time and money to train the staff to perform at such a high level of customer service continuously. I was more than surprised when he informed me that no money was spent on special training programs. Rather, providing quality service was an integral part of the organization's culture. It just came naturally because staff members took pride in what they were doing.

For the hotel there was no need to send out customer feedback forms. There was no need to hire expensive consultants to measure adherence to inputs or what others have deemed the indicators of a world-class operation. The hotel was in tune with what it takes to ensure high customer satisfaction. They measured the quality of their output daily. They knew when they were on track or off. Customer complaints were few and far between because the staff was fully aware of what was required of them, and they met the challenge. For the manager, QA measuring was more a task of watching, listening, and staying actively involved with his staff.

CONCLUDING COMMENTS

We covered a great deal of ground in this chapter. First, we discovered the value of pursuing a metrics-based approach. This is more than creating statistical measures. It encompasses the establishment of criteria that are business based. It demonstrates that strategies are fact based rather than opinion or assumption based. Within the framework of this analysis we saw that the initial base rests on a concept first developed in Chapter 1—the establishment of a risk assessment tool. This was followed by the integration of a staffing model that centers on a rational approach to allocation and deployment. Next we read about one consultant's approach to creating a measured baseline for security devices and systems. Finally, we reviewed an extract from the latest revision of my model services agreement. Together these three represented how a metrics approach can be applied to each of the fundamental components of a comprehensive asset protection program: staffing, state-of-the-art technology, and operating practices.

We saw that success is also incumbent on the manager's ability to establish critical buy-in by the end-user. This buy-in not only establishes advocacy but also minimizes unnecessary user demands and expectations. Before moving on, however, I want to note one word of caution. Security managers need to recognize that some issues, especially those that focus on workplace violence prevention need to be addressed carefully. Because this is a highly volatile human relations issue, especially in a world after 9/11, security directors need to walk a very thin line between pushing for allocations that are in the best interest of the organization and pulling back those that are more emotionally based.

Finally, we examined the need for rapidly deploying your program once it has been developed and obtained the necessary buy-ins. We also saw the need for developing a continuing quality assurance element—one that is not typically modeled after the failed efforts of Total Quality Management, which were so popular a few years ago. We saw that rapid deployment means "seizing the moment," because security is an organizational factor that rarely maintains the sustained interest of executives and the general rank and file.

When it is all said and done, I leave you with this simple challenge: If you want your program to be successful (e.g., readily accepted and its value appreciated) you need to sit face-to-face with the critical decision-makers and make sure they understand what you are doing—and why. It sounds obvious, almost simplistic, but so few security directors do this. We fail to see the importance of creating advocacy and ownership until it is too late.

Luck is the residue of design.

Vince Lombardi

Thought-Provoking Questions

1. For many security managers metrics-based performance has a negative connotation. After reading the three examples provided in this chapter, can you see how such an approach can work for an organization? Do you believe that each has an application for you based on your experience?

2. Thus far we have taken many steps in our journey toward achieving organizational success. These include identifying your risk level, defining which security program is most appropriate to respond to your threat(s), identifying the skill sets necessary for the team's leader, understanding the barriers that are in the way, and adopting a metrics-based approach. Are there others that you believe are necessary?

3. Can a statistically driven staffing model really work, or is it so antiseptic that it misses the nuances of the organization and can result in allocation and deployment of staffing that fails to meet the intents of security?

4. We reviewed what James Lucas had to say about the illusion of quality assurance and offered the notion that even though QA is an important management tool, it must be approached in a manner that is not input driven and based on negative-based criteria. What do you think? Does his approach make sense? What is the downside of his position?

Chapter 6

MOVING TO AN ERA OF TOTAL ASSET PROTECTION

Following in the light of the sun, we left the Old World.
Christopher Columbus

Primary Themes

- Global Security: The New Frontier and the Era of Total Asset Protection
- Business Risk Analysis
- Human Resource Security
- Global Operations Support

OPENING OBSERVATIONS

Early on we explored the evolution of private security. We noted that most security departments are somewhere between the physical security era and the corporate security era. This means that they are still managing uniformed security services, either directly or indirectly. Other common denominators include:

- **Developing employee awareness programs**, including a new hire orientation module on security related matters
- **Investigating a variety of corporate and criminal violations**, within certain parameters (e.g., drug violations, thefts below a certain value or organizational level, security related company policies)
- **Managing an executive protection program**, generally limited to travel advisories, providing or arranging protection for corporate VIPs and visiting dignitaries, residential alarm consultation and monitoring, and the executive driver program

- **Overseeing security for special events**, including such events as the annual shareholders' meeting, board of directors' meetings, new product announcements, and company employee get-togethers
- **Managing the organization's access control program**, which can include issuance and tracking of mechanical keys, developing electronic access levels and inputting or extracting card holders, and managing the photo identification card program; other components include visitor and contractor registration
- **Managing the organization's parking program**, the issuance of parking permits, writing citations, and providing employee escorts after hours
- **Working with corporate engineering on technology designs and applications** is generally limited to recommending particular devices and their locations.
- **Creating corporate policies related to security practices and procedures** can range from fire-life safety policies to listing security-related employee do's and don'ts.

Others, especially those within the corporate security era, may be involved in collaborating with their data security counterparts on information protection policies and programs. Additionally, they may be part of a workplace violence protection taskforce. For still others, their scope of responsibility may extend to applying any number of the above to their company's non–United States operations.

Even though this list is not intended to be all encompassing, it does represent the majority of security duties. On first glance such a delineation of accountability may appear to be impressive, and it is. Certainly today's security management teams are responsible for a wide variety of protections. Those who have achieved this level of responsibility should take pride in their contribution. The measure of success is not in what added duties one can assume, for adding more increases the opportunity for failure. As Theodore Roosevelt once advised, "Do what you can, with what you have, where you are."

I frequently receive telephone calls from frustrated security managers who believe their organizational role is inadequate. Some may have reached that point in their career where moving on is a logical conclusion. This is important to note because career development may mean seeking other opportunities. There are few things more frustrating than to be seen as having limited value for your organization; all too often senior managers and corporate executives fail to see that their security director, or the department as a whole, has the ability to make far more of a contribution than they have been allowed to make.

I think one of the best illustrations of this limited perspective can be seen in the assignment of managerial grade for a security manager. For those in the physical security and corporate security eras, theirs is always a struggle to be seen as a viable candidate for other company positions. I have asked many HR managers or other business unit heads if they would ever consider their security director for something other than security. It never ceases to amaze me when they stop to think about it for a moment and reply, "Well, I guess I never considered the security manager. You know, security is such an area of specialty and I guess I never pictured the manager doing much else but security."

Some organizations do not have such a limiting perspective, and security managers in those organizations have indeed seen their scope change. They have ventured into many non-security-related areas, ranging from overseeing facilities management to a host of other infrastructure units. Others have stepped entirely away from security, moving into completely unrelated fields. For example, in the financial services sector alone, I recall Randy Brock at Fidelity Investment Services, Mike Foyle at Mellon Bank, and Joe Magennis, before he retired from what was then Bank of Boston, now Fleet/Boston. These three individuals not only demonstrated management prowess beyond protecting corporate assets, but also worked for organizations that believed in developing talent from within, regardless of the professional sector assigned to them.

Some security managers' companies have moved to a higher corporate ground and require completely new answers to their business plans. These are the ones that have evolved to what I refer to as the *era of total asset protection*. That is the focus of this chapter. Here we explore what lies ahead for today's security management team. Some, as I have noted, have already begun to move into this era; others are only beginning to take it under advisement. Regardless, from where I sit, I see a new watershed forming, and it is exciting.

A few years ago I was asked to address a meeting of the security profession's Certified Protection Professionals. The meeting was held in conjunction with the annual meeting of the American Society for Industrial Security, security's largest professional association. I am not sure how many were actually in attendance, but the event sponsors put the number well in excess of 500. At this meeting I set forth a vision about what tomorrow's security department would look like. This vision was based on much of the work I was doing at that time. This work continues today and much of the vision is now a reality among a handful of corporations. In time, I truly believe the number will significantly multiply. It has too, if for no other reason than because this is the direction corporate America is moving.

Before examining this new frontier in detail, I want to revisit a position that I strongly took in Part I. For those who have either entered this new era or those at the very edge, I still believe that the events of 9/11 represented a major setback. Today there is a new emphasis placed on the need to protect people and physical assets. Such an emphasis, in many regards, is well warranted. Yet the tragedy of 9/11, as I pointed out earlier, is only one of many threats that face today's corporate world. I hope that this setback is temporary and that the trend will reverse itself once again as executives come to realize that protecting assets in a world of global e-commerce means far more than protecting bricks and mortar on the home front.

I know that the turnaround will come. After all, that is the very nature of an evolutionary process. My fear is that those who have ventured to a newer and higher level of corporate contribution will become disenfranchised at being called back to a former era of responsibility. As one Fortune 50 security director noted: "Since the WTC attack my role has been reversed considerably. I'm not a happy camper because I've been there and done that." This sentiment, I suspect, runs deep among the handful of others having experienced the same. What is perhaps most troubling is the fact that in assuming this role reversal, the security management team is being asked to turn its back on other known, and highly probable, serious threats.

I have asked my business management students over the past four years to identify what they believe to be the corporation's most valued asset. As you might guess, almost all of them respond by saying that is the human element—employees. Some will offer that a company's most valued asset is its customer base. I believe that the latter group is headed in the right direction, but they have not quite hit the nail on the head. Employees are certainly valuable, but they are not a corporation's most valued asset. Employees need to be treated with respect and reflected as a critical resource, but are they the most valued?

Allow me to suggest that in terms of the survivability of a corporation, the most valued asset is the company's intellectual property, that which positions them in the marketplace and allows them to remain competitive. Employees serve as the catalyst for assuring that this asset—intellectual property—is developed, used, and protected. IP, as it is commonly referred to, defines the organization's ability to stay profitable. Only with profitability comes the assurance of continuity, which translates directly into job security. Without profitability, as we have seen over and over of late, there are no jobs, which is another way of saying there are no employees—or at least far fewer than before.

Employees, including the most senior executives, are replaceable. This does not mean that they are not important, and perhaps even critical. But everyone is replaceable. Larry Ellison, the founder of Oracle, was once asked about his company's succession plan. He was being criticized for not taking the lead to clearly articulate who his successors should be. His answer took the analyst community by surprise when he said, "Does it really matter what I say or who I want? I'll be dead and the company will continue to move forward." Some thought this to be flip and irresponsible. I do not see it that way. I believe this showed keen insight. Ellison understands that companies go forward or perish for a number of reasons and not just because a key player is no longer present.

As you will see in the pages that follow, security's role is not to abandon the protection of people and tangible assets. These responsibilities remain—some under security's direct control, others under their strong influence. The new paradigm is one that calls for security to expand its role in two ways. First, security should collaborate with others in providing protection advice and direction in new ways involving their traditional areas of responsibilities. For example, a number of my clients have voiced concerns for protecting their assets and people within leased spaces. Their primary focus is typically centered on developing a program within their leased area. They are likewise concerned about the common area (hallways, lobbies, etc.), but believe they have little control over the landlord's area of responsibility. This is not necessarily so. For a program that is *total asset protection* oriented, the security management team has worked with the internal corporate real estate people to develop landlord requirements that must be met before the lease is signed, or concessions are specified that will allow their company to make the necessary changes to common areas with an offset to the negotiated lease rate. In other words, security's role has been expanded to collaboration with another business partner in assuring that people and assets are protected at the front end of the owner–tenant relationship instead of being limited to the terms and conditions of a conventional lease.

Second, the expanded security role involves new areas of responsibility altogether. We will cover some of these areas in greater depth shortly. For our purposes here, however, suffice it to say that a total asset protection oriented program is actively involved in matters of safeguarding intellectual property, competitive intelligence, and other business activities that require protection.

> *Every morning in Africa a gazelle wakes up. It knows it must outrun the fastest lion or it will be killed. Every morning in Africa a lion wakes up. It knows it must run faster than the slowest gazelle or it will starve. It doesn't matter whether you're a lion or a gazelle—when the sun comes up, you'd better be running.*
>
> *Richard M. Hodgetts*

GLOBAL SECURITY: THE NEW FRONTIER AND THE ERA OF TOTAL ASSET PROTECTION

Hodgetts is right. In today's world of turbulent business times and uncertain economic conditions, we must all learn to be runners—the faster the better. When I first began my corporate career, a trip overseas was the exception to the rule. Only a handful of employees were seen as international travelers on behalf of their company. For most organizations, even among the Fortune 1000, global business was but a fraction of their portfolio. That was less than 25 years ago. Today, even the smallest company is likely to be global in scope. Certainly the Internet has been a major contributor, but far from the only one. Chico, California, is about two hours north of Sacramento in the heart of the state's central valley. Their airport is classified as an international trade zone because of the number of small businesses that operate across the world from Chico. There are many Chico's across the United States.

To be competitive and stay profitable, companies of all sizes know that they must run, and run hard. Their very livelihood is dependent on delivery of services and goods to foreign ports of call. These have to be protected. Without a protection program they become targets of theft, sabotage, and other forms of loss. Some losses are the result of state-supported underwriting. For the past decade the FBI has testified before Congress that some of America's strongest allies are also some of American businesses largest thieves. But not all thieves are foreign nationals; some American businesses are not above stealing or destroying valued assets of their competitors.

And then there are events that are unplanned. Some are the result of natural disasters and others are the result of economic or political strife in various parts of the world. Such unplanned events can mean the loss of an American asset in the host country. American corporations have lost billions of dollars since the end of World War II to countries that have "repatriated" their resources by taking over American business interests. Energy companies have had their oil production facilities taken from them, hotel chains have lost large resort properties, and financial services have seen loan guarantees withdrawn as a result of coups or changes in a country's political system. How does one protect against these losses?

What follows is a model for your consideration. As a model, there may well be variations when it is applied to the real world of asset protection. This new paradigm consists of three primary pillars: business risk analysis, human resource security, and global operational support. Among those companies that have moved into this new era of asset protection, some have chosen to call these three units by other names. The name is not as important as the scope of responsibility. I might quickly add that not everyone has aligned the three units in exactly the manner I will be discussing. Again, alignment is also a matter of individual preference. The critical variable is that the accountabilities are reflected as part of this new organization.

The following lists briefly outline each area of functional responsibility.

Business Risk Analysis

- Current business risks
- New partner, product, and market due diligence
- Major fraud investigations
- Data security investigations
- Strategic fraud prevention
- Special request inquiries
- Competitive intelligence protection
- Intellectual property protection

- E-commerce threat management
- Geopolitical business profiling

This list of functional responsibilities reflects a professional role within the corporation that extends well beyond the traditional duty to undertake reactive investigations. It illustrates how security has integrated itself into the very mainstream of the company's business. It demonstrates that value comes in a variety of deliverables, ranging from participation in market-driven decisions to crossing organizational lines and partnering with those responsible for data security. It underscores security's value as a resource for others.

Human Resource Security

- Strategic partner qualification
- Security awareness and ownership
- International HR security
- New hire qualifications and orientations
- Executive protection
- Workplace violence prevention
- Ethical business practices

Human resources involves more than issues pertaining to resident staff. It encompasses the continuum of issues associated with the "people" side of the business. This includes both proprietary employees and the company's strategic partners. This is particularly important in today's dynamic business environment as companies continue to rely heavily on external providers. It also reflects two fairly new direct contributions: participation in the development of comprehensive programs aimed at workplace violence prevention, and ethical business practices. This means more than the development of policy statements for both. Rather, it reflects the commitment of resources, strongly advocated by the organization's executive tier.

Global Operations Support

- Corporate policy development
- Security standards and guidelines
- Uniformed security services
- Site compliance and quality assurance
- Systems design and research
- Special projects management
- Special events management

Security's role is rounded out through active involvement in supporting the company's enterprises, regardless of their global location. This area of concentration begins with developing corporatewide security-related policies, standards, and guidelines to be followed by business units. It is enhanced through security's direct responsibility for conducting QA reviews and working with "the field" in assuring proper systems design and applications. Like their counterparts of the corporate security era, they too oversee or provide support for a variety of special events such as director and shareholder meetings, companywide employee meetings, and new product introductions.

As noted in our initial discussion on selecting the right program to meet your corporation's asset protection requirements, staffing is limited to a small cadre of professionals and managers. Security's role is largely advisory, with a couple of noted exceptions in each category. For example, the investigative functions, executive protection, and systems design and research require the specific talents of dedicated security professionals. The delivery service system is based on collaboration. Global security need not necessarily have direct control over some of the areas delineated in the list, let alone ownership of the final products. Rather, global security becomes the catalyst for the organization to address issues and resolve them in a manner that reflects the best interests of all stakeholders.

Earlier I laid out the criteria for what I believe are the necessary business and technical skill sets to be a successful security executive in today's business world. Much of the same business acumen is necessary for an individual to assume the mantle of managing any one of the three units detailed in the following sections. Meeting the challenges of today requires more. No longer can a unit manager simply rely on expertise gained through academic pursuits or "putting one's time in." As Lohr, the outsider, accurately observes: "The job calls for a new kind of corporate security executive—one with breadth of experience, analytical skills, business acumen and leadership skills." But he does not end there. He adds: "The elusive ideal is an executive not only familiar with the physical security of people and property, but also fluent in the digital security of computers and information—roughly equal parts top cop, business manager and computer geek."

For years, many of us within the profession have been professing these concepts. I find it refreshing to read a nonsecurity writer parroting these ideas in an internationally recognized medium such as the *New York Times*. Such breakthroughs suggest that a crack in the wall of corporate indifference to security's role is beginning to emerge.

Lest we go wild with excitement, the road ahead is still fraught with many large potholes. One of the first to be encountered on the road to a new order of corporate recognition is understanding what security management teams purport to serve. A security staff may want to better serve their internal clients with a responsive set of deliverables, but lacking the necessary skill sets not only limits their capabilities but also sets them up for failure. Today's business executives demand experts who know how to quickly assess the causes of control variables and transform deficiencies into pragmatic solutions. They demand an investigative capability that can identify culpability and both build a case that will hold parties accountable and offer policy or procedural changes that mitigate the likelihood of future similar events. Can today's security team measure up to such expectations? As many security managers have discovered, current staff capability is often found wanting. What is the resolution? The answer is simple: either retool those on staff or replace them with those who can provide the needed abilities. To answer this dilemma, we need to first understand the elements of each component. Only then can the appropriate management decision be made.

Following are brief descriptions of each area of responsibility. Since this is a general management text, my purpose is to simply identify the components and explain how they are integrated into the whole of global security. A detailed examination of each, complete with examples drawn from the business world, would be served well as a separate text. For now, my purpose is to explain how the three pillars interrelate and the primary focus of each.

BUSINESS RISK ANALYSIS (BRA)

A global security unit does not necessarily address each of the following. Some incorporate many, and some incorporate only a few. Some involve areas that are not delineated here. But the purpose remains constant; there is a small cadre of individuals dedicated to assessing the organization's asset protection risk. The unit is headed by a manager. The risk analysis has a very specific focus and does not compete with other business units because the global security team concentrates on those aspects that can result in direct loss arising out of fraudulent practices or associations. The analysis can lead directly to a recommendation that the organization pursue legal remedies, whether they are criminal or civil in nature, or both.

Current Business Risks

An organization faces a number of risks. We saw earlier how one company developed a risk assessment for its properties and how such a model could be modified for use by any number of other corporations and public organizations. Current business risks might involve existing partners, products, or environments. For a global organization there is a need to continuously monitor foreign locations. Economic and political instability can change rapidly. Protectionist legislation can alter or threaten stable relationships. Much can be said on the domestic front, as well. Special interest groups such as animal rights organizations, environmental extremists, and labor unions can target, almost overnight, unsuspecting organizations.

One of the country's largest consumer product companies retained my services to assist them in developing a security program designed to protect their intellectual property. As a part of this analysis I discovered that a common practice for them was to hire nonemployee workers through a third-party temporary agency. Under the contract there was no provision for the temporary agency to screen those they assigned to my client. Nor was there a requirement to have the employees/agents sign a nondisclosure agreement. I also learned that this practice was commonly known within the industry. The temporary employees were typically assigned to the company's R&D facilities.

Shortly after beginning my engagement with them, I was informed that they had recently hired a security firm that specialized in the collection of competitive information. A few weeks later I was called into the office of the senior vice president for operations. He was extremely upset and informed me that the security firm had reported that instead of gathering information on his company's competitors, the security specialists learned that sensitive information regarding my client's soon-to-be released new blockbuster product was in the hands of their two major competitors. Moreover, one competitor had a significant lead on my client and would be introducing its version of the product weeks ahead of my client. It did not take long to discover the source of the leak. A simple risk analysis would probably have found this hole in their R&D process and remedied the situation before experiencing a loss.

New Partner, Product, and Market Due Diligence

Senior executives can redefine their market direction and open the company to unforeseen exposures. One large full-service financial institution recently shifted its focus from serving multibillion-dollar clients to serving midsized organizations with annual sales not exceeding $500 million. This meant suddenly seeking relationships with business owners and investors who were operating in a world where required disclosures are not the norm. Such new customers represented an inherent risk simply because their principals were largely unknown.

Likewise, when a company shifts markets and moves into uncharted territory, risks are bound to arise. Size of the potential new partnership or marketplace is not always an indicator that more or less risk is present. At the height of America's merger mania in the 1990s many Fortune 200 companies experienced the sting of inadequate due diligence. An effective global security program can actively participate by tapping into its own network to determine if prospective partners are legitimate or new markets are as stable as both may appear to be.

Major Fraud Investigations

The American stock market was rocked hard by the Enron disclosures and subsequent charges of wrongdoing by not only Arthur Anderson, but also by many other large companies and their respective accounting firm relationships. What differentiates a global security unit's investigative prowess from others is its ability to manage such large-scale frauds or other wrongdoings. Rather than focusing on infractions of significantly lesser value, this unit's responsibility is to concentrate on risks associated with internal or external threats that jeopardize the very existence of the company.

Less dramatically, a major fraud unit also concentrates on threats that could prove particularly embarrassing to the company or cause it to lose market share from a loss of customer confidence. Consumer product companies are highly sensitive to the issue of product contamination. Executive malfeasance can also be damaging, as with Tyco, whose chairman resigned in late spring of 2002 under a cloud of sales tax evasion. Many large corporations have felt the sting of an executive who converted corporate assets to personal use.

Data Security Investigations

Data security specialists typically rise through the ranks of computer technology. Although they are adroit at creating firewalls and platforms that can readily identify viruses and track hackers, rarely do they have the ability to investigate breaches that can lead to criminal prosecution. It is also not unusual for them to lack the ability to identify the actual wrongdoer. As we become more e-commerce oriented, such a risk only spells greater danger to a company, especially a company that is globally positioned.

The Computer Security Institute/FBI computer crime survey, conducted in 2000, reported that losses totaled more than $265 million among respondents. This was up from $123 million in 1999. They also reported that loss resulting from cybercrime sabotage approached $30 million in 2000, compared to approximately $10 million in 1999. Similarly, computer-related financial fraud rose from $40 million in 1999 to $55 million in 2000. Finally, Netspionage exceeded $65 million in 2000, compared to approximately $42 million the previous year. This level of data security threat warrants a corporate resource capable of investigating such losses with the clear intent to criminally prosecute. Global security can demonstrate significant added value if properly equipped.

Strategic Fraud Prevention

Many corporate executives do not want to wait until they have been victimized before combating losses. Consequently, several corporations have begun developing fraud prevention models designed to identify risks up front. Companies such as Fifth Third Bank of Cincinnati and Fidelity Investments have been working on programs that allow global security to monitor inappropriate employee activities based on a number of indicators. Their aim is to quickly identify suspicious activity such as account transfers that are not immediately preceded by customer requests. Such activity-based profiling alerts global security that behavior patterns are present that typically lead to a loss. This allows security, in turn, to track other indicators and enables them to shut down a potential loss while identifying culpability.

Strategic fraud prevention is key to the security department's success at being viewed as a contributor to mainstream business operations. It shifts the security function from being primarily a reactive support function to a critical front-end resource. Effective prevention models can be used as a marketing capability for companies and as another arrow in management's risk insurance quiver.

Special Request Inquiries

Special request inquiries can take on any number of forms and issues. The important point is that global security has a demonstrated capability to handle them—or at least knows where to find the appropriate resource. These inquiries may involve a confidential investigation of suspected wrongdoing on the part of a strategic partner or one of its principals. They may involve a discreet inquiry into the financial affairs of a corporate officer with fiduciary responsibilities. They may involve inquiries into safe houses for international travelers establishing legitimate business enterprises in an unstable environment. The list can go on as long as the imagination allows. Each inquiry varies based on the times, the need, and the particular circumstances that can affect the organization's business operations.

Competitive Intelligence Protection

This is an area of expertise that requires a double-edged approach. On the one hand, the company may be interested in ethically and legally obtaining information on one or more of its competitors. On the other hand, it may require skill sets for deflecting inquiries from one's competitors. Many large organizations have established specific units for the former, usually as a part of their marketing or R&D units. Global security's role may be that of a collaborative partner assisting other business units in gathering key information from their established networks. Global security can take on a more direct role by developing awareness and ownership programs for employees, designed to sensitize employees to the ways in which critical information is lost—both inadvertently and through deliberate deception.

Under the leadership of CapitalOne's former security director, Mike Arrighi, their security management team developed a program entitled *InfoLock*. This multidimensional program consisted of a number of initiatives ranging from simple placards placed atop each conference table warning that "loose lips sink ships," to contests that test an employee's knowledge of company policies regarding the protection of sensitive information.

Intellectual Property Protection

Just as global security can have a direct role in the protection of competitive intelligence, it can also play an active role in the protection of the organization's intellectual property. Many believe that IP is limited to patents and trade secrets. In reality, these comprise only a part of an organization's full IP portfolio. In *The Art* we discussed a number of added elements, including:

- Formulas and processes
- Machines and components
- Pricing strategies
- Industry sources
- Customer/client information

In some organizations, IP extends to:

- Employee records, including performance reviews
- Internal communications between business units
- Research and development reports and updates
- Pending and past litigation
- Supplier and strategic alliance agreements
- Reports and work products

Protection for each of these requires special expertise. Whereas the physical protection of many of these components is the responsibility of the business unit owner, global security can serve as both liaison among the various business units and as advisor as to the level of actual or potential threat and ways to mitigate the likelihood of loss.

E-Commerce Threat Management

A great deal is being written about the threats associated with e-commerce. Global security's role and organizational value is directly defined by the level of their direct involvement. Such involvement may concentrate on assessing new threats and defining ways to prevent them, or on attacking the threat head-on in conjunction with the aid of law enforcement. Often this requires established contacts in other countries and an understanding of what is legal there versus in the United States. E-commerce threats range from Internet abuse to automated systems capable of diverting resources from the organization. This might include credit card frauds, fictitious procurement arrangements, and fake inventory controls, to highlight but a few of today's more common loss vehicles.

Geopolitical Business Profiling

For some of today's larger global enterprises, having up-to-date—or, better yet, advance notification—of impending political strife can mean the difference between launching a major business initiative or not. It can radically alter an organization's marketing strategy and change the course of its business plans. Knowing the political leanings of future leaders is often more important than knowing those who are currently in control, because corporations often make large capital investments that require decades to realize their return on investment. Global security's role here is most likely to be advisory, drawing on established networks in the intelligence, military, and law enforcement communities.

Human Resources (HR) Security

As with business risk analysis, not all global security departments have responsibility for the following. Some have additional duties, and others have fewer. Nonetheless, this unit, too, is composed of a small cadre of professionals under the direction of a unit manager. This area of responsibility is largely advisory in nature. The primary customer base is corporatewide, but there is extensive interaction with human resources and legal departments because their purpose is to provide programs and input on matters that deal directly with the safety and well-being of employees, external partners, and customers. In short, they are the 'people end' of the business.

Strategic Partner Qualification

As more companies align themselves with third-party suppliers, it is not uncommon for many nonemployees to be resident at a corporate site. Companies such as Oracle rely heavily on their outside relationships. With the emergence of virtual companies, strategic alliances, and venture partnering, there is a need to ensure that the employees and agents representing these outside resources meet the same requirements as a company's own employee population. I noted earlier that external agents often have the same access to restricted areas and assets as company employees. The role of global security is threefold: first, to assist in developing the appropriate screening standards for all outside agents, including temporary workers and contractors; second, to serve as a quality checkpoint to ensure that the standards are being met; and finally, to provide the necessary investigative support when called on.

Security Awareness and Ownership

We have often heard that security is everyone's business. This is one of those basic organizational facts of life. Yet it is not uncommon for the general employee base to either abdicate or become very lax with this responsibility. The security industry has been assertive in promoting awareness programs. Today most employees are aware of the need for security and that they have some role in protecting themselves, their colleagues, and the company's assets. On the other hand, far fewer take active ownership. Often this is simply a matter of not knowing what to do. The HR security unit is accountable for developing such programs and assuring that they are carried out. Such programs typically have both incentives and disincentives to encourage full and equal participation.

International HR Security

As companies go global there is a need to address the security issues of employees and third-party agents in each location. Customs and practices differ widely, making it incumbent on the company to ensure that compliant programs are in place. Global security's role is to assist HR in developing policies and procedures that reflect both local customs and corporate policies. They also serve as a resource for those domestically based employees who travel outside the United States. Such services range from travel advisories and briefings for those being assigned to arranging the appropriate level of security for special events sponsored by the host locale.

New Hire Qualifications and Orientations

Many companies require some form of security clearance before an employee is hired. Sometimes this entails fingerprinting candidates or conducting other criminal checks. Often such checks are completed by HR as part of their responsibility. Regardless of who actually controls the process, global security is accountable for ensuring that the standards are developed and enforced. Some senior level positions or other sensitive positions may require a more detailed and discreet investigation into the person's background before a final offer can be made. The role of global security is to assist in completing these inquiries. This unit is also responsible for the development of new-hire orientation programs. Today many programs have specific modules that focus on workplace violence prevention, explaining the concept of intellectual property and how to protect it, and how global security can serve as an ongoing resource for employees.

Executive Protection

Executive protection has been a part of an overall security program for decades. The nature of the company, the profile of its executives (e.g., highly public or very low), and its position in the marketplace will drive the type of executive protection needed. Some companies require very sophisticated programs involving armored vehicles and armed escorts (e.g., energy companies operating in several Latin American countries). Others require very little security (i.e., a security officer posted along executive row, or a residential alarm system for the CEO). Regardless of the extent of protection required, global security is accountable for determining the appropriate level and following through to assure that it is in place and updated regularly.

Workplace Violence Prevention

Violence in the workplace continues to escalate. Beyond the threat of a terrorist attack, today's corporate sites remain a key locale for violence to erupt. I believe that this is largely due to the fact that the workplace has become, for many, their extended neighborhood or home. Today's employees know more about one another and bring more of their personal lives to the workplace than they do to their neighbors, churches, and families. Employees operate under stress, and interpersonal conflicts often arise. I am not a sociologist, but based on my experience, I would venture to say that many people place a lower value on life than ever before. All of this places a burden on the employer to do everything reasonable in mitigating the opportunity for a violent episode. Global security's role is to work with HR and business unit heads in developing a comprehensive program that extends beyond the creation of a policy alone.

Ethical Business Practices

In the early to mid-1990s a great deal was made of ethical behavior in business schools and texts. Corporations created entire units dedicated to assuring that their executives subscribed to the highest standards of ethical conduct. As the 1990s drew to a close, many of these programs went away. It was as though corporate America and their supporting halls of academia no longer saw a need for ethics. Then came 2002's disclosure after disclosure of unethical conduct both along executive row and in the boardroom. Beginning with Enron, company after company became the focus of a U.S. Justice Department criminal investigation. The Securities and Exchange Commission undertook separate probes, as did Congress. Apparently these corporate elite had either missed all of the ethical talk or turned a blind eye and deaf ear for their own purposes. Whatever the reason for these failures of ethics, the need for assuring ethical conduct remains stronger today than ever before.

Global security serves a role as both a resource for input into such programs and as investigator into wrongdoings. In 1998, First Tennessee Bank issued its *Matters of Principle*. This was an ethics program developed with considerable input from the security department. I still hold this as a model for any global security department concerned with the issue of moral behavior on the part of all organizational stakeholders.

Global Operations Support

This is the third pillar of a global security department that is concerned with total asset protection. As with the others, this subunit is made up of its own cadre of specialists under the direction of an experienced manager. Some programs have jettisoned responsibility for managing the company's uniformed security services division altogether. When this is done, the security officers are generally transferred to facilities management. I believe this is a smart move because managing this aspect of asset protection can be very time-consuming and can divert a great deal of a security department's limited resources. With proper guidance and quality review oversight by global security, facilities management is often better equipped to integrate uniformed security services into their operation.

Corporate Policy Development

One of the most valued contributions global security makes is its lead role in the development and dissemination of corporate policies aimed at protecting people and assets. A lack of clearly articulated policies creates its own risk for the organization. Policies create accountability and, as we saw in our discussion of strategic planning, employee empowerment. Together these attributes of policy development establish the framework for all else that follows. Through the development of policy statements, global security receives the endorsement of senior management, thereby creating a new level of awareness and ownership for the rest of the organization.

Security Standards and Guidelines

Throughout this text I referred to the three fundamental aspects of a comprehensive asset protection program. The establishment of security standards and guidelines serves as the centerpiece of this plan because it defines global security's desired security technology. Earlier we read how Steve Kauffer assisted one of his clients in articulating a set of security standards. These guidelines created a forum for nonsecurity decision-makers to better understand the why's and wherefore's of an effective and comprehensive security strategy. Whether global security assumes direct management of this function or serves in an advisory role, collaborating with corporate engineering, the measure of success is its ability to assure that security systems are designed in accordance with recognized best practices.

Uniformed Security Services

As noted earlier, some global security departments have retained this responsibility and others have transferred daily operational management to other corporate support units. Either way, global security cannot abdicate this key element of a comprehensive asset protection program. Regardless of which role it assumes, global security units provide key insights into the development of performance criteria and perform oversight reviews to ensure compliance with established corporate guidelines. When third-party providers are introduced, global security's point of accountability centers on identifying qualified candidates and participating in the development of a final service agreement. In those organizations that utilize a proprietary workforce, global security's role is to assure that the resident staff is knowledgeable and capable of handing all that comes their way in matters of employee security and asset protection.

Site Compliance and Quality Assurance

Today's businesses are becoming more functionally oriented. This means that corporatewide standards are in place to assure continuity. However, local decision-makers are given the responsibility of carrying out the organization's mission and business plans. To assure that local management remains compliant, global security is called on to conduct random site compliance visits. They become, in essence, a corporately sponsored QA resource.

Systems Design and Research

Technology related solutions to security problems continue to be introduced almost weekly. Whereas some might suspect this to be a slight overstatement, it does underscore how much the security industry has become dependent on systems and devices to solve operational issues. Researching the right solution or designing something altogether new is an essential backroom activity for global security. In finding the best answer, global security demonstrates its added value to the organization because the focus is on delivering service in the most cost-effective and efficient manner. Some global security departments are willing to serve as *beta sites,* or test locations, for a new product. This allows them to not only push the envelope in the pursuit of more responsiveness, but also puts them on the leading edge, making them the types of *rule breakers* we discussed in the section on strategic planning.

Special Projects Management

Global security often is called on to participate in the management of special projects. These are initiatives that are outside security's normal scope of responsibility. Sometimes the project is not related to asset protection at all, but security's demonstrated talents in handling other projects leads senior management or other business units to turn to them for assistance. Corporations that have adopted a matrix management approach will often drawn upon the skills resident within global security. Other times global security may be asked to assist one of the company's strategic partners or alliance relationships with a security issue. As more companies move into such unions, it is not uncommon to find one or more partners lacking a well-defined asset protection plan. Having global security serve as the focal point for such issues assures the host company that business objectives will not be impaired.

Special Events Management

Global security is routinely called on to represent the company's protection interests when special events occur. Global security is expected to provide added protection at corporate sponsored events. For example, John Hancock's security team is used for the Boston Marathon. Similarly, other global security departments have been deployed when their companies have sponsored charitable functions, sporting venues, and even political events.

Other Responsibilities and Reporting Relationships

At the outset of this latest discussion I noted that global security departments will vary in their areas of responsibility. I noted that some may have more responsibility and some may have less. Examples of those that might assume added responsibilities include aviation security, data security, and corporate safety. Those areas that are given to global security's charge reflect the organization's emphasis and the skill sets resident within the department. This, in turn, often drives the reporting relationship for global security. Many companies have opted to make it a part of the chief administrative officer's domain because of global security's widespread scope of involvement. Others have opted to make it a part of the legal department, audit group, or human resources. In short, there is no one reporting relationship that fits all organizations. Global security is, in this sense, a universal support unit that can fit under any one of many organizational hats. There is one key factor, however. To be effective, global security needs to remain a direct charge of a senior level executive. Failure to do so weakens its impact and renders much of its true value suspect. Those companies noted for their pursuit of best practices learned this lesson long ago.

We have to do the best we can. This is our sacred human responsibility.
Albert Einstein

Concluding Comments

The end of this chapter is also the end of Part II. Throughout these past three chapters I have attempted to define what I would refer to as the mechanical side of security management. We stepped into the arena where success is defined by those willing and capable to pursue a performance-based management style. We began with a call for employing a strategic planning approach to the business of asset protection. From there we examined three approaches to asset protection, each reflecting a core element and bound together by the use of a metric-based approach. Finally, we drew our attention to the emerging new asset protection model—a total approach that is both global in its orientation and functionally widespread in its scope.

In Chapter 6 we highlighted 24 key areas of responsibility for today's global security department. We noted that this was not intended to represent a complete delineation of responsibilities, noting that others have assumed direct responsibility for no less than data security, corporate safety, and aviation security—to name but three. The challenge facing today's asset protection teams can appear to be daunting if it incorporates all that is involved in the business of protecting people and assets, both tangible and intangible. Many would argue that no one department can, let alone should, be accountable for so much. Perhaps they are correct. What is certain, however, is that no one department head can lead such an undertaking without the able assistance of an experienced and professional supporting cast. Moreover, even they need assistance. Thus, we see the need to make asset protection a collaborative effort among all stakeholders. To achieve this, as I have pointed out a couple of times, requires both a high level of awareness and a higher level of ownership on the part of all employees—beginning with executive row.

The only test of leadership is if someone follows.

Robert K. Greenleaf

THOUGHT-PROVOKING QUESTIONS

1. Conventional security departments have been given considerable responsibility. In this chapter the author sets forth a case to expand this role even further. Do you believe the time has come for corporate America to embrace the concept of global security and an era of total asset protection?

2. To properly respond to the 24 areas of accountability contained within the author's three pillars of the new asset protection model, new skill sets will be required. Are today's security managers and professionals capable of stepping up to each? If not, what do you think needs to be done?

3. In Part I the author paints what some might call a dark side of today's security profession, not the least of which is the lack of support from executives. How does this square with his model calling for considerably more responsibility, and therefore, accountability?

4. Do you know of any security department that has achieved what the author refers to as the three pillars? If you do, what allowed them to

achieve this level? If not, perhaps you know of some that are well on their way. If so, what do these departments have going for them to allow them to eventually achieve this new level?

5. If companies fail to develop their security department to the level articulated by the author, who will fill the void?

PART III

THE ART OF MANAGEMENT AND THE SUCCESSFUL SECURITY MANAGER

Thus far our journey has taken us down some interesting paths. We have explored the need for a planned approach to the business of asset protection. Prudent business practices demand nothing less. Yet, as we have also seen, it is easy to fall into the trap of running from one crisis to the next and missing the opportunity to be masters of our fate, if you will, through a strategic approach. We can never be in total control of our fates because many of the driving factors that determine our organizational roles are not under our control. As noted earlier, executive management may elect to steer the company in a completely different direction, leaving the security department to redefine its deliverables and structure. The success of today's asset management is tied to being flexible and willing to change as quickly as the organization shifts.

In Part I we explored the underlying concepts and barriers that "get in the way" of effective asset protection. In the second section we explored what it takes to "get the job done" in a technical sense. In this last section we explore the art of managing a security program, or how asset protection managers can "get their due." These three "gets" define the continuum of a successful strategy. We need to understand what is in front of us, the good and the bad, to best define our strategy. We need to know what tools are available to us so we can draw upon them as the project unfolds. Now comes the last element, developing the knowledge to use these tools once we pick them up. This is the challenge that awaits us in Part III.

I would venture that many readers will find this last section the most enjoyable. In Chapter 7 there is a dramatic shift as I draw on the art of storytelling as a learning instrument. This is not to suggest that the chapter is made up of one "war story" after another. No, war stories may be interesting to tell and read, but they are often limited. Rather, here the storytelling is designed to serve as a vehicle to allow us the opportunity to explore many factors in an integrated way. You will be able to draw several lessons from each, even though each one has a dominant theme. I have chosen this approach because it offers a lighter read, yet is a powerful retention tool. If I am successful in this approach, you should be able to readily recall the story some time later and, in doing so, easily remember the lessons to be drawn.

Chapter 7 is not all about these stories. I have also chosen to insert midway through a sports analogy that contains many direct parallels to the art of management. I rediscovered the game of golf, as you may recall from an earlier chapter, a few years ago. And, like the other analogies I used in *The Art*, I find that there are several lessons that can be directly applied to the pursuit of effective security management. To assist us along our journey I have called on many of golfing's greats to share their insights.

In Chapter 8 I tackle head-on the issue of managing from the middle. Most security directors are middle managers. They typically occupy an organizational level that is three or four tiers below the CEO. Although many of today's asset protection managers actually occupy a higher position, most continue to occupy a place in the middle. The challenge is how one can effectively and efficiently manage from such an organizational perch. To help us I draw once again to one of my favorite management writers, Oren Harari. He has developed 11 rules for managing from the middle. Some of his ideas are bold and appear not to directly apply in an asset protection context—but they do, and we will explore how. From here I would like to take the reader on a side journey as we revisit what some of the great organizational practitioners and theorists have offered over the past century. You might be surprised at what they had to say then and how applicable it is today.

In Chapter 9 I conclude on an even more relaxed note. As many of you know, from 1999 to 2002 I had a monthly column entitled "Dalton's Tips" for *Security Magazine*. I have had the opportunity to share thoughts, ideas, and strategies on a wide range of topics for today's security manager and executive. In discussing this book with many of my colleagues and readers, there was a widespread interest in including something similar. So, in keeping with my golf analogy, I have entitled Chapter 9 "May I Play Through?"

It is a chapter composed of my best List of Tens (although some lists are not ten items long). Some lists are drawn from my previous columns, but a number are new or drawn from other sources. Either way, I offer them to serve as quick reference points, again in a format that will be easy to remember. Each list is accompanied by a few comments that tie one list to the next or offer explanation. All in all, I hope you find them both entertaining and informative.

Chapter 7

Have I Got a Story for You–And Maybe a Few More

You must be the change you see in the world.

Mohandas Gandhi

Primary Themes

- Management Lessons through Storytelling
- The Deer in the CEO's Headlights and *Panic du Jour*
- Collaborating versus Dictating and the Dreaded E's
- Talkers and Walkers
- Security and the Art of Golfing
- Lessons from Some of the Game's Greats

Three Added Management Requirements

- The Advantage of Creating Trust
- Education through the School of Going It Alone
- The Importance of Effective Communication

Opening Observations

I want to share a story with you. Actually, if you scan the pages of this chapter you will discover that I have several stories to share. I think storytelling is a wonderful learning tool. I believe it is one of the highest forms of learning an individual can be exposed to—something that great thinkers such as Mark Twain, Benjamin Franklin, and Aesop also believed. The New Testament centers on another great storyteller, the one many of us call "Teacher" today. My story is this:

Once a great war broke out between two powerful kings. One king had the larger army with many generals and far more captains. At the outset of the war one of the king's generals was considered to be very good. It didn't take long, however, before this general lost one of his very valuable captains. The king and other generals commented how unfortunate it was, but rallied the general on. Soon a second captain was lost, and then another. The king began to ask his other generals if something was wrong; none would come forward, though many suspected that there was. After all, there was honor among the generals and no one wanted to be seen as second-guessing a fellow officer.

Not long after that still another captain was killed. Becoming very concerned, the king sent his personal advisor to watch and report back. While in the general's camp, some of the general's remaining captains, lieutenants, and soldiers confided that the general was a weak leader and often made bad decisions or no decisions at all. The general discovered what had been said and just as the advisor was about to leave the general summoned him, saying: "Tomorrow you shall accompany me to the front line. Here you will see firsthand how difficult this war is and judge for yourself before return-ing to the king." At dawn they set out, and the advisor had walked into the trap. He was killed by one of the general's closest confidants.

The general sent his courier to the king with the following message: "Regret-tably, your advisor has been lost to the cause. He died at the enemy's hand in your honor. Here the war is difficult and the battles are hard fought. We have lost some good captains but have slain many in return. But do not fear. You have been generous in providing me still many others. I will call upon them all if needed in your defense."

The king responded: "Your battles must be difficult. As I have now lost an advisor and friend, surely the same can be said for you about your lost cap-tains. Fight on my loyal and trusting servant. God speed to you and all your brave men."

One of my former clients had a manager who was very frustrated. He knew he was good, but he kept butting heads with his boss's boss. The boss's boss could certainly talk the talk, but lacked some of the essential skills necessary to make him a trusted and competent senior manager. Out of frustration, the lower-level manager left. Before doing so, however, he called and asked for some advice. It was during this conversation that I told him the story about the wily general. I actually made it up some time ago when I, too, had a similar expe-rience and tried to make sense of what was happening. My departing words to him were: "May your generals be competent and your king wise."

You see, in today's organizations there are many so-called bosses who would not think twice of sacrificing a subordinate to save their own reputations and organizational souls. Perhaps you might recall in *Business Strategies* my introducing you to ELVIS. Mary Woodall first coined the acronym. It stands for Executive Level Vicious Infighting Syndrome. Briefly, she explains that there are many different types of ELVIS, but they all have the same agenda: blame someone else so you can succeed on the other's misfortunes. Her experience led her to conclude that ELVIS is alive and well in many executive suites today. I would agree.

There is an important lesson for subordinate managers to learn. When their executives begin slugging it out, lower-ranking managers need to know when to duck and weave. Or, as one of my former colleagues noted: "When the swinging starts, run and hide. Otherwise, someone is likely to grab you, pick you up, and throw you into the ring. Believe me, you do not want to be in the ring with someone who has longer arms, stands taller, and carries more weight." This quite colorful retort underscores the importance of getting out of the way when higher-ups choose to do battle. In these cases there are always winners and losers. The lightweight manager is simply no match for someone who has more experience and a better organizational position. Another way of viewing this is summed up in an earlier quote: "Never take a knife to a gun fight."

Security managers can miss this point altogether in their pursuit of what is ethically right or morally wrong. Security professionals have been trained to believe that there is a code of behavior that must be followed. Despite the generally sinister portrayals of security managers in the movies, the overwhelming majority of asset protection managers are highly desirous of being seen as true professionals. They typically abhor office politics and are committed to doing what they believe is the right thing. When corporate politics conflict with this approach, it is the security manager who can suffer the consequences, despite having taken the higher moral ground.

Does this suggest that to be successful security managers need to ratchet down their own moral code and mix it up with the big boys to succeed? Certainly not. But whether we like it or not, there is now, and will always be, a certain degree of back stabbing and infighting, especially among those who have significant power bases to lose. The successful manager, security or otherwise, learns to spot these people and manage around them.

If you are going through hell, keep on going.

Winston Churchill

In this chapter we completely shift gears. I hope you'll enjoy the change of pace. We will be looking at management from a different perspective, focusing on what I refer to as the *art-side* of management. Part II focused on some of the technical dimensions of being a successful manager. But that was only one side of the management coin. There is another side, and this is it. I think it is important to note that effective management, and therefore successful management, is a mix of variables. As we have seen, there are certainly some aspects that require technical knowledge such as using metrics-based strategies. Others are more subtle, employing techniques such as the fishbone and SWOT analyses we also discussed earlier. Some require the use of such approaches as the Fifth Discipline. However, successful management requires more. There is an innate component that drives an individual in the right direction. This sense of moving in the right direction cannot be neatly laid out as some established plan or written down like a formula or recipe. Sadly, that is what many management authors try to do. Many have tried to write their management version of the Holy Grail. Perhaps that is why their books are so popular; people want a simple step-by-step process that, if followed, will lead them to their "pot of organizational gold." If it were only as simple as that. But being a success at management requires being in tune with that inner sense in each of us that can guide us along.

To help us along the path I have opted to tell a few stories, to share some other insights offered by others with far sharper minds, wit, and writing prowess. Some of the ideas have been generated by my clients and students. So, with their indulgence (and permission) I want to share with you a composite of what I believe are some of the more fundamental pillars to effective management.

Are You the Deer in the CEO's Headlights?

One of my former bosses had a way of phrasing things. I never saw him "blow-up," but I did see him turn red from time to time. Bob was very calm, at least outwardly. He was the CAO of a major bank and one of the most professional administrators I have ever encountered. One day I advised him that I suspected one of my managers had been responsible for wiretapping several offices, including Bob's and mine. There was no doubt about the wiretapping—we had the physical evidence. All that was needed was to find the right culprit, and our investigation pointed squarely at my manager. After advising him, I could see Bob flush. He sat calmly, much like the character Nero Wolfe being advised by Archie about some recent twist in their latest caper. After a while Bob looked at me and said: "He's mentally terminated." I knew exactly what he meant.

We both understood that it would take time to build our case, but eventually we would snare him, if he was guilty. After several months our suspicions proved true and he was eventually confronted, confessed, pointed the finger at another manager, and both of them were terminated. During the entire investigation our prime suspect had many interactions with Bob. Business was as usual and he never suspected that we were on to him. Once I asked Bob how he could keep his composure. He simply responded: "He's mentally terminated." By this I came to realize that for Bob, interacting with our suspect simply meant going through the drill of the boss–subordinate relationship until the real agenda could be revealed.

Over my consulting experience I have had several other executives express the same perspective. They may not have used Bob's succinct phrase, but their intent was just as clear. The lesson to be taken away is that often security managers, like any other manager, may be engaging in an activity that has already spelled their organizational demise without their actually knowing it. The wiretapping episode is an extreme example; the others I have encountered have committed far less grievous actions. The end result remains the same, however.

Perhaps the most common managerial error I have encountered is obstructionism. I made a passing reference to this a few paragraphs back when I wrote about the strong moral conduct to which security managers subscribe. Again allow me to stress that there is no substitute for having high moral character— I only wish more executives subscribed to this approach. If they did, the spring and summer of 2002 would not have seen the scandals associated with so many large cap companies and their fall from investor confidence (e.g., Citicorp, Adelphia, Worldcom, Enron, etc.). It is not the moral ground that security managers take that can lead them into trouble. Rather, it is their style, their execution that ensnares them.

Perhaps another way of looking at this managerial failure is to realize that the root of their failure lies in their own arrogance. I have witnessed several occasions when the security directors were technically right, but their delivery—confrontational or simply ignoring what executives have directed— demonstrates that they are not team players. This leads to mistrust and it is not long after that one hears the murmur of "he's mentally terminated." So, what are security managers to do if they know they are correct? The answer is simple to write, but admittedly difficult to execute. It is called *salesmanship*.

Salesmanship is the art of selling one's position effectively and decisively. It moves an individual from one position to another. Some, it is conjectured, are natural born marketers. I believe there is some element of truth in this, but it is also a skill that can be acquired because there are many ways a person can influence another in positive ways. The ability to sell is rooted in the term *business savvy*. It is the ability to perceive what is happening and then develop an effective strategy to achieve the desired result. For security managers this means moving away from blustering or intimidating executives with threats that dire consequences will happen if one course of action versus another is not followed. We need only look to what has previously been discussed regarding how executives respond to such managerial techniques after a time (e.g., the snicker test).

Salesmanship also incorporates the use of advocacy building. I discussed this at length in *Business Strategies* and reinforced it in *The Art*. This should tell you something about the importance of this managerial tool. Simply stated, it is as essential as a hammer is in constructing a house. Without it, no structure can be built. Building advocacy does not require hardcore selling. It evolves, based on the elements of trust building between two individuals. Advocates want to support the manager because they have seen the manager's value, or subscribe to the same value, or hold the same position. Here is the link for successful management. Find your advocates and build the relationship. They can be found all over the organization. Some hold positions above yours, some are equal, some are in completely different sectors, and some are even below you but have influence with senior managers (i.e., administrative assistants, respected specialists, executive drivers, etc.)

> *The wise learn from the experiences of others, and the creative know how to make a crumb of experience go a long way.*
>
> *Eric Hoffer*

Panic du Jour

Earlier I introduced the concept of *panic du jour*. This is a management style that knows no organizational limit. Operating units, divisions, even executive rows have all fallen victim. In the world of corporate security, I routinely encounter it. I am not referring to an organizational climate that is in full-scale emotional panic. Sometimes this can happen, but *panic du jour* is more often an overriding approach to decision-making. Lacking a plan, managers find themselves literally running from one crisis to another. More alarming, they often create the crisis without realizing they are the cause. Whenever I hear the phrase, "I'm too busy fighting fires," I suspect a case of *panic du jour* in full operation.

In *Business Strategies* you may recall situational cases 11 and 12, "Preparing for a Riot that Never Took Place" and the "LA Olympics," respectively. Both of these cases underscore how excessive spending can result from panic. To the outsider, the actions of senior managers can be amusing, but often the consequences are serious and the impact on stakeholders can be devastating. In the case of the "Riot that Never Took Place" there was actually another part of the story that was left untold. Briefly, this is the case in which a large city was on the verge of electing its first African American mayor. The retail security manager in the story was convinced that, regardless of which way the election went, rioting was going to break out that night. It was bad enough that the manager incurred $185,000 (a considerable sum for an ailing retailer at that time) of expense for one night's preparation, despite repeated assurances that there was going to be no riot. He went so far as to hire off-duty police personnel from neighboring jurisdictions, equip them in black police SWAT uniforms with bright yellow dickeys, and station them in one of his stores that was directly across the street from the newly elected mayor's headquarters. When a passing patrol officer observed what he saw as terrorists taking up positions in the store, it was not long before the store was surrounded by the local police and a near-shootout began to unfold. Quick action and strong influence with the local press kept the entire episode from the public's eye. This was *panic du jour* in full operation.

It is almost inconceivable that the executive management team allowed the same manager to incur an additional $250,000 a few months later to assure that there would be no disruption to their distribution network in the Los Angeles area during that year's Summer Olympics. You may recall that his plan included renting an 18-wheel trailer truck and filling it with rations capable of equipping 50 security officers, complete with guns and ammunition. He also leased a helicopter to serve as an airborne point of coordination, despite being told in advance that the area had been designated as a no-fly zone by the Los Angeles Police Department. For six weeks his helicopter sat in a parking lot.

Despite the unbelievable nature of each example, the cost was staggering. One is left asking how this manager could have been allowed to go forward, especially in the second case when his first episode had been so disastrous. The answer is simple; in both cases his dire warnings of ruination panicked his executive staff. In this organization's case, they simply deferred to what they believed was his expertise. Could something as wild as this occur again? One only needs to turn to the events following 9/11. In the weeks following the attack, many executives assumed they knew what was best and ordered quick fixes at any cost. Other executives deferred to their security staff. Some security personnel were sensible, others were not. And the government was not then, nor is it as of this writing, very helpful. We have already reviewed how the Office of Homeland Security and the FBI kept America on edge in the year following the WTC with their threat warnings and cumbersome and ineffective airport security program.

Tragically, the *panic du jour* doesn't end there. In the summer of 2002 the U.S. Customs Department announced its Customs-Trade Partnership Against Terrorism (C-TPAT) security program. The agency gave corporate America less than four months to install a comprehensive program to "develop and implement a sound plan to strengthen security procedures throughout the supply chain for all cargo that is imported into and through (inbound cargo) the United States. Where you do not directly control a function within the supply chain you must make every reasonable effort to ensure compliance by the responsible party." With this preamble Customs then articulated two and a half pages of bulleted requirements ranging from operating procedures and physical security requirements to education and training awareness.

Imagine a retailer like Wal-Mart with tens of thousands of suppliers. Imagine Sealand Corporation with hundreds of thousands containers and hundreds of ships on the high seas heading to American docks daily. Imagine every other business that transports inbound goods across the country via rail and trucking. There is no standard auditing program offered by the Customs Department to determine if one supply chain carrier is in compliance. This means that Company A is left to assess Supplier B using whatever measure they deem appropriate. Supplier B has little or no say. If Supplier B is deemed a low risk by Company A, but a high risk by Company C because Company C uses a different measure, what does Supplier B do? What does U.S. Customs do?

Who is right? Who is wrong? Who assumes the liability for a wrong decision that causes significant delays? One retailer determined the per hour cost for delays at a single point of entry to be $16,000 per shipment. Multiply this across all shipments and the financial impact is staggering. What's even more troubling is that Customs set a compliance date for October 1, 2002—just in time for the peak Christmas shipments to start arriving.

This example illustrates how the government cannot only create its own *panic du jour*, but can spread it across the country with a single proclamation. I am reminded of what Nobel Award–winning economist Milton Friedman once observed: "If the government were put in charge of the Sahara Desert, within five years, they'd have a shortage of sand." For security managers, the lesson here is obvious. A reasoned approach that is well constructed needs to be a guiding principle, even when all those about you are lost.

> *Some men go through the forest and see no firewood.*
> *English Proverb*

Collaboration versus Dictation

"It's my way or the highway!" Have you ever heard this exclamation? Have you ever found yourself saying this? Today's organizational climate has little tolerance for the underlying attitude. I knew a security director—actually more than one now that I think a little more about it—who subscribed to this management style. Fundamentally, there is nothing wrong with such an approach. Often there is no right or wrong management style. One, from a purely value-less perspective, is just as valid as another. The problem arises in the application. A military style of organization may have a greater tolerance for an authoritarian approach, whereas an entrepreneurial start-up would find it totally out of place.

In his book, *Transforming the Way We Work: The Power of the Collaborative Workplace*, Edward Marshall notes:

> *Collaborative approaches to leading and managing, however, are not for everyone. There are a number of situations where this approach should either not be attempted or attempted with caution. In all of these situations there appears to be a common denominator: The fundamental values and beliefs of senior management are such that they do not accept that collaboration is the way in which they want their organizations to evolve; or they believe it is the wrong way to manage. In some instances management may intellectually understand the need for collaboration, but does not yet know how to implement it. Other organizations where collaboration may not work are those that have win-lose as their rule.*

Most of today's corporations have very little tolerance for pure authoritarian management styles, however. Despite examples that can be readily found to illustrate the presence of a dictatorial approach, even those that might be characterized as benevolent, most U.S. companies have committed to a management style that reflects some level of employee involvement in the decision-making process. The concepts of empowerment, work teams, matrix management, and the like are all indicators that the current climate tends to promote a more participatory form of management than a one-way street flowing from management to the line level.

A security manager who fails to intellectually or emotionally understand this is more likely to be doomed than to be praised, even among his or her peer group. Failing to collaborate among other support units such as legal, accounting, HR, corporate real estate, and so forth places the entire security program at risk. Yet many security management teams refuse to adopt a collaborative outlook, opting instead to "go it alone." It is little wonder when they later lament that they were the last to know, even though their expertise might well have brought significant value.

Take for example the case of the bank security director who refused to communicate his department's findings regarding the outcome of fingerprint checks on new hires. He had adopted a program in which his staff alone fingerprinted new hires, even at remote branch locations. His department would then forward the cards to the FBI for processing and had the results returned to security. His department would then issue a memo to the hiring manager indicating whether or not the employee passed this portion of their background screening.

The security manager argued that he alone was responsible for protecting the privacy of these new hires and that neither legal nor HR was qualified or charted. He had created a system without checks and balances, and his word was final regarding the acceptability of branch tellers or anyone else. It was not long before HR discovered that other banks took a much different approach and that before an employee was terminated for failing the fingerprint check, other departments were notified and the case was reviewed to assure that the bank was in compliance with regulations and that termination was actually warranted. The security manager dug in, taking his team with him. As the battle lines drew tighter and tighter, some branch managers began creating excuses for their new hires not to be available for fingerprinting. That drew the attention of regulators. Before long the bank found itself in a very precarious situation.

The resolution finally came when the bank's president intervened and asked the security manager to change and take on a more collaborative approach or face termination. The director called the president's bluff and was shown the door within two days. This story underscores the need to cooperate and collaborate. When managers fail to recognize the environment they are in, they can create more obstruction than added value. As companies move their asset protection programs along the evolutionary continuum, the call for more collaboration will be heard, if for no other reason than because security will lack the resources necessary to take the operational lead and hold it.

The Dreaded Two E's by Any Other Name Is Still the Dreaded Two E's

In the early 1970s I was a graduate student at Michigan State University. This was the first time I began reading about the concept of management by objectives, or MBO. I was fascinated by the thought that even then performance indicators were being developed and results could be statistically measured. A short time later I was introduced to Theory X and Theory Y as the new management tool. This was followed by Theory Z and the Japanese style of managing. Further along, I was exposed to a variety of management techniques, each professing to be better than the previous and more effective on organizational behavior and corporate results. By the 1990s we had total quality management (TQM) and continuous quality Improvement (CQI), followed by the Fifth Discipline, Six Sigma, and the ISO 9000 standards.

As I think back to each of them I cannot help but note that they all have two elements in common, and one consistent theme. It is what I refer to as the *dreaded two E's*. Why most learned management theorists and behaviorists go to great lengths to avoid the two E's, I am not certain. The E's are effectiveness and efficiency. These two concepts were introduced decades ago and popularized in American management texts in the early 1920s when Frederick Taylor and Frank Gilberth began reporting the efforts of their scientific management methods. The motion picture industry played on the popularity of time and motion studies that evolved from their work. Called *Cheaper by the Dozen*, the movie made lighthearted humor of a father who was able to achieve household productivity by employing Taylor's methods with his 12 children.

The underlying threads that tie the subsequent management strategies and theories together are the concepts of efficiency and effectiveness. Why the "bad rap?" Perhaps it is rooted in the idea that these concepts are associated with the early management schools which tended to stress mechanics more than the human element. It may also be that practitioners and theorists believe there ought to be a far more complex integration of multiple factors that explains why organizations either succeed or fail in the pursuit of productivity. It is not my purpose to dismiss all that has followed the work of the early twentieth century. Many new concepts have emerged that have significantly contributed to our overall prosperity. The problem is more one of losing focus. Many of today's management strategies are based on formula's that were originally designed to improve manufacturing processes. When trying to apply them to the human side of the equation, I fear they fall significantly short of the intended goal. Take for example the work associated with Six Sigma.

With the fall of TQM, Six Sigma advocates were quick to rush in and fill the supposed void in defining a quality-oriented process. Pande, Neuman, and Cavanagh, in their book *The Six Sigma Way*, tell us: "Six Sigma is revealing a potential for success that goes beyond the levels of improvement achieved through the many TQM efforts. Past quality programs fell victim to mistakes that hurt both their results and the reputation of TQM." I must admit that I agree in part with what they have to say—at least about how previous quality programs stalled because of their inherent flawed assumptions.

I recall when I was asked by John Hancock Insurance Company to address a group of their managers. I had been working with their security department on developing some very basic ways to assure that their service delivery was both effective and efficient. We had reviewed the TQM elements promulgated by senior management and I had advised setting them aside because they were internal-process oriented and missed the most basic metric of customer satisfaction. The security manager found this interesting because John Hancock had adopted TQM as their operational bible and spent millions developing a Quality College for their employees to attend. One of the basic tenants was that true quality was only achieved when there were literally no defects. In short, it was to be the mission of all of the company's departments to accept nothing less than 100% accuracy in all processes and deliveries. Bunk! Yet their senior management had accepted this because a so-called quality assurance consulting company had convinced them that this was an absolute.

Intrigued that I represented an alternative view, the security director arranged for me to conduct a workshop for nonsecurity managers. He cautioned that a senior vice president would be present, one of the key advocates of TQM and founders of the company's Quality College. After the group assembled we began with a discussion of what quality means and how it is to be accomplished. It was not long before the senior vice president grew impatient and announced that we were wasting a great deal of time. He then told us that he was going to define "quality." I will never forget his eloquent, but succinct, definition. He said: "Quality is delivery without error. And, our goal is to deliver 100% of the time without error." He smiled triumphantly, crossed his arms, and waited for each of us to hold him in awe. After all, he had introduced himself at the beginning as a student of QA and had taken all of the courses offered by the consulting firm that had developed the company's quality college. Because of this, he had learned from the best and understood exactly what they meant. I could not believe what I just heard and asked if there was no accounting for human error in the pursuit of daily operational activities? He firmly reiterated what he had just proclaimed and said to accept anything less was evidence that someone did not know anything about quality assurance.

I thought about this for a moment, along with the others, and then, hoping to lighten the discussion up, simply said: "If you are right, I guess I must be on major drugs." He did not see the humor in this. I went on to point out that the nature of human involvement will always mean that presence of some degree of error, nearly all of the time. Such a definition of 100% error free 100% of the time was absurd and could never be achieved because of its inherent assumptive flaw. He refused to accept this point and finally directed those in attendance to ignore what I had to offer since it was clear that I was "willing to accept that employees cannot achieve and sustain error-free delivery 100% of the time and therefore I was not really interested in quality." I could not believe that anyone interested in the concept of promoting true efficiency and effectiveness as the two fundamental tenants of assuring quality customer care could be so myopic and so misinformed.

Quality processing, as the Six Sigma advocates will readily agree, means that human involvement requires the acceptance of errors along the way. Success is defined by how these errors are addressed. To my way of thinking, this senior VP had to be under the influence of something. If this was what he and others were promoting to senior executives in not only this company but also many others, I knew it was only a matter of time before their lunacy would catch up with them. It did, and they—along with so many other TQM advocates—were cast aside. Sadly, in the process, millions of dollars and staff hours had been foolishly spent. This is what the advocates of Six Sigma meant when they referred to the TQM gurus as being injurious to programs that fell victim to mistakes that hurt both their results and the reputation of quality.

The *Six Sigma Way* authors go on to point out twelve TQM traps that their approach avoids. Nonetheless, even Six Sigma, as an applied human enterprise, is flawed because it is based on a process that is largely built on the manufacturing processes associated with products. Security service companies cannot be viewed strictly in terms of Six Sigma tenants, nor can any other service-oriented organization. When an organization relies on human interaction, those in charge of delivery need to understand the nuances of motivation, morale, equity, spirit, and soul. These are the artful aspects of management and need to be understood if an organization is to optimize what it defines as effectiveness and efficiency. Trying to apply $X + Y = Z$ or some silly Greek letter/symbol is cute, but that is where it ends. *Efficiency* means pursuing that which is economically most value-added. *Effectiveness* means pursuing that which yields the best result in the most efficient manner. Some may wish that there were a simple formula for achieving both. To truly understand that no two organizations are the same and therefore no two approaches can be measured the same is to understand the folly of those who seek to find universal strategies.

If a man does his best, what else is there?

George Patton

SEPARATING THE TALKERS FROM THE WALKERS

By now I will assume that you have heard the expression "There are those who talk the talk, and there are those who walk the walk." The intent is fairly clear. We have, no doubt, come across those who say all the right things and those who set their words aside and let their actions speak for themselves. In the world of security management, we, too, have talkers and walkers. My experience is that most talkers seem to occupy fairly high-profile positions while most walkers go about the business of getting what needs to be done, done. In my own profession, security consulting, I know many who are quick to talk the talk. We visited a few of them a couple of chapters back in our discussion of the so-called expert witness—those who enjoy a national profession, but say some of the most outlandish things and believe that just because they said them, they must be true. On the national level, former President Clinton is a great talker and former President Carter is a walker. I do not particularly care for either, but we have Clinton telling a group of Jewish supporters in Toronto, Canada, "The Israelis know that if the Iraqi or the Iranian army came across the Jordan River, I would personally grab a rifle, get in the ditch, and fight and die." This from a person that the *Sacramento Bee* notes avoided the Vietnam War. Carter, on the other hand, has continued to promote both political and humanitarian reforms by actually getting involved.

Closer to home, there are security managers who are likewise quick with the words and short on their delivery. I recall one manager who always knew what the latest management buzz term was and bragged about all that his department accomplished in the pursuit of the latest metric for success. His company was in financial services, and he boasted of how his department had been converted from a corporate division to a wholly owned subsidiary. In this capacity, he and his management team were to be measured on their "contribution to the company's bottom-line performance."

One day I asked him what that actually meant. He told me that his contribution was defined in terms of dollars delivered "to the overall profitability of the company as measured in pre-tax earnings." This sounded very good. I pressed him as to what that meant and how his department's performance was exactly measured. He went on to tell me that his deliverables were measured in terms of "their proportionate share of the corporation's projected annual earnings." Now, this was getting interesting. I asked if he could help me better understand by defining what that meant and give me a couple of examples of how this was measured. With a wave of his hand to indicate that he was growing tired of my annoying and silly inquiries, he said: "Our company defines contributions as those deliverables that can be measured against its current earnings to those of the same period in the previous fiscal quarter. So, when our loss recoveries equal or exceed that of the same quarter the year before, we have made a significant contribution." I asked his indulgence one last time to explain because I was not certain I understood what he was saying. He answered: "Well, you need to understand, we are just at the threshold of a new way of defining our security services deliverable. To say that we have accomplished all that we have targeted would be not completely accurate." I turned, smiling as I walked away, and recalled what George Stephanopolous once told the press: "The President has kept all of the promises he intended to keep." In the same way, I think this security manager had kept all of the commitments he thought he understood. It was not long after that his executive management team reorganized the security department a second time, but this time under new stewardship.

The brain is a wonderful organ; it starts working the moment you get up in the morning and does not stop until you get into the office.

Robert Frost

Security Management and the Art of a Good Golf Game

It has been said that some of the greatest business deals have been made on the golf course. I'm not so sure I would agree with this. I have been in the business world since 1979 and playing golf for the past five years. I've been matched with many golfers, and none of them has ever spent the round discussing business, let alone making big deals. Off the course, I have talked to hundreds of executives, many at the most senior level. I have never heard any of them make the comment that their latest big deal was hashed out on the links or even over the nineteenth hole on a bar tab. Nevertheless, golfing is a sport that is enjoyed by many corporate executives and has likely helped define the types of people they are dealing with back at the office.

Golfing and management have some interesting parallels. One does not have to be a golfer to see what I mean. As a game, golfing is about sportsmanship, honor, integrity, and having a strong sense of humor. It involves strategy, patience, knowledge of the technical rules, and competition. For those inclined to wager, it can mean high stakes or, at the very least, bragging rights. Early on I told you my "Mike's Dad" golf story. Even though the intent was to illustrate how timing plays an important role in everyone's life, there's more to the story. It also serves to remind us of the need to pay attention to details, such as where did I leave those clubs? It teaches us about appreciating the value of resources and taking responsibility for our actions. In other words, it does not take digging very deep into the game to find remarkable parallels to the real world of management. Following this analogy, I have found it helpful for my students and clients to draw on what some of the game's greatest players have had to say about golfing and adopt their words to managing an organization. You have already seen a few examples in the previous chapters, so I thought you might enjoy further elaboration.

Sportsmanship

Over the course of the past few years I have read a number of golfing books. After a while each has melted into one another. Whereas I may not exactly remember who wrote what, I do remember the lessons I derived from them. I suppose that is the truer mark of a great book. In any event, I recall the story of one golfer who had spent a lifetime trying to break his best score of 80. On one particular round his caddie mistook the golfer's ball for another player's. The gentleman golfer was on the final hole and needed only one shot to accomplish his life's dream. He took it and sunk the ball solidly. A broad smile spread across his face until he reached in the cup and discovered the mistake. Looking at the caddie, the golfer quietly pointed out the error as they left the green and headed for the locker room. The caddie was devastated and asked the golfer what he intended to do. He simply replied, "I guess I'll have to take the penalty and start again tomorrow. See you then."

What a wonderful lesson this can teach any manager. One moment the golfer felt an incredible high, the next true disappointment. He could have let the score stand, justifying that the mistake was not his. He could have simply pocketed the ball and posted the score, and no one—not even the caddie—would have known. Instead, he was a true sportsman and followed the rules, knowing the consequences. He went further, however. He knew the caddie had innocently made a mistake. There was no harsh rebuke, no chastisement, no end of the relationship. The golfer knew he was accountable for a proper score and that the caddie would most likely never commit the error again, having learned his lesson. Together, they moved forward and did not dwell on the past. It was a closed episode, something a true gentleman, sportsman, or manager understands.

A successful manager dwells on the facts and deals with the human dimension in a way that allows the person to save face and learn from the mistake. All too often security officers feel the brunt of an angry manager or corporate executive. People make honest mistakes, and those who are in responsible positions can feel the sting, but this does not justify shifting the blame.

It is good sportsmanship to not pick up lost golf balls while they are still rolling.

Mark Twain

Integrity

"To find a man's true character, play golf with him." P.G. Wodehouse, British humorist and golf enthusiast, once made this observation. There is nothing funny in this observation, however. He was being serious at the time and his words remain, I believe, just as serious now. Golf is a unique sport because it allows the player many opportunities to cheat without anyone knowing. The game of solitaire is similar. In both, when you cheat you are only cheating yourself. The lesson for managers should be obvious. Yet, as the summer of 2002 demonstrated, honor is a value that has been absent from more than one executive row. As of my last count, more than a dozen major corporations had experienced stock prices plummeting because of dishonest or highly questionable practices.

Unlike golf, however, in business the probability of eventual discovery for cheating is significantly higher. Sadly, the history of the security profession is checkered with acts of dishonest managers. Some have been publicly reported, yet, like so many other professions, most have been quietly attended to and the offending manager released. Whether it is a public trial or an administrative action, the profession is hurt every time a manager exercises poor judgment and falls to some dishonest temptation or engages in outright criminal activity.

> *I never pray that I may win. I just ask for the courage to do my best.*
>
>   *Gary Player*

Honor

The good news is that the security industry can boast of far, far more honorable people than people who have caused it dishonor. One of the most dramatic tests was the number of security personnel who sacrificed their lives at the WTC. This included several security managers, one of whom had just started and owed no real allegiance to anyone but himself. Nevertheless, he chose to stay and render what assistance he could to save others. This was certainly a proud time for security professionals everywhere. But there have been many more honorable people that preceded these brave security people.

Some have turned away from bribery attempts, and others have simply relinquished what might have technically been theirs (e.g., equipment, a better working schedule, a more favorable post) to simply help another officer in need. Some security personnel have stood their ground to protect the constitutional rights of an accused person even when the evidence clearly pointed to wrongdoing. These are only a few examples and are cursory at best. For managers, especially nonsecurity executives, there is a need to recognize those who dedicate themselves to the organization—often as third-party contractors. Unfortunately, they are often overlooked. It is therefore incumbent upon the security management team to bring attention to these honorable people.

> *Golf is a game of honor. If you're playing it any other way, you're not getting the fullest satisfaction from it.*
>
>   *Harvey Penick*

Sense of Humor

John called his friend and said, "My doctor says I cannot play golf." The friend answered, "Oh, he's played with you too." Golfing requires a strong sense of humor. I tell people that since taking up the game I have earned my fourth degree. I now have a Masters Degree in inconsistency. Golfers learn to laugh at themselves quickly. Some precede their laughter with fits of anger and frustration, but eventually one cannot help but find the humor in his or her inabilities. Security managers need to do the same.

Successful people stress the fact that success can come only when the individual has the ability to see the total picture; this includes the funny side as well as the serious side. Doctors and other health specialists have long ago told us that the ability to laugh, especially at ourselves, is necessary in maintaining a balanced well-being. I recall one client who was a security manager with no sense of humor at all. I spent days with her, attending meetings and developing strategies. We were together long hours each day and I never saw her laugh, even when others laughed. Once we were working on something and, even though I cannot remember what was exactly said, it certainly was funny. I began to laugh and she looked blankly at me. Then, quietly, she said: "Dennis, security is serious business. There is no room for laughter." I wish this was a solitary episode, but other security managers have held similar perspectives.

When I first took the helm at Continental National Bank in Chicago in the mid 1980s I recall asking the manager in charge of the security officers why they never smiled while on duty, especially when greeting the bank's customers. He told me that there was a standing order for them not to smile or laugh. He too told me that security was serious business and that an officer found smiling or laughing would be disciplined. I reassigned the manager and issued a new directive.

Enjoy the game. Happy golf is good golf.

Gary Player

Strategy

Humorist Kin Hubbard once observed, "Lot's of folks confuse bad management with destiny." Quality guru W. Edwards Deming adds a slightly different perspective. He notes: "Survival is not mandatory." Both are correct. Hubbard tells us that many hold the fatalistic attitude that there is a destiny for all organizations. Some have a positive destiny, reflected by good managers and their strategy. For others, their destiny is not so positive, and that too is the result of management. I wish it were so simple. Deming, on the other hand, challenges us to consider a most risky proposition. He simply notes that the survival of an organization is not mandatory. Yet, many—especially those in government—believe it is their destiny to save corporate America from its own ruination. Would that they could only turn such a destiny-driven attitude toward themselves.

The direction, let alone survival of an organization, is more a factor of smart strategic planning than of destiny. We have already covered this at length in a previous chapter. Suffice it to say here that, for a security manager, Jack Nicklaus offers his own brand of sage advice: "Success depends almost entirely on how effectively you learn to manage the game's two ultimate adversaries: the course and yourself." For managers, the first adversary is their own organizations. This often means the security department itself. For others it means the company. I am a firm believer in the fact that many allow the organization to consume them, therefore rendering them organizationally impotent.

Like the game of golf, management involves the art of knowing where one wants to hit the ball next. To simply get up and swing away is reckless and will most definitely cost. In golf, it is a stroke, but in management it may well mean loss of credibility on one end and the potential for serious harm (economically, professionally, and sometimes personally) for others. Again, it is Nicklaus who challenges us by asking, "How many shots would you have saved if you never lost your temper, never got down on yourself, always developed a strategy before you hit, and always played within your own capabilities?"

If you can't hit a driver, don't.

Greg Norman

Patience

I talked about this when discussing the execution of your strategic plan. I am far from being considered anything but a weekend hacker as a golfer. One thing I have learned, however, is that if one wanted to change the name of the game, *patience* would be a strong contender. Golfing is all about letting the game come to you. If you overpower the ball to make it go longer, it is just as apt to go astray or dribble weakly out in front of you. Every golfer understands the old (though now somewhat sexist) rule that if your tee shot does not clear the women's tee box, you must play the remainder of the game with your pants down. Although I have yet to actually see this, I have seen many a Samson-like player swing for all he is worth only to watch the ball miserably trickle out halfway to the women's tees. Why? Because they failed to be patient and allow their swing to be natural and let the club do the work.

Similarly, when golfers are in a hurry to play through another group that has allowed them to do so, most invariably rush their shots, only to end up with a bad hole. This is then followed by the mumbling comment, "I hate that. Whenever I hurry through, I always end up with a lousy score on the hole. I'll never play through again!!" And they do not—or at least not until they are invited to do so the next time. I have read about the importance of having patience, I have seen how important it is and I have experienced it. Yet like the other duffers, I too need a lesson in patience more than a lesson in the proper swing technique.

The same can be said for security managers. We hurry our decision-making, or we fail to have the patience to see our strategic designs through to their natural conclusions. Executive management is often a driving force (no pun intended) for quick fixes, lacking the patience to manage processes in an orderly and systematic manner. Patience is nothing more than an exercise of waiting— not to the point of becoming obstructionist or out-of-step with the rest of the management team, but long enough to evaluate the here and now and what is required next.

Nobody asked how you looked, just what you shot.

Sam Snead

Knowledge of the Technical Rules

The rules of golf are many, often arbitrary, and sometimes rather convoluted. Management draws a direct parallel. Yet without the rules, chaos would reign. Having someone on hand who knows the rules assures success for both. Golf professionals know the rules, but still rely on their caddies. The same can be said for administrators and managers. Many know the rules of their profession or organization, but it is often a more prudent route to follow those who know the technical rules.

Another golfing great, Arnold Palmer, noted, "Golf is deceptively simple, yet endlessly complicated." I suspect this can be said of many things, and chief among them is the art of managing people and programs. It is certainly true for the security industry. Whenever I sit with my clients for the first time, they invariably comment that they had no idea what went into the business of asset protection management. I recall one senior executive commenting that he thought security was only about a uniformed guard standing in the lobby. He was amazed to discover that protecting assets is a complex world of integrating people with state-of the-art technology and operating practices. I believe he was intellectually aware of several security-related elements, but he had never taken the time to actually stop and put them all together.

I raised the issue of the courts' decisions in matters of premises liability in an earlier chapter. This is a form of technical knowledge, one that can save significant operating expense if properly followed. Similarly, knowing about the latest security devices and their capabilities offers a greater range of decisions. Managers must either develop this knowledge on their own or know where to find it. Those who have long been recognized for their pursuit of best business practices understand the importance of being surrounded by technical experts who know the latest and greatest, or what is doable and what is not. Borrowing from an old adage, one security director commented that his technical group was worth their weight in gold.

Never bet with anyone who has a deep tan, squinty eyes and a one-iron in his bag.

Dave Marr

Competition

The world of business is all about competition. This is one of the basic dynamics of what defines corporate America. It is all about obtaining market share and holding it. Golf is the same way; even if you are not competing in a major tournament, there is the element of competing with yourself. Harvey Penick, one of the more colorful professional golfers advises: "Instead of worrying about making a fool of yourself in front of a crowd of 4 or 40,000, forget about how you look and concentrate instead on where you want the ball to go." Successful security managers well understand that competition is more about beating themselves than having others do it for them.

Competition can make the manager sharp. It forces smart thinking and calculated strategies. It allows the best in an individual to rise. Competition creates the opportunity for the security management team to demonstrate what they can do and how they can be effective. Arnold Palmer steps forward again and suggests, "There is a philosophy of boldness—to take advantage of every tiny opening toward victory." In *Business Strategies*, I pointed out Jim Meisenheimer's five ways to beat the competition and how they apply to the world of asset protection management.

Strategy #1: Outbid

In competing with other department heads for limited capital and operating monies, the object is not to demonstrate that your programs may cost the company less. The truer objective is to demonstrate that your programs have, or will bring, an increased value to the organization on the whole. This means more than sugar coating. The best way to win approval is to posture the program's features and benefits as something the decision-maker strongly relates to and sees the value. Meisenheimer suggests that these value adds should be placed strategically in any presentation requesting funding—just before the cost of the program or requested capital expenditure is identified.

Strategy #2: Outdistance

He goes on to suggest that the successful manager is one who is prepared and willing to do the work. He suggests that there's no easy way to go the extra mile. If it were easy, everyone would be doing it. By putting in that extra effort, you immediately differentiate yourself from the other department heads.

Strategy #3: Outlast

Remember that a large part of business management is the competition for limited resources; therefore, it is important to be persistent. Many managers are willing to give up too early or run from resistance, because they can't bear to hear the word no. Meisenheimer suggests that those who persevere tend to be the winners in the long run.

Strategy #4: Outfox

Successful managers take seriously the notion of thinking like their customers think. It is also important to think like your competitors think. In doing so, you're more apt to be able to outfox them, especially in very competitive situations. Essentially, ask yourself how the competition has reacted in the past, who they got involved, and why they considered certain options, to assist you in achieving your end result. In most organizations, the same department heads come to the capital planning committee or meet each other in the budget process on an annual basis, and invariably some department heads are continuous winners, while others are left shaking their heads and simply suggesting that "maybe next year it will be my turn." Those who are consistently successful know the tricks of the game and how to play it.

Strategy #5: Out of Step

Meisenheimer suggests that the quickest way to lose those who are in the ultimate decision-making position is to begin with an explanation of your services, instead of identifying their problems. Corporate executives make decisions based on the problems currently facing them. They're not necessarily interested in buying or encouraging a total service package. Most executives want effective solutions to those challenges facing them, and if your programs are perceived by them to be the answer, the chances are very high that approval will be given. In short, the challenge is to get into step with senior management and align yourself with their needs. Meisenheimer concludes by suggesting the following, "If you want to finish third, show your customers how little you offer. If you want to finish a close second, place a priority on extra effort. If you want to win, strive to outbid, outdistance, outlast, and outfox your competition, and never be out of step with your customers."

No one remembers who came in second.

Walter Hagen

Risk Taking

Sometimes the manager, like the golfer, needs to set the conventional approach aside momentarily and take calculated risks. Note that I have included two key words: *momentarily* and *calculated*. These two words are powerhouses in the world of effective and successful security management. It is easy for a manager to get caught up in the excitement of risk taking and make it a primary decision-making strategy. Risk taking is successful only if it is incremental and designed to accomplish a specific end result. Tommy Armour once noted, "There are no blind holes the second time you play them." That is because there is no element of risk; the course's secrets are now known. This means the second time around there is a new strategy, perhaps a more conventional approach because the risk element is no longer there. Until the course can yield no more secrets, there will always be the element of risk. It must also be calculated risk, which simply translates to an affordable risk. Here's what I mean.

Gene Littler observes: "Golf is not a game of great shots. It's a game of the most accurate misses." With this observation we can say that Littler is spot on in understanding how risks play to the manager's advantage. Security managers with experience have certainly felt the exhilaration of successfully winning an organizational battle or taking a risk that was proven to be accurate, be it an investigation, a new staffing model, or a capital project. Unfortunately, it is common for the same managers to press their luck in another area when the factors that led to success in the previous battle or challenge are not aligned properly or are absent altogether. I refer to this as being *mis-assumptive.* We will explore this in more detail in the pages ahead. For now suffice it to say that risk taking needs to be understood in its incremental, or transactional value. Risk taking cannot sustain itself as a management strategy that is successful over the long term. Why? Walter Hagen provides us with a little more insight: "You don't have the game you played last year or last week. You only have today's game. It may be far from your best, but that's all you've got. Harden your heart and make the best of it." You might argue that Hagen's words tend to support more risk taking than not. If so, I think you have missed a very subtle point.

Hagen recognizes that reality is what is in front of you at the time. Relying on strategies that worked previously is a game of chance—they may work or they may not. If the previous strategy was based on risks that exceeded the norm, the chances are that the manager will fail. If the strategy is consistent with a determined game plan—one developed based on the collectivity of experience and past successes, the probability of success increases dramatically. Nonetheless, there comes a time when risk taking is the most appropriate course of action. I recall one episode that might best serve to illustrate the how and when.

Where Did the Files Go?

There was a time when the United States was a major supporter of Iran. The Shah of Iran, before he was dethroned by the radical left and exiled, encouraged capitalism and corporate America's involvement in the area. There was a major financial institution at the time that provided the necessary infrastructure and funding to support a number of enterprises. With the Shah's overthrow, there was considerable upheaval in not only Iran, but many other parts of that area. One of them was the ongoing war between the Christian forces and Muslims, most notably in Beirut. After considerable shelling and fighting between the two groups, it became obvious to the bank that it should withdraw its presence immediately and reestablish itself in a more friendly environment.

As the warring factions carried on, the bank's former regional offices suffered considerable damage. It was felt that many of the bank's more sensitive files left behind in the manager's hurry to get out would be discovered by those unfriendly to the United States' interests. Because the files contained business transactions and names of individuals, the bank's executive management felt it was necessary to retrieve the files and secure them in another part of the world. To accomplish this, however, required that a team go into the area and secret them out. The files were rather voluminous, consisting of more than 40 file drawers. Simply driving a moving truck up, loading the files, and driving away was regarded as suicide and fraught with risks. Yet because of the unorthodox nature of this assignment, perhaps a direct approach might be best.

The risks were considerable, considering that Caucasians in an Arabic city would draw immediate attention. Using Arabic operatives was also risky simply based on the trust factor. Moreover, with daily fighting in the streets, there was always the possibility of someone getting shot. But the contents of the files were so sensitive that some risks would be required. Finally a plan was devised using a third-party security team with considerable experience (remember the comments above regarding the engagement of those with the technical expertise?).

The plan called for a team of screened Arab operatives to drive up to the building, enter the heavily shelled offices, inventory the contents, pack them up and, through bribing the port master (the airport at that time was closed to all but a handful of diplomatic carriers, none of which were American), have the files secreted onto an outbound ship as some form of other cargo. Unfortunately, as the plan was finalized, fighting in the area increased. This meant that no fewer than four separate runs at the building were required. Once the team made their way to the office containing the files, they discovered the door locked. In the bank manager's hurry to vacate the office he had taken the time to close and lock it. The problem now was that the Arab team felt it was against their religious and cultural heritage to simply break in, even though the building had been nearly destroyed as a result of recent shelling. Without the key to open the door properly, they were not entering.

The mission was halted until the key could be located. Two weeks later it was found in the desk drawer of a branch manager in Paris. (That is another long and unrelated story.) Suffice it to say that the key was retrieved and sent to the team, and they were successful in their efforts shortly thereafter. The cargo, however, was not sent via ship. Rather, it was boarded on a diplomatic courier airplane and flown to the designated location. Why was the there a shift between the ship and the airplane? It had always been the intention of the team to do so. Fundamentally, such operatives do not trust anyone, even their client, so there was a bait and switch element built into the plan.

This real-life story underscores several points about the use of risk taking. First, the task at hand required an approach that could not have been accomplished through conventional means. Second, though this is an admittedly unusual example, it demonstrates that risks involve costs: sometimes in human life, sometimes in time, and most certainly in expense. Third, risk taking means having the ability to react to changes and unplanned events. Fourth, risk taking is designed to achieve positive results. Weigh the probabilities carefully before launching a risk based plan; in other words, undertake a very thorough cost/benefit analysis before launching the plan. Finally, risk taking requires the use of experienced people who have the resources necessary to accomplish the task.

A game of golf is not as dramatic as secreting files out of a besieged city, but it too has its elements of high risk. Some of the more notable examples that come readily to mind are several of the recent major tournaments. In their efforts to beat Tiger Woods, many second-place holders have taken high-risk shots or employed unconventional strategies in hopes of gaining the upper hand. Their plans have been successful on a few occasions. However, more often than not, the plan has imploded, leaving them to drift lower and lower in the standings on the final day. The net effect: the loss of hundreds of thousands of dollars at the end of a single day's play. Had they focused on maintaining their second-place spot, they would have been significantly further ahead in terms of winnings and overall rankings. Risk taking is adventurous but it is also what the name implies—risky—and therefore dangerous.

The most rewarding things you do in life are often the ones that look like they can't be done.

Arnold Palmer

Resource Management

Another parallel between business management and the game of golf is resource management. Once again, I harken back to Mike's Dad story. This was all about my careless use of his father's clubs. I envision a day when there will be a built-in detector that signals a golfer when he or she has left a club behind in the fairway or on the green. Even though forgetting clubs is an easy thing to do, there is really no good excuse for doing so. The same thing can be said for many business decisions.

I also pointed out earlier that many nonsecurity executives take a myopic view of the management abilities of their security directors. Seeing asset protection as a specialty area, they fail to see through the specialty and measure the individual's ability to make even more contributions in another or an expanded capacity. Security managers themselves can fall victim to mismanaging their own resources. In reviewing their operations, I find it common for a security director to push hard for additional staff, especially in administrative functions. Take, for example, the function of inputting access cards for new hires or voiding those of employees recently separated from the organization. Often the case is made that this time-consuming but time-sensitive activity requires considerable staff time, therefore the need for an added staff person. When I hear this, I ask about the workload of the midnight shift console operator. Since this generally is a low activity time, I find that the operator will often be in a position to augment the input/output activity of access control. In other words, the security director has failed to review all of the available resources and think in new ways that can lead to more effective use of existing resources.

Golf is a thinking man's game. You can have all the shots in the bag, but if you don't know what to do with them, you've got troubles.

Chi Chi Rodriguez

Taking Responsibility

Finally, there is the parallel between the lessons of golf and business management regarding the manager's willingness to take responsibility. Previously I related the story of the gentleman and his caddie who mistakenly identified the wrong ball, with the result that the golfer missed his chance to break a long-standing score. There we saw that the golfer understood the rules of the game and accepted responsibility. Recently, a professional golfer lost a major tournament by one stroke because his caddie mistakenly allowed him to start the match with one more club in his bag than the rules allowed. The golfer lost more than $250,000. Again, the golfer accepted responsibility because it was his game and he was ultimately accountable for the proper number of clubs.

I wish I could say that accepting such responsibility was widespread in business. President Truman popularized the phrase, "The buck stops here." Yet example follows example in which other organizational executives, including U.S. presidents who followed Truman, failed to accept accountability for their actions and those of their staffs. Over the spring and summer months of 2002 our country saw chief executive after chief executive appear before Congress, grand juries, and the media denying responsibility for their failures and shifting the blame to someone else. In California, the great power crisis that turned a $12 billion surplus into a $23 billion debt in one year became a political football between the governor's office, federal regulatory agencies, and the state's legislature. These examples serve to illustrate that perhaps the leaders of our organizations need to take one more golf lesson—that of accepting responsibility for their actions.

Successful managers know that there are times when they must step forward and "face the music," even when they know that they could not fully control the actions of others. Regardless, they appreciate the reality that they are in charge and, as such, are the unit's leader. A true leader accepts the good and bad. Instilling confidence means that others look to the security manager to take the higher road, even if it means a setback. That is because the leader sees the bigger picture and focuses on the longer-term success.

> *Most golfers prepare for disaster. A good golfer prepares for success.*
>
> *Bob Toski*

Before closing this chapter, I would like to share three other short management stories. Each demonstrates a different characteristic of a successful manager, one that is acquired through experience and sensitivity to others. Collectively they illustrate that accomplishing an organizational goal requires interactions with others and the learning that it brings.

DEMONSTRATING TRUST

In the midst of America's merger mania two large organizations became one. A new security director was hired, much to the surprise of many within both companies. Each heretofore separate organization was sure their director would be given the nod to head up the new department. Shortly after the new director arrived he set out to bring in more new managers, in essence creating his own team. One of the previous directors resigned, and the other, Dan, accepted a lower-level position as manager of the combined investigative unit. One of the new director's hires was John, who was put in charge of several units, including investigations.

Six months into John's tenure a large internal fraud was discovered in one of the company's out-of-state operations. The security director asked John to take personal charge of the inquiry. John accepted, but realizing he would need help, told his boss that Dan would be accompanying him. The director reluctantly gave his approval, cautioning John that Dan was very popular in the field and might talk negatively about the new security team behind John's back.

As the two flew to their destination Dan asked John why he had been selected. John replied that he considered three things in making his choice. First was experience, and Dan certainly had that. Second was someone who knew the department under investigation well, and that was Dan. Finally, he needed someone he trusted and respected as a professional. Dan was taken aback and commented, "I thought your boss considered me part of the old team and there was no room for me on the new team." John looked at him and replied, "I don't know anything about new teams and old teams. I do know about my team and you're a critical part of it."

The next day, while meeting with a senior manager, John was summoned to the telephone to handle a breaking emergency. Upon departing John said to Dan, "I may be a while, I'll meet you in the break room for a cup of coffee when you finish here." The call did not take as long as John had anticipated. Completing it, he began to walk back into the senior manager's office. As he approached the door he heard the executive comment: "Dan I'm real sorry you didn't get the top job. We were really behind you. Is there anything I can do?" John waited for Dan's reply, recalling what his boss had cautioned him about. That's when Dan said: "No, I'm on a new team and really think the best decision was made. I intend to support them any way I can and would simply ask you to do the same." John knew his return was not required, so he turned and headed for the break room to await Dan's arrival.

Trust. It is a simple word, but it requires a great deal to exercise it. John knew well the danger associated with mixing old team members with new team members. More often than not the mix will fail if vested interests are still very much alive. Yet John put his trust in Dan and told him as much. John respected what Dan had to offer and saw him as a valuable resource. He made it a point to let Dan know this. Dan was mature enough, smart enough, and experienced enough to reciprocate with the same degree of trust and confidence given to him.

THE UNIVERSITY OF GOING IT ALONE

A few years back a corporate security manager was hired by the company's vice president for risk management. This VP had a number of units reporting to him, including audit, insurance, compliance, security, and quality assurance. It was not long before the security manager, Tom, realized that the VP had a serious drinking problem. The other department heads warned him that the VP's "MO" each day at noon was to call one of his managers and suggest they go to lunch to discuss some business matter. Unless the manager had some prior engagement, he or she would be roped into going along. There the boss would order at least two or three martinis and ask the subordinate to sign the check. Because the VP had signing authority for the expense, the lunch would pass through accounting as a business expense and the manager would be reimbursed accordingly.

Consequently, Tom's colleagues went out of their way to set up other arrangements to avoid lunch with the boss. Tom chose another route. When he got a call, he would always go. Tom didn't drink and never said anything to his boss about the number of martinis the VP consumed. After a number of months, the company's human resources department received an anonymous call suggesting they look into the VP's noon behavior. It was not long after that the VP entered a rehabilitation program. After three years with the company, Tom was approached by another firm, which offered him greater responsibility, more staff, and considerably more money. He accepted.

Shortly after joining the company, his new boss commented how experienced Tom was in handling a variety of very sensitive matters, especially considering he had not had that much "real-life" experience. Tom replied that it was largely the opportunity given to him by his former boss. The new one remarked, "I might be wrong, but I thought he had a drinking problem and spent more time off the job than on it." "That's true," Tom replied. He went on to comment: "You see, when he needed me, I was there. It wasn't long before he trusted me and basically let me do my own thing. Sure, I made some mistakes along the way, but I learned and I didn't have a boss looking over my shoulder and second-guessing me every step. He eventually got help and when he returned he knew he didn't have to watch over me like he felt he had to with the others. I was there in ways I suspect he'll never know. In return, he wasn't there hounding me every day. He allowed me to become the manager I am today."

Tom understood a basic factor in human relationships. Building trust in another allows that individual to build trust in you. Tom was astute enough to know that the VP needed help and that to get it he needed to trust those near him. Perhaps the VP's definition of help may have been misguided at the outset, but the need was there and Tom discovered a way to meet it. Along the way he also discovered that as his boss addressed his personal affairs that meant more time for Tom to develop into a stronger manager through experiencing the art of decision-making the tough way. Tom was once asked who his best boss ever was. He told the inquirer that it would be difficult to pick one, but the VP had to be among the top because he allowed Tom to graduate from the University of Going It Alone.

JUST WHAT DO YOU WANT?

Kelley's boss was anything but effective in trying to communicate what he wanted. It started when he informed her that the time had come to order the new security vehicles. The leases on the current fleet were coming to an end and the company's policy was to reorder as the term drew to a close. Kelley asked her boss if he wanted anything special. "No," he replied. "We usually get Fords. I see no sense in changing." Armed with that comment, she asked one of her employees to handle the project and put it out of her mind as she went about the business of managing the security department's administrative support section.

A few days passed and her subordinate filed a status report indicating the make, color, and so forth of each new vehicle. She forwarded it to her boss for his final okay before processing the order. A day later he called her in and informed her the colors were wrong. He told her he wanted all white cars and these were dark blue. She apologized and returned to adjust the order. The next day she again sent the package to her boss only to receive a call saying that he was not satisfied. She went to him again, and he told her the cars were two-doors and he wanted four-door models. Again she apologized, asked if there were any other issues he had with the order, and after being told no, set out to readjust the readjusted order. A third time she forwarded the package for his approval. And, as before, he called her in saying he was still not satisfied. This time he was not satisfied with the size of the engines. Irritated, she blurted out,

"But you told me there no other concerns!" She went on: "At the outset you told me you were satisfied with the current fleet. They are all dark blue, are two-door models, and have V6 engines. You have changed everything along the way!" The boss responded: "Well, I'm sorry, I didn't know I had so many options. You should have told me up-front!"

A couple of months later he called her into his office and said: "Kelley, I've been thinking about the ties our officers wear. I would like a change. Come back with something new and we'll go with it." It was not until she returned to her office and began thinking about her latest assignment that she realized that there are club ties, solid color ties, stripes than run left-to-right or right-to-left, ties with logo's, clip on ties, bow ties. . . .

My father-in-law once humorously told my wife and me that he always knew when my mother-in-law was mad at him. Before leaving work she would call and ask him to stop and buy a pound of sugar. "Sugar? How does that demonstrate she was mad at you?" I asked. He responded, "Have you ever bought sugar? There is white sugar, pure cane sugar, granular sugar, lump sugar, brown sugar, and so on and so on." All of these point out the necessity for clear and accurate communication. Managers often assume that their subordinates know what they want. They expect team members to read their minds and get it right the first time, every time. It simply does not work that way. Success requires that the stream of communication be succinct and understood by all stakeholders. This is pretty basic, but like so many of the other basics, managers lose sight of them and begin executing them poorly. As I draw this chapter to a close, I need to hurry along. I am to meet my wife for dinner and she asked that I stop and buy her a six-pack of soda along the way.

CONCLUDING COMMENTS

This chapter has been a departure from the classic security management texts. This was done by design, in hopes that the stories and analogies will allow you to think longer about them and the many lessons that can be drawn from each. This is not to suggest that the other chapters have not contained equally important information. Rather, when discussing the softer side of managing an asset protection program, or any other program, conventional approaches can sometimes miss the more subtle nature of what is intended. A great deal of material was covered in this chapter. Educational experts advise that using a story-based format allows the writer to cover a great number of lessons more efficiently and allows the reader to remember them more effectively. Hopefully, this is the case here, because there have been many topics covered.

- The importance of trust was presented in three ways: first with the king's general, in John's treatment of Dan, and Tom's relationship with his alcoholic boss.

- Managers can fall into the trap of their own arrogance, which can lead their bosses to "mentally terminating" them.
- Managing from a panic mode is very disruptive, yet remains common.
- Collaboration needs to replace a management style of dictating.
- The importance of staying focused on the simplicity of effectiveness and efficiency is inescapable, despite how they are masked under the latest and greatest new management theories.
- Successful managers go about the business of walking the walk while others master only the art of talking the talk.
- The parallels between a good golf game and a successful business manager include the ability to demonstrate:

  strong sportsmanship

  integrity and honor

  a strong sense of humor

  strategic management

  patience and endurance

  a positive competitive spirit

  knowing when to take calculated risks

  an ability to accept responsibility
- The opportunity to manage without continuous direct intervention from the boss is of great value.
- Communicating your desires clearly and thoroughly is of the utmost importance.

With each of the items in this list, a stage has been developed for what follows. By setting forth a series of lessons that a manager will find useful, a baseline is created for a much broader exploration of what it takes to be a successful manager in today's global economy–driven world of business. We can better understand what other writers have to offer because some of their observations and conclusions reflect many of the lessons presented in this chapter.

Never let the fear of striking out get in your way.

Babe Ruth

THOUGHT-PROVOKING QUESTIONS

1. Are you the deer in your CEO's headlights? Or is there someone else that you know either inside the organization or in another that may be in this position? If so, what can be done to avoid being hit?

2. This chapter explores in more depth the concept of management by *panic du jour*. Is your organization actively partaking in this entree? If so, what can be done to stop this method of operating? If not, what are you doing to avoid this deadly course?

3. The author makes a case for maintaining a focus on the two E's of effectiveness and efficiency, and avoiding the trappings associated with management writers' so-called latest and greatest new strategy. What do think about such an approach?

4. Many parallels were presented between the game of golf and organizational management. What are your thoughts? Can you add any more parallels? What other sports analogies are there? What characteristics do they share with successful organizational managers?

5. The chapter concludes with three management stories that highlight the importance of building trust, the value of learning on your own, and the need for clear and concise communication. Is there a story you know that illustrates an equally important management lesson?

Chapter 8

GUIDELINES FOR SUCCESS

If I have seen further it is by standing on the shoulders of giants.

Isaac Newton

Primary Themes

- Apply Morris's Seven C's to Achieve True Success
- Lessons from Past and Present Giants
- Harari's 11 Rules for Bold Leadership from the Middle

OPENING OBSERVATIONS

In this chapter we continue our journey, focusing on the art of management. We covered a great deal of territory in Chapter 7; we will do the same here. We will not cover new management theories, but will focus on the basics because I believe we have strayed far enough away from them as to become lost. Tiger Woods says that just before a major tournament he focuses on the basics because having command of the basics separates the winner from all others. Effective management means having the ability to stay in touch with core principles and values that can serve to guide us in new directions. Without these managers cannot hope to achieve success, even if they possess all of the technical know-how. Here's a quick example.

I received a call from a client who wanted to know everything I knew about "knowledge management." She went on to say that this was the new thing in her organization and she did not want to be out of the loop. "Oh by the way," she added, "can you also give me a five-minute crash course in decision-making analysis using the Kepner-Tregoe process? We're starting to use of lot of this stuff and I'm going to need to get up to speed quickly if I'm going to survive."

Something was missing. I felt she was masking something deeper by throwing out some of today's jargon in hopes of demonstrating that "she really was in the know," that she was *one of them.*

Jargon is a powerful tool, if it is used correctly. Jargon helps create clarity between two professionals, allowing them to connect quickly and efficiently when they are both using it correctly. But jargon is only a communication instrument. It does not indicate an individual's capacity to effectively manage. Knowing the latest and greatest in techniques and strategies is not sufficient, either, and even knowing how to implement them in the technical sense is no measure. To be successful, a manager must be grounded in the basics of understanding human relationships. This is why we will spend time on the thoughts of those who have gone before us.

I begin by revisiting Tom Morris. I first introduced him in my previous book, *The Art,* which I ended with his Seven C's for Success. When I first set out to write this book I originally intended to start with the following discussion. As this latest endeavor began to unfold, however, it made far more sense to put it here. I follow this discussion with a return visit for some of you to such giants as Deming, Peters, McGregor, Follett, Bennis, and Drucker. Each in their own way has helped shape what we call management today. Finally, I want to conclude with a paper authored by Oren Harari entitled "Managing from the Middle." This is a provocative article that addresses the issue of how one manages from a mid-management position, which is where most security managers find themselves.

REVISITING TOM MORRIS

As noted, I finished *The Art* by drawing the reader's attention to Tom Morris's Seven C's for Success. I thought it was appropriate then because he offers a different perspective on what it means to be successful. As I understand, he has stepped away from his role as a philosophy professor at Notre Dame and is now a management consultant and motivational speaker. One of his other books is entitled *If Aristotle Ran General Motors.* As in his previous book, *True Success: A New Philosophy of Excellence,* which is centered around his Seven C's, he challenges corporate managers to take a different perspective toward their pursuit of business excellence. He defines a new corporate spirit, one that revolves around truth, beauty, goodness, and unity.

In *Aristotle,* he begins by observing: "The philosophers of the centuries, from Plato and Aristotle to the present day, have left us the equivalent of a huge bank account of wisdom that we can draw on for a wealth of insight applicable to both business and the rest of life. We can invest this intellectual capital in our own careers and experiences and reap tremendous returns of new wisdom as a result." He continues: "I believe that a few simple but powerful ideas drawn from Aristotle as well as from many other great philosophers of the past can help us re-energize our ways of doing business, reinvigorate our workplaces, and reinvent corporate spirit for our time. Ultimately, greatness is rooted in simplicity, if we make consistent use of the most fundamental, simple concepts and truths about excellence as foundations for everything we do."

By this time, I think it no surprise that I endorse his notion of simplicity. From the first chapter of this book the concept of simplicity rings loud and clear, because I too believe that success is achieved through simple planning and staying focused on what needs to be done. Yet, more is required. Success requires a context, a framework that allows individuals to stay centered in all that they do. For me, Morris's Seven C's provide one such context. They are:

1. We need a clear *conception* of what we want, a vivid vision, a goal or set of goals powerfully imagined.

2. We need a strong *confidence* that we can attain our goals.

3. We need a focused *concentration* on what it takes to reach our goal.

4. We need a stubborn *consistency* in pursuing our vision, a determined persistence in thought and action.

5. We need an emotional *commitment* to the importance of what we're doing, and to the people with whom we're doing it.

6. We need a good *character* to guide us and keep us on a proper course.

7. We need a *capacity* to enjoy the process along the way.

Listing them allows us to read each and take a few moments to reflect on them. I would, however, like to expand our reflection by making a few comments about each.

A Clear *Conception* of What We Want, a Vivid Vision or Goal Powerfully Imagined

Earlier we explored the concept of vision as that which guides us. But from where does this vision originate? Does it just materialize one day as we engage in something else? Perhaps, but it most probably found its genesis in some prior experience or thought process. A clear conception of what we want begins with the deliberate exercise of contemplating what *is* versus what we *want*. Many security managers can easily define what their world is and whether they like it or not. The successful ones are those who see clearly the disparity between their reality and what could be. Robert Kennedy popularized the saying, "Some men see things as they are and ask why. I dream things that never were and ask why not?"

With these words, Kennedy defines what Morris means by powerfully imagined. That which is powerfully imagined requires time for thought. A manager requires time alone—solitude. If properly used, this time alone allows one to think about realities and how things need to be changed. During my corporate years I spent many an evening staying back after everyone else left. This time alone allowed me to walk around the office to think about the challenges currently facing the department and consider alternatives. Now, as a consultant, I do the same for my clients. Time alone can force one to think differently. Some of my best thinking occurs when I am running, whether it is beside a road, along a path, or on a treadmill. Location is secondary; time is primary. Out of these experiences arise new perspectives, new ideas, new visions.

I recently met with David Gibbs at a client site. We were discussing some of the latest security technology and he began telling me of a new product that would soon be available. Then he smiled and commented that I had talked about the same idea over ten years ago. I had taken the time then to see what was needed and think about it. The technology was not available then, but that did not stop someone from considering the possibilities. Great ideas spring into being only when time is given for them to jell in someone's mind.

Imagination is more important than knowledge.

Albert Einstein

A Strong *Confidence* That We Can Attain Our Goals

One of my father-in-law's favorite childhood rhymes goes like this:

Somebody said that it couldn't be done
But, he with a chuckle replied:
That maybe it couldn't, but he would be one
That wouldn't give in till he tried.
So, he buckled right in with a bit of a grin on his face,
If he worried he hid it, and he started to sing as he tackled that thing
That couldn't be done and he did it.

He kept this ditty in his office until the day he retired. He was with the same company for 44 years, starting out as an errand boy for the purchasing department. When he retired the company had grown to the world's largest dental conglomerate and he had 13 presidents reporting to him. You may think of the rhyme childish, yet it served him, as it does my entire family today, as a reminder that despite the difficulty of many things, most anything can be accomplished if one has a strong sense of confidence.

Establishing goals is only the beginning. Lacking the confidence to achieve them is nearly as bad as not having defined them in the first place. Today's business world is fraught with uncertainty. I have noted before that life is only 1% what is dealt to us. The other 99% is how we deal with it. It seems to me we all have three options: We can choose to go part way and give up; we can stay where we are, blaming others for our being stuck; or we can commit to making a difference and accomplish what we set out to achieve. I do recognize, however, that life's events sometimes draw us away from one goal to another. When this happens we need to embrace what E.M. Forster said: "We must be willing to let go of the life we have planned, so as to have the life that is waiting for us." Either way, we demonstrate a strong confidence that we can attain our goals.

The greater the difficulty, the greater the glory.

Cicero

Focused *Concentration* to Reach Our Goal

It is easy to get sidetracked. I suspect that is why I am a strong advocate of keeping management principles as simple as possible. Simplicity allows us to maintain our concentration; it allows focus. Morris sums this up best in commenting: "The quest for success is a journey, sometimes difficult, sometimes easy, occasionally brief, but often long, a journey of effort, frustration and joy. At its best, it is a journey of heart, mind, and body. It's an adventure of challenge and triumph. Most people who fail in life just fail to prepare themselves for the journey. They lack any focused concentration on what it will take to reach their goals. Or, as another catchy aphorism has it, they don't plan to fail, they just fail to plan."

Hence, we find yet another reason why planning is so important for a manager. What Morris tells us about success in life certainly has a direct application for managers. Planning allows us to stay focused, to concentrate on what we set out to achieve. Drawing from my own experience, I had a plan that guided me to achieving my career goals. I knew the day I started a new job that in three years I would move to the next level of my professional career. I did not always achieve it exactly in accordance with my original timeline, but more often than not I did. People are amazed when I tell them of my last corporate experience. On my first day I gathered the staff, introduced myself, and told them that over the next three years we were going to accomplish things they had yet to even think about. We were going to have fun along the way, but more importantly, we would be demonstrating our corporate value over and over. They became excited because they knew that I knew we had goals to achieve.

Before we ended the meeting I told them one additional thing. I said that three years from that day I most likely would be moving on, having accomplished what we were about to undertake. They were shocked to hear their new boss say such a thing. But I had a plan and that plan included my moving on. And, just as I had done with every other job but one, exactly three years later I moved on. (The one exception took me almost four years to the date I was hired.) I had a plan and understood the concept of focused concentration. I knew that to achieve my personal goal, we needed to achieve what we set out to do as a security tem. When all was said and done, to do so required a commitment on the team's part—to maintain that commitment required focus.

Morris leads us to another important consideration: sometimes the journey involves detours. Since we are not complete masters of our destiny, external variables do arise. But does this mean we will miss our target, and we can lose focus? Far from it. Morris tells us: "A detour is nothing more than a different way to get where we are going. We just can't usually see it as such unless we have that goal clearly in view and we understand the unavoidable unpredictability involved in any interesting journey. It may take us longer than we had planned. But then again the detour may end up being the scenic route, allowing us to see things we might not otherwise have been able to appreciate. And traveling it may enhance our skills."

We are not retreating. We are advancing in another direction.
Gen. Douglas MacArthur

A Stubborn *Consistency*—a Determined Persistence in Thought and Action

Note that Morris says a *stubborn consistency*, which not the same as a foolish consistency. Stubbornness can be a positive attribute if it is not exercised to an extreme. If it describes a person's doggedness, such stubbornness is an attribute. Conversely, stubbornness can also describe intransigence. The latter situation, as we noted earlier, is far more likely to put the manager squarely in line with the CEO's headlights. A stubborn inconsistency can also describe what I referred to in *Business Strategies* as organizational cancer—a cancer that results commonly in the death of the organization. I am speaking about complacency, the attitude that "we have always done it this way, so it must be okay." Complacency kills drive, kills imagination, kills the organization's spirit.

On the other hand, a stubborn consistency is another way of describing the manager's determination, or as Morris himself refers to it, *firmness of purpose*. Success comes to those who can change as conditions warrant without being driven away from unchanging principles. The dogged manager knows what is ethically correct and does not break under the pressure of the politically expedient or a view that is espoused by even the majority, if the majority is wrong.

To help us, Morris offers his Five-I Framework for Positive Change. He notes that one of the major obstacles to achieving firmness of purpose is the persistent inconsistencies in our lives. These are caused by:

- **Ignorance:** Not being aware that there is a problem even when everyone else is
- **Indifference:** The "I don't care" attitude
- **Inertia:** Being stuck in a rut and not knowing how to get out

To overcome these three self-destructive inconsistencies requires the introduction of:

- **Information:** Being receptive to data that may come from one or more sources such as colleagues, customers, bosses, books
- **Imagination:** Being receptive to new and bold ideas renews our ability to care

The Bible tells us the story of a traveler who arrived late at the inn. He pounded on the door until he awoke the innkeeper, who rebuked him and turned him away. But the traveler persisted and continued to knock loudly until the innkeeper could no longer take it. The innkeeper let him in, knowing that only this would satisfy the traveler and enable the innkeeper to go back to bed. This is positive persistence or stubborn consistency.

To keep a lamp burning, you have to continue to put oil in it.
Mother Teresa

Emotional *Commitment* to What We're Doing, and to the People with Whom We're Doing It

A few paragraphs back I told you about my three-year plan. You will recall that I told my staff at the outset that I intended to move on after three years. Some readers may have thought, "so much for loyalty and developing a commitment." Let me add a footnote to that anecdote. To my surprise, approximately two years later I received *Security Magazine's* Executive Achievement Award. It was the journal's first national award recognizing the contribution of a manager in our industry. I was nominated by my entire staff without me even knowing such an award was possible. They nominated me because of what I had done for them. As surprised and happy as I was to receive the award, I told the *Security Magazine* journalists that the true story lay with what my staff had accomplished. In the two years since assuming the helm of the security department, I had watched each individual grow and perform at levels they had never dreamed possible.

The day after the award ceremonies several staff members and myself were talking about the recent events. It was then that I reinforced my pride in them and told them they were the ones who deserved the recognition. One them thought about that comment for a moment and then said, "No Den. You showed us the power of being committed. Your commitment to us and the goal is what drove us." I had never thought about it that way. It was true enough, but it was they who had followed, and together we had charted a path that could only lead to one end—success. For me it was a powerful lesson about being committed—on everyone's part. Ralph Waldo Emerson once noted,

"Nothing great was ever achieved without enthusiasm." Managers need to understand that enthusiasm is required of everyone—not one person, not a few, but everyone.

Morris tells us that he has come to believe that successful living and successful working are a process of self-discovery, self-invention, self-discipline, and self-indulgence. By self-indulgence he means the process of engaging in that we love to do whenever we can. Sometimes this means changing what you are doing; sometimes it may mean simply changing the way you view what it is that you are doing. He reminds us of the story about three men hauling stones in wheelbarrows. When asked what they are doing, the first says, "I'm hauling rocks." The second says, "I'm helping put up a wall." The third replies, "I'm building a cathedral." In short, emotional commitment is rooted in one's perspective on life.

Enthusiasm is the electric current that keeps the engine of life going at top speed.

B.C. Forbes

A Good *Character* to Guide Us and Keep Us on a Proper Course

Goethe once noted, "The history of a man is in his character." As I write this I cannot help but be saddened by how strongly this Seven C element resonates with the American public. Whatever one's politics, few would disagree that former President Clinton's personal character was an embarrassment. Public figures such as O.J. Simpson and many other sports celebrities, Hollywood stars, and other entertainers, have cast the shadow of questionable character upon themselves. As though this was not enough, the summer of 2002 found us reeling from one scandal after another involving Roman Catholic priests and their bishops. And when we thought we could go no lower, corporate executive after corporate executive found themselves the target of federal probes involving fraudulent or deceptive activities.

Good character is an inescapable ingredient in an organization's success. Greed, which is often the root cause of failure, may gain near-term success in the marketplace, but it cannot sustain success over the long run. We need to be cautious in even using the word "success" to describe the near-term end results. On one dimension we can say a manager is successful if targeted goals have been met. But if these accomplishments are the result of fraud or deception, then such successes are less than paper thin. They are more of an illusion because they lack a sound foundation but have only a surface appearance that leads to the conclusion that success is there. I liken such results to a movie set. When viewed on the screen, many structures appear to be real. In reality, they are only sets and consist of an exterior facade only. The same can be said for many props or stunts performed by the star. All appear to be what they are not.

Lacking good character is the same. Scoundrels and unethical managers can achieve fame and wealth. History and today's events are testimonies to this. But such measures fail to be what Morris believes is "true success." By this he means that "success which is deeply satisfying, that involves making the most of our potential, and that is sustainable over the long run, the sort of success that contributes to all forms of health and human flourishing." I suspect he would not object to my adding that it is also that which is noble and can withstand the scrutiny of another's judgement. True success can stand on its own, apart from the one(s) that may have caused it to come into being. I know this may sound fairly philosophical, and admittedly it is to some extent. But it is more than just philosophy. Success, if it is true success, creates a lasting trust. I can be confident in buying a product or service from a company because they have earned my trust. This trust fosters higher earnings for the company, which in turn defines their success.

The case of Martha Stewart is an excellent example of the trust–success relationship. As of this writing she remains someone who is only suspected of wrongdoing. Nonetheless, her character has been brought into question, and even though her actions were in no way associated with her company, the value of the company's common stock plummeted. Why? Because of a break in the stockholders' trust.

Having good character seems so basic to the human enterprise that one is tempted to ask why it is even necessary to have to even write about it. Sadly, it is required for, as Morris observes, "It is no surprise that in our time the most neglected condition of success may be our condition number six: the necessity of a good character to guide us and keep us on a proper course. The kind of character that will give us sound guidance in our choice of goals and of the means to those goals." He wrote these words in the early 1990s. Now, more than a decade later, they ring just as loudly. Long before that, Alexander Bebel pointed the rebuking finger at corporate enterprises and accused: "The nature of business is swindling." Despite all of the evidence to suggest otherwise, I do hope this point of view is jaded and does not reflect the majority's approach to business management.

Should our halls of academe insist on teaching business ethics? Of late, many business schools have dropped courses dedicated to ethical behavior altogether. Most contend that, as a topic, ethics is integrated into many other courses. Whether this is the case or not, I am no longer certain that having it as a separate course of study or is essential. When schools began to move away from teaching ethics as standalone courses, I was offended because I am one of those who teach business ethics. Teaching ethics was a hot topic for business schools in the 1990s, but now the 1990s are cynically referred to as the decade of greed. Likewise, the cynical side of me thinks, "So much for ethical behavior taking root through our academic institutions." I am not alone. Regarded by many as one of our country's leading management minds, Peter Drucker comments: "Ethics stays in the preface of the average business science book." Again, I hope that the actions of a few represent only the actions of a few, and are not a reflection of a much deeper and widespread erosion in executive row.

Much earlier I made the point that those who are inherently ethical know how to act accordingly and do not need laws to govern their behavior. Others who are not so ethical will simply find ways to manipulate the laws to their personal advantage. I believe the same can be said for the need to set time aside for specifically addressing ethical conduct in a business school environment. If the purpose of such academic pursuit is to critically analyze the nature of what is and what is not ethical and its consequences, then there is definite academic value. If the purpose is to somehow convince students that ethical behavior and decision-making is the proper course of action, then this is an indictment on those who have gone before university professors and college instructors.

Before turning our attention to Morris's final condition, I want to offer another factor that underlies much of today's unethical corporate behavior. I am speaking about the pressure associated with "making our numbers." Over the past decade I have watched as stock analysts and the media seem to compete with one another in a feeding frenzy over corporate performance. Company executives know that their firm's performance is measured in 90-day increments. If there is a perceived stumble, the stock is battered. Note that I say perceived, because the stumble is not always the reality.

Senior management has fallen victim to allowing the proverbial tail (stock analysts) to wag the dog (the company). The 1990s saw an explosion of day trading, a highly volatile and risky practice that often served as the driving force for major swings in stock prices. It was also the decade when the term *whisper number* came into vogue, that make-believe number that analysts *wanted* to see as opposed to an otherwise legitimate number based on actual earnings. Along with analyst whispering came the use of projected earnings as a measure of future performance that somehow or other equated to, or exceeded, actual value. There were many other so-called value-added metrics that served as barometers of corporate performance. If the companies were perceived as falling behind, stock options and other compensation programs were at severe risk. Drucker observed many years ago: "Stock option plans reward the executive for doing the wrong thing. Instead of asking, 'Are we making the right decision?' he asks, 'How did we close today?' It is encouragement to loot the corporation."

This short-sighted, high-stakes game (90-day performance) has become the catalyst for doing what it takes to make the books look good. Couple such a strategy with an economic downturn and the mix is right for any shell game to be discovered. It is no wonder that more than $7 trillion was lost in retirement accounts in a matter of weeks. The corporate calamity of 2002 demon-

strated that the system is inherently flawed. Yet, true reform based on addressing this basic system flaw (e.g., *what have you done for me these past 90 days?*)
is not even under consideration.

A man's own character is the arbiter of his fortune.

Publius Syrus

A *Capacity* to Enjoy the Process along the Way

Of Morris's Seven C's, this is my personal favorite. So much is written about
the need to enjoy what it is that we are doing, and yet I dare say few of us actually do. Morris is not talking about "following your passion." This fairly new,
but overused, expression has misled more well-intentioned managers and professionals than almost anything else. Following passion is filled with traps and,
more often than not, frustration. The art of passion following is difficult to
pursue and sustain. We have all heard of the starving artist. There are just as
many starving writers, actors, inventors, and even professionals. By now you
know of my keen interest in golf. Among the books I have in my library is one
that is fully dedicated to the hardships endured by excellent golfers pursuing
their passion of trying to break into the big time of the PGA tour.

Dismissing the concept of pursuing one's passion as a general course of
pursuit is not to suggest that we should just "buck up and be content with what
life has given us." On the contrary, having the capacity to enjoy means having
the ability to consciously make choices, one of which may mean pursing
another line of work altogether. Many security managers have sought my advice
regarding their organizational sense of worth and happiness. To some I have
had to point out that career development meant moving on. Managers who
continue to stay where they are not happy, when they believe that more is out
there, need to understand that their feelings will translate directly into how they
manage.

Unhappy or insecure managers are about as injurious to their organization
as are complacent employees. Both invariably spiral the organization downward. Such a direction can only have one outcome—*crash and burn*, as marketing gurus are wont to call it. Morris's definition of the capacity to enjoy
focuses directly on the ability to enjoy the present. He tells of an exchange
between the Greek thinker Diogenes and Alexander the Great. In this discourse,
Diogenes asks what Alexander hopes to achieve. Alexander tells him of his plans
to conquer Greece and, having accomplished this, do the same with Asia Minor.
After that, his goal is to conquer the world. Diogenes pursues it one step further:
"Then what?" Alexander replies that he will relax and enjoy himself. To which
Diogenes finally asks: "Why not save yourself all of the trouble by relaxing and
enjoying yourself now?" As Morris notes, Alexander never got the point.

Having the capacity to enjoy means enjoying what you are doing now. I must
admit that as a classical A-type personality, many years slipped by that I did

not truly enjoy. I find myself still struggling with this, but I know that I am on the right path. My friends and family look at me and tell me I have never looked so relaxed. They tease me about having moved to the country, and I tease them back because I no longer have a mortgage.

Some readers may say, "Yes, for him it works because he's been at it for more than 30 years and has his house paid for." If only it were so simple. Along my journey I can recall many a manager who had found that capacity to enjoy, including those who had far fewer years of experience and even larger mortgages. Morris points out that children instinctively know how to enjoy the present moment. As adults, on the other hand, we gear our lives toward rushing into the future. It is a profound thought.

> *You can't control the wind, but you can control your sails.*
>
> *Chinese Proverb*

A Guide to Managing the Basics

W. Edward Deming

In *The Art* you may recall that I spent time discussing Deming's views regarding the pursuit of quality. As a part of that discussion I also examined his Seven Deadly Diseases that can affect an organization. Each can sideline a security manager's program without much effort. In rereading what I wrote in 1997, I was struck by the similarity with several of the points I have raised in this book. Apparently change is a very slow process indeed!

Deming recognizes that the organization is a holistic system, including all of its influencing factors—internal and external customers, suppliers and competitors. His seven deadly diseases that can impact an organization are:

1. **Failure to develop a long-term purpose:** As noted above, American businesses are driven by quarterly and/or annual results. Success is measured based on how well one performs this year as compared to the previous quarter or year. This absence of a longer view makes employees and managers feel insecure in their jobs and this then feeds directly to the second deadly disease.

2. **Focus on near-term profits:** American businesses define their success based on quarterly earnings. Public companies are driven by expected returns from the investment community. This preoccupation with profit for the sake of profit erodes concern and attention for the longer view. Resources that are designed to feed the future suffer for the sake of near-term profit.

3. **Conducting annual performance reviews:** Annual performance reviews rarely measure true annual performance. Rather, they reflect

the last "you done me wrong" or "atta-boy." Employees soon discover that performance criteria are a way of punishing more than encouraging. Deming believes these measurements have the opposite impact on morale and productivity for both managers and workers. They promote fear, inequities, internal competition, anger, and discouragement. After spending three decades in both the public and private sector, I heartily agree that more negative effects occur than positive outcomes.

4. **Management exodus:** Deming points out the traditional migration of high-level managers from one company to another. Whether they are dedicated executives who have become disenfranchised or just opportunists, managers are not developed with the "big picture" in mind. Over the past several years, corporations themselves have unwittingly turned on themselves with the wholesale elimination of middle and senior management layers. In their pursuit to achieve lower operating expenses, they jeopardized their own continuity and the talent once hired to create their future.

5. **Missing the hidden value:** A company's success is just as linked to intangible values as it is to the empirical, or known, data. Unfortunately, many companies miss the former altogether in their pursuit of the latter. As Deming explains, some of the most important figures for a company are "unknowable." They include the multiplier effect of a happy or unhappy customer, the absence of that "extra mile" by motivated managers and workers that makes all the difference, and the hours saved in front-end planning and communicating.

6. **Lack of emphasis on healthcare prevention:** Even though many companies are turning to healthcare prevention programs, the vast majority of American businesses have yet to make the transition. The evidence clearly demonstrates that significant savings can be achieved in premium reductions when prevention becomes the front line of choice. These include wellness programs, anti-smoking programs, paid workouts and/or health club memberships, and annual medical check-ups.

7. **Substituting CQI (continuous quality improvement) for warranties:** It has become easy for companies to offer warranties. But the real value of their product or service is not reliance on a system that is driven by "customer satisfaction guarantees." Although warranties provide assurance that the company is concerned about the quality of the product, the real value is in establishing error-free systems altogether. Companies that commit to quality and error-free work realize savings during a warranty period because of very few nonanticipated services. In other words, the warranty is the consumers' safety net—it is not the company's substitution for CQI.

These seven deadly sins have clear applications to security providers. Even though each has a specific lesson for the third-party supplier, the underlying principles apply to resident security programs as well. Security decision-makers need to become focused on the longer-term strategy for providing asset protection. This is best illustrated in their systems purchases. I find that all too often the procurement process is driven by answering the here and now need. As the company grows or alters its course, today's "new" security system quickly becomes obsolete.

Focus on short-term profits can be just as deadly. In today's litigious society, premises liability has become big business for attorneys. Deferring action until better economic times are evident can place the organization at greater risk. There are many ways to creatively finance capital expenditures or budget operating expenses. One of the more overlooked approaches, for example, involves splitting the cost over a longer budget period (e.g., extending the budget cycle from 12 months to 18 months).

Deming's belief that annual performance reviews work more against the employer–employee relationship than for it is worthy of particular note. He is not advocating that performance ought not be reviewed. Rather, it is the current approach that he and other quality specialists find troubling. More effective are peer reviews, group assessments, quality circles, demonstrable contributions, and so forth. These and other strategies are addressed later in our discussion of the journey toward future success.

One of the more difficult challenges facing corporate America and the security profession is the issue of management mobility. It remains true that a company's success is linked to its ability to inject fresh ideas and new perspectives on a regular basis. It is equally true that success is linked to the company's ability to maintain a balance of continuity. Longevity is not bad.

Security programs are built on earned trust and proven reliability. Whether the people are proprietary, outsourced, or a combination of both, success directly corresponds to demonstrated capability. This is difficult to measure, but it is very real. You can't measure it, you can't even see it most times, but you know it's there—you can feel it.

Deming's last two deadly diseases speak to a reliance on traditional approaches and their inherent traps. There was a time when healthcare benefit costs were an insignificant part of the compensation formula. With runaway costs, however, this is no longer the case. Rather than shopping for lower premiums among competing carriers, the better answer requires a change in strategy altogether. By seeking an alternative healthcare approach, the cost associated with escalating expenses is attacked at the root level. The end result is a lower cost all around. The question to be asked is whether or not the same type of thinking can be applied elsewhere.

In a like vein, warranties have become a standard business practice. There was a time when guarantees inherently forced employees to think error-free. The corporation understood the cost associated with having to redo or resupply a defective product. Over time, warranties have become the employee's safety net. After all, they reason, the company can afford a few mistakes. Besides, how many people really go through the effort to take us up on our warranty? Such misguided, and what I term "lazy thinking," misses the very point of offering a guarantee. Such lazy thinking is a direct result of lax management.

I have found this even among my consulting colleagues. To become an associate of my firm, one needs to demonstrate a commitment to quality improvement. Part of this is an acceptance that if the client is not satisfied (satisfaction being defined by the client), then neither the consultant nor I receive our fee. The incentive is very high for both of us. The only way I can assure success is to do an excellent job myself and be very selective in choosing the right associates. If compensation is the primary driver, we will not be successful. Rather, to accept such a risk is to be committed to producing a quality product for the sake of a quality product. Stated another way, it's a willingness to engage in something in which the intrinsic motivation transcends the monetary value.

In our pursuit of quality strategies, I'd like to complete our discussion of Deming's contribution with a review of several obstacles he has identified. These obstacles plague organizations because they are grounded in management mindsets that work against their best interests. Yet because of America's obsession with short-term fixes, executives and business unit heads frequently find themselves heading down a path that leads to anywhere but success. Security managers are no exception.

- **The Quick Fix:** Deming cautions that one cannot simply put a quality process in place overnight. When I was asked to assist a security services company in developing a corporatewide QA program, I suggested that the transformation would begin to bear its first fruit three years out. The president blanched and then rested back after a moment's reflection. Then he commented, "If then." That insightful response demonstrated that he was on the right road.

- **Reliance on Technology as the Great Problem Solver:** Technology is an administrative tool. Nothing more. Real quality arrives when the tools are used by skilled specialists. As one observer notes, "The future includes high-tech as well as high-touch."

- **Following the Leader:** Organizations that wait for "the other guy" to chart a new course and then follow their lead will always be behind. Each organization is unique. It is important to learn from the lessons of those who have gone before, but it is only when they blend the nuances of their culture with the maps of those who have gone ahead, that real qualitative progress can be made.

- **Accountability for QA Is Limited:** A security supplier was asked to describe her company's QA program. She proudly told the selection committee that her company had a great program. She then went on to describe how they had a QA director, a QA council, and a QA mission. When pressed to describe the process, she said she would have to get back to them because that was something the QA people would have to answer. And then she asked, "Why are you concerned about QA, we've done that and moved beyond." Quality assurance is a continuously unfolding process. It is not a commodity or one-time event left to those who specialize in it. It belongs to everyone, all the time.

Tom Peters

Tom Peters became a management icon in the 1980s. His bestselling book, *In Search of Excellence*, captured the attention of corporate executives because of its simple but powerful message. At the start of that decade he delineated his eight attributes that characterize outstanding performers. They are

1. A bias toward action
2. Simple form and lean staff
3. Continued contact with customers
4. Productivity improvement via people
5. Operational autonomy to encourage entrepreneurship
6. Stress on one key business value
7. Emphasis on doing what they know best
8. Simultaneous loose–tight controls

Each of these principle characteristics, I believe, is self-explanatory. This is because they are so basic, so simple. Like Deming's diseases, they read as though they were written for 2000 and beyond. This reflects the timelessness of what is being offered. Sound management begins with building blocks that support an organization for a very long time. To do this, the blocks need to be solid and long lasting themselves.

Peters notes: "Although none of these sounds startling or new, most are conspicuously absent in many companies today. Far too many managers have lost sight of the basics—service to customers, low-cost manufacturing, productivity improvement, innovation, and risk-taking. In many cases, they have been seduced by the availability of MBAs, armed with the "latest" in strategic planning techniques. MBAs who specialize in strategy are bright, but they often cannot implement their ideas, and their companies wind up losing the capacity to act."

Peters wrote this nearly a quarter of a century ago. When I rediscovered this last year, I set out to ask my clients and MBA students what they thought. Since that time I have offered his remarks to well over 200 managers, some from emerging high-tech companies and many who are associated with the Fortune

500. A great deal has happened over these 25 years. TQM has come and gone, globalization has strongly emerged, resizing and merger mania have become corporate staples, we have had three recessions—each with its own call for smarter ways of managing in order to stay competitive. When I ask today's managers if what Peters has to offer applies to them, I more often than not receive this interesting reply: "Oh, I didn't know Peters had a new book out. What is this one called, I'd like to read it, maybe even pass it along to my boss in hopes that he/she will learn something."

Douglas McGregor and Mary Parker Follett

In his book, *The Human Side of Enterprise*, Douglas McGregor introduces us to his Theory X and Theory Y. Stemming from his work in the 1950s, he was intrigued by the inconsistencies of management behavior. He concluded that mainstream management theorists at that time believed employees have an inherent dislike for work and this, in turn, requires management to employ coercive measures to get employees to work, and that the average worker wants to be directed. These three assumptions represented his Theory X.

Conversely, his Theory Y purports:

- Effort spent on working is as natural as effort spent on play or resting.
- Coercive inducements are not the only motivators for achieving productivity.
- Commitment is a result of the perceived rewards attached to accomplishing the objectives.
- Employees, when properly encouraged actually seek out responsibility.
- Creativity and ingenuity can be found throughout the organization and are not limited to a few.
- An employee's intellectual capacity is only partially being tapped.

These six assumptions set in motion many of the basics that define today's management–employee relationship. He was not alone in advocating a shift in the way managers exercise control over their subordinates. Mary Parker Follett articulated the core of McGregor's theory as early as the 1930s, at a time when Frederick Taylor was developing his scientific management school and Henri Fayol was espousing the attributes of strong management control over employees.

For today's security manager, understanding the early work of McGregor and Follett helps to define the emphasis on collaboration and cross-functional teams. Classic military and paramilitary models have historically paralleled the scientific school of management. Hence, managers holding steadfast to the latter over the former find themselves creating their own conflict. Even today's military models are more in line with team management principles than the one-way controlling techniques previously employed.

Before moving on, it is important to note that Theory X, as Gayle Porter notes, "is not an evil set of assumptions, but rather a limiting one. Use of authority to influence has its place, even within Theory Y assumptions, but it does not work in all circumstances." Porter goes on to note that the critical challenge for managers is to honestly examine the assumptions that underlie their own behavior. Fully understanding the implications of both can best determine which approach is best. A few years ago I worked with one client whose security team was so nonproductive that the assumptions underlying Theory X were blatantly obvious. Over the short term, a management control strategy that was built on Theory X was essential. It was not until a number of key individuals had been replaced before the security department could even begin to think in terms of Theory Y management, let alone Deming's precursory work to Theory Z.

Warren Bennis

If the title Dean of Business Management Thought were to be conferred, Warren Bennis would be one of the two most likely recipients. He is a prolific writer whose insights have served many executive teams well over the years. Drawing from his academic and real-world experience, along with his work involving leadership, Bennis has made a number of major contributions. In researching a book on leadership, he came to some rather simplistic but incredibly profound conclusions.

1. Leaders are people who do the right thing, managers are people who do things right.
2. Organizations throughout the industrialized world are under-lead and over-managed.
3. Leaders have an ability to draw others to them, not just because they have a vision but because they have a sense of outcome, goal, direction.
4. Leaders make ideas tangible and real to others, so they can support them.
5. Leaders instill trust. Their constancy and focus allows others to count on them.
6. Leaders know themselves; know their strengths and how to nurture them, while also knowing their limitations and how to leverage them.

I think Bennis would agree that leaders also recognize when they have made mistakes and know what it takes to make it right and avoid similar missteps in the future. Or, as Thomas Edison once noted: "I have not failed. I have just found 10,000 ways that won't work."

Peter Drucker

The other candidate for the title of Dean of Business Management Thought would most likely be Peter Drucker. Noted for his often brash comments, he has always had the ability to cut through the obfuscation laid down by many other so-called theorists and writers and "tell it like it is." Following are 12 of his observations that ought to serve any manager well. Several have been tabulated by John J. Tarrant in his treatise entitled *Drucker: The Man Who Invented the Corporate Society*. It was written in 1976. How much of what he said before 1980 is still highly relevant today? The others are snippets of Drucker's that I have collected over the years and continue to use today.

1. So much of what we call management consists of making it difficult for people to work.
2. Fast personnel decisions are likely to be wrong.
3. Start with what is right, not with what is acceptable.
4. Long-range planning does not deal with future decisions, but with the futurity of present decisions.
5. There is an enormous number of managers who have retired on the job.
6. If you make the organization your life, you are defenseless against the inevitable disappointments.
7. It takes years to build a management team; but it can be depleted in a short period of misrule.
8. It is necessary and urgent that we think through what really defines a manager and who should be considered management.
9. Setting objectives, organizing, motivating and communicating, measuring, and developing people are formal, classifying categories. Only a manager's experience can bring them to life, concrete and meaningful.
10. An organization will have a high spirit of performance if it is consistently directed toward opportunity rather than toward problems.
11. No professional, be he doctor, lawyer, or manager, can promise that he will indeed do good for his client. All he can do is try. But he can promise that he will not knowingly do him harm.
12. Management has no choice but to anticipate the future, to attempt to mold it, and to balance short-range and long-range goals. It is not given to mortals to do well of any of these things. But lacking divine

guidance, management must make sure that these difficult responsibilities are not overlooked or neglected but taken care of as well as is humanly possible.

We have already established that most security directors are middle managers. I have selected these insights because I believe they are particularly noteworthy for middle managers. They range from personnel matters to strategic planning. In sharing them with others it is always interesting to hear which one(s) they find particularly appealing. This is obviously a reflection of each middle manager's particular experiences and current views. I find the last three most significant.

Number 10 encourages managers to take the high road and see opportunities instead of problems. Asset protection often involves the darker side of organizational life. It is easy to see a world filled with problems. Add to this the challenges we explored in Part I and it becomes even easier to see organizational dynamics through dark gray glasses. Yet, Drucker challenges us to change our perspective. His soft admonition is very similar to Morris's views about looking for the positives to build on. People want to have a positive outlook on life, particularly at the work site. If they didn't, most sensible people would never complain, opting instead to simply show up and follow instructions, just as Theory X advocates contend. But any experienced manager knows just the opposite is true.

Number 11 again parallels Morris's concept of good character. Drucker notes that this first responsibility of a professional dates back more than 2,500 years to the Hippocratic Oath: *Primum non nocere*—above all, do no harm. Managers at all levels need to recognize that this is truly their first responsibility. By pledging to do no one harm, the manager acknowledges a basic respect for subordinates, peers, and superiors. Operating from the perspective of respecting others sets the stage for all else to follow. Just think how small corporate HR manuals would be if managers would commit to this tenant as their first priority.

Finally, number 12 establishes management's ultimate accountability. It is incumbent on them, regardless of their level in the organization, to know and embrace the future. Short-term goals can only be defined in terms of how they set the stage for intermediate goals, and ultimately the longer-term future. Recently a senior executive told me that the company had hired one of the larger consulting firms to assist them in strategic planning. The consultants told the executive team that their product assured them a positive outlook for the future, both over the intermediate and longer terms. Therefore, all that was needed was a strategy to get through the short term.

I asked him if the consultants had defined "short-term." It was defined as the next 12 to 18 months. I asked if he and his team agreed with this. "They're the experts, and God knows we're paying them enough to be the experts. They better be right. What do you think?" he asked. "Candidly?" I asked back. "Certainly," he responded. "Sorry, but I think you just got taken if you believe that,"

I answered. I explained my reasoning. First, how did they determine such a neat window as short term versus any other length of time? Second, and far more important, until the company understood their long-term mission and each preceding step as a building block leading to that mission, all so-called short-term strategies were little more than empty, incremental steps that assured nothing in the end. I asked: "Does one build a house without a plan or is the house simply an outcome of a series of short-term solutions such as erecting a wall here, a wall there, and so on?" No, Drucker is correct: Management has no choice but to anticipate the future, to attempt to mold it, and to balance short-range and long-range goals. They must make sure that these difficult responsibilities are not overlooked or neglected but are taken care of as well as is humanly possible.

A speculator is a man who observes the future, and acts before it occurs.
Bernard Baruch

MANAGING FROM THE MIDDLE

Earlier I mentioned Oren Harari's concept of leading from a middle-management position. In February 1999, he introduced this concept in an article entitled "Leading Change from the Middle" for *Management Review*, the American Management Association's trade journal. In the article he sets forth 11 rules for being an effective change agent when you occupy a middle-management position. From the outset I need to point out that they are bold and require tenacity, perseverance, and a willingness to consider alternatives, even changing organizations.

1. Let the customer drive your change process.
2. Develop standards, measurements, processes, and rewards based on your customer feedback and follow-up discussions.
3. With rare exceptions, don't ask for permission.
4. Stand by your convictions and stay the course.
5. Make your moves quick, continuous, and public.
6. Don't shirk from challenging sacred cows.
7. Act the part of a coach.
8. Demand some quick payoffs.
9. Embrace perpetual change by looking ahead to tomorrow's customer.
10. Stay ahead of change; don't try to manage it.
11. Prepare for a daily grind.

Let's took at each in more detail and see how they apply to today's world of asset protection.

Let the Customer Drive Your Change Process

For a security supplier, this appears to be fairly obvious. For the corporate security manager it may be a little bit more subtle, but it remains just as relevant. There is one word of caution for the supplier, however. Have you defined who the customer actually is? Many believe that it is the person who signed the contract, but in a typical large organization the supplier serves multiple customers. The same is true for a proprietary operation. For the supplier, customers are local managers who are directly affected by the daily operation of a security program. Internal customers can also be found among senior managers whose responsibility may include oversight responsibility for a local campus. Customers are also those customers of the client. In a banking environment this means the account holders. In healthcare it is the patients, and so forth. For in-house programs we can define a customer as anyone who uses the services of security or makes use of one of security's products.

Having a clear definition of who the customer base is, a change-oriented security manager needs to involve customers in the process of leading change. Customers have expectations and needs. Both are uniquely different. One or the other may not be realistic and could require education. But once customers understand the direction of the existing security program, they can be powerful lobbyists for change. To achieve change requires ongoing contact and listening to what they say. Harari suggests that listening is critical for four reasons: to gain strategically critical and timely information, cultivate a collaborative relationship, provide a valid direction, and build in-house credibility and momentum.

Develop Standards, Measurements, Processes, and Rewards Based on Your Customer Feedback and Follow-Up Discussions

This should not be new information. Chapter 5 lays out a detailed rationale for using metrics for building a business case for performance. The same principles apply when pursuing changes. To effect change, such metrics might involve customer care, turnover, response, or any one of the elements we discussed in the looping model. Once the metrics have been defined, resource allocations can determine if the objectives can be accomplished. If they are, rewards should be sufficiently high to foster efforts designed to raise the bar. If they cannot be accomplished, the metrics may serve as the baseline for building the business case for change. Harari cautions us to remember that change is an ongoing process, and therefore it requires an ability to keep score.

Asset protection is one of those organizational functions that is easy to measure. Uniformed services can be defined in terms of any number of activities, ranging from patrol duties to console operations. Investigative units can be measured from the number of cases opened and closed to dollars recovered or losses thwarted. Activities associated with competitive intelligence gathering or defense can be translated into direct effects on bottom-line performance. Participation in due diligence inquiries can be measured in terms of impact on the final sale price. In other words, I harken back to the basic concept that security's value needs to be defined and measured in terms of the organization's core deliverables. If this can be accomplished, even a middle manager can demonstrate significant contribution.

With Rare Exceptions, Don't Ask for Permission

This is admittedly one of the bolder steps, which may not be readily available to every security manager. But, I suspect Harari would challenge you to try it, at least initially in safe areas. Harari acknowledges that some decisions are going to require permission, such as large capital projects. However, I agree with his suggestion that your method of operation is better off if you adopt an approach based on, "If I haven't been specifically told not to do it, I'll go ahead and do it." Middle managers who push everything upstairs to their bosses find their ideas stalled or bogged down in turf battles, bureaucratic delays, and opposition from those who believe their job is to say no. This also applies to those career naysayers resident on your staff.

It is important to note that this active form of circumvention is not a slap in the face of collaboration. Working with others remains a necessity. By now you, as a middle manager, have no doubt learned that security cannot go it alone and hope to achieve ultimate success. On the other hand, today's turbulent time requires quicker action than before. Here is what Harari has to offer: "If you are challenged, explain your actions on sound business principles and then continue to act without asking for permission. Let your results convince people. Prudently pick your battles, but don't fall into the trap of playing it safe." Is this strategy risky? Simply put, yes. But, you might ask, if your company rebukes your efforts for positive change, is it perhaps time for you to consider a change?

I fear that I am about to date myself. In one of my previous corporate positions there was a need to automate years of investigative files. This was the mid-1980s, and desktop computers were still considered more of a novelty than a serious office tool. Aside from what was then referred to as "management information systems" (today's information technology), no other department had desktop computers. I ordered one and shortly thereafter ordered a second, then a third as I realized the value of automating several other functions of security. All were purchased within the approved operating budget. Not long thereafter the word had spread among other departments. A short while later I received a visit from my boss, inquiring about the desktops. His boss, who also had the head of MIS reporting to him, was upset that security was automating at a pace equal to his own department. My boss listened, smiled when we demonstrated what we were accomplishing, and said he would talk to his boos. I never heard another word, but it was not long after that many other department heads began placing their orders for desktop PCs.

Stand by Your Convictions and Stay the Course

This is perhaps one of the most difficult tasks for any middle manager. When pursuing change, especially change that will alter the organization's perception of security or require a shift in relationships, resistance will be great. Power brokers may want more than the middle manager believes is possible, or key decision-makers may openly oppose the change. Don't give up. Success comes at a cost, but it must also be earned.

To achieve change requires being right. That means having built your business case first, tested it to assure its validity, and then gathering your resources. Battles are individual occurrences. In other words, they have a beginning and an ending. In some battles progress is made, and with others ground is lost. Or, as one of the quotes noted earlier: "We are not retreating, we are just advancing in another direction." Compromise, even if it is small, is more common than full victory. But that is advancement. Harari advises that middle managers cannot wait for top management to find religion. Today's battle cry for thriving (beyond simply surviving) is *Change or die!*

In *Business Strategies,* I introduced the concept of the 180-degree rule, that there are often two ways to approach a challenge. The first is the traditional way. I referred to it as going through the front door, the way that works most of the time and is tried by everyone at the outset. Yet, when most fail to gain entry they either continue trying the door or give up altogether. But there is another way that is equally effective: the back door, which is 180 degrees from the front, its opposite approach. Try it and you will be surprised. Many great generals have won decisive battles employing this simple principle.

The 180-degree rule is particularly effective in times of crises. Internal bureaucracies can quickly bog down timely decision-making. In cases involving natural disasters, standard purchasing procedures may need to be set aside. While this is no license for reckless purchasing, it may be necessary for a security manager to go directly to suppliers for necessary emergency assistance. More often than not, the resourceful security manager is rewarded by senior managers for thinking smartly and taking the initiative even though lower-level purchasing agents and managers may loudly object. Similarly, when looking for ways to reduce operating expense, the savvy security manager will look to redefine core deliverables, consider alternative workforce configurations, or extend funding projects across multiple fiscal years as opposed to focusing on a one-year payback.

Make Your Moves Quick, Continuous, and Public

Organizational change is often painful. It may even be fatal to someone's organizational way of doing things or perceiving how things ought to be done. One cynical manager put it bluntly this way: "If you are to be the catalyst for such change you have two options: with a knife to the back or a dagger to the heart." If you are to follow this strategy, I would suggest the latter. But, more often than not, there is no need for political intrigue, secret deals, or hand-wringing. Change ought to occur out in the open, for everyone to view. This means posting results, sending memos, hosting meetings, driving for results. Effecting change also means that the plan needs to be continuously unfolding. Progress needs to be seen as flowing out—sometimes rushing, sometimes slow, but always flowing. A change agent cannot afford to sit back and analyze a situation forever; we call this *analysis by paralysis* for a reason, and it is not good. Here, change and action are synonymous.

I recall a security manager who created a security department newsletter and posted it on the company Web site. Each week there was an update on what was happening within the department. As new programs unfolded, the Web site highlighted the changes with bold headings. The Web site had a question and answer section. When anticipated questions regarding new operating practices or policies were not forthcoming, she created a questioner and published the make-believe inquiry with its corresponding answer just to draw more attention to the changes. She had her staff create posters promoting the Web site and had them posted in public areas, and made up flyers that could be picked up at each lobby desk staffed by a security person. She told me how she despised hearing employees remark, "Gee, I didn't know that." So she went out of her way to make certain no one could claim they did not have the opportunity to become informed. Her public notifications and open communication literally disarmed her critics because they could not accuse her of "playing office politics," or trying to "make an end run." Her strategy worked.

She borrowed this strategy from classic political books. By making her moves public, if someone objected to something she could rely on others to act as her advocates. In some cases her advocates responded to the objector by saying: "I am confused. Why are you just now objecting? Security has been open about this all along. You had your chance in the past to object, why now?" In other cases, objectors were met with: "Wait a minute, this is old news. Why didn't you object sooner?" In either case, by going public, she was able to deflect criticism while keeping everyone informed of what was happening.

Don't Shirk from Challenging Sacred Cows

Harari suggests that if people are not questioning your sanity, you are probably not pushing hard enough for necessary changes. I did caution you that some of his positions are bold. His point, nonetheless, is valid. Sacred cows represent vested interests, and even security management teams have them. They can take on a variety of forms. Most common are programs that have been long established or are promoted by a senior executive. Others take on the form of customers, corporate policies, or operating practices.

Before attacking sacred cows, one caution is in order: Never tear down a fence until you know why it was built. My father first told me this when I was a small boy. In our country's agrarian days farmers learned that fences keep livestock separated for a variety of reasons. To the casual passerby the purpose of the fence may not be evident, but it serves an essential function. Organizational fences are operating practices, divisional units, and so on. Asking why the "fence" is in place is very legitimate, even necessary. But this is not a license to indiscriminately tear it down. If the reasons for its existence are no longer valid, certainly take it down. But if it still serves a purpose, leave this sacred cow alone.

This caution aside, most sacred cows can, and do, get in the way. A security director with strong business management skills is adroit in challenging such "untouchables." I have a client whose former security director believed that all lobby posts required a uniformed security officer. His persuasive skills prevailed and it was not long before the guard in the lobby became an institutional fixture. From executives to line-level employees, it was just assumed that this staffed position was a basic requirement. In reality, many lobbies do not need an officer's presence, especially during the late evening hours when the building is closed and no one is present; technology is then a reasonable alternative for effective coverage.

There is a new security director now, the previous one having recently retired. Before this organizational fence can be torn down, a new perspective needs to be established. Given the organization's desire to reduce operating expenses where it can, I suspect that establishing this new perspective is not long off. Yet it will create an initial sense of retrenchment, given the attitudes reinforced since 9/11. Regardless, the new director understands the value of challenging one of his own department's sacred cows. Once successful, his own credibility should be increased as he sets out to challenge other revered organizational bovines. After all, if he is willing to challenge his own, he may have a new perspective that could yield other positive changes outside the direct control of his department.

Act the Part of a Coach

An informed employee is better prepared to act and more easily commits to the projects at hand. Informing them can be done through commands, but most staff members will resent the one-way communication and not fully commit. Coaching, on the other hand, involves two-way communication; there is a chance for the subordinate to ask questions and provide feedback. Coaching is more, however. It is a style of communicating. It involves a role beyond that of the conventional middle manager. Harari suggests that the manager become a professor, hosting seminars or workshops for employees. He also pushes the envelope further by suggesting that enthusiastic public recognition be given for superlative results. Coaching is not about preaching or scaring personnel with doomsday scenarios. Rather, it stresses the positive and builds on the one big success and not past failures. It does, however, use setbacks and mistakes as opportunities for learning.

Demand Some Quick Payoffs

Success for the middle manager requires that the team produce results sooner rather than later. Results, in and of themselves, are organizational arrows to be drawn from the manager's quiver when necessary. Senior-level executives will not support change unless they see the proof. Results, even if not complete, demonstrate in a strong and empirical way, the likely outcome. They become the proof that the manager's team is on the right track.

We read earlier about the security manager who spent months developing her plan and not producing anticipated results. The delay cost her time and credibility. Harari cautions that in today's fast-paced business world, results are essential. If they cannot be demonstrated, he suggests reviewing Rules 1 and 6. I would add that a quick, but unhurried, root cause analysis be undertaken to determine if the hold-up is internal or the result of some external factor. Either way, the middle manager needs to know why results are not forthcoming and what can be done to spur the change along.

The security manager for one of our country's largest retail chains implemented a new program for detecting under-ringing. This is where a cashier intentionally bypasses the automated price checking system and enters a lower retail sale. This is often done as a favor to family members or friends. A prestudy revealed that under-ringing was costing the company nearly $600,000 a year. To test the value of his new program, he needed early results, good or bad. If the results were positive, he knew additional funding would be made available and this would put security in a favorable position with senior management. After 30 days, there were no reported outcomes. After 45 days, the same. He pressed his staff, only to discover that one of his analysts had intended to hold back the test results until a 180-day period could be established. Her reasoning was sound, under normal times, but she had missed the criticality of providing preliminary results. The situation was corrected and the security director, a middle manager, was given the green light to expand the program after 60 days of testing because the preliminary results were overwhelmingly convincing.

Embrace Perpetual Change by Looking Ahead to Tomorrow's Customer

Harari tells us that this rule is huge. He notes that today's customer is not necessarily the same as tomorrow's. A large security supplier totally missed this rule. The supplier had developed a long-standing relationship with their client's representative. Over time, the supplier reduced their contact with this person to once a year, at the most. Unfortunately, there was a reorganization and a new contact person in a different department was named. The supplier missed the change altogether. When it came time to renew the contract, the new customer saw the supplier as just one of the many, and a new request for proposal was sent out. A more aggressive supplier was quick to respond and eventually won the contract; a contract valued at more than $20,000,000 in annual billings.

Internal security managers can miss the same opportunity. We have seen how asset protection programs are on a continuum of change. Those wanting to move from one position to the next need to understand that change in core competency will most likely require addressing the needs of new end-users (e.g., internal customers). This, in turn, requires knowing something about what their business entails and how corporate security can bring them value. This rule of Harari's illustrates the integrated nature of effective management. Recognizing customers is one thing, but knowing what they need and planning in advance is another. How to respond to that need weaves nicely into the concept of strategic planning and all of the subsets we discussed in a previous chapter. In short, customers do not suddenly appear. They are anticipated; therefore, preparation for them today better positions the middle manager to be effective.

Stay Ahead of Change; Don't Try to Manage It

You may recall the old Chinese proverb I quoted earlier: "You cannot control the wind, but you can control your sails." We spent time in a previous discussion addressing the internal and external variables that affect a manager's decision-making process. We also raised the point a couple of times that life is 1% what is dealt to us and 99% how we manage it (or what you choose to do with it). This is what Harari is saying. It is interesting how often this theme arises in any discussion of management, especially middle management. Several times in this book we have read how one author after another draws our attention to the fact that it is not so much the organizational position that you hold, but how you manage from it.

Drucker notes: "One can't manage change. One can only be ahead of it." In responding to this, Harari draws his own conclusion.

"Managing change" sounds nifty because it suggests there is an orderly, linear and predictable path to change. It's perfect fodder for bureaucrats and for consultants peddling this year's fad: Wrap change around a technique and an orderly structure—in other words, "manage" it—and you'll be successful.

It's all nonsense. Change is unruly, chaotic and unpredictable. It wreaks havoc on plans and egos. It rips an organization inside out. It's not an analytically detached process; it's an emotional process—both painful and exhilarating. You should have goals, a broad plan of action. But realize that you can't control or predict either the unfolding events or the outcomes. So rather than worry about the inevitable chaos, you should expect it, revel in it, deal with it.

Prepare for a Daily Grind

One of my favorite riddles is, "How do you eat an elephant?" The answer, of course, is "One bite at a time." The same can be said about successfully managing change; it can only be accomplished one step at a time. Or, as one rock star remarked after being asked what it was like to be an overnight success, "Not bad, considering it only took me 15 years of practice and hard work."

One of my former bosses lamented as the year drew to a close that our department had not accomplished very much over the past 12 months. Shortly thereafter I shared what he had said with one of my colleagues. A few days later the colleague called and suggested that we pool our collective thoughts and create a list of all that the department had, in fact, accomplished. His plan was to create a large parchment and present it to the boss at the department's Christmas party. We did. Much to my amazement, we had listed almost 365 successes—an average of one a day! Granted, some were small, but others were fairly large. The boss had missed them because of his concentration on the daily grind.

Change comes slowly. You have already read my lamentations about how slowly our industry is moving forward, sometimes through our own faults, sometimes because of others. Yet, I must admit that significant progress has been made over the three decades I have been privileged to serve. The fact that I can talk about a continuum of progress from an era of night watchmen to mainstream business contributors speaks volumes about our progress. When I first began teaching in the early 1970s there were only four books on private security. Today there are thousands. The private security sector has exploded from a multimillion-dollar business to a multibillion-dollar industry.

Change comes slowly, but it does come. Harari concludes: "It demands ingenuity and innovation, to be sure, but above all it demands attributes like daily discipline, persistence, thick skin and thick-headedness. Milestones will be celebrated, successes will be reveled in, memories will be sweet. That's all the good stuff. But, for the (successful) leader, the unsexy, daily reality is that change requires a ton of hard, often less-than-thrilling work. This is why so many (other) leaders prefer to delegate change to someone else. It's why so many leaders embrace *fads du jour*, and why so many change interventions fail."

Yours is not to be the middleman. Rather it is yours to be in the middle of it all.

Anonymous

CONCLUDING COMMENTS

I noted at the outset of this chapter that we would cover a lot of territory. I think we did. It is important to note that this chapter harkens back to what has been said by many of those who preceded us (some are still with us). What they said sometimes decades ago still resonates well today. In our hurry to find that magic elixir, that holy grail, if you will, that contains the one true formula, we miss the sage advice of those who have experienced our same frustrations and offer keen insights.

Please understand that I am not opposed to new management strategies. It is just that I grow tired of today's latest fads. I also realize this creates somewhat of a catch-22. One could argue that any new strategy must first be introduced and that its early popularity is what makes it a "fad." This is true enough, but a truly effective strategy is demonstrated to have lasting power. That is why the basics have changed so little. Tragically, many executives and security managers live their organizational lives according to the gospel of McKinsey or some other large consulting house. They spend millions listening to what recent business grads have to regurgitate from what was fed to them by one of their so-called enlightened professors who, in turn, have only a modicum of true organizational experience or who have been out of the business world for decades.

The basics are the basics because they work. New strategies need to be built on them. If they do not, they will most certainly collapse, as so many have already. I was recently reading two of the recent bestsellers in business management. The first was John C. Maxwell's *Failing Forward: Turning Mistakes into Stepping Stones for Success*. The other was by Michael Useem, professor of management and director of the Center for Leadership and Change Management at the Wharton School of the University of Pennsylvania. His book is *Leading Up: How to Lead Your Boss so You Both Win*. These two books do not really offer anything new. They do, however, present what they have to offer in new ways. Each, in its own right, relies on proven basics. For this reason, their texts make a valuable contribution to management writings. They have taken what has gone before them, twisted it, and applied it to new environments and new challenges. And it works.

In this chapter we visited Tom Morris and his ideas for achieving true success. We explored his Seven C's and found that they can serve as beacons along our sometimes-murky journey. We followed this discussion with a review of several organizational giants. Briefly, we explored how the likes of Deming, Peters, McGregor, Follett, Bennis, and Drucker have helped in defining the basics that serve middle managers well in their pursuit of effective change. We concluded with a review and application of Harari's 11 rules for the middle manager. With all of this to serve as our guide, we turn our attention to the last chapter, one that continues the theme of pursuing organizational success. Combining the lessons of what we have explored thus far, we can begin to see how finely woven each element is with the other.

Let it be borne in mind how infinitely complex and close-fitting are the mutual relations of all organic beings to each other and their physical conditions of life.

Charles Darwin

Thought-Provoking Questions

1. Tom Morris provides us a guideline to success with his Seven C's. After reviewing them, can you add one or more of your own C's? Is his blueprint achievable, or do you believe that it is too altruistic and not reality based?

2. The author explores six organizational giants (Deming, Peters, McGregor, Follett, Bennis, and Drucker) who have provided some basic wisdom for achieving organizational success. Can you think of others? Based on your experience, is sticking to the basics better than pursuing the latest management strategy? Is true success found in a combination of both?

3. Think about your situation. Of all of the basics that were discussed in this chapter, which represent your strengths? Which need improvement, or more attention? Which need to be pursued more assertively with your boss?

4. Harari gives us his 11 rules of managing from the middle. Which are most realistic for you? Which are not? Of those that are not, is there any way to positively manipulate your circumstances to allow them to become real possibilities?

5. Thinking over the material covered in Chapters 7 and 8, which hit the strongest cord for you? Were there any that made for enjoyable reading, but were really not applicable to your situation? Why? Could anything be done to make them more relevant?

Chapter 9

MAY I PLAY THROUGH?

The man who wants to lead the orchestra must turn his back on the audience.

James Cook

Primary Themes

- Ten Basic E's
- The Ten Commandments for Clients and Suppliers
- Ben Franklin's Guide to Effective Management
- Traps Effective Managers Avoid
- Dalton's 20 Axioms for Success, and 20 More

OPENING OBSERVATIONS

A number of years ago I discovered a reprint of eight rules for office workers dated 1872. Even though it was intended to be a very serious document then, today we might find it quite amusing. I start each of my management classes by handing a copy out to all of my students. It does not take long before you can hear them begin laughing aloud. When they finish reading and we have all had our good time with the rules, I remind them that their work site rules are probably a little less demanding. Here are the eight rules from 1872:

1. Office employees each day will fill lamps, clean chimneys, and trim wicks. Wash windows once a week.

2. Each clerk will bring in a bucket of water and a scuttle of coal for the day's business.

3. Make your pens carefully. You may whittle nibs to your individual tastes.

4. Men employees will be given an evening off each week for courting purposes, or two evenings a week if they go regularly to church.

5. After thirteen hours of labor in the office, the employee should spend the remaining time reading the Bible and other good books.

6. Every employee should lay aside from each pay day a goodly sum of his earnings for his benefit during his declining years so that he will not be a burden on society.

7. Any employee who smokes Spanish cigars, uses liquor in any form, or frequents pool and public halls or gets shaved in a barber shop, will give good reason to suspect his worth, intentions, integrity, and honesty.

8. The employee who has performed his labor faithfully and without fault for five years, will be given an increase of five cents per day in his pay, providing profits from business permit it.

These eight rules actually serve as more than an ice breaker for each new class. They point out how far management has come over the years, at least in some areas. It is also interesting to note that in 1872 there was the concept of contributing to a retirement plan (Rule 6) and profit sharing (Rule 8). My favorite is Rule 7 because it demonstrates how much society's values have changed—what were once considered dens of questionable behavior are now respectable places of business and entertainment. One of my students remarked that even though she and her colleagues are not required to bring in a scuttle of coal, they are expected to change light bulbs, sanitize the restrooms, and clean the floors. She works for a Fortune 500 company. So I guess some things do not change, or at least change very slowly.

Establishing office rules is only one function of management. Although it is important to assure a healthy work site and honest employees, there are other responsibilities that define the success or failure of management. Along the way I have mentioned a number of arrows for your management quiver. Two of them are *effectiveness* and *efficiency*. Having a working understanding of each keeps a manager focused. Along my professional journey, I have found ten additional E's that need to be included. Over the years I have had to draw on each many times. In golf only 14 clubs are allowed in the golfer's bag. We should be thankful that in management our quiver can have an unlimited number of arrows. The actual number depends on the size of your quiver. Some managers try to go through their professional careers with a very small one. It ought not be surprising then to hear that they didn't get very deep into the business jungle before they were either forced back, ran up a tree for safety, or were eaten by one of the many animals roaming the jungle floor.

The American Indians taught the early trappers well. They showed how arrows could be fabricated along the journey, carved from tree branches and attached to stone heads. But they also taught the trappers that without anything to carry the arrows, the trapper was limited to a small handful. It was essential to find the appropriate animal hide to carry the necessary arrows to assure a successful hunt. The trapper also had to avoid making his quiver too large and overstocking it with too many arrows. In short, there was a perfect size—one that carried just enough arrows to get the trapper to the hunting ground, secure his catch, and return home safely. An overstuffed quiver became burdensome. More important was the likelihood that the trapper would become overly dependant on the arrows if he had too many and fail to develop his skill as a true archer.

The skills of the early trappers have a modern day parallel. When my daughter was growing up, she and all of her friends enjoyed playing Nintendo. One of the earliest games was called the *Legion of Zelda*. The object was to maneuver a small treasure hunter through a series of mazes in search of a lost treasure. Using the joystick and control keys, they would rapidly maneuver the hunter through one obstacle after another. Many times the hunter would become stuck or encounter a monster of one sort or another. To successfully defend himself, he would have to rely on arrows and other lifesaving tools called power sources he found along the way. Sometimes it was necessary for the hunter to actually set the treasure hunt aside for a time while he went in search of one particular power source. Without that power source, my daughter knew he could go no further. Sometimes there were clues along the way or she would learn tips from others who had played the game. But often she had to rely on trial and error to find the magic lifesaving potion or golden arrow that would enable the hunter to overcome the next challenge. In the end, the treasure hunter would have to face the dreaded demon in a small chamber in a fight to the finish. If the player put the hunter in the room without the right resources and skill set, death was assured and the treasure would remain lost.

I think you can see the parallel for today's organizational trappers. They need to carry the right type and number of management tools. Equally important, they must learn how to use them adroitly lest they become victims. What follows is a series of lists. I begin with the ten additional E's and move through a number of others. Each list in its own way represents a set of management tools. Some may be used daily and others may be rarely used, but when the circumstances warrant, they are there and their value is immeasurable. Some of the lists have appeared in my other publications, most notably in my management column with *Security Magazine*. I have chosen to alternate these tips between those that are general in nature and those that are more specific to the security manager. I have done so just to keep the mix flowing and therefore (I hope) more interesting.

One final note: You might be asking yourself about the strange title for this chapter, "May I Play Through?" In previous chapters I have drawn on the golfing analogy and quoted a number of the sport's greats. In playing the game, it is not uncommon for one or more players to catch up with the group ahead of them. The courteous thing is for the slower group to allow the faster ones to play through. That allows everyone the opportunity to continue enjoying the game. I chose this title because the chapter is constructed to allow you a quick read, should you desire it. Others of you may want to go through at a slower pace.

Where is the wisdom that we have lost in knowledge? Where is the knowledge we have lost in information?

T.S. Eliot

Ten Basic E's

By now you know there are actually 12 E's, the first two being effectiveness and efficiency. I have accumulated the remaining ten over the years and ranked them in the order that I feel is important. However, in the final analysis, establishing a ranking is secondary because all of them are required and each must unfold simultaneously with the others.

1. **Ethics:** This is the first building block because it defines character and how things are to be governed.

2. **Energy:** This is second because progress can only be made when there is an energy force present. Without it, people are lethargic and become easily stuck.

3. **Experience:** We've made this point before. Experience takes away the mystery, the unknown, and allows us to set our fears aside because we know what to expect and how to handle it.

4. **Enthusiasm:** This is the fuel that drives success. It allows everyone to focus on the positive and avoid getting bogged down on previous setbacks.

5. **Environment:** The environment defines our circumstances. If it is supportive and nurturing, we can accomplish a great deal. If it is not, it needs to be changed or abandoned. Remember, some environments are not going to change despite our best efforts—their time has not yet come (or has passed).

6. **Entrepreneurs:** Successful management requires bold thinking and calculated risk taking. We have covered both throughout this text. It defines our creativity and willingness to forge ahead.

7. **Enabling:** Smart managers know they cannot go it alone. This, too, we have covered. It merits repeating because the level of success depends on how much respect we have in others and confidence in ourselves.

8. **Enlightenment:** This is a successful manager's ability to see that which is only envisioned. It defines the framework on which we build plans, programs, and projects.

9. **Enjoyment:** Success requires a happy frame of mind, a capacity to enjoy what we are doing.

10. **Enforcement:** This brings order and structure. It allows ideas to become realities. Enforcement demonstrates commitment.

Author's Note: My wife, Linda, points out there is actually another E. She points out that it is the secret E, Excedrin. She notes that when any of the preceding E's give you a colossal headache, as they often will, use of the secret E works—to use her words—"pretty damn fast."

Each of the E's help the manager stay focused on what is important in the running of an organization. Collectively they define a framework to pursue strategies designed to yield the results a manager wants. Next, I would like to draw your attention to my second and third lists of management principles. They are more technical in nature because they focus on the relationship between a client and supplier. Both parties need to subscribe to their own set of rules or commandments. Failure to do so not only jeopardizes the relationship, but also creates an atmosphere of distrust and reluctance, both of which can only spin the relationship into a no-win situation.

THE CLIENT'S TEN COMMANDMENTS FOR EFFECTIVE PARTNER RELATIONSHIPS

Over time a great deal has been written about the relationship between client and supplier. Most of it has been from the perspective of what the supplier needs to do to assure quality customer service. There is no doubt about the importance of this element in the customer service formula. However, I might suggest that we often overlook another significant variable—the obligations that the client has toward their supplier. Just as the supplier has responsibilities toward their clients, the same holds true for the other side of the relationship.

Clients believe they drive the relationship. "After all, we pay the tab, we therefore have the lead position," is all too commonly argued. Such positioning reminds me of the Golden Rule of Business—e.g., *I have the gold, therefore I make up the rules.* Ah, that it were so simple. Unfortunately, successful relationships are built on trust earned over time on the part of both parties. Clients need to recognize they too have rules—or a set of commandments, if you will—that require adherence.

1. **Define your expectations and needs up front.** All too often, managers who serve as the client contact assume that their supplier knows what they want or need. Or, the manager may provide only a partial list, believing that they have covered everything. More often than not this is more a reflection that not all of the manager's internal customers have been adequately canvassed for their particular wants/ needs. Soon after the supplier relationship has been established, to the chagrin of both the primary client contact and the supplier, these internal customers surface with the cry: "What good are these guys? They don't even know what I need or want." This results in people becoming defensive and a loss of credibility.

2. **Don't drive the relationship based on cost.** This is perhaps the most commonly violated commandment. It's easy to fall into the trap of *best pricing* equates to *lowest pricing*. Wrong! Best pricing means *best value*. The front-end cost may be higher, but it is the *return on the investment* that needs to drive the relationship. Relationships that are cost driven operate from the misguided perspective that security—its services and products—are corporate commodities. When I hear someone use this term, I usually find that the person is more in tune with the latest corporate fad than in truly seeking a quality relationship.

3. **Allow room for errors to occur.** This is fairly straightforward, but is often missed. Security is about the *people business*. Whether the supplier represents a service or a product, the bottom line is that people make up the business. With this comes the inevitable opportunity for mistakes. Suppliers need to be judged on how well they correct their errors and initiate safeguards against allowing the situation to surface again. Here's a simple question for a hardened client: "Would you like to be judged that harshly the next time you make a mistake?" After all, that day will come, sooner or later.

4. **Require accountability through performance measures.** Talk is cheap. We have heard this dozens of times and experienced it even more often. Success can—and should be—demonstrated. To demonstrate success requires a means of measuring what we achieve against an established baseline. Measured proofs pave the way for further funding, stronger support, and widespread advocacy. The lack of measured proofs can create doubt, second-guessing, and weak credibility.

5. **Seek a partnership, not just a supplier relationship.** Supplier relationships—sometimes referred to as vendor relationships—are cut and dried formal business relationships. Their very labels plainly suggest this. A partnership, on the other hand, demonstrates a paradigm based on trust, a willingness to work together with shared input and decision-making. Partners respect one another and join

resources to achieve a common end. In short, partnership is a two-way street, reflecting gives and takes on both sides.

6. **Share the rewards and the risks.** Partnerships reflect shared risks and shared rewards. Service and product suppliers alike should be willing to demonstrate their commitment by accepting part of the front-end costs in exchange for a meaningful back-end reward. The clients must also be willing to demonstrate a like commitment. Partnerships reflect a long-term perspective and a desire to "make it work." Absent these two critical variables, sustained success is tenuous at best.

7. **Establish routine feedback sessions.** People need to know how they are doing. This is a concept taken right out of Relationships 101—so simple, but probably the second most overlooked or abused commandment. If the service is not meeting expectations or the product is inadequate, the partner needs to know. Likewise, when the service or product is on target, this needs to be shared as well. Good ideas and approaches can provide the same base for improvement in other areas just as learning from past mistakes is a well-known teacher.

8. **Identify your partner's limitations.** Partners cannot meet all expectations or needs under all circumstances. Good partners know their limits and are willing to share them. Few security providers offer a full range of services or products. Even those industry giants who do also have their limitations. It is critical to know your partner's true capabilities if the relationship is going to be successful. How does the adage go? "He was a jack-of-all-trades and a master of none."

9. **Integrate your partner's employees.** Often I hear that "for legal reasons, we cannot allow our suppliers' employees to enjoy the same benefits we have for our own." This is unbelievable. There may be legal reasons for not wanting to create a precedent, but I am not aware of any legal restrictions, per se. People need to believe that they belong. If you sponsor a company picnic, invite your partner's employees. If there is a corporate discount program on goods and services, allow your partner's employees the same advantage. This creates loyalty and a sense of self-worth. To do otherwise is simply an indication that the manager has rolled over on an aggressive, and highly misinformed lawyer who needs to return to law school.

10. **Aggressively pursue a continuous quality-oriented program.** Partners need to experience your commitment to continuously pursing quality service. More important, they need to actively participate—even if it is something new for them. Security product distributors have the upper hand over their service industry counterparts. This is because they are more in tune with quality driven production stan-

dards. In time, however, more service providers will see the necessity for developing quality-oriented programs. Market competition will demand nothing less. As a receiver of their services, it is to your benefit to encourage the development of these programs.

Deal with the faults of others as gently as with your own.

Chinese Proverb

THE SUPPLIER'S TEN CARDINAL SINS

Over the past couple of years I have had the opportunity to benchmark dozens of large corporations for my clients. This activity has taken me across a wide spectrum of the corporate continuum, ranging from retail and health-care companies to manufacturing and property management firms. Despite the diversity of comparators, one theme seems to emerge above all the rest: the things suppliers do to upset their clients. There appears to be no one standard complaint, but there are some common themes. Their regularity is so predictable that I would suggest they rise to the level of "cardinal sins," or the breaking of ten supplier commandments.

1. **Failing to focus on the relationship instead of the price.** Price is without a doubt a cornerstone in any client–supplier union. Yet what really sells products and service is the ongoing relationship. Focusing on day-to-day needs builds confidence and trust. Once this is established, clients see value and develop advocacy, all of which leads to long-term loyalty over pricing.

2. **Not demonstrating their strong commitment to ethical practices.** Ethical behavior, despite what we may see being played out in certain sectors of our society and business community, is strongly expected in the corporate theater. Such behavior extends to everyone involved—especially suppliers. How suppliers conduct themselves is critical to their success in both the near and long term. Despite the fact that the security profession is approaching a $50 billion industry, it remains a small community when it comes to word-of-mouth referrals. Absent an ethical reputation, a supplier's business will soon wane.

3. **Not understanding that clients want results, not association with big names.** I think it is part of our nature to want to be associated with celebrities and big names. But when such associations do not yield the results we want, we are also quick to abandon them. The same holds true in the corporate world. When a supplier flaunts their "big name" client list, it can sound impressive. But if they cannot deliver, even the most enamored client can quickly turn. I could retire

early if I had a quarter for every time I have heard "I don't understand what Corporation X sees in this supplier. You would think a company that big would see the supplier for what they are. Well, I have learned my lesson and I'm moving on."

4. **Not realizing that high-profile, low-margin accounts rarely net their full market value.** Associated sin #3, it is easy for a supplier to fall into the trap of pursuing big name accounts for their market value. In reality, this approach more often than not represents a losing proposition. Even if one argues the concept of "loss leader," the reality is that the supplier is trying to defend a position based on loss. Far more impressive, especially for the investor, is a company with sustained earnings—which means acceptable margins across the board.

5. **Not realizing that clients want the function managed, not simply supplied.** Today clients look for suppliers to be more than purveyors of product and services. They want the supplier's expertise. With outsourcing, the expectation is that external suppliers need to step up to the partner podium and take on more of a management role.

6. **Not realizing that 90% of all accounts lost are directly related to account management. Conversely, 90% of all long-term relationships are directly related to account management.** We have already raised this point, but it needs to be raised again because of its importance. This is directly related to point #5. The reality is that effective account management is not limited to the security industry. I dare say it is a fundamental law of suppliers, because client–supplier unions are about relationships, and the pivotal point of this relationship is the account manager.

7. **Not recognizing that clients typically have misconceptions about the supplier's industry.** It is the rare client that understands totally what a supplier can and cannot do. The same holds true for the industry at large. Recognizing that most purchasers of security services and products are not security professionals, it is easy to understand why there are so many misconceptions. Clients can develop expectations that may be totally inappropriate for their application or for something that is beyond technology's current capability. Therefore, it is incumbent upon the supplier to assume the role of educator.

8. **Not understanding that clients want to take pride in their suppliers.** Clients want to take pride in their suppliers' products and services. A recent experience of mine serves as an excellent example. Accompanying my client to one comparator site, I found it fascinating that the client openly talked about how his supplier's product represented the latest state-of-the-art technology. When visiting a second comparator we again listened to the comparator talk

with pride about his security service provider. Such pride leads to directed referrals.

9. **Not knowing when to say no to a potential or current client.** We have all heard of "trying to put a square peg into a round hole." I see this daily when it comes to suppliers. Wanting to "land the sale," it is very tempting to say: "We have the product or service you need." I frequently get called about consulting on certain sectors of the marketplace. Obviously I cannot serve every sector. I need to recognize when I can be of help and when it is appropriate to say no. Passing along a valued referral has residual impact. People respect companies that know their limits and remember them the next time around.

10. **Not understanding that client relationship extend beyond customer satisfaction and stretches into customer loyalty.** Clients want more than satisfaction. They may not necessarily articulate this, but they do. Specifically, they want to become loyal to a particular supplier. That's right, *they want to be loyal to you.* Loyalty makes their life so much simpler. The challenge for a supplier is to develop a strategy for building loyalty and understanding that customer satisfaction is a subset of loyalty building. But suppliers need to earn their clients' loyalty, and this means building a relationship about more than price. Relationships built on price are the most tenuous.

Fortune magazine's May 27, 2002, edition featured an article by Ram Charan and Jerry Useem entitled "Why Companies Fail." I find it interesting that what they have to offer could well serve as a supplement to my list of supplier sins. Here's their list.

1. Softened by success
2. See no evil
3. Fearing the boss more than the competition
4. Overdosing on risk
5. Acquisition lust
6. Listening to Wall Street more than to employees
7. *Strategy du jour*
8. A dangerous corporate culture
9. The New Economy death spiral
10. A dysfunctional board

It is easy to become soft when you have scored a series of back-to-back successes. Organizations can get lulled into the trap of believing they can do no wrong, and their blindness can cause them to miss any number of lurking evils. As we witnessed throughout the summer of 2002, greed certainly crept into many proud companies and caused them to stumble or, for a few, fall down altogether.

When employees fear their boss more than the competition, there are serious problems present. I have seen this all too often among the ranks of the uniformed personnel. They commonly fail to act even when they recognize they should, for fear of being rebuked by their boss. A group of my students shared the following poem from an unknown source. It shows the difference between a boss and a true leader.

> *The boss drives his men; the leader coaches them.*
> *The boss depends on authority; the leader on goodwill.*
> *The boss inspires fear; the leader inspires enthusiasm.*
> *The boss says "I"; the leader says "We."*
>
> *The boss says: 'Get here on time;" the leader gets there ahead of time.*
> *The boss fixes blame for the breakdown; the leader fixes the breakdown.*
> *The boss knows how it is done; the leader shows how.*
> *The boss says: "Go"; the leader says: "Let's go."*
>
> *The boss uses people; the leader develops them.*
> *The boss sees today; the leader also looks at tomorrow.*
> *The boss commands; the leader asks.*
> *The boss never has enough time; the leader makes times for things and people.*
>
> *The boss is concerned with things; the leader is concerned with people.*
> *The boss lets his people know where he stands; the leader lets his people know where they stand.*
> *The boss works hard to produce; the leader works hard to help his people produce.*
> *The boss takes the credit; the leader gives it.*
>
> *When people go to work, they shouldn't have to leave their hearts at home.*
> *Betty Bender*

We have talked a great deal about risk—and still have a few more things to say about it. Nonetheless, an otherwise well-intentioned company can overdose on risk. There is smart risk taking that has a calculated return. There is also foolish risk that endangers all that has been achieved. One excellent example is Charan and Useem's fifth reason for failure: acquisition lust. Acquiring or merging is an intelligent strategy if it is executed for the right reasons. Sadly, many companies expand for the wrong reasons, the most common, and most deadly of which, is to either avoid being acquired by an unwanted suitor or seeking to achieve the number one position simply for the sake of being number one. Look at AOL/Time Warner as one quick example.

When companies listen more to Wall Street than to their employees or their market, they are on the brink of sure disaster. As we discussed earlier, effective strategy development demands a well-thought-through plan. Running from one strategy to another, or as the authors refer to it, pursuing the *strategy du jour,* is an indication that management is responding to artificial forces and not the core values that made them successful in the first place. Such pursuits can often lead the organization into a culture that is both counterproductive and harmful to the bottom line. When executives and board members spend more time slugging it out among themselves for power and recognition than seeking new ways to enhance revenues, it is time for the smarter ones to jump to safer ground, even if it means going over to the competition.

Finally, suppliers need to recognize that the "new economy" is not an end in and of itself. It is simply a new way of doing some aspects of their business. Investments in new technologies are wise if there will be a true return on the investment. This is particularly so of support unit managers. In security there is a newfound enthusiasm for emerging software products and hardware devices that are supposed to increase productivity and reduce operating expense. In some cases this is true, but in many it is not. Security suppliers and in-house managers are being aggressively pursued by "new economy" representatives who are more charlatans than valued resources.

MANAGING ACCORDING TO THE WIT AND WISDOM OF BEN FRANKLIN

Turning our attention back to a more general focus, I have been a fan of Ben Franklin for many years. Few Americans know that he was one of our country's earliest and most successful businessmen. We typically think of him as a founding father, career diplomat, or inventor. He was most certainly all of these, but he was also more, not the least of which was a successful man of business. Author and university professor Blaine McCormick captures the business side of Franklin in his book, *Ben Franklin's 12 Rules of Management.* He notes that many other business giants have modeled their careers in part after Franklin. Among them are Andrew Carnegie and Thomas Mellon, Warren Buffet and his low-key silent partner at Berkshire Hathaway, Charles Munger.

I like to tell my clients and students that if you ever want to stop someone in their proverbial tracks, say something that sounds insightful and credit it to Ben Franklin. No one will ever challenge your wisdom; such is the power and mystique of Franklin even today. Here are the 12 rules of management that McCormick has extracted from Mr. Franklin's own autobiography, coupled with my interpretation and application to our industry:

Ben Franklin's 12 Rules of Effective Management

1. **Finish better than your beginnings**. Ordinary managers well understand their own beginnings and can make a number of excuses for accepting their "lot in life." Franklin noted that God helps those that help themselves. He cast aside the obstacles—they were many and great—and sought a better life for himself and those around him. He saw that it was his destiny to rise above his beginnings and make both contributions to his fellow man and himself. Security managers need to hold Franklin out as a model for overcoming what I call *organizational bracketing*. This occurs when other corporate executives can see the security manager only as an asset protection specialist. The successful security manager pushes these executives to see him or her in a broader context, therefore achieving an ending that is greater than his or her beginning.

2. **All education is self-education.** Despite our business world's obsession with formal degrees, all true education remains a function of self-education. Even in the classroom or cloistered away reading a textbook, students need to learn for themselves. Professors and workshop facilitators can provide materials, debates, and lectures, but the individual needs to be open to what is presented for learning to occur. The same can be said for managing. Successful security managers understand the need for "going it alone," just as we saw in Chapter 7 with Tom and his often inebriated boss.

3. **Seek first to manage yourself, then to manage others.** Only when we know ourselves, our limitations and our strengths, can we begin to know how to manage others. We have all fallen victim, at one time or another, to either the insecure or the overly arrogant manager. Neither of them knows themselves, and therefore cannot manage themselves. This failure translates directly to the mismanagement of others. What is interesting about this Franklin rule is that as a manager learns more about self-management, there is the tendency to allow others to manage themselves. Today we would call this *empowerment*. Security managers need to "let go" and trust that their employees will succeed, despite the occasional misstep.

4. **Influence is more important than victory.** Managers, including asset protection managers, spend a great deal of time and energy positioning themselves solidly in the organizational pecking order—the higher, the better, many believe. This is not always so. The person who is in the best position to influence outcomes is often far more successful than one occupying a given organizational position. One of my professors once commented: "Put me in charge of an organiza-

tion's budget and training program and I can rule with far greater influence than a CEO." He was right.

5. **Work hard and watch your costs.** Successful managers in all professions have learned this lesson long ago. This is particularly true in good economic times. I have a property management client who has hired me as the confidential consultant regarding physical security advice for one of their clients. Their client has spent recklessly. During strong economic times the security manager allowed his operating budget to go unchecked. As the company grew, he continued spending. Within a very short period of time his annual operational budget exceeded $10 million. Recently the company's stock tanked and their revenue stream collapsed. An opportunity for smart management based on hard work and watching costs has risen. Our analysis shows that the same deliverable can be achieved for $3.4 million annually. The security manager is in trouble and will most likely lose his job—fair warning to all over-spenders.

6. **Everybody wants to appear reasonable.** No one wants to appear as an obstructionist, but often actions come across as such. Sometimes obstructionism is obvious to everyone and resentment is quick to follow. Other times, it is far more subtle. Today's security manager needs to be particularly alert for this. Some business unit manager may either envy the manager or disdain what security stands for, but be sophisticated enough to come across as an advocate in front of the manager while engaging in subversive activities behind the manager's back. Other times employees can dig in, especially if they are unionized and labor negotiations are underway. McCormick suggests that the manager remember his "exchange theory." He cites the experience of his infant son who was holding the living room couch hostage by bringing in a glass of milk and climbing up, when he knew this was expressly forbidden. Any attempt to reason or try to snatch the milk away was out of the question so McCormick negotiated an exchange—the glass of milk for a couple of favorite toys. This experience calls to mind the strategy of finding areas of mutual interest between two parties. Here the aim is to set aside areas of difference and try to resolve matters under dispute by focusing on the areas of like-mindedness.

7. **Create your own set of values to guide your actions.** Franklin knew his core values and stuck by them, particularly in times of uncertainty. Stated another way, if you fail to develop a set of values you will manage to the set that comes your way. Values are closely linked to integrity. In the following list of sayings borrowed from Franklin's *Poor Richard's Almanack*, I provide ten examples of what Franklin had

to say about the pursuit of integrity and his insight on justice and virtue.

8. **Incentive is everything.** People need to be motivated. I live in California. Recently a major intersection was completed as part of the state's highway upgrades. The new section was completed in record time, finishing nearly 18 months ahead of schedule. The politicians and officials were delighted beyond belief. They credited the project's success to a new strategy: they offered the contractor a major bonus for coming in under budget and ahead of time. The contractor accomplished both, because there was an incentive. This is something the private sector learned about centuries ago.

   But not everyone in the private sector has developed this basic under-standing of the power of incentives. *Business Week* magazine recently reported that K-Mart's executives have found a strategy they believe will significantly contribute to their efforts of emerging from bank-ruptcy. They have stumbled on the idea of having merchandise in stock when they run an advertisement for it! In short, customers return when they have a reason to do so, just as suppliers perform when they are given the proper motivation. Pretty basic stuff, but so often missed. Providing incentives is also key in the client–supplier relationship.

9. **Create solutions for seemingly impossible problems.** In Franklin's autobiography he tells of a plan he and a colleague devised to procure a much-needed cannon. The early assembly was continuously under the control of Quakers, who were pacifists. The two conspirators devised a plan to introduce a bill calling for the purchase of a fire engine. Once the assembly approved, Franklin immediately spent the money on a cannon, reasoning that the cannon, after all, was a "fire engine." This plan is admittedly deceptive and I would not recom-mend deceit as a strategy, but Franklin's approach was undeniably creative. The important point here is that security managers need to search out, or at least be open to, alternative approaches. Early on we discussed how myopic other executives are in terms of both defining the manager's role and allocating resources. Even in good times, asset protection is often forgotten when it comes to designing new facili-ties, venturing into new markets, developing new products and ser-vices. The lessons of 9/11 also illustrate that even a major disaster cannot sway effective decision-making when the economy is lacklus-ter or recessed. Creativity is needed to survive, let alone thrive. If you are not the creative genius in your department, offer incentives to others who can develop creative solutions that are effective and efficient.

10. **Become a revolutionary for experimentation and change.** This management arrow of Franklin's harkens back to what has already been raised several times in one form or another. It also helps me set the stage for the central point of my epilogue. In short, we need to experiment more and test the very basic assumptions we operate on. As we saw in the WTC disaster, we need to test the validity of sending people above and below a disaster site as opposed to a full evacuation. Responding units were able to get through despite the presence of tens of thousands of fleeing individuals. Or, on another track, do armed security personnel really deter robberies, or do we just think they do because common sense says so? This is an important question because the very rules that govern common sense are changing and our societal values have been changing rapidly over the past two decades (e.g., the value of human life appears to be diminishing, as seen in school shootings, terrorism, road rage, workplace violence).

    As security managers we build elaborate programs and ask for large sums of operating and capital dollars. But do—or will—our companies receive their return on investment? In both *Business Strategies* and *The Art* I raised this question and I still encounter, more often than not, security managers who pursue strategies based on assumptions. Franklin, we must remember, was one of our founding fathers. This is to say that he was a revolutionary. He had a vision that was outside of the norm and he pursued it. I think we are all familiar with his keen interest in experimentation to prove his hypotheses. (Remember the kite, key, and electrical storm?) To this end, he serves as a wonderful role model for today's security manager.

11. **Sometimes it's better to do 1001 small things right than only one large thing right.** Attention to detail is a critical component to success. One of my former bosses once said, "I'll take success one step at a time." He was very successful in the end. I am also reminded of the great football quarterback, Joe Montana. I always enjoyed it when he came into the game in the last two minutes when his team was down. Invariably, he would chip away at the opponent's defense with short yardage passes or run patterns that forced the ball out of bounds, giving him the necessary time to march his team downfield. Step by step he would lead them until the necessary scoring opportunity presented itself—and then he struck! His success rate was phenomenal because of his measured strategy.

    Earlier we called this dogged persistence. Great golfing drives are exciting to watch, but the smart golfer knows that the shot before him or her is only the prelude to the next one. To reach the hole in as few strokes as possible, the strategy is much more dependant on placing one good, well-placed shot after another. Security managers can learn a great deal by watching a sports legend in action, whether it is the *Tour de France* or a baseball game. Each is about taking incremental steps along the road to victory. As Helmut Schmidt noted: "Whoever wants to reach a distant goal must take many steps."

12. **Deliberately cultivate your reputation and legacy.** When the day comes for you to leave your organization, what will be your legacy? This is a difficult question to answer, but a responsible security leader dares to ask it—and more importantly, has the ability to answer it. Legacies are good things. Recently, the concept has been tainted with the scandals of previous government and business executives. Yet legacy building forces us to focus on what it is that we want to leave behind. Most want a positive remembrance, but that is not enough. A true legacy provides something for others to build on. It represents our heritage. There is the saying of a true leader: "It is he who, when gone, his followers say 'We did this ourselves.'" A legacy ought not be confused with one's reputation. A reputation is what people think about you while you are here. A legacy is what they think about you when you are gone.

With each of my corporate positions I knew I wanted to leave something behind. I want the same for each of my consulting clients. I think I succeeded in most cases. I say this not in any braggart way. Rather, legacy building was another one of those management arrows I keep referring to along our journey. It keeps me focused and provides a framework for assuring that measurable contributions will result. Why go to work each day, put in a hard effort, and leave in the end with only a paycheck? When I hear security managers tell me that they are proud of what they have accomplished, I am proud too. They can point to having accomplished more than having earned a fair day's wage for a fair day's work. Progress is defined on the back of our collective legacies.

These then are *Ben Franklin's 12 Rules for Effective Management*. Interestingly enough, he did not end there. As noted earlier, he was a statesman, an author, a scientist, a businessman, and an inventor. He was also a humorist and philosopher. One of his more famous writings was *Poor Richard's Almanack*. In the following list I have extracted three areas in which he provides sage advice for any success-oriented manager. I have chosen what I consider to be his ten best sayings in each area. You may have others. Each is self-explanatory and needs no further elaboration. I share these with you in hopes that they, too, will help guide you along the path of success.

Lessons from Poor Richard

Written in the mid-1700s, Franklin's words ring as relevant now as then. What impresses me most is his balance. On the one hand he can leave us shivering a little at his Machiavellian suggestions in dealing with others. On the other, he leaves us in awe over what he has to say about the virtuous person. I've extracted some of my favorite sayings, copied here just as he originally wrote them, grammar and all. I have limited his comments to the three areas that I believe challenge most managers. I hope you find a great deal of wisdom and practical advice in each.

On Managing Others

1. Kings and Bears often worry their keepers.
2. Fools make feasts and wise men eat 'em.
3. Beware of the young doctor & the old barber.
4. Distrust and caution are the parents of security.
5. Great famine when wolves eat wolves.
6. There is no little enemy.
7. Anoint a villain and he'll stab you, stab him & he'll anoint you.
8. Beware of meat twice boil'd, and an old foe reconcil'd.
9. Three may keep a secret, if two of them are dead.
10. To whom thy secret thou dost tell, to him thy freedom dost sell.

The worst wheel of the cart makes the most noise.

On Being Careful What You Say and Do

1. Great Talkers, little Doers.
2. He has chang'd his one ey'd horse for a blind one.
3. The heart of a fool is in his mouth, but the mouth of a wise man is in his heart.
4. Better slip with foot than tongue.
5. Blame-all and Praise-all are two blockheads.
6. Approve not of him who commends all you say.
7. There's many witty men whose brains can't fill their bellies.
8. Weighty questions ask for deliberate answers.
9. There's small revenge in words, but words may be greatly revenged.
10. Sloth and silence are a fool's virtues.

Of learned Fools I have seen ten times ten, Of unlearned wise men I have seen a hundred.

On Pursuing Justice and Virtue

1. The poor have little, beggars none, the rich too much, *enough* not one.
2. He is ill cloth'd, who is bare of virtue.
3. Snowy winter, a plentiful harvest.
4. In success be moderate.
5. Without justice, courage is weak.
6. To be humble to superiors is duty, to equals courtesy, to inferiors nobleness.
7. Sell not virtue to purchase wealth, nor liberty to purchase power.
8. The noblest question in the world is *What good may I do in it?*
9. You may be more happy than princes, if you will be more virtuous.
10. The nearest way to come to glory, is to do that for conscience which we do for glory.

If you would not be forgotten,
As soon as you are dead and rotten,
Either write things worth reading,
or do things worth the writing.

MAXWELL'S TRAPS THAT MAKE PEOPLE BACK AWAY FROM RISK

Before leaving Ben Franklin, I want to share one last point raised by McCormick. He notes that a few decades back a sociological survey was taken of people nearing their century mark. They were asked if there was anything they would do differently if they had the opportunity to relive their lives. These near-centurions stated that they would risk more, reflect more, and create a lasting legacy. For a group that survived two world wars and a great depression, I find it interesting that their first wish was to have taken greater risks. This leads directly to what follows.

John C. Maxwell, in his book, *Failing Forward: Turning Mistakes into Stepping Stones for Success*, notes that there are six traps that people can easily fall into, and, in so doing, avoid risks that could otherwise propel them to a higher level. After reading and reflecting on what Maxwell has to offer, here is my take on how these six traps can affect a security manager's ability to effectively lead.

1. **The Embarrassment Trap:** We do not want to embarrass ourselves. We do not want to be perceived as losers or, worse yet, *wacky*. But risks require our ability to put such an outcome on the line. We all know that with high risk comes high reward. Sometimes we have to step outside the safety of conventionalism and take a high risk. Most times such high-stakes risk taking is not necessary. Calculated risks—those with a degree of certainty—can also yield success. But, you have to begin by taking the risk.

2. **The Rationalization Trap:** One of my former bosses was the master of rationalization. He could rationalize himself into complete inaction. I often thought of him as organizationally catatonic because he could never make a timely decision. For him there was always a reason why one should not do something. If he thought doing one thing might lead to another, he would soon spin himself into an anxiety attack trying to figure out what the outcome of the second thing would be and how that would create a third and, in turn, a fourth, and so on. One of my colleagues told me the boss gave him headaches just listening to his litany of rationalizations. I thought he was joking at first. Then one day after one of those dizzying episodes I saw him return to his office and take several high-powered aspirin! (Perhaps they were Excedrin.)

3. **The Unrealistic Expectation Trap:** Many of my students have fallen into this trap, and I have seen many a security manager do the same thing, especially those who are first-time security directors. It is an easy trap to get into. We want things to be as we perceive them and we can become blind to what they are in reality. So blinded, we continue to act as though our perception is reality and fail to venture out and test the validity of our perceptions. That is, until it is too late. I know of security managers who fail to recognize the vulnerability of their own position, believing that since they are in security, their position is safe. After all, they reason, "How can our company go on without a security director?" The 1980s and early 1990s are testimony to such flawed thinking.

4. **The Fairness Trap:** In *Business Strategies* I first introduced the concepts of organizational competence versus organizational politics. We have been raised to believe that the world is fair and if we work hard and demonstrate our competence, we will be rewarded. Sometimes this is so, but sometimes it is not. Why? Because organizations—all organizations—have some degree of politics. With politics come decisions that are not always fair or based on one's competency. Yet our upbringing is so strong that we find it difficult to understand that organizational politics is just as powerful a force as the force of competency or fairness.

We pass the concept of fairness along to our children and become appalled if our teachers, clergy, friends, and civic leaders suggest otherwise. Security managers, as a profession, want what is fair because most of us have come from a world of law and order. We have been trained in matters of justice and a sense of fair play. When decisions are made not to prosecute those proven to be culpable, we can become jaded or discouraged. This, in turn, lessens our willingness to take appropriate risks because we believe that we will not be supported.

5. **The Timing Trap:** Another adage is, "An idea whose time has not yet come." This is a reflection of the timing trap. Timing, in many cases, is everything. In *The Art* I shared with you the analogy of fly fishing and security management. I referred to it at the beginning of this book. You may recall that the success of your ideas is closely related to the speed of the fisherman's water (translation: the organization's timing). In other words, is the organization at a point where its senior management and/or line-level employees are ready to accept the idea? Sometimes they may not be, but the only way to find out is to take the risk and "float the idea out there." Politicians are masters at this. A successful manager soon learns this skill as well.

It is easy to sit back and simply say that the time is not right. But how do you know? Do you really know for sure, or is it your assumption? I recall the time I needed a new security console. My company was in a severe turnaround mode. The cost of the new facility was projected to exceed one million dollars. Everyone told me that it would never survive the capital budget review committee. Even the CEO had sent word that he would not support such an idea. Well, my management team did its homework and built a compelling business argument. We tactfully approached some of our advocates and tested the case on them. At first they resisted, but then they began to see why the idea had merit. We risked more and went out further to others. They agreed as well. Soon we had our army of supporters. The CEO relented and we had our project approved.

6. **The Inspiration Trap:** Managing in hard times can be more fun than managing in good times. This may seem to be an oxymoron, but it is true. Hard times generate opportunities for creative thinking—new ways of doing things and managing people. Good times can lull us into complacency, and we know how that can lead to organizational cancer. Ask yourself this simple question: When was the last time either I or someone on my team had a true inspiration? Hopefully, you can think of one or perhaps several over the near past. If not, this ought to prod you to further question whether you and your team are getting the most that is there to receive.

Ten Ways People Get in Their Own Way

To help us along this part of our journey, Michael Useem offers ten ways in which we can get in our own way. In his book, *Leading Up: How to Lead Your Boss So You Both Win*, he shares with us the following list:

1. Poor people skills
2. A negative attitude
3. A bad fit
4. Lack of focus
5. A weak commitment
6. An unwillingness to change
7. A short-cut mind-set
8. Relying on talent alone
9. A response to poor information
10. No goals

Each of these is self-explanatory. I am sure there are at least ten, and perhaps twenty more that come to your mind. Regardless of the number, Useem's point is that we must be aware that there are ways that we defeat ourselves. As I first reviewed the list, I not only thought of individuals I have encountered, but also saw how I had tripped myself up in the past. He offers us a short, but powerful list to consider as we evaluate our own management style.

Dalton's 20 Axioms for Managerial Success

In putting this chapter together, several of my professional colleagues asked if I had developed any new axioms for success. In *Business Strategies*, I identified my 20 Axioms and made a few comments on each. They were

1. Sometimes the boss is a jerk.
2. Don't tell me what I know, show me what I don't.
3. Without controversy there can be no success.
4. In any organization there are always two spheres: politics and competency.
5. Despite all the evidence, there are those who continue to believe that all is well, or this, too, shall pass.
6. Organizations, like water, seek their own level.
7. Organizations begin to die the day the sense of urgency begins to fade.

8. Security ought not be that department where an individual goes to get the answer no.

9. Radical ideas blossom when line and staff merge.

10. Document!! Document!! Document!!

11. Success comes to those who orchestrate it.

12. An organization's greatest cardinal sin is to allow the norm "we've always done it this way" to exist.

13. Nature didn't give the buck its antlers just for looks.

14. Women need to be better prepared if they are going to survive, let alone make it to the top.

15. There are some events that are simply out of your control.

16. Ask a manager where he or she wants the organization to be in ten years. If the answer is not significantly different from how it is now, you know you're talking to a maintenance manager.

17. There's a lot to be said for those who can survive.

18. Organizations are like waves. Some crash, some just fade; yet one thing is for sure, all waves crest and end.

19. The best way to enter a building is not necessarily through the front door.

20. Never attend a meeting without bringing the agenda.

Over the past few years I have added to this list. Again, most of the items are fairly self-explanatory, but a few can be better explained with a couple of additional thoughts for your consideration.

21. If managers know so much, how come there are so many below them who do so much better?

22. The level of success for managers is directly related to how well they manage perceptions.

23. There's a difference between quitting and knowing when to move on. When a security manager or professional calls to let me know that they have grown tired of where they are working, there is the inevitable second part: Do I know of anything open? Whether I do or not, I always ask if they are running from something or running to something. There is a significant difference. Sometimes good career development means moving on, especially in turbulent times.

24. Most managers listen with the intent to answer why they are right, few with the intent to truly understand.

25. Keep an eye on your enemies, and an ear to your friends. This axiom actually swings both ways. Enemies can make strange partners when

the occasion is right. The effective manager keeps a careful eye on them to pick up this subtlety and use it wisely. Conversely, listening to your friends can tell you whether they have your best interest at heart or have shifted allegiances.

26. An effective manager understands that a desk is a dangerous place from which to lead people.

27. Good leaders don't need to explain their vision, they simply need to have their staff stand beside them on the hill and see for themselves what lies beyond.

28. Success means falling down, a lot.

29. Be open and apologetic about your shortcomings. People will forgive quickly. This gives you more time to show the rest of your shortcomings.

30. Being smart is when you find your boss' error. Being wise is keeping your mouth shut. Many up and coming managers are quick to show everyone, especially their boss, how intelligent they are. They want to impress, thinking this will lead to acceptance. Wise is the experienced manager who bites his or her tongue and guides the boss in such a way as to allow the boss to find the mistake. After all, if managers are as smart as they believe themselves to be, their time will come.

31. Zig Ziglar notes that confidence is going after Moby Dick and taking the tartar sauce with you.

32. We must all hang together, or assuredly we shall all hang separately (Ben Franklin)

33. There is nothing that says we cannot change, so long as it is for the right reason.

34. Manage your staff as if they were your customers.

35. When you focus on one thing, that is all you can possibly achieve.

36. To thine own self be true, even if it means accepting a loss.

37. I don't have a monopoly on brains, that's why I borrow as many as I can.

38. It is okay to pursue your passion, but far better to pursue what you do passionately.

39. That which is best is that which is simple to understand.

40. Failure is not falling down. Failure is not getting up.

Success comes before work only in the dictionary.

Vidal Sassoon

CONCLUDING COMMENTS

In this chapter we have examined many of the ideas offered by those intent on showing us how we can be more effective managers. Even though there are several direct references to security managers, I think you would agree that what has been presented here has application for every profession. I have done this by design. In my opening remarks in *Business Strategies* I stressed that success is more a reflection of our ability to demonstrate business acumen than security expertise. Three books and several years later, the same holds true.

Security management is more than learning the technical aspects of running an asset protection unit. There are plenty of books that can teach us this, and from my publisher I understand many more are on their way. There is nothing wrong with this. For that matter, it is necessary to achieve balance. But, in our pursuit to be proven security professionals, we must never lose focus on own primary responsibility—to be savvy business leaders who are ethically bound to core principles.

In Chapter 9 we have read what Ben Franklin teaches us about ourselves and our professional careers. We visited some relatively new authors on organizational success, including Ram Charan, Michael Useem, Blaine McCormick, and John Maxwell. I also provided some of my own thoughts regarding client and supplier relationships via their respective ten commandments and sins of execution. Finally, I hope that you found revisiting my original twenty axioms with twenty new ones both enjoyable and thought provoking. As we draw to a close I leave you with two added comments, one from Helen Keller and the other from Bruce Barton. Both have served me well over the years. I hope they do the same for you.

One can never consent to creep when one has an impulse to soar.
Helen Keller

When you're through changing, you're through.
Bruce Barton

THOUGHT-PROVOKING QUESTIONS

1. Clients commonly believe they control the relationship between themselves and their suppliers. The author raises the concept of partnering and how no one partner is in total control. Do you believe this approach has merits, or will suppliers seize upon this as an opportunity to deliver less than promised?

2. Suppliers can fall into a number of traps or commit a variety of sins, according to this chapter. From your experience, are there other traps or sins that today's security supplier ought to be aware of?

3. The chapter draws upon the wit and wisdom of Ben Franklin. Who else can you think of who has as keen an insight on both human nature and the nature of business? Are there any other sayings of Ben Franklin that can serve as a guide to effective management?

4. John Maxwell and Michael Useem offer us a number of traps or ways in which we can stumble as managers. Based on your experience, do these make sense? Are there others that need to be raised as well?

5. Finally, the author provides us with 40 axioms for success. Your reaction? Are they helpful? Do you have any of your own?

EPILOGUE

We are at the end of our journey. In the last chapter I have deliberately shifted gears. This is not your conventional ending to a book on security management. But then, I hope the entire book has been unconventional. We live in very turbulent times. I mean more than just being in what security historians will most certainly call the *Post 9/11 Era*. The start of this new century has rocked America with scandals from boardrooms and the emergence of new threats that represent even greater harm than the WTC tragedy. I am referring to cybercrime and the threats associated with loss of intellectual property. Neither carries the emotional weight of the loss of nearly 3,000 lives, but each is capable of destroying the professional and personal lives of those dedicated to their professions and organizations. This means literally tens of thousands.

Today's asset management team needs to be in tune with these threats, many of which are only beginning to appear on corporate radar screens. Gone should be the day when security is defined simply in terms of physical asset protection. Unfortunately, 9/11 has set this new focus back. My hope is that it is a temporary setback, but indications are that this may not be the case. I do hope I am proven wrong. Security's value needs to be measured in multiple ways on different corporate stages. Physical protection is only one stage. The true measure of long-term success will come only when we challenge many of our current assumptions and test their validity. To do this we need to seek the assistance of those outside our industry.

Bold thinking requires bold resources. Corporate grants are needed, as are research efforts originating from within our industry and academic institutions. I wonder if I shall see the day when business students from Harvard, Wharton, Stanford, or the University of Michigan will undertake serious research on some of our industry's most fundamental assumptions. For example, do security officers really deter crime through their actions? If so, to what extent? What does the empirical evidence really indicate about building evacuation plans? The events of 9/11 certainly tell us that thousands can be evacuated into a crowded space and emergency units can still rapidly respond without their interference. There are other equally fascinating areas that demand a more business-directed approach based on sound criteria that measure a solid return on the organization's investment. Following are some examples.

What, if any, is the crime prevention value of a uniformed security officer?
Preventative value has been a long-standing issue, even in law enforcement. From studies that have been done, it would appear that the presence of uniformed personnel has little deterrent value. Yet, the level of staffing and debates as to which are more effective, third-party providers or proprietary workforces, continue to be two of the central axes of an asset protection plan. Clearly more research is needed to address this issue given the dollars involved. Industry experts know that uniformed security officers do not have a legal or ethical obligation to put themselves in harms way. This is not generally understood by corporate executives and their employees. Consequently, they often will call for additional security staffing believing that more officers means more safety. Similarly, *how should security officer be deployed?* We saw one example of this in a previous chapter, but even this is admittedly not without its subjective flaws. I recognize that asset protection has an inherent degree of subjectivity, but what is the proper ratio of subjectivity to objectivity?

Are there roles for private security personnel in law enforcement operations?
We know there is an application in our correctional system, but is that all? City, county, state, and even federal administrators should be offered proven alternatives if they are to take their fiscal management responsibilities seriously. This means having the data that counters the emotionally vested interests of sworn personnel. If security officers can detain people with proper safeguards, why not extend this to an actual arrest?

What is the proper mix between using state-of-the-art technology and allocating uniformed security personnel?
Corporate executives swing from one end of the pendulum to the other without a clear strategy. There are no clearly defined criteria that can be offered to them. Some overspend on personnel because their security director comes from this school. Others want to replace all officers with cameras, alarms, and card readers. While such an approach is appealing because it significantly reduces annual recurring expenses, it is foolhardy at best. Yet, just what is the proper strategy? It is incumbent upon us to seek out the correct formula. Just as it is appropriate to ask about the deterrent value of security staffing, the same can be asked about the use of technology. All too often I find camera installations that purport to view an exit, monitoring who comes and goes and what, if any-

thing, they may be carrying. Yet, the cameras have been mounted facing the door, thus rendering an excellent view of the backs of people as they exit, not to mention no real way of discerning what they may be carrying. In other words, we assume that the camera is providing a deterrent value when in fact it is of little value, even for investigative purposes.

Is there really such a thing as an effective proactive criminal investigation?
A few companies have tried to develop proactive investigative models in an effort to mitigate loss before it happens. The idea is sound, but it lacks proof of its effectiveness. Some have tried to work with artificial intelligence, and others have tried historical trend analyses. Either one of these, or something entirely different, may be the answer, but we need commitment from executives and researchers to pursue this. Why? The cost of internal fraud alone represents a multibillion-dollar challenge for businesses.

Can we do better at determining threat levels, especially those associated with terrorism and loss of highly confidential information?
I sincerely believe the answer to both is a resounding yes. But, it requires a sustained research effort. We know that color-coded threat matrices are not the answer—they only obfuscate the real issue. In the world of information technology, we know that building firewalls is only a partial solution. We need a process that addresses the unique nature of each of these threats and others. We need to understand root causes and challenge underlying assumptions before we can develop effective responses. This is critical, because these answers are what drive the ultimate management decision-making process.

Recently the Office of Homeland Security announced that airports should randomly screen arriving automobiles for explosives. Moreover, major airlines agreed to economically profile passengers at the time passengers purchase their tickets to assure that they are not potential suspects. To do this, the airline screeners would rely on a passenger's banking account and credit card history. This is a very, very dangerous infringement on our right to privacy. Yet, the American public seems willing to roll over and allow this under the fear that to object is somehow un-American. Coupled with the loss of other protections against governmental intrusion, all under the cloak of protecting Americans against terrorism and assuring freedom, I believe we have stepped to the edge of losing that which we cherish the most—true freedom. Why are we allowing the government to do this? Because we believe that they know best and have our best interests at heart. So did Joseph McCarthy and J. Edgar Hoover. Potential abuse does not rest with political leaders and government agency heads alone. As noted earlier, many corporate and even religious leaders have the ability to abuse individual rights.

The irony is that invasive profiling and screening is based on assumptions. Where is the empirical proof that such approaches really accomplish what they are intended to do? The reality is that such proof is lacking. For that matter, I suspect it is non-existent. Responsible security executives should be screaming that our liberties are being trodden upon for the sake of supposed security.

What do all of the assumptive approaches have in common? They illustrate that ours is still largely an industry that is based on the art of what ought to be done and not the scientific "what if." The correct plan of action, therefore, appears to be obvious. We ought to call a time-out and seek the resources necessary to challenge these assumptions. I raise only a handful of them to illustrate how much needs to be done. If asked, both you and I could fill many more pages. However, to do so only serves to illustrate the amount of work that lies ahead. Suffice it to say, ours is a profession with ample opportunity for meaningful research that can challenge even the most gifted for a long time to come. I see this as a really exciting time, because there are so many challenges before us. In short, what I am calling for, as I have done in each of the preceding two books, is the deliberate, systematic, study of what we call asset protection and not the collective assumptions of the well intentioned or those with vested interests.

Before God we are all equally wise and equally foolish.

Albert Einstein

Appendix A

A Model Request for Security Services Proposal

This appendix presents a model Request for Proposal designed to solicit a strategic partner. Even if you opt to pursue another relationship, most of the material contained in the model RFP can be used.

Introduction

We are seeking quality-oriented service providers to assist us in meeting our security requirements. Together they will constitute a strategic partnering network. We are committed to assuring our tenants, visitors, customers, and employees that every reasonable effort is being extended to provide them a safe and secure working environment. To meet this commitment, we recognize that our security providers play a critical role. It is for this reason that each provider must demonstrate an ability and commitment.

Our strategy for selecting qualified suppliers to participate in our strategic partnering network is an interactive process. You will be given several opportunities to share with us your abilities and your ideas for improving our security program. Here is an outline of the process:

1. Selected suppliers will complete the quality service assessment and submit it with the proposal.
2. Selected suppliers will be invited to participate in a proposal conference to ask questions and seek further clarification.
3. Proposals will be submitted and reviewed by our taskforce using a variety of value-driven assessment measurements.
4. Final candidates will be invited to appear before the selection committee to answer questions arising out of their submitted proposals.
5. After a final selection is made, the candidate will sign a letter of intent to serve as an interim agreement until a final contract can be negotiated and begin immediately working with our project manager to implement the project.

Profit Margin, Pricing, and Best Offer

At the outset, we want to address our commitment to seeking qualified vendors who will become our strategic partners. We recognize that the traditional approach to providing security service is to competitively bid one supplier against another using pricing as the bottom line. That is not our intent here. We want you to make a reasonable profit—for that matter, we expect it. If you cannot do so, you will become a *reluctant warrior* and will not be able to fully participate in the relationship. We do not want reluctance, for it breeds mediocrity.

There are two ways you can price this account: a) submit an hourly rate reflecting your costs and profits, or b) submit a proposal reflecting your costs and a management fee which reflects a reasonable profit. We prefer the latter for several reasons. In either case, we will expect full disclosure of your total costs and profit.

Here's a word of caution: We intend to step through this process aggressively. Therefore, we do not want to get bogged down in discussions of profit margins. Simply tell us what you believe is a reasonable margin and we can address this up front, professionally and judiciously.

Finally, it is not our intent to spend a long time negotiating a final price. Therefore, consider your submittal as your best and final offer. You should also note that we are not interested in any form of progressive pay rate for your officers that is spread over a year. Rather, we expect that you will set a pay range for your officers and each will receive an annual merit raise based on successfully completing measured performance standards. In other words, we want a starting wage that will remain fixed for one year. We do not want a step scale based on an initial probationary rate followed by an increase 90 days later and then followed up another 90- or 120-day pay increase. We expect our partner to hire qualified people up front, train them accordingly, assess their performance throughout the year, and then reward them appropriately at the end of the year.

Management/Service Approach

Alternatively, for locations in multiple markets, please complete the attachment that details the locations and current hours of coverage. Remember, even though you may not currently have a branch office in each marketplace, there is nothing to prohibit you from subcontracting to another supplier. If so, know that we expect the same standards as set forth in our agreement to be applied to each of your subcontractors.

Our goal is to position ourselves with one company who will serve as the overall security business partner. Our partner needs to know the local marketplace, be familiar with existing ordinances and laws and recent civil litigation impacting security coverage for the area, and be able to best serve our needs. Our partner will work with us to establish annual operating budgets, assist in capital projects involving security systems, develop local procedures and audit for compliance, and, when appropriate, assist in investigating related incidents. In short, we are looking for a partner willing to assume management responsibility first and operational performance second. In this way the partner is not necessarily limited to drawing on their own internal resources.

RFP Contents

The Request for Proposal is divided into five major sections. The first is a prequalifier exercise designed to show us your commitment to providing quality-directed services. After completing the exercise you will know whether or not you will want to continue to be considered, because your ultimate success will be largely measured against the criteria detailed here.

The second section asks for a series of documents. These include an acknowledgment letter, a company profile, your latest audited financial statement, a list of current and past clients, a time and action plan, and other material you may feel is relevant. These documents will assist us in getting to know you better. They also serve as a means of allowing us to better understand what you do and how you compare to your competitors.

The third section is a list of our basic terms and conditions. The fourth section is a list of expectations that will become part of the final agreement. These expectations have been developed to mirror our quality management process. They serve as an ongoing measure of your accomplishments and contributions to our security program. Over the course of time these expectations will change, but the process and scoring system will remain constant. As a business partner, it is our assumption that you will take an active role in defining future expectations.

The final section is a copy of the intended agreement. Although this is not the final agreement, we are providing it up front to allow you to know what we want so you can make an informed decision about partnering with us. We believe that the agreement is the core connector to our mutual success. This document will serve to bring us together and clearly set forth our mutual expectations.

Categories of Consideration

The selected supplier will be the one best able to present a proven track record in each of the following six categories:

1. Management of the account
2. Supervision of the account
3. Recruitment of personnel for the account
4. Training of assigned personnel
5. Administrative support to the account
6. Cost of servicing the account

We have ranked them in the order of their importance to us. Each is briefly described in the following sections so you will know what we mean by each and why we have ranked them as we have.

Management of the Account

To effectively provide quality-oriented security service, we believe that the supplier's most critical capability is effective account management. This means that the account manager needs to be a proven business manager. This person must be able to interact effectively with our management and line personnel. The individual must be able to effectively interface with our employees and customers.

To accomplish this, the account manager needs to be supported by a strong district and regional manager. He or she must have access to resources beyond those resident on the account. This entails more than access to higher-level managers. It includes online capability to the corporate library and other automated systems and electronic databases. For example, if we should request development of a comprehensive time and action plan for a given project, the account manager should be able to generate such a plan drawing on the resources of those above him or her.

As a minimum, the successful supplier will be able to demonstrate the following:

1. An account representative directly responsible for the management of our security program. This manager will have demonstrated executive business management experience. This person will have a working understanding of the concepts underlying Continuous Quality Improvement (CQI) and demonstrated success in applying them to client accounts. They will be familiar with the difference between strategic partnering and being a provider of contract services.

2. An on-site manager or supervisor(s) who will oversee the account will have a minimum of 2 to 3 years of demonstrated security business management and/or supervisory experience.

Supervision of the Account

We believe that the second most critical variable is the ability to effectively supervise those assigned to this account. Supervision requires people with proven security experience. It also requires the development of measurable performance criteria to be applied to all posts and officer classifications. Effective supervision means knowing how to be an appropriate role model. It requires an ability to teach, guide, and direct. It means knowing every operational aspect of the business and being able to perform them well—consistently.

We believe that supervisors should, for the most part, emerge from within the ranks of those assigned to the account. This achieves continuity and assures that experienced officers are at the forefront of protecting our employees, customers, visitors, and assets, both tangible and intangible. To accomplish this requires the account manager to have in place criteria that objectively identify the most-qualified individuals.

Recruitment of Personnel for the Account

Effective security service ultimately rests with those charged with providing this service on a daily basis. That is why we believe recruitment is the next highest variable. Quality service can only be delivered by a quality-oriented workforce. This is not something that can simply be taught. There must be a core value intrinsic to the individual. We will look closely at this process to assure ourselves that the selected supplier understands its importance.

Officers assigned to this account will be assessed based on their aptitude for customer relations. They will be expected to conduct themselves in a professional manner, both in demeanor and bearing. They will need to be experienced in handling conflict resolution, possess a high measure of self-reliance, and know how to make appropriate discretionary decisions and act on them accordingly.

Training of Assigned Personnel

Even quality-oriented people need to be taught the basic expectations of a client. Moreover, they need to be properly shown how to carry out their duties to meet the client's expectations. For this reason we believe that training is critical. The successful supplier will demonstrate the existence of each of the following types of officer training:

- IOT (Initial Officer Training)
- OJT (On-the-Job Training)
- AOT (Advanced Officer Training)
- SOT (Specialized Officer Training)

Each type of training will be explained in detail and examples of current client usage will be expected. We will assess the appropriateness of such training and its application for meeting the needs of this account. Such training should reflect a multimedia approach involving classroom training, audio and video learning, computer-aided instruction, and on-the-job execution, each complete with samples of testing and scoring.

Administrative Support to the Account

Critical to any successful operation is the level of administrative support. This entails an established infrastructure at the district, regional, and corporate levels. This will include, but not be limited to:

- An automated payroll and scheduling system
- A regional or corporate training program, complete with instructors specialized in customer relations and asset protection strategies and practices as required by this account
- A reference library directly accessible to the account manager for quick retrieval of documents necessary to support the management of this account
- An online capability to the regional and corporate offices for E-Mail assistance and information exchange
- An established background and selection procedure capable of meeting the requirements as set forth in this RFP

Cost of Servicing the Account

In today's competitive marketplace, cost is always a consideration. We, too, are concerned with rising costs, but that is not the only driver. We will pay for value. This is our investment to assure a strong place among our competitors. But value must be received. We will look seriously at the supplier who can work with us to achieve lower operating expenses without loss of quality.

We want high-energy workers, committed to supporting our business aims. This means we must be willing to invest in them. Our mutual success depends on your willingness to share in the risks and the rewards. Through incentives for identifying cost efficiencies, we will look seriously at the supplier that can demonstrate the ability to work with us.

Section One: Quality Orientation

We see strategic partnering as a critical management tool for improving efficiency and effectiveness. By partnering with selected third-party suppliers, we believe that the overall quality of security will be enhanced. To achieve this, however, we recognize the need to make the relationship a two-way street. To be successful, both of us need to be willing to share in the success and the risks associated in achieving that success. The partnership needs to be defined in terms of a working relationship that provides shared benefits to the mutual satisfaction of the parties in terms of creating value, long-term business growth, continuous improvement, problem resolution, and information access.

We also recognize that a successful partnership is based on earned mutual respect. Part of this mutual respect acknowledges that each partner has a core function uniquely its own. As a leading provider in a highly competitive marketplace, we need to protect our people and assets. As a supplier of security services, we look to your core competency and count on your organization being a well-managed, professionally oriented provider of asset protection.

Demonstrating Quality Improvement Processing

To allow us to better understand your capabilities and set forth what we expect from you in this relationship, we are asking that you respond to each of the following.

1. Quality values: Submit a narrative description of your Quality Service Values, explaining how they are projected to your clients in a consistent manner, and how they are determined and reinforced.

2. Public responsibility: Describe how you extend your Quality Service Values into the external community; e.g., serving professional associations, public agencies, volunteer groups, etc.

3. Quality goals and plans: Describe how your Quality Service Values are translated into action plans for meeting your client's short-term (1–2 years) and longer-term (3 years or more) needs. Explain how this differentiates you from your key competitors in this marketplace.

4. Employee involvement: Describe the means available for all employees to contribute to meeting your company's quality objectives; summarize trends and current levels of involvement.

5. Quality education, training, and performance: Describe how you decide what quality education and training is needed by employees and how this is transferred to meeting current client needs. Provide samples of detailed performance criteria for security officers with existing clients. These should be specific to site location responsibilities and be measured in value-added terms.

6. Determining customer requirements and expectations: Describe how you determine current and future customer requirements and expectations. This might include performance information on your services, how complaints are managed and corrective action taken, gains and losses of customers, customer satisfaction, and competitors' performance.

7. Customer relationship management: Describe how you provide effective management of the relationship you have with other customers and how you use the information gained from customers to improve products and services as well as customer relationship management practices.

8. Customer service standards and resolution for quality improvement: Detail your most important customer service standards and how you handle complaints, resolve them, and use them for quality improvement and prevention of future problems.

9. Determining customer satisfaction: Describe your methods for determining customer satisfaction, how satisfaction information is used in quality improvement, and how methods for determining customer satisfaction are improved.

Also compare your customer satisfaction results and recognition with those of your key competitors.

Once you have completed this exercise, you should have a basic understanding of what we expect in a service provider. Please attach your responses to your proposal and proceed to the next activity, if you elect to continue.

Section Two: Supporting Documentation

The successful contractor will complete the following.

1. Submit a letter and designate it as Attachment A, signed by an authorizing agent, attesting to having read the RFP and its attachments and agreeing to meet and comply with their requirements as a condition of being awarded this account.
2. Complete the company survey (Attachment B).
3. Provide a current client list identifying accounts in excess of x hours per year of security coverage as administered and managed by the office or branch to be responsible for this account. The list shall identify the total hours of service per year, nature of the account, and the name of a contact person and that individual's telephone number.
4. Provide the names of three previous clients served by the office or branch intending to manage this account. Each previous client shall have been provided security service with no less than x hours per year. The list shall include the identity of the former contact manager and telephone number. These clients should represent the type of account similar to that addressed in this RFP.
5. Provide proofs of insurance as outlined in the following section.
6. Submit a proposed conversion schedule as outlined in the following section.
7. Submit resumes of one to three potential account managers capable of meeting the basic requirements as outlined in Section One who would be available for immediate assignment to this account.
8. Supply any additional material that may assist us in making an informed decision.

Section Three: Terms and Conditions

Submission Requirements

Each bidder is required to submit one bound copy and one unbound copy. All copies are to be received sealed by (DATE, TIME). The copies are to be sent to: (INSERT NAME & ADDRESS).

Such submissions may be in person or by mail. It is our intention to reach a final decision on or before (DATE). Should we determine that value will be added by having prospective contractors make a presentation, two or three semi-finalists will be invited to make such a presentation prior to (DATE). The selected contractor will be notified by telephone within 48 hours of the final decision. Unsuccessful bidders will be notified by mail.

Conversion Schedule

The contractor should prepare a proposed conversion schedule, unless the selected contractor is the current contractor. Such a schedule should reflect the activities necessary to assure staffing and training from the time the contract is awarded through the actual conversion. The schedule should reflect projected dates of completion for particular tasks and assignments, and identify the person(s) responsible for such actions. *A time and action plan must accompany the conversion schedule.* If some of the current security staff will be retained (assuming they meet the contractor's hiring requirements), the contractor will also reflect how these individuals will be hired, integrated, and trained as a part of the new team. *The schedule should reflect a 24-hour client-specific training program for all assigned personnel—including 8 hours of customer services training—prior to anyone being assigned to this account.*

Uniforms and Equipment

The selected contractor will supply all uniforms as specified by us and assure that they are continuously cleaned and maintained. The cost will be borne by the contractor and is to be reflected in the stated billing rate outlined, separating out the cost for procurement and cleaning. The contractor will not structure any type of program that requires employees to advance or draw from their wages any cost associated with their uniforms, particularly during their probationary employment.

The contractor will supply, at its expense, all weather gear, leather gear, flashlights, pagers, and other equipment as is mutually agreed upon between us and the selected contractor, to meet the requirements of this account. The contractor will have use of our internal radio system.

The contractor will replace or repair at its cost any client-owned equipment (such as, but not limited to, communications equipment, fire and safety equipment, locks and keys, access control systems, CCTVs,) damaged or lost through abuse or neglect by the contractor's personnel.

Use of our telephone system for personal use is prohibited. Telephone calls will be audited. The contractor will be either billed for such calls or the cost of such usage will be deducted from the monthly payment, at our discretion. We will furnish office space and those supplies necessary to operate and manage the account on a daily basis.

Hours of Coverage

The selected contractor can anticipate providing up to (STATE APPROPRIATE NUMBER) hours of unarmed uniformed security service per year. In addition, there will be (STATE APPROPRIATE NUMBER) hours per year of uniformed supervision and 40 hours of account management. In total, we anticipate (STATE APPROPRIATE NUMBER) hours of security service per year. We anticipate that hours of coverage will be met largely by use of full-time personnel.

Staffing

The selected contractor should read carefully the conditions governing overtime, staffing assignments, turnover, and post assignments. The selected contractor should understand that the terms and conditions associated with the turnover rate will be adhered to strictly. Turnover is defined as beginning 60 days after the start of the account and as a percentage of total full-time equivalency of those assigned.

Duties and Responsibilities

Customer service is a critical component of our business strategy. Security is viewed as an integral part of accomplishing this objective. Therefore, the primary responsibility of each officer, supervisor, and manager will be to provide quality customer service. Typical duties will involve providing directions and assisting customers, visitors, employees, and vendors. On occasion, escorts may be required. Answering telephone inquiries and serving as a central or visible source of information is a significant part of the job. Therefore, each officer, supervisor, and manager must exercise courtesy, respect, and professionalism. In addition, the selected contractor must be able to assure that each of its assigned personnel will comply with the duties and responsibilities as outlined in attached contract.

Quality Standards

The selected contractor will have read and understood the terms and conditions contained in the agreement. Particular attention should be given to those articles that outline the development of specific performance objectives and their application toward merit pay increases for personnel assigned to this account.

Insurance

Prior to selection, the contractor shall provide Certificates of Insurance indicating the coverages as prescribed by the agreement. The contractor will assure that we will not be liable for the payment of any premiums or assessments with respect to the coverages described above.

Thirty (30) days' prior notice of cancellation or reduction in coverage is to be furnished to us. Further, our officers, agents, and employees shall be named additional insured with respect to the named insured's activities on or about the premises of the property. The policy shall be endorsed to provide that this insurance shall be primary and not contributing with any other insurance available to said additional insureds as respects any and all liability, loss, claims, damages, or expense arising out of the negligence or alleged negligence of the named insured.

Method of Payment

The contractor shall submit monthly invoices. Each invoice will be accompanied by originally signed timesheets and other documents, as may be required by us, demonstrating proof of purchase for items needed and approved prior to the purchase by us. The terms and conditions for payment by us shall be in accordance with those outlined in the agreement.

Incentives

Security personnel who consistently perform in an excellent manner or who perform over, above, and beyond their duty in a singular incident may be eligible for special recognition by us and/or selected contractor. Such recognition may involve, but not be limited to, financial rewards, supervisory consideration, and/or other awards or commendations as mutually agreed upon between us and the selected contractor.

Compensation Rates

In an effort to take full advantage of current economic conditions, the selected contractor will supply a billing rate based on a starting wage for security officers between (IDENTIFY DESIRED MINIMUM STARTING WAGE) per hour and (IDENTIFY DESIRED UPPER STARTING WAGE) per hour. Similarly, the contractor will establish a rate for supervisors using a base wage between (IDENTIFY DESIRED MINIMUM BASE WAGE) per hour and (IDENTIFY DESIRED UPPER STARTING WAGE) per hour. Likewise, the selected contractor will determine a rate for the account manager based on a starting wage they believe commensurate with the duties and responsibilities associated with this account. Billing rates and/or management fees are to be determined based on the contractor's ability to assure that all the terms and conditions of this RFP and accompanying attachments will be met.

Proposal Format

All proposals will follow the format outlined below:

1. Table of Contents
2. Completion of the Quality Improvement Processors 1 through 9 as outlined in Part One
3. The Company Survey, Attachment B—(Detailed Below)
4. Copy of Certified Financial Statement, Attachment C
5. Proofs of Insurance, Attachment D
6. Letter of Attestation, Attachment E
7. List of Current and Previous Clients, Attachment F
8. Resumes of Potential Account Manager Candidates, Attachment G
9. Conversion Schedule with Time and Action Plan, Attachment H
10. Added Material, as deemed appropriate

Section Four: Expectations

Vision of Security

We define the vision of security as follows: "To create and maintain a security program that encompasses our corporate values as well as those of our strategic security partner. Through outstanding performance, allow our strategic partner to fully manage and operate the security program."

Customer Relations

Establishing a strong and positive customer relations program is one of our highest priorities, and therefore expectations of security. Regardless of the time of day, day of week, or location, security is expected to be guided by and follow the precepts set forth in our quality service programs. Performance criteria are to be designed so they can be measured and documented. All of the expectations that follow should be updated through our Quality Assurance Criteria.

Lobby Management

The lobby operation has been defined as one of our critical positions. All lobbies, however, are not the same. Some require concierge duties and others require managing limited access control and monitoring a variety of devices and systems. The lobby is a sensitive position, one which in many cases is our most impressionable point for an employee (current and prospective), customer, tenant, or visitor. The range of skills required to staff this post varies, depending on the specific lobby and time of day.

The lobby receptionist represents our mutual image. First impressions are formed whether the contact is made in person or over the phone. Every individual lobby contact must be handled professionally and courteously. This means that every individual making contact with the lobby receptionist will be left with a favorable impression. Figuratively speaking, the lobby receptionist is the "narrow point in the hour glass" through which the outside world passes into our world; this is the bridging point.

Telephone Management

Types of contacts vary by hour of day. For instance, during the day shift most contact is with tenants, visitors, and contractors. During the day, operators handle all incoming business calls. After hours—swing and grave shift—the on-site contact is still an issue with contractor arrivals and departures. The phone responsibility, however, shifts from the operator to the security lobby receptionist. All incoming emergency phone calls are handled by security. The dispatch capability is truly a critical element in the overall emergency response plan. Therefore, the highest professional response capability is an expected norm.

Access Management

Management of access to our buildings and grounds for the most part involves levels of access control depending on the time of day, day of week, and location within the property. The essence of the program involves administering the rules that determine how access can be gained to the property, by whom, and when.

Proper access distinguishes between who is allowed on-site versus who is not allowed. In this violence-prone era it is imperative that our people are protected from unwanted individuals gaining entry to our property. Other undesirable actions by individuals not allowed on our property include vandalism and theft. For those individuals rightfully admitted to the property the process must be administered in a friendly, effective manner. The business atmosphere must not be compromised due to distractions created by individuals gaining unauthorized access to our property.

Incident Case Management/Fact Finding/Preliminary Investigations

There is a need to expertly characterize each incident as fully as possible. Documentation of the facts around the most important critical incidents is therefore essential. All written communication must be objective, concise, and able to withstand the scrutiny of legal review. Security personnel need to understand the necessity for accuracy and timeliness in generating and submitting their investigation results.

Patrols, Observe, and Report Management

During normal business hours, our principal means of communicating unusual events is through the on-site presence of our employees, tenants, contractors, and visitors. During these normal business hours security's patrol, observe and report activity is at its lowest level. After-hours, however, when there are so few people on-site, it is incumbent on security to be the facility's "eyes and ears." The main business-hours responsibility is to be dispatched to a scene for report writing purposes, initial control of the incident scene if required, and proper notification. After hours, security will be both the observer and then follow through with the customary report writing responsibility, associated security event handling activities, and making appropriate notifications.

The need for building patrols is a necessary part of doing business. It is important to be familiar with all the normal conditions within an environment. Beyond recognizing an abnormal condition, there must be an equally impressive ability to obtain an adequate response to correct the situation.

Data Management

Contract security has been characterized as being very process/procedure oriented. There is a huge amount of information that is generated from these processes and procedures. It is critical that the output be effectively managed. Many of the security processes and procedures result in data-oriented output (i.e., number of thefts, number of machine failures, etc.). There are incident reports, clock rounds (and associated findings), number of permitted accesses, and so on. Much of this output data should be used to control resources and identify problems. Knowing what to control, how much to control, when to control, and what type of problem has originated depends on the ability to analyze and interpret the data. Equally important is the ability to make recommendations in a timely, proactive manner and/or take the appropriate action.

Program Management

Effective program management utilizes process management techniques aimed at continuously improving service levels and satisfying customers. This includes developing and adhering to processes designed to manage to financial targets. Program management incorporates a reward system that recognizes contribution, not just time in grade. Personnel are therefore expected to be properly trained to meet the expectations, be positively oriented, and be deployed in the most effective manner.

Emergency Response Program Management

ERP management involves demonstrating the ability to maintain a quick and safe response capability when and where necessary. This includes complete familiarity with local response agencies, their services, and our expectations. Processes are expected to be put into place rapidly to allow for superior interfacing capability between us and a local responding agency. Expertise in Incident Command System protocols is necessary for the local responding agency to serve as incident commander during initial phases of an incident.

To assure such integration, security must be familiar with our ERP and Environmental Health and Safety audit criteria for emergency response. This includes complete familiarization with the Emergency Action Plan section of our Life Safety Manual and the Emergency Response section of our Management Services Guide. This includes violence in the workplace protocols. In total, response capability to such events must be continuously demonstrated. Communication procedures and hardware are to be maintained in ready status.

Public Affairs

Security's success is tied to its ability to properly respond to and handle issues involving public affairs and employee communication. Often security will be the first to arrive at the scene of an emergency or serve as a public contact point because of their presence at lobby desks or the entrance gates. This requires complete familiarization with our public affairs/employee communication (PA/EC) program. It also requires thorough familiarization with our PA/EC personnel, their backups, and how these personnel can be contacted.

Security Awareness

Because of security's limited size, it literally cannot be everywhere all the time. This is obvious. Equally obvious, therefore, is the need to build both awareness and ownership of security issues by all employees. This means an ability to distribute, through the most appropriate means, awareness information for use by our employees. This involves utilizing management information memos and, when appropriate, making your presence known, including making your services and contributions known.

To achieve timely communication we expect security to take advantage of the most appropriate technology to communicate needed information and ensure that our population is reminded, on an as needed basis, what their security roles are. This may include attending staff meetings, conducting security orientation for larger groups, and developing a package for security awareness.

Security Surveys/Assessments

Quality service is directly tied to an ability to develop an appropriate feedback mechanism. This would include, but not be limited to, a performance audit. Surveys and assessments should focus on the most meaningful security-related issues. Such efforts should reflect a strong correlation between what is focused on and the significant business issues within this operation. Surveys and assessments are geared to improving the most significant security-related problems, and a strong ability to justify necessary improvements.

Violence in the Workplace

Security requires complete familiarization and adherence to our Workplace Violence program. This means developing programs that limit site access to authorized personnel only. Security vehicles are to be provided with Emergency Response maps showing them where to respond and the quickest, safest route to each location. It also involves a structure to direct media personnel to our appropriate spokesperson and to the area specified by us. Moreover, there is an ability to secure the site through access closures and the capability of isolating and containing the incident area without jeopardizing safety of personnel. Security also needs to have an ability to identify potential violent incidents and notify our designated management representatives immediately. This includes providing additional security personnel as needed.

Environmental Concerns

We expect our business partners to be environmentally conscious. Contractors should be active in addressing environmental issues and introducing solutions to them. This includes assuring that their environmental vision is a part of our corporate philosophy. When appropriate, security must demonstrate that proper disposal techniques are followed for hazardous material.

Retail Centers Only: Teen Management

Teenagers and young adults are a major customer base for our retail centers. They are to be treated respectfully and courteously. They, too, are expected to abide by the established rules of conduct for the retail center. Any infraction will be dealt with according to the center's regulations and the laws governing juvenile and young adult rights.

Retail Center Programs

The retail center is designed to attract customers and encourage return visits. Security is expected to assist in developing and enforcing those rules designed to assure that customers and visitors can do so safely and securely. This entails rules governing proper attire, loitering, proper consumption of food and drink items, etc. Security is expected to assist in keeping benches, walkways, entrances, main aisles, and parking facilities clean at all times.

Parking Lots and Structures

Security is expected to routinely patrol parking lots and structures to assist customers and deter criminal activity. Customer assistance will be defined within the limits set forth by each retail center. These might include, but not be limited to, escorts, traffic control and enforcement, vehicle location assistance, and traffic accident investigation. Security is expected to remain particularly vigilant for suspicious activity and take the appropriate action.

Attachment B: The Company Questionnaire

1. DATE
2. COMPANY NAME
3. CORPORATE ADDRESS
4. CORPORATE OFFICER RESPONSIBLE FOR THIS ACCOUNT
5. CORPORATE TELEPHONE NUMBER
6. EMPLOYER TAX ID NUMBER
7. YEARS IN BUSINESS
8. BRANCH OFFICE TO SERVICE THIS ACCOUNT
9. BRANCH OFFICE ADDRESS AND TELEPHONE NUMBER
10. PARENT COMPANY
11. PARENT COMPANY ADDRESS AND TELEPHONE NUMBER
12. BRANCH MANAGER
13. BRANCH MANAGER'S IMMEDIATE SUPERVISOR'S NAME, ADDRESS, AND TELEPHONE NUMBER
14. TOTAL NUMBER OF EMPLOYEES CURRENTLY EMPLOYED IN THE BRANCH INTENDING TO SERVICE THIS ACCOUNT
15. ARE ALL COMPANY AND EMPLOYMENT TAXES CURRENT? (IF NOT, EXPLAIN ON SEPARATE SHEET)

Appendix B

MODEL SERVICES
AGREEMENT

AGREEMENT
By and Between
CLIENT COMPANY Inc.
and
(SECURITY COMPANY NAME)

This agreement is made and entered into this DAY of MONTH, YEAR between CLIENT COMPANY Inc. (hereinafter CLIENT), a corporation organized and existing under the laws of STATE having its principle place of business at ADDRESS, and SECURITY COMPANY, company organized and existing under the laws of STATE having its principle place of business at ADDRESS.

WHEREAS, CONTRACTOR engages in the business of providing uniformed security services, and is willing to provide these services to CLIENT under the terms and conditions hereinafter set forth; and

WHEREAS, CLIENT desires to have CONTRACTOR furnish uniformed security service for CLIENT at its location; and

WHEREAS, CONTRACTOR agrees to furnish such service on the terms and conditions set forth below;

Now, THEREFORE, in consideration of the mutual covenants and agreements herein contained, CLIENT and CONTRACTOR agree as follows:

ARTICLE 1. CONTRACTOR'S GENERAL DUTIES

During the term of this agreement CONTRACTOR shall furnish CLIENT with up to (HERE FILL IN THE TOTAL NUMBER OF WEEKLY HOURS PER CLASSIFICATION OF SECURITY PERSONNEL REQUIRED; e.g., SECURITY OFFICERS, SHIFT LEADS, SUPERVISORS, CONSOLE OPERATORS, etc. ALSO, IF SITE REQUIRES AN ACCOUNT MANAGER AND/OR ASSISTANT ACCOUNT MANAGER, THESE HOURS NEED TO BE DEFINED). The Account Manager/Site Supervisor shall be responsible for direct management/supervision of CONTRACTOR'S personnel furnished to CLIENT pursuant to this Agreement and shall be available at reasonable times to consult with CLIENT or its designated representative regarding the services rendered or to be rendered under this Agreement.

The duties and responsibilities of CONTRACTOR'S officers, supervisors, account manager, and agents shall be those specified in herein, including all Exhibits. CONTRACTOR'S employees assigned under this Agreement shall conform to such rules and regulations and shall perform such other duties as may be mutually agreed upon in writing from time to time by CONTRACTOR and CLIENT.

ARTICLE 2. TERM OF AGREEMENT

A.2.1. Length of Agreement and Renewal

The term of the contract shall be an initial three (3) calendar years commencing the date all parties endorse the CLIENT COMPANY Inc. ('CLIENT COMPANY') Independent Contractor Agreement. An additional three (3) option years of one (1) year each are included at the end of the initial three (3) year period but may only be exercised with the mutual agreement of both parties. Notwithstanding the foregoing or any breach or termination of the Agreement, as stated in the CLIENT COMPANY Communication Inc. Independent Contractor Agreement and the next paragraph of this document titled "Termination" shall remain in full force and effect.

A.2.2. Termination

This Agreement shall terminate should CONTRACTOR default in the performance of this Agreement or materially breach any of its provisions or should the results of any background and security investigation be unacceptable to CLIENT. At CLIENT's option, CLIENT may terminate this Agreement by giving written notice to CONTRACTOR. For the purpose of this paragraph, material breach of this Agreement shall include, but not be limited to, the destruction of CLIENT property, breach of any Confidentiality Agreement entered into by CONTRACTOR and CLIENT, dishonesty or theft, or failure to perform the services and/or services described in related Purchase Orders to CLIENT's satisfaction.

In addition, this Agreement may be terminated immediately by CLIENT upon 30 days written notice to the other party and by the other party upon 60 days written notice to CLIENT, for any reason, notwithstanding that the non-terminating party is in compliance with all delivery, performance, or payment requirements. Notwithstanding the foregoing or any breach or termination of the Agreement as stated in the CLIENT Communication Inc. (CLIENT COMPANY) Independent Contractor Agreement shall remain in full force and effect.

Each party to this Agreement may terminate this Agreement immediately upon written notice in the event of default by the other party in the payment of any monies due hereunder or in the event at any time during the term of this Agreement there shall be filed by or against the other party in any court pursuant to any statute, either of the United States, or of any state, territory, or possession, a petition in bankruptcy or insolvency or for reorganization or for the appointment of a receiver or to receive all or a portion of such party's property, or similar or related relief, or if such party makes an assignment for the benefit of creditors, or if either party shall be approached and accept an offer for sale, merger, or acquisition by another party.

CLIENT may terminate this Agreement immediately upon written notice in the event of a strike or other labor disturbance against CONTRACTOR by CONTRACTOR'S employees. Further, CLIENT may terminate this Agreement immediately upon written notice if CONTRACTOR fails to maintain insurance coverage in accordance with the conditions of this Agreement.

Termination of this Agreement shall not affect the obligation of either party to the other to pay any fees or reimburse any amounts due and payable at the time of termination pursuant to this Agreement and shall not affect the obligation of CONTRACTOR to indemnify CLIENT in accordance with this Agreement.

ARTICLE 3. DEFINITIONS AND RELATIONSHIP BETWEEN PARTIES

A.3.1. Definitions

A.3.1.a. "Contractor Employee" is defined as: any person lawfully employed by the Contractor under the terms of this agreement that performs work in the capacity of Security Officer, Supervisor, Investigator, Supervisor, or Manager.

A.3.1.b. "CLIENT Corporate Security Department " is defined as: any CLIENT COMPANY employee in the position of Supervisor, Manager, Director, or Vice President assigned to the CLIENT COMPANY Corporate Security organization.

A.3.1.c. "Assignment" is defined as: Performance of duties under normal supervision rather than under direct training supervision.

A.3.1.d. "Certification" is defined as: Formally approved for assignment at CLIENT COMPANY after successfully completing a job knowledge examination and skills demonstration.

A.3.1.e. "Site" is defined as: any CLIENT COMPANY, Internet Data Center, Facility, Office Building, Suite, Warehouse, or Property.

A.3.2. Relationship

The relationship of CONTRACTOR, its security officers, supervisors, and account managers to CLIENT shall be that of independent contractors. The CONTRACTOR'S officers, supervisors and account manager furnished pursuant to this Agreement shall be employees of CONTRACTOR, an independent contractor. CONTRACTOR shall exercise complete and exclusive control over all aspects of their employment and conduct. Such control to include evaluation and the resolution of complaints and grievances.

CONTRACTOR shall pay all payrolls, payroll taxes (including but not limited to, Federal Social Security Taxes, Federal and State Unemployment Taxes and State Workmen Compensation Taxes), insurance premiums, license fees, fingerprinting costs, outfitting expense, and all other expenses of CONTRACTOR or such employee in performing this Agreement.

ARTICLE 4. LICENSES

CONTRACTOR, its employees and all others acting under its direction and control, shall be duly licensed and will obtain all necessary permits to perform services where service is to be performed. Costs for all licenses and permits and background and screening costs are the sole responsibility of CONTRACTOR. Throughout the term of this Agreement, CONTRACTOR shall maintain current licensing. Potential for license suspension, revocation, or limitation must be reported to CLIENT with ten (10) days of notice from state, county, or city licensing boards.

ARTICLE 5. COVERAGES

Assignment of hours per shift will be mutually agreed upon between CONTRACTOR and CLIENT prior to such assignments.

ARTICLE 6. STANDARDS OF CONDUCT

CONTRACTOR'S employees assigned to this account will have personal contact with staff, visitors, and vendors of CLIENT and, though independent contractors, may be deemed by some staff, visitors, and vendors as direct representatives of CLIENT. Accordingly, it is agreed that said CONTRACTOR employees shall meet high standards of appearance and demeanor, and shall at all times treat staff, visitors, and vendors of CLIENT with the utmost courtesy and respect, all as is appropriate to the environment and business of CLIENT.

It is understood that CONTRACTOR'S employees may have access to areas that are restricted to CLIENT staff, visitors, and vendors, provided CONTRACTOR'S employees have met the requirements as set forth by CLIENT in accordance with CLIENT'S standards for procuring and maintaining such admissibility requirements.

ARTICLE 7. GENERAL DUTIES AND RESPONSIBILITIES

Customer service is a critical component of CLIENT'S business strategy. Security is an integral part of accomplishing this objective. Therefore, the primary responsibility of CONTRACTOR'S assigned personnel will be to provide quality customer service. Each employee or CONTRACTOR agent must exercise courtesy, respect, and professionalism. In addition, CONTRACTOR will assure CLIENT that each of its assigned personnel will comply with the following added duties and responsibilities:

A.7.1. Provide security, as defined by CLIENT, for its staff, visitors, and vendors.

A.7.2. Provide process controls over the movement of employees, customers, visitors, materials, and equipment into and out of the facility and maintain accurate records and reports reflecting the activity.

A.7.3. Enforce the rules and policies concerning prohibited items such as, weapons, alcohol, cameras, explosives, and recording devices and others as stated in the policy; respond to and investigate incidents and violations involving security policy and unlawful acts; protect all physical properties, information, and assets from theft, misuse, abuse, or other improprieties; control vehicle parking and traffic flow (if applicable) to ensure appropriate accommodations and safety of personnel; assume reasonable leadership in cases of accidents or injuries on CLIENT property and other reasonable duties assigned by CLIENT'S Corporate Security Department.

A.7.4. Enforce control over removal of CLIENT property, documents, or any vital material as identified by CLIENT. Administer CLIENT'S Non-Disclosure Agreement process.

A.7.5. Use reasonable effort to deter, or only when absolutely necessary, detain persons observed attempting to gain or gaining unauthorized access to any of CLIENT'S facilities.

A.7.6. Respond to suspicious incidents and take reports. When necessary and deemed appropriate, follow incidents to their conclusion, including court appearances. Promote a safe and secure work environment by detecting and immediately reporting situations and/or events where it appears criminal, unauthorized, and/or unsafe acts may occur or may have occurred.

A.7.7. Cooperate with and assist law enforcement agencies in connection with crimes committed against CLIENT, including maintaining the scene of a crime to protect possible evidence in accordance with established procedures.

A.7.8. Respond to and provide assistance in security and/or safety related situations, demonstrating common sense and good judgment and in compliance with CLIENT'S policies and practices.

A.7.9. Make all reasonable efforts to actively detect, report, and mitigate the occurrence of fires, explosions, structural failures, and other hazards by close and detailed observation of buildings, building equipment, products, supplies, vehicles, and personnel within controlled and uncontrolled areas. Identify and report unsafe or potentially unsafe conditions or activities and restrict or prohibit admission to hazardous and/or unsafe areas to minimize risk to persons and property.

A.7.10. Participate in the Emergency Response Team. Contribute to the success and effectiveness of CLIENT by responding to fires, explosions, bomb threats, medical emergencies, hazardous material spills and/or gaseous releases incidents, utility interruptions, executive protection incidents and other related incidents human or naturally caused. Assist in the protection of personnel, physical and intellectual property, summon appropriate assistance, and notify personnel and agencies in accordance with established procedures to assist in restoring personnel or the area to a safe condition and secure status.

A.7.11. Provide security services at meetings and other events, construction sites, labor disputes, or other situations that may occur on a scheduled and/or unscheduled short-notice basis.

A.7.12. Foster an environment that greatly discourages the commission of crimes of violence against persons and the illegal use, sale, or possession of illegal/controlled drugs and substances on CLIENT property by observing and immediately reporting the incident to CLIENT'S Corporate Security Department and, as required by law, the local police department.

A.7.13. Prevent damage, misuse, theft, or other improper or unlawful acts against the assets of CLIENT and its employees; or acts of espionage or sabotage in accordance with applicable security plans, by providing:

1. Constant or frequent personal surveillance of the secured areas.
2. Close observation of persons within secured areas to detect evidence of trespass, damage, misuse, or theft of CLIENT or Customer assets.
3. Monitoring of equipment deliveries and removals and construction contractor activities.
4. Close visual inspections of persons and vehicles entering and exiting CLIENT'S property to ensure that nothing is either introduced or removed without proper permission and documentation.

A.7.14. Assume additional responsibilities, though not specifically enumerated herein, as may be set forth in CONTRACTOR'S special orders or manuals and procedures issued by CLIENT.

A.7.15. Maintain training and certification of those items, skills, concepts, and other requirements as outlined above and defined through mutual agreement by CLIENT and CONTRACTOR.

A.7.16. Maintain knowledge of appropriate federal, state, and local statutes and ordinances and regulatory requirements, including periodic updates provided by CLIENT.

ARTICLE 8. STANDARDS OF PERFORMANCE

As a condition of this agreement the following standards will be required of CONTRACTOR. All personnel assigned to this account will:

A.8.1. Possess proof of having met the requirements Private Security Guards as required by (STATE or DISTRICT).

A.8.2. Possess a high school diploma, GED, or equivalent training or job experience.

A.8.3. Demonstrate the ability to read and write in English equivalent to a high school graduate. Have the ability to verbally communicate in English; particularly in emergency situations requiring clear and definitive articulation to assure confidence, control, and safety of those involved.

A.8.4. Have the ability to demonstrate psychological stability under a variety of conditions as illustrated by passage of appropriately administered testing consistent with national standards and as allowed by law.

A.8.5. Pass a physical fitness examination, including drug testing, by a licensed physician or laboratory, which demonstrates an ability to meet the requirements of this account.

A.8.6. (IF DESIRED BY CLIENT), Possess CPR and First Aid certification as set forth by the American Red Cross or equivalent association.

A.8.7. Pass a test on Customer Service Relations, to be set forth by mutual agreement between CLIENT and CONTRACTOR and undergo periodic training as agreed to from time to time by CLIENT and CONTRACTOR.

A.8.8. Receive a 24-hour course of advanced officer training annually, the curriculum to be mutually agreed upon between CLIENT and CONTRACTOR, reflecting changes in law, customer relations, corporate policies, etc.

In addition:

A.8.9. CONTRACTOR is responsible for providing, at a minimum, all legally required employment benefits to the CONTRACTOR employees. These costs shall be included in the overall bill rate to CLIENT Corporate Security.

A.8.10. CONTRACTOR employee duties and responsibilities shall be performed in accordance with (i) the duties and responsibilities and the rules and regulations contained in the site-specific Security Procedures for each site being serviced, and (ii) any subsequent additions, deletions or revisions to the Procedures which CLIENT'S Corporate Security Department, at its discretion, may make from time to time. CLIENT'S Corporate Security Department shall promptly notify the CONTRACTOR, or its representatives, of any such additions, deletions, or revisions.

A.8.11. CONTRACTOR is to ensure that its personnel are dressed in the complete uniform, appropriate for the assignment; that they present a neat appearance, paying particular attention to their personal hygiene, bearing, uniform, and equipment; that they are prepared for and are performing the assigned security duties in accordance with established operational procedures and policies; and that they prepare and submit all required recorded and reports.

A.8.12. CONTRACTOR shall require CONTRACTOR employees to comply with all CLIENT policies and procedures related to the personal conduct of individuals working at CLIENT facilities.

A.8.13. CONTRACTOR shall ensure that CONTRACTOR employees do not tamper with personal papers, desk, or cabinets, or use CLIENT telecommunications or computer and related network systems or any other equipment or systems except as authorized by CLIENT'S Corporate Security Department.

A.8.14. Except with the written consent of CLIENT'S Corporate Security Department, CONTRACTOR shall not permit any CONTRACTOR employee to possess, on CLIENT premises, a firearm, night stick, club, liquid and/or aerosol mace, or any other device, object, or instrument reasonably considered for use as a weapon which may be used against another person while on CLIENT premises and while engaged in providing Security Services under this Agreement.

A.8.15. CONTRACTOR shall promptly assign a qualified CONTRACTOR employee to fill the position of any CONTRACTOR employee who fails to report for duty, is absent from his/her assigned post, or requires relief from his/her assigned duties. CONTRACTOR employees shall be both qualified and available to personally staff assignments immediately when a CONTRACTOR employee fails to report for duty (or such assignment otherwise becomes vacant) and shall remain at the assignment until such time as a CONTRACTOR employee is made available.

A.8.16. CONTRACTOR shall use its best efforts and all available resources to promptly furnish temporary CONTRACTOR employees requested in the event of unforeseen emergencies. CONTRACTOR shall be capable of providing a minimum of two additional certified CONTRACTOR employees (per shift) on 24 hours notice. These personnel may be billed at a premium rate not to exceed 1–1/2 times the contracted billing rate for the work being performed and only for a maximum of 48 continuous hours.

A.8.17. CONTRACTOR shall not permit CONTRACTOR employees to work on CLIENT premises in excess of 12 consecutive hours in a 24-hour period, or more than 48 hours during any five-day work week, unless specifically requested or authorized by CLIENT'S Corporate Security Department and Senior CONTRACTOR Management. Nor shall any security officer report for duty with less than 12 hours off from having worked a previous shift, unless such reporting is necessitated by an emergency. Further, no security person may be assigned to work a post or work site alone without first having been tested and successfully demonstrated a comprehensive knowledge of the job functions and responsibilities.

A.8.18. CONTRACTOR employees assigned to CLIENT shall not be assigned to any other CONTRACTOR accounts while such employees are regularly assigned full-time to CLIENT.

A.8.19. CONTRACTOR shall promptly inform CLIENT'S Corporate Security Department of any and all incidents that require or appear to require investigation. CONTRACTOR shall not conduct investigations in which CLIENT is a party unless approved by CLIENT'S Corporate Security Department. CONTRACTOR shall inform CLIENT'S Corporate Security Department in the event they conduct an investigation of any CONTRACTOR personnel assigned to CLIENT. CONTRACTOR shall cooperate fully in any investigation conducted by CLIENT'S Corporate Security Department.

CONTRACTOR shall install at its expense and use an automated management reporting system comparable to the PPM 2000 product to track incidents and generate reports for CLIENT'S Corporate Security Department. This system will be interfaced with CLIENT'S Corporate Security Department, allowing them direct access as necessary and appropriate.

A.8.20. CONTRACTOR shall supervise and administer CONTRACTOR employees through designated on-site and off-site supervisory personnel, who will be responsible for the performance of the security services. These supervisory personnel shall have operational and administrative experience in security services at a level commensurate with the scope of work of this Agreement and shall be responsible for maintaining high standards of performance, professional appearance, and conduct. Off-site CONTRACTOR supervisory personnel shall inspect on-duty, on-site CONTRACTOR employees a minimum of once per week, including CONTRACTOR employees working weekends and holidays.

A.8.21. CONTRACTOR management personnel shall be available 24 hours a day at designated locations and telephone numbers provided by CONTRACTOR to the designated CLIENT'S Corporate Security Operations Center (SOC) and designated CLIENT'S Corporate Security Department Representatives.

A.8.22. CONTRACTOR managers, where they directly or indirectly manage the site security, shall accomplish daily coordination with the CONTRACTOR employees assigned to the responsibility for security at the protected site, to ensure that the requirements/needs of CLIENT'S Corporate Security Department Management are met.

A.8.23. CONTRACTOR shall maintain an office within 15 miles (or its equivalent in kilometers) of the CLIENT site to be serviced. It is possible that additional facilities may be occupied by CLIENT during the term of this Agreement and may require CONTRACTOR services there as well. CONTRACTOR shall, upon request of CLIENT'S Corporate Security Department, provide a Supervisor on any specified CLIENT site within one (1) hour, a Manager on site within two (2) hours, or an Executive officer on site within four (4) hours. A current copy of CONTRACTOR'S organization chart is to be continuously on file with CLIENT'S Corporate Security Department. If CONTRACTOR is part of a multilocation organization, CONTRACTOR shall demonstrate, in writing, how the local office fits in the corporate structure, and identify the reporting lines between management at the local level and corporate.

A.8.24. CONTRACTOR shall provide a detailed plan to CLIENT'S Corporate Security Department which states how Key Performance Indicators will be measured and results reported and the strategies employed to ensure the continued quality and improvement of the CONTRACTOR. Key Performance Indicators are attached as (EXHIBIT X).

A.8.25. CONTRACTOR shall develop and submit a one-year business plan prior to the start of the contract. This plan shall clearly detail the strategies, tactics, milestones, and execution methodologies that will be employed by the CONTRACTOR during the plan period, which will ensure the successful management and support of this critical element of the CLIENT'S Corporate Security Department Program.

A.8.26. CLIENT'S Corporate Security Department shall have the sole and absolute right to prohibit any CONTRACTOR employee from entering CLIENT premises or to eject any CONTRACTOR employee therefrom without stating cause.

A.8.27. CONTRACTOR employees must read, understand, and endorse CLIENT'S Non-Disclosure Agreement (NDA). CLIENT'S Corporate Security Department shall maintain completed NDAs.

A.8.28. Prior to commencement of services under this Agreement, CONTRACTOR shall furnish CLIENT'S Corporate Security Department with description of the uniforms to be worn by the CONTRACTOR'S employees and satisfactory evidence that such uniforms comply with legal requirements. CONTRACTOR shall, at CONTRACTOR'S expense, provide any other clothing or equipment required in the performance of the services. CONTRACTOR shall require each CONTRACTOR employee to wear the complete and issued uniform at all times while engaged in providing services.

A.8.29. CONTRACTOR shall periodically review operational policies and procedures intended to ensure optimum performance and submit recommended changes to CLIENT'S Corporate Security Department.

A.8.30. CONTRACTOR shall collaborate with CLIENT'S Corporate Security Department in establishing and implementing mutually satisfactory procedures for meeting the needs of the site to which Security Services are provided.

A.8.31. CONTRACTOR shall take receipt of, secure, and account for all property and equipment assigned to the CONTRACTOR by CLIENT. CONTRACTOR shall maintain and care for such property and equipment and replace or compensate CLIENT for property and equipment that is lost, stolen, or damaged by CONTRACTOR Employees. CONTRACTOR shall conduct a semi-annual inventory of CLIENT property assigned to the CONTRACTOR and submit a written report to CLIENT'S Corporate Security Department.

A.8.32. CONTRACTOR shall advise CLIENT prior to any CONTRACTOR employee being assigned to or reassigned, disciplined, promoted, or transferred within or away from the account.

A.8.33. CONTRACTOR shall assure CLIENT all staffing will be in compliance with established EEO standards for the geographic area.

A.8.34. CONTRACTOR shall provide annual testing of all assigned personnel on CLIENT'S emergency procedures plans.

A.8.35. CONTRACTOR shall assure CLIENT that all personnel assigned to operate a motor vehicle or other such equipment requiring special licensing shall have such certification and appropriate levels of insurance.

A.8.36. CONTRACTOR shall assure CLIENT that all assigned personnel have passed a comprehensive preemployment background reference check.

CONTRACTOR shall submit to CLIENT, within seven (7) days before the commencement of service or concurrent with assignment, a background investigation report for all personnel assigned to CLIENT under the terms of this agreement. The background investigation report will include, but not be limited to:

- Police record check
- Credit check (if permissible)
- Confirmation of previous employment
- Verification of all application information

The criminal history check as prescribed in this document is to be updated annually in the anniversary month of each year of the contract for all CONTRACTOR employees assigned to CLIENT. In the event a misdemeanor or felony conviction is discovered, CLIENT Corporate Security Department shall be informed immediately for consultation. CONTRACTOR shall institute requirements, which will obligate CONTRACTOR employees to "self report" interactions with Law Enforcement that result in arrests resulting in either misdemeanor or felony convictions.

A.8.37. CLIENT reserves the right to fingerprint and photograph all personnel assigned under terms of this agreement. If CONTRACTOR receives an unsuitable report on any of CONTRACTOR'S employees subsequent to the commencement of service, the employee will not be allowed to continue work, or be assigned to work, under the terms of this agreement.

A.8.38. CONTRACTOR shall provide CLIENT with a Letter of Affidavit on each person assigned to the account certifying that the individual has met all of the hiring and training requirements as set forth in this agreement.

A.8.39. All services, equipment, or material furnished or utilized in the performance of services and quality of service provided by CONTRACTOR shall be subject to inspection and testing by CLIENT without notice. Such inspections and testing will be conducted in a manner so as not to unduly interfere with CONTRACTOR'S ability to carry out the terms of this agreement.

Should CLIENT determine, as a result of these inspections and testing, that services and/or equipment or materials used by CONTRACTOR are not satisfactory, CLIENT shall inform CONTRACTOR in writing. CLIENT reserves the right to: (a) require CONTRACTOR to take immediate action to bring such matters into compliance with the terms of this agreement; and (b) impose monetary deductions in accordance with a schedule to be mutually agreed upon between CLIENT and CONTRACTOR prior to the initiation of this agreement.

A.8.40. Should CONTRACTOR fail to take necessary measures to ensure conformity with the requirements of this agreement, CLIENT reserves the right to (a) procure or furnish services as required by CLIENT and charge CONTRACTOR any cost that is directly related to the performance of such services; or (b) terminate this agreement for default in accordance with the terms set forth in Article 2.2 governing Termination of Agreement.

A.8.41. Further, within 60 days of the initiation of this agreement, CONTRACTOR will develop a set of measurable performance objectives for CONTRACTOR'S employees. These objectives will be developed for each position assigned to this account. Personnel assigned to this account must satisfactorily complete each of the performance objectives to be eligible for an increase in base wages. Performance objectives will be evaluated on an annual basis and be responsible for 75% of any consideration for an increase in wages. The balance of the performance evaluation will be based upon the officer's compliance with general orders, absenteeism, personal bearing, and professionalism.

A.8.42. Each security person will receive an interim evaluation every 90 days, to be administered by the selected contractor. This evaluation will be a brief overview to allow the officers to know and understand the quality of their performance. A thorough review of performance will be conducted every 180 days.

A.8.43. CONTRACTOR employees shall read, comprehend, and satisfy all training, certification, and vetting requirements set forth in this document and/or the attached Exhibits prior to assignment to any CLIENT site unless specifically permitted an exemption by CLIENT Corporate Security Department in this document or a formal letter.

With the prior approval of CLIENT Corporate Security Department, CONTRACTOR may temporarily assign CONTRACTOR Trainee Employees who have not satisfied the qualifications required of CONTRACTOR employees under this Agreement. Provided, however, that such temporary assignments shall be made only for the purpose of preparing CONTRACTOR Trainee Employees for regular assignments as CLIENT assigned employees. Or, such CONTRACTOR Trainee Employees are accompanied at all times by a certified CONTRACTOR Employee who satisfies all qualifications required under this Agreement. CLIENT shall not be charged for CONTRACTOR Trainee Employee services.

A.8.44. CONTRACTOR shall require CONTRACTOR employees to comply with all CLIENT policies and procedures related to the personal conduct of individuals working at CLIENT.

A.8.45. No CONTRACTOR employee, including those serving the CONTRACTOR in a managerial capacity, or those controlling the CONTRACTOR through stock ownership or otherwise, shall have been convicted of a felony or have been dishonorably discharged from any branch of the Armed Forces. Affidavits are required for each CONTRACTOR employee attesting to meeting this requirement as well as accomplishing background checks.

ARTICLE 9. STAFFING

A.9.1. Overtime
CLIENT will pay for only that overtime it authorizes. CLIENT will pay CONTRACTOR a rate of one and a half times the base rate of pay for each person assigned on each of those calendar days designated as CLIENT holidays. Overtime requests for special events or times of the year that require in excess of 40 hours per week of additional service will be billed at the normal base rate, provided CLIENT gives 30 days advance notice.

A.9.2. Overfills
Overfills occur when CONTRACTOR supplies too many individuals, or individuals for longer periods than required, or at a higher level—as defined by a schedule mutually agreed upon by CLIENT and CONTRACTOR at the outset of this Agreement or anytime thereafter in advance of such overfills. CLIENT will pay for only the services requested.

A.9.3. Shortfills
Shortfills occur when CONTRACTOR supplies unqualified personnel. CLIENT reserves the right to refuse CONTRACTOR'S personnel whom CLIENT determines not to be qualified. Overtime will not be paid to CONTRACTOR to compensate for shortage of personnel.

A.9.4. Shortfalls

Shortfalls occur when the required services are not supplied at any post or work site. CLIENT will pay for only time actually worked. If a security officer arrives late for work or leaves early for any reason, overtime will not be paid when CONTRACTOR fills the vacancies so created. Moreover, the absence of a security officer at a post or work site without a replacement constitutes a shortfall for a portion of a shift and a proportional reimbursement will be charged.

CONTRACTOR shall promptly assign a qualified CONTRACTOR employee to fill the position of any CONTRACTOR employee who fails to report for duty, is absent from his/her assigned post, or requires relief from his/her assigned duties. CONTRACTOR employees shall be both qualified and available to personally staff assignments immediately when a CONTRACTOR employee fails to report for duty (or such assignment otherwise becomes vacant).

A.9.5. Double Banking

Whenever it becomes necessary to assign or reassign an individual to a post for the first time, CONTRACTOR shall arrange, at its expense, to have the new individual "double bank" with an experienced employee prior to having the inexperienced individual take over any post alone. CONTRACTOR will bear the associated expense for this double banking.

A.9.6. Turnover

Turnover is the number of security personnel hired to replace those leaving or dropped from CONTRACTOR'S workforce. For purposes of this account, the turnover rate will be expressed in terms of the actual number of hired replacements. Turnover will be calculated on an annual basis and a turnover rate in excess of the established rate will be considered unacceptable and may be cause for the termination of CONTRACTOR'S services. The acceptable turnover rate for any one or more of CLIENT'S sites will be negotiated and attached as (EXHIBIT X) of this agreement account.

A.9.7 Incentives and Penalties

A.9.7.a. Awards/Penalties: CLIENT reserves the right to award incentives to CON-TRACTOR'S employees for outstanding performance. Such incentives will be paid by CONTRACTOR and billed to CLIENT at CONTRACTOR'S cost without any mark-up. Penalties for failure to adhere to the terms and conditions of this agreement or failure to take appropriate remedial measures on any reasonable request by CLIENT shall be mutually agreed to by both parties prior to the commencement of this agreement. Such penalty schedule shall be attached to this agreement as (EXHIBIT X).

A.9.7.b. Recognition Events: The CONTRACTOR shall independently sponsor and hold Quarterly Employee Recognition Events for CONTRACTOR employees assigned to CLIENT COMPANY consisting of Recognition Awards, catered meals, and beverages.

A.9.8. Staffing Analysis

The staffing of contract security positions (Key Performance Indicator) is absolutely critical to the continued success of CLIENT'S security program. Therefore, given the critical nature of this requirement, any failure by CONTRACTOR or CONTRACTOR'S employee's to provide CLIENT a certified Supervisor or Officer for a position and/or to allow any position to be unfilled at any time during a shift shall be considered a significant adverse event and shall be reported to CLIENT'S Corporate Security Department immediately.

CONTRACTOR shall conduct a review, establish the root cause of the failure, and provide a formal report to CLIENT'S Corporate Security Department within 24 continuous hours of the failure. The report shall also include specific corrective actions the CONTRACTOR will complete to ensure future failures are avoided. CLIENT'S Corporate Security Department shall review the report and the corrective actions, and determine their acceptability. The review shall also include a determination as to the need for any additional actions to ensure contractual compliance. This may include a review of the CONTRACTOR'S ability to meet present and future staffing obligations. If it is concluded that the CONTRACTOR is unable to meet the staffing requirements, CLIENT'S Corporate Security Department may consider limiting the amount of work required of the CONTRACTOR and or reducing the level of work. Any such reduction shall trigger the use of another CONTRACTOR as stated in next paragraph.

It shall be understood that it is the responsibility of the CONTRACTOR and its employees to protect and safeguard CLIENT employees, premises, information, material, facilities, and property. In the event of any strike, work stoppage or other interference, CONTRACTOR employees will continue to report for duty, remain at their posts, and discharge their duties in a professional manner and perform such other security services as are determined essential and proper under such circumstances as directed by CLIENT'S Corporate Security Department. Should they not do so, or should any other circumstances prevent their performance under this Agreement, CLIENT'S Corporate Security Department may resort to whatever measures it deems appropriate under the circumstances for the protection of CLIENT employees and assets.

CLIENT'S Corporate Security Department reserves the right to employ an alternative Service Provider in the event positions are not staffed for any reason by CONTRACTOR or CONTRACTOR employees and to charge the CONTRACTOR in the full amount (including premium rates) of the replacement officer services including supervision and management costs.

ARTICLE 10. ADDITIONAL PERSONNEL

CONTRACTOR shall assure CLIENT that CONTRACTOR will maintain a fully trained cadre of (X) backup personnel ready to assume assignment at CLIENT'S location(s) on request by CLIENT. By "fully trained" it is meant that such personnel will meet CLIENT requirements.

CONTRACTOR shall maintain manpower levels capable of meeting the call-back requirements as defined in Article 8.23 without regard to any riot, war, act of God, the enactment, issuance or operation of any municipal, county, state or federal law, ordinance or executive, administrative or judicial regulation, order or decree, or any local or national emergency, or any other similar cause outside of the control of CONTRACTOR.

CONTRACTOR shall use its best efforts and all available resources to promptly furnish temporary CONTRACTOR employees requested in the event of unforeseen emergencies. CONTRACTOR shall be capable of providing a minimum of two additional certified CONTRACTOR employees (per shift) on 24 hours notice. These personnel may be billed at a premium rate not to exceed one and a half times the contracted billing rate for the work being performed and only for a maximum of 48 continuous hours.

ARTICLE 11. EQUIPMENT

CLIENT will furnish the necessary office space and supporting equipment necessary to service this account (telephone, copier, desk and chair, basic supplies, radios, etc.). CONTRACTOR will supply, at its expense, all weather gear, leather gear, flashlights, pagers, and other equipment, as is mutually agreed upon between CLIENT and CONTRACTOR, to meet the requirements of this account.

CONTRACTOR will assure CLIENT that CONTRACTOR will replace or repair at its cost any CLIENT-owned equipment (such as, but not limited to, communications equipment, fire and safety equipment, locks and keys, access control systems, CCTVs, etc.) damaged or lost through abuse or neglect by CONTRACTOR'S personnel. Use of CLIENT'S telephone system for personal use is prohibited. CONTRACTOR will be either billed or the cost of such usage will be deducted from the monthly payment, at the discretion of CLIENT.

ARTICLE 12. CONTROL OF PREMISES

It is hereby understood and agreed that CLIENT, as owner of its property and facilities, has the exclusive right to control and deny access to same to any individual including, without limitation, an employee or agent of CONTRACTOR.

ARTICLE 13. AUDITS AND BILLING RATES

A.13.1. Audits

CLIENT Corporate Security Department shall conduct periodic scheduled and unscheduled performance audits to evaluate CONTRACTOR services to determine current effectiveness and compliance with this Agreement and established procedures. The audits shall also be utilized to determine if a change in the scope of work is warranted to improve the effectiveness and efficiency of the services or to terminate services.

CONTRACTOR shall submit, if requested by CLIENT Corporate Security Department, to an annual audit of all financial records regarding the costs, revenues, and profits generated from services rendered by the CONTRACTOR under this agreement. CLIENT shall select and compensate the accounting firm performing the audit. If the audit determines that CLIENT overpaid CONTRACTOR, CONTRACTOR shall compensate CLIENT the full amount of overpayment and shall also pay one half of the total costs incurred by CLIENT for the accounting firm's services.

A.13.2. SEE EXHIBIT X (to be negotiated based on date and location).

ARTICLE 14. METHOD OF PAYMENT

CONTRACTOR shall submit a monthly invoice for services rendered in accordance with the terms and conditions of this Agreement. Invoicing will be submitted to CLIENT'S electronic accounts payable system. CONTRACTOR will maintain originally signed timesheets and other documents, as may be necessary, demonstrating proof of purchase for items needed and approved prior to such purchase by CLIENT. Such retention will be for a period of not less than 3 years, unless litigation is pending, in which case retention will be required until disposition of the litigation.

Said invoice and relevant documentation shall be e-mailed to such office as directed by CLIENT and are payable by CLIENT at the address specified on the invoice within 30 days of receipt. Should CLIENT contend any such invoice as incorrect, CLIENT shall notify CONTRACTOR in writing within said 30 days and specify the reasons for such contention. CLIENT shall pay the amount mutually agreed upon on settlement of such dispute and shall not be deemed in default.

ARTICLE 15. INSURANCE

At all times while performing the services, and for two (2) years after the cancellation or termination of this Agreement, CONTRACTOR shall maintain, at its sole cost and expense, at least the following insurance, from insurance companies and in a form satisfactory to CLIENT with limits of liability not less than stated below. CLIENT shall have the right to inspect and review the policies and shall be provided with copies upon request. Certificates of Insurance shall be in the name of CLIENT and each such certificate shall list CLIENT as additional insured. Certificates of Insurance shall be delivered to CLIENT ten (10) days prior to the inception of the Agreement and any change or cancellation shall not be valid without thirty (30) days prior written notice to CLIENT. CONTRACTOR shall provide to CLIENT, promptly upon receipt by CONTRACTOR, renewal notices regarding such insurance policies.

A.15.1. Commercial General Liability Insurance
Combined single limit for bodily and property damage of not less than $5 million for each occurrence and annual aggregate providing:

A.15.1.a. Broad form property damage coverage

A.15.1.b. Broad form contractual liability coverage

A.15.1.c. Products and completed operations coverage

A.15.1.d. Personal and advertising injury coverage

A.15.1.e. Such policy to include CLIENT as additional insured for all activities arising out of the performance of the services. This policy shall be primary for all purposes to other insurance coverage, whether such other insurance is stated to be primary, contributory, excess, contingent, or otherwise.

A.15.2. Comprehensive Automotive Liability

A.15.2.a. Combined single limit for bodily injury, death, and property damage of not less than $1 million per accident.

A.15.3. Workers' Compensation and Employer's Liability Insurance

A.15.3.a. With limits of liability for Workers' Compensation of not less than those required by law, and with limits of liability for employer's liability of not less than $1 million each accident, $1 million disease—policy limit, $1 million disease—each employee.

A.15.4. Contractor's Third-Party Fidelity Bond in the amount of $150,000 for each occurrence covering all employees of CONTRACTOR.
CLIENT will not be liable for the payment of any premiums or assessments with respect to the coverages described above. Further, CLIENT, its officers, agents, and employees shall be named additional insured as respects the named insured's activities on or about CLIENT'S premises. The policy shall be endorsed to provide that this insur-

ance shall be primary and not contributing with any other insurance available to said additional insured as respects any and all liability, loss, claims, damages, or expense arising out of the negligence or alleged negligence of the named insured.

ARTICLE 16. CONFIDENTIALITY

CONTRACTOR understands that during the term of this Agreement, its employees and agents may produce or have access to confidential information, records, data, specifications, trade secrets, customer lists, and secret inventions and processes of CLIENT. All records, files, drawings, documents, or copies thereof, relating to CLIENT'S business, which CONTRACTOR shall prepare or use, or come in contact with, shall be and remain the sole property of CLIENT, and shall not be reproduced, transmitted, or removed from CLIENT'S premises without its written consent, and shall not be disclosed to any persons, or business entity without the written approval of CLIENT. CONTRACTOR shall hold all such information contained in or derived from any of the sources described above in trust and confidence for CLIENT except as authorized by CLIENT in writing.

CONTRACTOR agrees to adopt and maintain procedures reasonably calculated to ensure that only such employees of CONTRACTOR that have a need to know such information in order to discharge CONTRACTOR'S obligations hereunder have access to such information. Upon cancellation or expiration of this Agreement, CONTRACTOR shall return to CLIENT all written or descriptive matter, including but not limited to drawings, descriptions, or other papers or documents that contain any data or information of the nature described above.

ARTICLE 17. EMPLOYMENT RESTRICTIONS/LIMITATIONS

CONTRACTOR will not require its employees assigned to this account to sign any document prohibiting them from seeking employment with another security contractor for any period of time either during or subsequent to their employment with CONTRACTOR.

ARTICLE 18. USE OF CLIENT'S NAME

CONTRACTOR shall assure CLIENT that CONTRACTOR will not, without CLIENT'S prior written approval, publish or use any advertising, sales promotion, or publicity matter relating to services equipment, products, reports, and material furnished by CONTRACTOR wherein the name of CLIENT is mentioned or its identity is implied.

ARTICLE 19. INDEMNIFICATION

Except as otherwise provided and limited in this Agreement, CONTRACTOR shall indemnify, defend, and hold harmless CLIENT, Manager, and their respective partners, directors, officers, employees, servants, agents, representatives, and affiliates from and against any and all claims, liabilities, demands, actions, suits, damages, losses, injuries, costs, and expenses (including without limitation reasonable attorney's fees) involving any personal injury or property damage suffered or incurred by CLIENT, caused by the negligent or wrongful acts or omissions of CONTRACTOR. CONTRACTOR'S duty to indemnify and hold harmless CLIENT is limited to the proportionate share of such damages, losses, and expenses attributable to the aforesaid acts and omissions of CONTRACTOR, its employees, agents, or representatives.

ARTICLE 20. FORCE MAJEURE

"FORCE MAJEURE" as used in this article shall mean an act of God, industrial disturbance, exclusive of those related to labor disputes, act of the public enemy, war, blockage, public riot, lighting, fire flood, earthquake, explosion, government restraint, unavailability of equipment, and any other cause, whether of the kind specifically enumerated above or otherwise, which is not reasonably within the control of the party claiming suspension of those services enumerated herein this Agreement.

If either party is rendered unable, wholly or in part, by Force Majeure to carry out its obligations under this Agreement, such party shall give to the other party prompt written notice of the Force Majeure with reasonably full particulars concerning it; thereupon, the obligations of the party giving notice, so far as they were affected by the Force Majeure, shall be suspended during, but no longer than, the continuance of the Force Majeure. The affected party shall use all possible diligence to remove the Force Majeure as quickly as possible. In the event CONTRACTOR is unable to carry out its obligations under this Article, CLIENT may upon thirty (30) days written notice cancel this Agreement in whole or part without any obligations or liability to CLIENT.

ARTICLE 21. EQUAL EMPLOYMENT OPPORTUNITY AND AFFIRMATIVE ACTION

CONTRACTOR represents that it is in compliance with all applicable federal, state, and local laws, regulations, and orders with respect to Equal Employment Opportunity and Affirmative Action, and either has previously provided or will provide to CLIENT the certifications and representations regarding same that CLIENT may require under such laws, regulations, and orders.

ARTICLE 22. IRCA COMPLIANCE

CONTRACTOR agrees at all times to remain in strict compliance with all terms, provisions, regulations and rulings relative to the Immigration Reform and Control Act of 1986 (IRCA). All employees of CONTRACTOR assigned to the Properties will have had their identity and eligibility for work within the United States properly verified. Within three (3) days of receipt of a written request from CLIENT, CONTRACTOR shall provide CLIENT with copies of the I-9 form or such other documentation as may be appropriate to satisfy CLIENT as to CONTRACTOR'S compliance with IRCA.

CONTRACTOR agrees to defend, hold harmless, and indemnify CLIENT, its affiliates and subsidiaries, directors, partners, officers, agents, representatives, and employees from and against any claims, costs, including but not limited to reasonable attorneys' fees, actions, suits, or proceedings of any type whatsoever to the extent caused by CONTRACTOR'S breach of the terms of the paragraph immediately above.

ARTICLE 23. PROVIDING DUE NOTICE

CONTRACTOR shall assure CLIENT all logs, incident reports, and daily reports will be completed and submitted in accordance with the schedule as set forth by CLIENT. Further, CONTRACTOR shall assure CLIENT receives adequate notice of hazards, safety violations, or other conditions that warrant an unsafe condition, as may be discovered by CONTRACTOR'S personnel in the performance of their security duties so CLIENT may take appropriate action in an expeditious manner.

ARTICLE 24. METHOD OF NOTICE

Any notice or other communication provided hereunder shall be given in writing and shall be deemed to have been duly given when delivered by hand, or five (5) days after being mailed, postage prepaid, certified with return receipt requested, addressed to:

If to CLIENT: (••)

If to CONTRACTOR: (••)

Or to such other address as either party may specify to the other in writing.

ARTICLE 25. PENDING ACTIONS

CONTRACTOR certifies that no lawsuits, legal proceedings, administrative proceedings, or other actions, whether voluntary or involuntary, are threatened or pending against CONTRACTOR or any of its officers or employees which may have a material impact upon CONTRACTOR'S ability to perform this Agreement.

ARTICLE 26. SUBCONTRACTING AND ASSIGNMENTS

This Agreement shall not be assigned or subcontracted, in whole or in part by CONTRACTOR. Nor shall CONTRACTOR assign any monies due or to become due hereunder without prior written consent of CLIENT. Any attempted assignment or subcontracting hereunder without the prior written consent of CLIENT shall be void.

No contract shall be made by any Contractor Employee with any other party, for furnishing any of the work or services herein contracted for or any work or services, without the approval of CLIENT COMPANY. Approval must be in writing, and obtained prior to entering into a contract. This provision should not be taken as requiring the approval of employment between the Contractor and Contractor Employees assigned or services provided.

ARTICLE 27. ENTIRE AGREEMENT; AMENDMENTS

This Agreement supersedes all previous agreements entered into between CONTRACTOR and CLIENT and represents the whole and entire Agreement between the parties. No other agreements or representations, oral or written, have been made by CONTRACTOR. This Agreement may not be altered, modified, or amended, except in writing and properly executed by CONTRACTOR and CLIENT. Any purchase order or similar document issued by CLIENT simultaneously with or subsequent to this Agreement, and related to the subject matter of this Agreement, shall be subject to and governed by the terms and conditions hereof which shall supersede any conflicting terms or conditions of such purchase order or similar document.

ARTICLE 28. BINDING AGREEMENT

This Agreement shall not be binding upon either party until executed by its duly authorized representative.

ARTICLE 29. NO WAIVER

The failure by either party to enforce at any time any of the provisions of this Agreement or to require at any time performance by the other party or any of the provisions herein shall in no way be construed to be a waiver of such provision or to affect the validity thereof.

ARTICLE 30. SEVERABILITY

Whenever possible, each provision of this Agreement shall be interpreted in such manner as to be effective and valid under applicable law, but if any provision of this Agreement is held to be prohibited by or invalid under applicable law, such provision shall be made to conform to the law and this Agreement shall otherwise continue in full force and effect.

ARTICLE 31. APPLICABLE LAW

This Agreement shall be governed by and construed under the laws of the (APPLICABLE STATE AND/OR DISTRICTS).

ARTICLE 32. SURVIVABILITY

CONTRACTOR understands and agrees that the following Articles of this Agreement survive the expiration, cancellation, or termination of this Agreement:
[INSERT ARTICLES THAT LEGAL COUNSEL DESIRES TO SURVIVE]

IN WITNESS WHEREOF CLIENT AND CONTRACTOR have caused this Agreement to be executed by their respective duly authorized representatives as of the date first above written.

Client:

Contractor:

REFERENCES

Deans, G.K., Kroeger, F., and Zeisel, S., *Winning the Merger Endgame* (New York: McGraw-Hill, 2002).

Associated Press, "Clinton: I'd die for Israel," *Sacramento Bee*, August 2, 2002.

Brill, Stephen, "Ridge Against the Machine," *Newsweek*, March 18, 2001.

Charan, R., and Useem, M., "Why Companies Fail," *Fortune*, May 27, 2002.

Clayton, Susan, *Sharpen Your Skills in Developing Strategy* (London: McGraw-Hill, 1997).

Dalton, Dennis, *Security Management: Business Strategies for Success* (Boston: Butterworth-Heinemann, 1995).

Dalton, Dennis, "What Should Security's Function Be," *Security Management*, June 2001.

Dalton, Dennis, *An Analysis of Civilian Management in Urban Police Departments* (Doctoral Dissertation, University of Southern California, 1979).

Dalton, Dennis, *The Art of Successful Security Management* (Boston: Butterworth-Heinemann, 1998).

Dessler, Gary, *Management: Leading People and Organizations in the 21st Century*, 2nd Edition (New Jersey: Prentice Hall, 2001).

Gibbs, David, "Dominate Your Data," *Security Management*, June 2002.

Gulick, L., Urwick, L., *Papers on the Science of Administration* (New York: Institute of Public Administration, 1937).

Hamel, Gary, "Strategy as Revolution," *Harvard Business Review*, July/August 1996.

Harari, Oren, "Leading Change from the Middle," *Management Review*, February 1999.

Hawn, Carleen, "The Man Who Sees Around Corners," *Forbes*, January 2002.

Kline, Peter, and Saunders, Bernard, *Ten Steps to a Learning Organization*, 2nd Edition (Arlington, VA: Great Ocean Publishers, 1998).

Lemay, Leo, *Franklin* (New York: The Library of America, 1987).

Lohr, Steve, "In New Era, Corporate Security Looks Beyond Guns and Badges," *New York Times*, May 27, 2002.

Lucas, James R., *Fatal Illusions: Shredding a Dozen Unrealities That Can Keep Your Organization from Success* (New York: Amacom, 1997).

Marshall, Edward, *Transforming the Way We Work, The Power of the Collaborative Workplace* (New York: Amacom, 1995).

Maxwell, John C., *Failing Forward, Turning Mistakes into Stepping Stones for Success* (Nashville, TN: Thomas Nelson Publishers, 2000).

McCormick, Blaine, *Ben Franklin's 12 Rules of Management* (Irvine, CA: Entrepreneur Press, 2000).

Morris, Tom, *If Aristotle Ran General Motors* (New York: Henry Holt & Co, 1997).

Morris, Tom, *True Success: A New Philosophy of Excellence* (New York: G.P. Putman's Sons, 1994).

Nola M. v. University of Southern California, 16 Cal.App.4th 421, Cal. Rptr.2nd (June 1993).

Pande, P.S., Neuman, R.P., and Cavanagh, R.R., *The Six Sigma Way* (New York: McGraw-Hill, 2000).

Pearce, John A., and Robinson, Richard, B., *Strategic Management*, 7th Edition (New York: Irwin McGraw-Hill, 2000).

Pierce, J.L., Newstrom, J.W., *The Manager's Bookshelf: A Mosaic of Contemporary Views* (Reading, MA: Addison-Wesley, 1996).

R. Goffee, and G. Jones, *The Character of a Corporation* (New York: Harper Business, 1998).

Robbins, Stephen, *Organizational Behavior* (New Jersey: Prentice Hall, 2001).

Schreyogg, G. and Steinmann, H. "Strategic Control: A New Perspective," *Academy of Management Review* (No. 12, 1987).

Shein, Edgar, *Organizational Culture and Leadership*, 2nd Edition (San Francisco: Jossey-Bass, 1992).

Tarrant, John, *Drucker: The Man Who Invented the Corporate Society* (Boston: Cahners Books, 1976).

Useem, Michael, *Leading Up: How to Lead Your Boss So You Both Win* (New York: Crown Business Publications, 2001).

INDEX